BRAVES FIELD

MEMORABLE MOMENTS
AT BOSTON'S LOST DIAMOND

P96 1929 first Sunday game in Boston exhibit Between RS & Braves 4/14
P99 1929 4/29 ∞ Bos Braves (Not Fenway) BRS vs A's—
P103 1929 5/5 ∞ Bos Braves v pits first ~~regl~~ Sunday gm Bos Braves

Edited by Bill Nowlin and Bob Brady

Associate Editors Greg Erion and Len Levin

SOCIETY FOR AMERICAN BASEBALL RESEARCH, INC.
PHOENIX, AZ

Braves Field: Memorable Moments at Boston's Lost Diamond
Edited by Bill Nowlin and Bob Brady
Associate editors Greg Erion and Len Levin

ISBN 978-1-933599-93-9
(Ebook ISBN 978-1-933599-92-2)

Cover and book design: Gilly Rosenthol

Front cover photograph courtesy of Bob Polio
Back cover photograph: *Boston Post*, 1953.
Courtesy Bain Collection, Library of Congress: 33, 40, 44, 45, 51, 52, 53, 77.
Courtesy Boston Braves Historical Association (BBHA) archives: 2, 4, 5, 7, 16, 17, 18, 47, 54, 61, 75, 79, 84, 87, 92, 93, 104, 107, 109, 114, 117, 118, 135, 136, 138, 141, 143, 144, 147, 157, 160, 162, 165,166, 167, 173, 174, 176, 177, 179, 183, 188, 194, 195 (both), 200, 201 (both), 202, 203, 207, 201, 222, 224, 229, 235, 238 (both), 239, 242, 243, 245, 247, 248, 254, 258, 267, 268, 271 (bottom).
Courtesy of Boston College Athletic Photographs: 30, 63.
Courtesy of Boston Public Library: 8, 88, 131, 144, 156, 163, 214, 216, 217, 226, 227 (top), 270 (top).
Courtesy of Boston Public Library, Leslie Jones Collection: 23, 37, 71, 81, 110 (both), 121, 122, 128, 132, 134, 139, 146, 148, 151, 152, 153, 159, 175, 182, 184, 186, 187, 204 (both), 218, 219, 220, 223 (both), 230 (both), 231, 234, 237, 241, 250, 251, 253, 260 (top), 262, 263.
Courtesy of Boston Public Library, Michael T. "Nuf Ced" McGreevey Collection: 119.
Courtesy of Bob Brady: 3, 5, 6, 9, 260 (bottom), 261 (bottom).
Courtesy of Jonathan Fine: 215, 227 (bottom).
Courtesy of The Jimmy Fund and Dana-Farber Cancer Institute: 190, 191 (both), 192 (both).
Courtesy of National Baseball Hall of Fame: 20, 56, 58, 66, 78, 108, 213, 233.
Courtesy of Noir Tech Research: 169.
Courtesy of Bill Nowlin: 269.
Courtesy of Bob Polio: 261 (top).
Courtesy of Sports Museum of New England: 266.

Society for American Baseball Research
Cronkite School at ASU
555 N. Central Ave. #416
Phoenix, AZ 85004
Phone: (602) 496-1460
Web: www.sabr.org
Facebook: Society for American Baseball Research
Twitter: @SABR

TABLE OF CONTENTS

INTRODUCTION

BY BOB BRADY

And there used to be a ballpark
Where the field was warm and green
And the people played their crazy game
With a joy I'd never seen
And the air was such a wonder
From the hot dogs and the beer
Yes, there used to be a ballpark, right here.1

Yes, there used to be a National League ballpark in Boston! Braves Field was the home turf of Boston's Braves from its opening on August 18, 1915, until the team's final major-league game at the site on September 21, 1952. Abandoned after the ballclub moved to Milwaukee in the spring of 1953, the park assumed a second life when Boston University transformed it into a sports complex and rechristened it as Nickerson Field. Fortunately for followers of baseball history, the university preserved the distinctive Braves Field administration building that had served as the ballpark's main entrance. Also retained was a portion of the old right-field pavilion so that a century after the ballpark was built, those attending campus athletic events and graduation ceremonies could sit where Braves Field patrons once witnessed the memorable events described between the covers of this book. Other than the still-active fellow centenarians Fenway Park and Wrigley Field, no other steel and concrete baseball stadium of this era has similarly survived.

The Wigwam, as it was affectionately known (or the "Beehive" during the Boston Bees years), was the site of Boston's first big-league Sunday game and its first night game, as well as the host to its first All-Star Game. It was borrowed on two occasions by the neighboring Red Sox for World Series play and per-

formed that duty for the Braves in 1948. Baseball's longest big-league game ended in a tie on its playing field. The immortal Babe Ruth graced its diamond as a member of the Red Sox, Yankees, Braves, and Dodgers. The Sultan of Swat signed his last player contract with the Braves in 1935 in the still-standing administration building. The Splendid Splinter, Ted Williams, made his Hub debut on this diamond during a 1939 preseason Braves-Red Sox City Series exhibition tilt. Braves Field was where Boston's baseball color line was first broken when Jackie Robinson visited the Wigwam with the opposing Dodgers in 1947 and Sam Jethroe debuted in the Tribe's outfield in 1950.

The ballpark's rich history includes many events outside of the national pastime. It was the birthplace of professional football's Washington Redskins and New England Patriots. Rocky Marciano boxed there on the way to becoming the undefeated heavyweight champion of the world. Famed artist Norman Rockwell sought inspiration within its confines for an iconic *Saturday Evening Post* cover.

Through the collaborative efforts of 43 members of the Society for American Baseball Research (SABR), memorable Braves Field moments have been retrieved from the haze of the distant past and reported here in glorious detail so that anyone perusing the pages of this book will gain an appreciation that, yes, there used to be a ballpark here.

NOTE

1   From "There Used To Be A Ballpark," as sung by Frank Sinatra on the 1973 Reprise album, *Ol' Blue Eyes Is Back* and written by Joseph G. Raposo. The song, in its entirety can be heard at https://www.youtube.com/watch?v=TgPPLHPx8PU.

A BIOGRAPHY OF BRAVES FIELD

BY RAY MILLER

INTRODUCTION

Braves Field was a marvel when it opened in 1915: "the perfect ballpark" (*Boston Globe*[1]); "the world's largest ballpark ever" (team owner James E. Gaffney); "baseball's first superstadium" (historian Michael Gershman). It was where Babe Ruth made his first World Series start, and it was his final baseball home nearly 20 years later. It was the site of the first major-league game ever played on a Sunday in Boston, and Ted Williams made his Boston debut there, going hitless in a City Series game on April 15, 1939. It was the site of Boston's first major-league night game, the 1936 All-Star Game, and three World Series. Although it was often derided as too big, too chilly, and too dirty, old Braves fans still declare that, in the early 1950s, at least, it "was the prettiest park in the majors."[2] Certainly, during the Braves' last hurrah in Boston, Braves Field was a fine place to take in a baseball game, but ultimately it was doomed by a series of strategic miscalculations at its inception—coupled with the fact that in 23 of its 37 seasons, the team finished in sixth place or lower.

The team that was to become the Boston Braves had been *the* most successful National League club in the nineteenth century. No other NL team won as many championships during that era (eight), and only the Providence Grays had a better winning percentage. This powerhouse played at the South End Grounds, a tiny wooden facility in northern Roxbury that was wedged between Columbus Avenue to the south and the New York, New Haven, and Hartford railroad tracks to the north. In its final incarnation, between 1894 and 1914,[3] it was a drab, poorly maintained facility that could not be enlarged because of its location. By the 1910s it was, in Harold Kaese's memorable phrase, "an ugly little wart,"[4] while the "few [fans who] wanted to watch the luckless Braves hated to make the trek to the field, which was badly located and had no modern conveniences."[5] When New York contractor and Tammany Hall insider James E. Gaffney bought the moribund team in December 1911,[6] he immediately renamed it the Braves (after the Tammany syndicate's symbol, Delaware Chief Tamanend), and started looking for a new ballpark site. In the meantime, he made some alterations to the South End Grounds for the 1912 season,[7] and brought his team to the Red Sox' Fenway Park for their Memorial Day doubleheader in 1913.

And then came 1914. Everyone knows the saga of the Miracle Braves: In last place on the Fourth of July, they suddenly caught fire and were in first place to stay by September 5. They won the pennant by 10½ games and swept the defending champion Philadelphia Athletics in the World Series. The Red Sox let the Braves use their sparkling new stadium for their September run and for their two home Series games. (They never did return to the South End Grounds.)[8] In the end, the club led all National League teams in attendance for 1914. If he hadn't known already, James Gaffney now understood just how profitable a pennant-winning baseball team could be—and if they

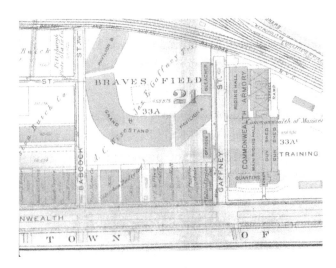

Braves Field plot plan circa 1916.

could outdraw their rivals while playing most of their home games in a dump like the South End Grounds, what could they do in a big, modern stadium that was easier to get to? The time to build was now.

As late as November 13, the *New York Times* could report a rumor that Gaffney had sold the South End Grounds and "would have to depend on the generosity of [the Red Sox] to use Fenway Park." In actual fact, at this time he was negotiating the purchase of the western portion of the old Allston Golf Club on Commonwealth Avenue, about a mile west of Kenmore Square.[9] The size of the lot was 13 acres, and it cost $100,000. Gaffney announced the purchase on December 4.[10] Ruzzo writes that Gaffney "became immersed in the details" of his new sports palace: He wanted nothing less than "the world's greatest ballpark" for his world-champion club, and he had some definite ideas about what that should look like.

BUILDING BRAVES FIELD

To bring his visions to life, Gaffney turned to the Osborn Engineering Company of Cleveland, a firm that had recently made a name for itself in ballpark construction: No fewer than 11 teams had recently built modern concrete-and-steel parks, and Osborn had been involved with six of them.[11] Although, according to Ruzzo, the Braves owner had pored over the plans of these "jewel boxes"[12] in order to "incorporat[e] the best features of each into" Braves Field, it really did not look much like these other stadiums. First, it lacked the quirky features that urban topography foisted on many of these other parks (for example, the short right-field wall in Ebbets Field, and Fenway's now-famous left-field wall); Gaffney felt that they just interfered with the way the game was "meant to be played." He loved inside-the-park homers, and thus wanted "the playing field to be so large that it would be possible to hit [them] in any direction"[13] He also demanded the largest seating capacity in the majors—in other words, a cash cow to exploit the team's new success. The lot he purchased was certainly big enough, and Osborn was able to deliver on both counts. Gaffney first revealed how the

Surviving portion of architect's original ballpark model.

Braves' new home was going to look when he showed a nine-foot-square architects' model to "members of the press and invited guests at team headquarters on March 8, 1915."[14] The public got its first glimpse of what was to come the following day, in a *Boston Globe* article, "Here's How the Braves New Home in Allston Will Look" the architects' model was subsequently displayed in a downtown department-store window.[15]

Ground was broken on the old links on March 20, 1915; the grand opening was originally scheduled for September 1. The diamond was sunk 17 feet below street level, and "[p]ainful attention was paid to making sure that drainage was superb."[16] The infield sod came directly from the South End Grounds. According to oft-quoted statistics originally provided by Kaese, 750 tons of steel and 8.2 million pounds of cement went into the new park, and that it cost the team $600,000 to build.[17] Work progressed rapidly and the grand opening was moved up to August 18. The club invited 10,000 schoolchildren and several thousand other guests, some of whom received a florid formal invitation with Chief Tamanend's profile embossed in gold at the top.[18] Fourteen Massachusetts mayors were among the dignitaries, as was Governor David I. Walsh. Paying customers numbered 32,000, with at least 6,000 people turned away at the gate. The grand total was estimated to be around 42,000, the largest crowd ever to attend a baseball game up to that point, although a far cry from the grandiose official proclamation of 56,000. The formal raising of the 1914 championship banner took place immediately before the game, which the Braves won, 3-1.[19] Later that year, World Series attendance records were set in Games Three and Four, when the Red Sox defeated the Phillies. The American League team also took over the Braves' home in 1916, in the first, second, and deciding fifth games of the World Series against Brooklyn. Babe Ruth made his first Series start there in Game Two, a 14-inning, six-hit masterpiece that is still considered one of the greatest pitching performances in postseason history.

THE STRUCTURE OF BRAVES FIELD

As it was originally conceived, Braves Field was to have a covered single-deck grandstand that extended around the playing field from foul pole to foul pole, with a sizable bleacher section in right field stretching from the end of the grandstand almost to straightaway center.[20] In this configuration, it would have seated about 45,000 spectators. However, in the end Gaffney "trimmed his design" to save money.[21] When the first "bugs" entered Braves Field on August 18, they beheld a covered single-tiered grandstand that curved from first base to third base; this was flanked on either side by enormous mirror-image pavilions, each with unroofed seating on benches for 10,000. Finally, the right-field bleacher section had shrunk: it was now a tiny stand in straightaway right that could hold up to 2,000 fans.[22] This became Braves Field's most famous

Aerial view of Braves Field and neighboring rail yard.

section, known to one and all as the Jury Box, after a waggish sportswriter counted just 12 people in it one day. Simple arithmetic shows that the seating capacity was thus reduced to 40,000, which was still greater than any baseball stadium up to that time.

For players used to the tiny South End Grounds, writes Harold Kaese, coming to Braves Field "was like moving from a modern three-room apartment into a nineteenth century mansion." The new field had gargantuan dimensions: According to *Green Cathedrals*, it was over 402 feet down the left-field line; 375 feet in right; 461 feet to straightaway center field; and a jaw-dropping 542 feet to the farthest point in right-center.[23] The park was surrounded by a 10-foot concrete wall; a large scoreboard was built into this wall in left-center.[24] Fans entered Braves Field through arches in the handsome stucco ticket office on Gaffney Street, just behind the right-field pavilion. The team offices were on the second floor; Ralph Evans says that:

"The ticket sellers never had to handle large sums of money: there were trap doors in the ceilings of each ticket booth, and they would put the money they took in into baskets, and these would be drawn into the offices above. That not only made things easier for the ticket sellers—it meant the treasurer would … have the proceeds for the day's game counted by the fifth inning."[25]

Cognizant of the problems fans had had getting to the South End Grounds, Gaffney added a special convenience for them in his new park, an "in-stadium transportation facility," courtesy of the Boston Elevated Railway: trolleys came in off Commonwealth Avenue via Babcock Street and deposited fans onto the same courtyard pedestrians entered through the arches off Gaffney Street. This feature was greatly appreciated, as we see from reminiscences in the literature.[26]

EXPERIENCING BRAVES FIELD

While the initial reaction to Braves Field was gushingly positive,[27] at the core of Gaffney's vision were several miscalculations (exacerbated by some of the cost-cutting measures that altered his original plan) that ultimately affected the fan experience adversely. Not all were his fault, certainly: As we shall see, the game simply changed not long after the stadium was built, and Braves Field was "relegated ... to premature functional obsolescence."[28] In any event, the next two games in the new plant drew only 9,300 souls combined, and this was a sad harbinger of things to come.[29]

Ruzzo and others credit Gaffney for taking the economically canny step of funding construction in part by selling off the valuable Commonwealth Avenue frontage and setting Braves Field at the back of the lot, down by the Charles River and the Boston & Albany train yards. However, in the end this proved to be a penny-wise, pound-foolish move: Fans soon realized that a chilly east wind frequently blew in off the river over the outfield walls, and that it carried with it acrid, sooty smoke from the railroad tracks. Kaese quips that the team thus did local "cleaners and launderers a good turn," and one old fan asserts that a dry cleaners was eventually located next door to the park for this very reason.[30] It is true that the builders were able to take advantage of the steep ravine that cut across the lot (and had driven down the asking price): The slope created a good pitch for the right-field pavilion. And Ed Burns, in his 1937 profile of the park for the *Chicago Tribune*, asserted that "[e]very seat [in the covered grandstand] gives an excellent view of the entire playing field;"[31] indeed, the expansive roof was supported by only 16 posts, fewer than in other new ballparks, so that there were fewer obstructed seats.[32] However, some fans found the sightlines in the facility less than ideal: "The grandstand had a very gradual slope to it. So consequently people sitting in these seats had difficulty seeing the action."[33] Unlike in the original plan, half of the seats were on benches and exposed to the elements in those vast pavilions, and the seats toward the top were far from the action: Ruzzo estimates that there was a whopping quarter of a mile between the top rows of the left- and right-field stands. People seated in the pavilions close to the covered grandstand had to crane their necks. Finally, the angle formed by the curvature of the grandstand was more obtuse than in other parks,

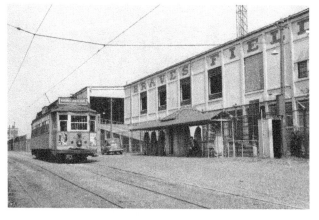

Braves Field had its own internal streetcar stop.

resulting in relatively more foul territory—and more seats farther away from the diamond.

James E. Gaffney sold the Braves in early 1916, making a handsome 267 percent profit on his original investment.[34] (His estate continued to own Braves Field, however, until the 1940s, although the NL took over the lease in 1935.) In 1919 the local syndicate that bought the team from him sold it to a New York group, which five years later sold it to yet another New York-based outfit that included the colorful magistrate Emil Fuchs, who over the course of the next decade became a local sports legend for all the wrong reasons.[35] None of these ownership groups was financially strong or willing to spend money to make the team a winner. (Fuchs himself was wealthy, but he did not know how to handle money and "owning the team [drove him] into bankruptcy.")[36] The National League finally forced Fuchs to sell his interest in the club in 1935; the group that took over from him was too large and unwieldy to work effectively.[37] For the most part, throughout the 1920s and '30s, "the Braves were broke,"[38] and generally could not field a competitive team. Although Braves fans showed they would come to park when the team had promise—in 1933 and 1934, for example, the team finished fourth in both the National League standings and in league attendance—"Braves Field [in this period] became a deserted village."[39]

If anything, the stadium only made the Braves' situation worse. Compounding the discomforts discussed above was the fact that this parade of weak owners

Ornate Braves Field aisle seat stanchion.

could not afford to maintain this "perfect ballpark" in good condition. Even more significantly, the style of baseball people wanted to see changed forever about five years after the cavernous park opened. Thanks to the exploits of Babe Ruth, people now wanted to watch baseballs soaring over the fences, not bounding toward them over a vast, green pasture. To put it mildly, Braves Field was not suited to the new power game. Kaese quotes Ty Cobb's famous reaction after seeing the place for the first time: "One thing is sure: Nobody is ever going to hit a ball over those fences."[40] The first homer hit there (August 23, 1915) was a fluke: Pittsburgh's Doc Johnston hit a ball that "got by the right fielder and rolled under a gate in front of the bleachers."[41] Other players bounced home runs through openings in the left-field scoreboard (e.g., "Bedford Bill" Rariden of the Reds on July 11, 1919). The first time a batted ball left the park was on May 26, 1917, when Walton Cruise of the Cardinals put one into the Jury Box. (It was Cruise who hit the second there, on August 16, 1921, this time for the Braves.) No one cleared the left-field wall on the fly until Frank Snyder

of the Giants did it on May 28, 1925, almost 10 years after Braves Field opened. According to Kaese, this was a majestic 430-foot blast that "cleared the top of the fence by about 20 feet, some 15 feet from the foul pole."[42] Otherwise, the vast majority of home runs hit at Braves Field in the first 12 years of its existence were in fact of the inside-the-park variety: for example, according to Price, 34 of the 38 home runs hit at the park in 1921. The Giants once even hit four IPHR's in one game there, on April 29, 1922.[43]

Starting in 1928, the Braves tried various stratagems to make their stadium feel cozier for hitters and fans: Inside fences were built, bleachers were added in left and center, home plate was moved around. The outfield dimensions changed — literally — on almost an annual basis into the 1940s, and Braves Field never looks the same in any two photographs from this period. Table 1[44] below gives you an idea of the extent of these constant renovations:

Table 1

Year	Left Field	Center	Deepest Point	Right
1915	402.5 feet	461 feet	542 feet	375 feet
1928	320/353.5	387/417	*	310
1936	368	426	*	297
1946	337	370	*	340/320

Different figures are given for 1928 because Judge Fuchs had built "papier mache"[45] stands in left and center to increase home-run production before the season opened, and then had them gradually disassembled after the opposition hit twice as many round-trippers as the home team. ("Anything hit into the skeleton of the great home run creation," writes Burns, "was adjudged a two-base hit.")[46] Meanwhile, home plate was turned to the right in 1928, moved 15 feet closer to the backstop in 1936, then tilted right again in 1937 and 1946. When they moved the dish in 1937, they had to blast a notch out of the right-field pavilion in order to accommodate the shifted foul line. This notch is clearly visible in photographs of Braves Field, and helps to date them. After the addition of bleachers in front of the distant left-field wall, a new scoreboard was built over the Jury Box, where it remained till the team left town.[47]

Important events transpired in Braves Field in the 1920s and '30s. This was where Joe Oeschger of the Braves dueled Leon Cadore of the Brooklyn Robins for 26 innings on May 1, 1920, the longest game by innings in major-league history. The first Sunday games ever played in Boston took place there early in 1929.[48] Braves center fielder Earl Clark set a record with 12 putouts on May 10 of that same year. The NFL team now known as the Washington Redskins played their inaugural season in Braves Field in 1932, when they, too, were known as the Boston Braves. Babe Ruth made Braves Field his final major-league home in 1935, and homered and singled off Carl Hubbell there on Opening Day. There were the inevitable farcical moments, as well. For example, in 1926, "irregularities in the … turnstiles cost the club as much as $50,000."[49] Then, at the NL meetings in December 1934, Judge Fuchs floated the idea of having dog racing at Braves Field in 1935: The track would be built around the playing field, and the races would take place at night. Needless to say, Commissioner Landis did not approve.[50] In 1936 the post-Fuchs regime tried to change the team's fortunes by renaming them the Bees. Of course, that prompted the temporary rechristening of the ballpark, which received the resoundingly dull official new sobriquet National League Field, although the Beehive inevitably became its unofficial nickname.[51] The newly christened Bees hosted the first All-Star Game in Boston that year on July 7. The National League won its first-ever All-Star Game, 4-3, defeating Lefty Grove. Cubs outfielder Augie Galan bounced a homer off the right-field foul pole for the decisive run. Alas, even here the team could not avoid tragicomedy: a newspaper mistakenly reported that the game was sold out, although there were plenty of pavilion seats available, and only 25,556 showed up—the smallest crowd in All-Star Game history. The Great Hurricane of 1938 hit Boston during the Bees-Cards game of September 21—umpire Beans Reardon held off calling the game until "Tony Cuccinello yelled for a pop fly behind second base, only to have [catcher] Al Lopez wind up catching the wind-blown ball almost against the backstop."[52] Finally, Burns adds some interesting details about the Braves

Field experience in the '30s: the right-field pavilion was a haven for gamblers; the park featured "the only concession stand in the majors which carrie[d] a full line of chewing tobacco"; and the press box on the grandstand roof was "'Earache alley'—the noisiest … in baseball."[53]

THE THREE LITTLE STEAM SHOVELS AND BRAVES FIELD'S LAST HURRAH

The last decade of the team's existence was arguably the happiest in its history. Three of the franchise's small army of stockholders got "sick and tired of putting money into a constantly losing proposition"[54] and staged a bloodless coup in early 1944, buying out the rest of the numerous syndicate. Lou Perini, Guido Rugo, and C.J. Maney were wealthy local contractors who soon became lovingly known as the Three Little Steam Shovels. They made every effort to make the club (by then once again called the Braves) a winning proposition, on the field and at the gate.[55]

Starting in May 1944, when the team was on the road, the aggressive new owners made the physical renovations to Braves Field that gave it the appearance best remembered today. They shortened the distances in the outfield by installing a graceful two-level wooden inner wall from the corner of the left-field pavilion to right-center, with a low chain-link fence in front of the Jury Box to the big right-field stand.[56] Light towers were installed for 1946, and the first night game

Braves Field during its glory days.

Painters replace "Braves" with "University" on outer outfield wall, 1954.

in Boston was played on May 11, "with neon foul poles and shimmering sateen uniforms that made the players look like a men's chorus."[57] To improve the sightlines from the grandstand, the plate was once more turned to the right for 1946, and the infield was lowered 18 inches during a two-week road trip in June 1947.[58] A huge new scoreboard was installed in left field for the 1948 season; and "Sky View Boxes" on the grandstand roof were also added around this time.[59] Finally, the upper half of the inner wall in center was removed in 1951, and fir trees planted behind the fence "to hide … the huge clouds of … locomotive smoke" from the railroad yards beyond.[60]

For all the renovations the team's different owners made to Braves Field over the years, "they still [couldn't] find a way to move 8.2 million pounds of concrete stands closer to the playing field,"[61] but Perini et al. might have come the closest with the intangible changes they introduced that made the stadium the beloved "Wigwam" fondly remembered today. Braves fans realized that a new era had dawned after Opening Day 1946, when the team turned what could have been perceived as a "same-old-Braves" gaffe into a public-relations bonanza. Due to unfavorable weather conditions, the fresh paint on some of the grandstand seats had not dried by game time, and several thousand spectators left the park with green stains on their clothes. "An Apology to Braves Fans" immediately appeared in local papers in which the team offered to

reimburse dry-cleaning expenses. Nearly 13,000 claims poured in from far and wide, and the club eventually paid off over 5,000 of them, at a cost of nearly $7,000.[62]

From that point forward, led by their new publicity director, Billy Sullivan, the Braves became "the team that called their fans 'family.'"[63] Fans had "a warm feeling" at Braves Field in the late '40s, and "felt like [they were] at home"—"even the ushers were friendly!"[64] Sullivan introduced Fan Appreciation Day, and the Braves Minstrels (a/k/a the Three Little Earaches), who serenaded fans throughout the park. The Braves gave away cars and teamed up with local hotels and restaurants on special promotions for night games.[65] Concessions were upgraded, and came to include "the best fried clams … in all baseball."[66] The team in those days also fielded likable players who were happy to interact with the fans, especially Tommy Holmes who became the favorite of the vocal denizens of the Jury Box—to the point where they would harass any Braves player who took his place in right field![67]

The most famous individual fan in these happy days was probably the redoubtable Lolly Hopkins, who shouted encouragement to the home side through a big megaphone, and brought Tootsie Rolls to every game for the players on both teams. It is emblematic of the relationship between the team and its fans that the Braves players presented Lolly with a bracelet before a 1947 game, as a token of their appreciation.[68]

The pinnacle was reached in 1948, when the Braves won their first pennant in 34 years and hosted the Cleveland Indians in the World Series. Three Series games were played at the Wigwam, the Braves taking Game One and dropping the other two, including the decisive Game Six. The team set a home attendance record by drawing over 1.45 million fans. Overall, 5,970,324 people visited Braves Field between 1946 and 1950, by far the only stretch in the park's history that the team was able to exploit its large seating capacity so profitably.[69] The park itself, according to Ralph Evans, was, at the end, "the prettiest … in the majors—I defy anyone to say it wasn't!"[70] Ever progressive, the Steam Shovels integrated Boston baseball in

The still intact old Braves Field main entrance and administration building today serves as the university's police station.

1950, when they brought outfielder Sam Jethroe to Braves Field.

Alas, this momentum simply could not be maintained. In 1951 the Braves finished fourth, as they had in the previous two seasons, but drew only 487,475 fans to their home games; that was fewer than any other NL team, almost only half as many as they had drawn in 1950. The 1952 figures were even worse: They finished seventh, and had a home attendance of 281,278; only 4,694 souls showed up for Opening Day. Mort Bloomberg remembers that "[c]rowds were so small that people's voices would reverberate throughout the park. If you sat on the first base side, you could hear individual fans' comments on the third base side."[71] He also felt that "[t]he park itself did not help draw fans": For one thing, "[p]arking was non-existent."

The sad fact was that the Braves had a slimmer margin of error than most other major-league teams: they had long been the "other team" in Boston, the Red Sox were now perennial contenders, and no one was willing to come to Braves Field to watch a mediocre team, no matter how friendly the ushers were. Perini finally threw in the towel and moved to Milwaukee immediately before the start of the 1953 season. (Only 420 season tickets had been sold.) Game tickets for

1953 were dumped onto the field, where they were burned.[72] Some people certainly took the move hard, of course. A group of local teens who called themselves the Mountfort Street Gang broke into the deserted stadium one night, shortly after the move was announced and

"using nothing but their bare hands, they dug home plate out of the clay. Mind you, it was sunk 17" into the ground, and they had only their hands! … All these years, it was hidden in cellars, in attics, under beds, and then, all of a sudden, this guy brings it out and presents it to us [at the 40th reunion of the 1948 pennant winners in 1988]!"[73]

Many old Braves fans agree that if Perini et al. had been able to hang on for one more year, they just might have been able to hold on in Boston: The team had a strong nucleus of good ballplayers, and they wound up winning the NL pennant only six years after leaving New England. Ralph Evans claimed that there were plans to renovate Braves Field thoroughly in 1954-55, but Peter Gammons reported on ESPN in 1997 that Lou Perini had planned to abandon the park in the early 1950s for a new facility at Riverside in Newton; this plan fell through when Tom Yawkey refused to let the Braves use Fenway Park.[74]

AFTER THE MOVE

Boston University purchased Braves Field for the back taxes on July 29, 1953. It stood vacant for several months, though fans would occasionally come to the empty park to meditate. Once one of them took a home movie, which has been uploaded to YouTube. Eerily silent, it shows the outfield wall in its final incarnation, with the fir trees standing behind left-center, an overgrown infield, and high grass in the outfield. The BU Terriers football team played their home games in a virtually unaltered Braves Field until 1955, when over the course of several months the inside walls were removed, and the Jury Box and left-field pavilion were torn down. (The giant scoreboard was shipped to Kansas City for the use of the just-transplanted A's.) Several curious overhead photographs exist showing a truncated Wigwam in this football configuration. A young Johnny Unitas made his first NFL start on this field during a Baltimore Colts-New York Giants exhibition game in 1956. The final baseball game was played there in the spring of 1959, between Boston University and Boston College.[75]

The old grandstand was finally razed in late November 1959. The football field was realigned to run parallel to the right-field pavilion, which now became the southern grandstand. The notch blown out of the pavilion in 1937 was filled in, and the opposite end was squared off to extend seating further toward the end zone. Eventually, dormitories and the Case Athletic Center were built where the grandstand and left-field pavilion had once stood, and the facility was renamed Nickerson Field. Meanwhile, the distinctive ticket office became the headquarters of the BU campus police department. In this configuration, James Gaffney's sports emporium became the first home to the Boston (later, New England) Patriots, who played the first game in American Football League history there on September 9, 1960, as well as an assortment of other professional sports teams: the Boston Minutemen of the North American Soccer League (1975); the U.S, Football League Boston Breakers (1983); another Boston Breakers, of the Women's United Soccer Association (2001-2003); and the

Boston Cannons of Major League Lacrosse (2004-2006). It was last renovated in July 2009, when a four-lane track was put in around the playing field. Now, BU boasts that Nickerson Field is "a 10,412 seat, FIFA-approved Field Turf facility."[76]

You can still take a tour of Braves Field: More of it was left standing than of any of the other classic steel-and-concrete ballparks built between 1909 and 1923 and subsequently abandoned. The old office building and right-field pavilion still stand; until the summer of 2010, you could see much of the original concrete wall in right, or at least what was left of it.[77] Ralph Evans is able to indicate exactly what remains of the old plant and what was subsequently added by Boston University, and he can point out the approximate location of home plate, the third-base dugout, where the grandstand wall stood, and other important points of reference.[78]

SOURCES

"Atlanta Braves Team History & Encyclopedia". Baseball Reference.com

baseball-reference.com/teams/ATL/.

"Boston the Way It Was—Part 3: The Boston Braves." Video, accessed at

youtube.com/watch?v=JycSH_ouRfc.

Brady, Bob. "Model View," *Boston Braves Historical Association Newsletter*, Spring 2010, 3-4.

-----. "A Streetcar Named Braves Field," *Boston Braves Historical Association Newsletter*, Spring 2010, 4.

-----. "Going, Going …," *Boston Braves Historical Association Newsletter*, Summer 2010, 4.

Burns, Ed. "Burns-Eye Views of Big Time Parks. Braves Field," *Chicago Tribune*, 1937, accessed at Behindthebag.net behindthebag.net/category/burns-eye-views-of-big-time-parks/page/2/.

Gershman, Michael. *Diamonds. The Evolution of the Ballpark* (Boston and New York:

Houghton Mifflin Co., 1993).

Hirshberg, Al. *The Braves: The Pick and the Shovel* (Boston: Waverly House, 1948).

Johnson, Richard A. *The Boston Braves* (Charleston, South Carolina: Arcadia Publishing, 2001).

Kaese, Harold. *The Boston Braves* (New York: G.P. Putnam's Sons, 1948).

Lowry, Philip J. *Green Cathedrals* (New York: Walker & Company, 2006).

Mack, Gene. "Braves Field," *The Sporting News*, January 15, 1947, 11.

-----. "Braves Field," *National Baseball Hall of Fame & Museum Yearbook*,

Cooperstown, New York, 1984, 53.

Marazzi, Rich. "Four decades after their departure, the Braves (and their park) are

fondly remembered by fans," *Sports Collectors Digest*, September 29, 1995,

90-92.

Miller, Ray. *A Tour of Braves Field* (Boston: Boston Braves Historical Association,

2000).

-----. "South End Grounds," *The Northern Game — and Beyond. Baseball in New*

England and Eastern Canada, edited by Mark Kanter (Cleveland: SABR, 2002), 36-38.

"Nickerson Field." Boston University Terriers Athletics Website,

goterriers.com/facilities/nickerson.html.

Palacios, Oscar A., and Eric Robin, Grant Blair, Ethan Cooperson, Dan Ford, Tony

Nistler and Mat Olkin. *Ballpark Sourcebook* (Skokie, Illinois: STATS Publishing,

1998).

Price, Bill. "Braves Field," *Baseball Research Journal*, Vol. 7 (1978).

research.sabr.org/journals/archives/online/40-brj-1978.

"Remembering the Wigwam: Braves Field & Nickerson Field." Video: Boston

University. Accessed at youtube.com/watch?v=r9q-MdefG-c.

"Remembering the Wigwam." Boston University website,

bu.edu/today/2012/braves-field-remembering-the-wigwam-2/.

Ritter, Lawrence J. *Lost Ballparks* (New York: Viking Penguin, 1992).

Ruzzo, Bob. "Braves Field: An Imperfect History of the Perfect Ballpark," *Baseball*

Research Journal Vol. 41, No. 2 (Fall 2012), 50-60.

Sullivan, George. "Memories of Braves Field," *Boston Globe*, "Sports Plus," September

30, 1977, 16-20.

Vincent, David W., ed. *Home Runs in the Old Ballparks* (Cleveland: SABR, 1995).

NOTES

1   "Here's How the Braves' New Park in Allston Will Look," *Boston Globe*, March 9, 1915; quoted in Bob Ruzzo, "Braves Field: An Imperfect History of the Perfect Ballpark," originally published in Society for American Baseball Research, *Baseball Research Journal* (Fall 2012), 50-60.

2   Quote is from an interview with Ralph Evans of the Boston Braves Historical Association conducted on May 21, 1997, and used as the primary source of Ray Miller, *A Tour of Braves Field* (Boston: Boston Braves Historical Association, 2000), 11 (also see below); all subsequent quotes from Evans are from this interview. No one knows Braves Field better than Evans: he came from a family of dyed-in-the-wool Braves fans, and worked as a clubhouse boy at Boston University from 1955 to 1961, after the university had acquired the facility: "I would come to work early and just walk the park, up and down"; ibid., 1.

3   Whether you see the South End Grounds as one park extensively renovated two times, or as three different parks that bore the same name at the exact same location is probably a matter of personal preference. Ballpark historians now prefer the latter approach, and refer to the different plants as South End Grounds I (1871-1887), II (1888-1894), and III (1894-1914). For a brief history of the park, see Miller, "South End Grounds" in *The Northern Game — and Beyond* (SABR, 2002), 36-38.

4   Harold Kaese, *The Boston Braves* (New York: G.P. Putnam's Sons, 1948), 101.

5   Al Hirshberg, *The Braves: The Pick and the Shovel* (Boston: Waverly House, 1948), 15.

6   See Ruzzo, "Braves Field: An Imperfect History," for more on Gaffney and the details of the purchase of the Boston NL franchise.

7   Kaese, 129.

8   There had been some disagreement about when the team left its old park in Roxbury. Kaese held that the Braves returned to the South End Grounds in 1915, playing there "until they began to move the infield sod over to their new park." (Kaese, 173). However, all modern Sources agree that they played in Fenway Park from mid-August 1914 until the grand opening of Braves Field.

9   See Ruzzo, "Braves Field: An Imperfect History." The state eventually built the Commonwealth Armory on the eastern half of the golf course. A familiar landmark standing directly across from the right-field wall, the armory was demolished in 2002 to make way for Boston University's Student Village.

10 See Ruzzo, who includes details of the purchase in footnote 21. Kaese states on page 173 that Gaffney's big announcement came on December 1.

11 Namely, League Park in Cleveland and Comiskey Park in Chicago (1910); the Polo Grounds V in New York and Griffith Stadium in Washington (1911); Navin Field in Detroit; and Fenway Park (1912).

12 Ruzzo uses the term "jewel box ballpark" for all the classic concrete-and-steel stadia that were built between 1909 and 1915 (presumably counting Wrigley Field in Chicago, which was built in 1914 as Weeghman Park for the Federal League Whales). Gershman, on the other hand, reserves the term only for Fenway Park, Ebbets Field, and Wrigley Field (106), while classifying Braves Field, along with Yankee Stadium and a few other facilities, as a "superstadium." See Michael Gershman, *Diamonds. The Evolution of the Ballpark* (Boston and New York: Houghton Mifflin Co., 1993), 126 ff.

13 Kaese, 173.

14 See Bob Brady, "Model View," in the *Boston Braves Historical Association Newsletter*, Spring 2010, 3.

15 Ruzzo, "Braves Field: An Imperfect History." The fate of this model is heartbreaking: According to Brady, the model "gather[ed] dust in the attic of the former Braves administration building" (currently the Boston University police station) until 1992, when a university employee decided to smash it to pieces in an overzealous effort to clean up the area. A fragment of the model was saved in the nick of time by another employee who happened to be associated with the Boston Braves Historical Association and had planned to display it at the group's first meeting on October 4 of that year. See Brady, "Model View," 4.

16 See Ruzzo, "Braves Field: An Imperfect History." Drainage could have potentially been an issue because there had been a large pond in this section of the old golf course; see Bill Brady, "An Engineer's View of Braves Field in 1915," *Boston Braves Historical Association Newsletter*, Summer 2014, 3-4.

17 Bill Price, in the article "Braves Field" (originally published in *Baseball Research Journal*, Vol. 7 [1978]), quotes a figure of "approximately $1,000,000." He does not cite a source for it, or address the discrepancy with Kaese's book, on which he otherwise relies for much of his information. Gershman (129) does call Braves Field the first "million-dollar ballpark," but there is no indication that he intends this epithet to be taken literally. The Price article may be accessed online at research.sabr.org/journals/archives/online/40-brj-1978. Incidentally, *Ballpark Sourcebook* mentions the legend that draft animals were killed during the construction and remained buried under the area of third base (Oscar A. Palacios et al. *Ballpark Sourcebook* [Skokie, Illinois: STATS Publishing, 1998], 16). Ralph Evans also mentioned this story in the interview of May 21, 1997. A photograph of the ballpark under construction showing horses and mules at work hangs in the lobby of the Case Athletic Center at Boston University, in the general vicinity of where the left-field pavilion once stood.

18 The Braves' invitation is reproduced in full in Richard A. Johnson, *The Boston Braves* (Charleston, South Carolina: Arcadia, 2001), 38.

19 Many Sources include the details of the grand opening of Braves Field. See, inter alia, Kaese, 174.

20 See Miller, *A Tour of Braves Field*, 6b, for an image of Braves Field in this original configuration. This is a photograph of a model made according to the Osborn Engineering blueprints that has been displayed from time to time at meetings of the Boston Braves Historical Association. The model is identified in this earlier publication on 6 as representing renovations planned for 1954-55. It is possible, however, that any future expansion of Braves Field would, in fact, have reinstated the features dropped by Gaffney in 1915. See note 22 below.

21 Ruzzo, "Braves Field: An Imperfect History." Brady, "Model View," 4, suggests that another reason for cutting back was to "keep the project on its quick pace."

22 This might have been a late modification. Ralph Evans points out that the right-field wall looks unfinished to the left of where the Jury Box once stood, as if the builders intended to extend the stands to that area. See photo #13 on page 4 of the "Photo Tour Gallery" toward the back of Miller, *A Tour of Braves Field*. Brady reports that the club had merely "set aside for later" extending the bleachers and grandstand roof, and that "such enhancements were under consideration during the Perini regime." (Brady, "Model View," 4). All this explains Ralph Evans's contention that the model mentioned in note 20 was of what the park would look like after renovations in the mid-'50s.

23 *Ballpark Sourcebook* (17) generally agrees: it has 402 feet, 375 feet, 440 feet, and 550 feet respectively. Gershman, 130, displays a photograph taken during the 1916 World Series. It clearly shows a low fence extending from the Jury Box to the center-field wall and cutting off the deepest corner from the rest of the field. Whether this was a permanent arrangement or set up for the standing-room Series crowd is unclear.

24 See photo in Lawrence S. Ritter, *Lost Ballparks* (New York: Viking Penguin, 1992), 20.

25 See Miller, *A Tour of Braves Field*, 8.

26 See, for instance, the interview with Boston Braves fan Mort Bloomberg in Rich Marazzi, "Four decades after their departure, the Braves (and their park) are fondly remembered by fans," *Sports Collectors Digest,* September 29, 1995, 91. Consult Ruzzo, "Imperfect History," and Bob Brady, "A Streetcar Named Braves Field" (*Boston Braves Historical Association Newsletter*, Spring 2010, 4-5), for specific details of the Braves Field trolley service.

27 Ruzzo quotes an article in *Baseball Magazine* that calls it "the world's greatest ballpark," as well as NL President John K. Tener calling it "the last word in ballparks." See Ruzzo, "Braves Field: An Imperfect History." Both quotes are referenced in note 33.

28 Ruzzo, "Braves Field: An Imperfect History."

29 See Baseball Reference.com: baseball-reference.com/teams/BSN/1915-schedule-scores.shtml; scroll down to the games of August 19 and 20.

30 Kaese, 173; Marazzi, 91.

31 From the series, "Burns-Eye Views of Big Time Parks," by Ed Burns of the Chicago *Tribune*. There were 15 one-page articles in

all, one for each park. (Sportsman's Park served both St. Louis teams; incidentally, League Park and Cleveland Municipal Stadium are covered together in article No. 11.) They contain Burns's own rather whimsical drawings of each park's layout (with several captions), plus two columns of text that combine factual data with the author's editorial comments. The website Behind the Bag has digitalized versions of Nos. 1-11 in the "Burns-Eye-View" series at behindthebag.net/category/burns-eye-views-of-big-time-parks/; they are given in descending order, which means you need to scroll all the way down for the Braves stadium (referred to by Burns as "National League Park"), which was first in the series. (For fans of the Red Sox, Fenway Park is covered in No. 8.) The article was originally published in the *Chicago Tribune* on June 6, 1937, on page B4.

32 See Lowry, *Green Cathedrals* (first edition, Reading, Massachusetts: Addison-Wesley Publishing Co., 1992), 113.

33 Marazzi, 91. Ralph Evans vehemently disagrees with the allegation of faulty sightlines, but he remembers the more "fan-friendly" Braves Field of the last years.

34 See Ruzzo, "Braves Field: An Imperfect History." Also Kaese, 174 ff. Gaffney accepted an offer of $500,000 for the team after paying a mere $187,000.

35 See Kaese (190-233) and Hirshberg (25-66) for entertaining accounts of the judge's many misadventures. Kaese (193) empha-sizes, however, that Fuchs also introduced a lot of fan-friendly features to the Braves experience, such as the first "broadcast-ing contracts for the Boston clubs" and a Knot Hole Gang for kids. The late George Altison, who served for many years as the president of the Boston Braves Historical Association, can be seen reminiscing fondly of his time in the Knot Hole Gang in "Boston the Way It Was — Part 3: The Boston Braves," part of a television series about Boston in the 1930s and '40s that first aired in 1995. It can be accessed on YouTube at youtube.com/watch?v=JycSH_ouRfc.

36 Ruzzo, "Braves Field: An Imperfect History." Also see Kaese, 192.

37 This group originally included Charles F. Adams, founder of the Boston Bruins hockey team; however, as he owned the Suffolk Downs race track, Commissioner Landis eventually forced him to sell his stock (1941); and then, "[s]o many stockholders took over the team that it became a standard gag around the press room that owners out-numbered newspapermen at the bar after every ball-game" (Hirshberg, 75); on the convolutions of the Braves ownership situation between 1935 and 1944, see Hirshberg, 63-77.

38 Hirshberg, 31.

39 Hirshberg, 38.

40 Kaese, 173, 174. Ruzzo, "Braves Field: An Imperfect History," includes another quote from the same interview that is telling: The Georgia Peach declared that the Braves' new home was "the only field in the country on which you can play an absolutely fair game of ball without the interference of fences." James Gaffney

was not the only person in America who preferred "inside base-ball" and thrilling extra-base hits in the 1910s.

41 See Price, "Braves Field."

42 Kaese, 197. Two months after Snyder's historical clout, Bernie Neis of the Braves outdid him by launching a drive in a game against St. Louis all the way onto the railroad tracks. Kaese writes that no one had hit a ball over the left-field wall even in batting practice until Neis did so on April 10 of that same year, four days before the 1925 season started.

43 Ritter, *Lost Ballparks*, 22. In all, there were 1,925 home runs of all types hit at Braves Field; see David W. Vincent, ed. *Home Runs in the Old Ballparks* (Cleveland: SABR, 1995), 12. For the record, the last homer at Braves Field was hit by Roy Campanella on September 21, 1952.

44 Figures are from Philip J. Lowry, *Green Cathedrals* (New York: Walker & Co., 2006), 32, which graphically proves that the dimensions by no means remained constant in the periods between the years chosen for reference! Some comments: after the renovations of 1937, the right-field foul pole stood 376 feet from home plate; left-field figure for 1946 is technically from 1944, but Ritter claims that it remained constant into the 1950s (*Lost Ballparks*, 24). He also writes that the deepest point after the last major renovations in the mid-'40s was 390 feet to "deep-est center." By the way, there is no explanation given for the two different distances listed for right field in 1946.

45 The epithet is Ed Burns's, from "Burns-Eye-Views of Big Time Parks," *Chicago Tribune*, 1937.

46 "Burns-Eye-Views of Big Time Parks," *Chicago Tribune*, 1937.

47 On the shifting of home plate and the concomitant alterations, see Ritter, *Lost Ballparks*, 24; the 1992 edition of *Green Cathedrals* (112), and Kaese, 235. On the right-field scoreboard (and the low esteem it was held in by Braves fans), see Hirshberg, 180-81; it is clearly visible above the Jury Box in photos and film footage from the final years.

48 Judge Fuchs passionately supported the referendum that passed in November 1928 to allow baseball on Sundays (Kaese, 207). The Braves were supposed to play the first Sunday game ever in Boston on April 21, 1929, but the game was rained out. It was the Red Sox, in the end, who had the privilege, losing to the A's in Braves Field on April 28. (Due to a provision of the new law that still forbade Sunday ball in fields close to churches, the Red Sox had to play their Sunday home games at Braves Field until May 1932. See Kaese, 221.) The Braves finally played their first Sunday home game on May 5, 1929. Incidentally, Ruzzo, in "Braves Field: An Imperfect History," contends that in 1918, "Gaffney and Red Sox owner Harry Frazee discussed the possibility of sharing Braves Field," so that the latter could make a killing on the real estate market by selling Fenway Park.

49 Kaese, 200.

50 Hirshberg, 50-51. Also see Kaese, 227-28. Kaese suggests that the plan was to use the park exclusively for racing, with the Braves moving their home games to Fenway Park ("'[o]ver my

dead body' was the equivalent of Tom Yawkey's quick reply," Kaese, 227).

51 Bob Brady points out (email of December 5, 2014) that the full official name emblazoned on the ticket office/administration building during the "Bees" era was "National League Baseball Field," but Burns uses the shorter name in his 1937 ballpark profile, and this is also what is listed as an alternate name of the facility in *Green Cathedrals*, 31. To further muddy the waters here, both Hirshberg (71) and Kaese (236) write that Braves Field was called "National League *Park*" at this time.

52 Kaese, 244.

53 "Burns-Eye-Views of Big Time Parks," *Chicago Tribune*, 1937.

54 Hirshberg, 117.

55 On Perini, Rugo, and Maney, see Hirshberg, 116-25, and Kaese, 254-69.

56 See Kaese, 257, and consult the outfield dimensions given in *Green Cathedrals*, 32.

57 Kaese, 261, 263; aerial views of "The Wigwam" at night can be seen in old newsreel footage included in the short Boston University video "Remembering the Wigwam: Braves Field and Nickerson Field," which can be accessed on YouTube at youtube.com/watch?v=r9q-MdefG-c.

58 Kaese, 263. Also Hirshberg, 180, who adds that this "job … was done while a rodeo was performed at Braves Field"!

59 On the new scoreboard, see Hirshberg, 180-81. None of the Sources consulted state when exactly the boxes were installed on the grandstand roof, but Brady, in his November 15, 2014, email, informed us that the building of the "Skyview Boxes" was announced in a late 1947 issue of the team's publication, the *Braves Bulletin*. Originally, they were only on the first-base side of the roof; a late 1948 issue of the Bulletin declared that Sky Views were being added to the third-base side for 1949. Also compare the two versions of the drawing of Braves Field by Gene Mack. The first was published in *The Sporting News* on January 15, 1947, 11, and shows no left-field scoreboard or seats on the grandstand roof; the second was a later revision, and is reproduced in *National Baseball Hall of Fame and Museum Yearbook* for 1984, 53; it shows what is labeled the "new scoreboard" and the Sky View box seats on the first-base side of the roof, and mentions the Braves pennant of 1948. We have not yet found publishing information for this later drawing; the 1984 Hall of Fame yearbook states only, on 53, that this and the other ballpark cartoons it is reproducing are "courtesy of Mrs. Ruth (Mack) O'Toole." The original drawings of 1946-47 can be viewed at baseball-fever.com/showthread.php?84778-1946-47-Sporting-News-Sketches-of-Major-League-Parks-by-Gene-Mack-Full-Set-of-14.

60 Marazzi, 91. The date is from Ralph Evans.

61 Kaese, 174.

62 See Kaese, 263-64; Hirshberg, 182; Marazzi, 91; also George Sullivan, "Memories of Braves Field" (*Boston Globe*, "Sports Plus," September 30, 1977), 20. Kaese quotes a final outlay of "nearly $6,000," while Hirshberg claims "the whole business cost the Braves over $7,000." *Green Cathedrals*, 33, erroneously reports that the Braves had to play their remaining April home games at Fenway Park because of this incident; in fact, the team played the Dodgers at Braves Field on the following day, and held only their April 28 doubleheader vs. the Phillies at the Red Sox' home park.

63 Quote from "Boston the Way It Was." *The Braves Family* is also the name of the team film that Sullivan produced after 1947: the first-ever color film made by a baseball team. (Extensive footage from this film can be seen in "Boston the Way It Was.") The black-and-white *Take Me Out to the Wigwam*, the first postseason film ever made in major-league baseball, appeared the previous year. Both films are available digitally through Rare Sports Films and contain priceless footage of Braves Field. Sullivan later became famous as owner of the New England Patriots NFL team.

64 From reminiscences in "Boston the Way It Was."

65 For more on Sullivan's many promotions, see Kaese, 262-64, 268 ("Three Little Earaches" on 263); Hirshberg, 178-85; Sullivan, 18; Marazzi, 91.

66 See the first edition of Philip J. Lowry, *Green Cathedrals* (Reading, Massachusetts: Addison-Wesley Publishing Co., 1992), 112.

67 See Hirshberg, 104-113.

68 On Lolly Hopkins, see "Boston the Way It Was," which includes film footage of her receiving her bracelet (in turn, this presumably comes from *The Braves Family*).

69 Total home attendance for this five-year period was 5,728,659; we have subtracted the home attendance for the games of April 28, 1946, when the Braves used Fenway Park after the "Wet Paint Incident" of Opening Day. The only years they drew over 1 million in Boston were 1947-1949.

70 Interview of May 21, 1997; see Miller, 10.

71 Marazzi, 92.

72 See photograph in "Remembering the Wigwam: Braves Field and Nickerson Field."

73 Miller, *A Tour of Braves Field*, 10-11. The Braves Field plate is now in the Sports Museum of New England.

74 As reported on August 31, 1997; the same story appeared in the *Boston Globe*. Of course, if this were true, why wouldn't the Braves just use Braves Field while their new park was being built?

75 Ralph Evans interview. According to Sullivan, "(C)ollege baseball attracted big crowds there in the '20s." Sullivan, "Memories of Braves Field," 16.

76 See the page on the Boston University Athletics website: goterriers.com/facilities/nickerson.html. For more of the history of Nickerson Field from a BU perspective, see the article

"Remembering the Wigwam" on the university website, at bu.edu/today/2012/braves-field-remembering-the-wigwam-2/. During the late 1990s, when Evans and this author collaborated on the print edition of his annual Braves Field tour, there was concern that BU was going to tear down all of what was left of the old ballpark. See Miller, *A Tour of Braves Field*, 11.

77 See Bob Brady, "Going, Going …" in *Boston Braves Historical Association Newsletter*, Summer 2010, 4.

78 Evans says "he paced every square foot" of the park after starting to work as the BU clubhouse boy in 1955: "I would come to work early and just walk the park up and down." He also was able to study the original blueprints.

OPENING GAME ON NEW BRAVES FIELD

The rivet tappers are silent,
The grumbling crusher is still
And here is the thing they've fashioned,
The work of the noisesome mill.
Tier upon tier it rises,
A gray and a lofty pile,
As grim in its stony casings
As the mark of a Gorgon smile.

But it ain't any further, kid, from the plate to second;
It's big an' gran' an' elegant, but get this in yer dome:
Them sacks are measured out jus' like you always reckined
And it's the same ol' erround' from home-ta-home.

—R.E. McMillin, *Boston Evening Journal*, August 17, 1915.

Main entrance under construction.

THE FIELD IS THE STAR

AUGUST 18, 1915: BOSTON BRAVES 3, ST. LOUIS CARDINALS 1 AT BRAVES FIELD

BY BRIAN DAVENPORT, PHD

A brief glance at the box score for the mid-August game between the Boston Braves and the St. Louis Cardinals makes it appear that the Braves' 3-1 win was a standard affair. However, the August 18, 1915, contest between these two teams was anything but normal. While the game flowed in fairly typical fashion, with a nice pitchers' duel resulting in only a handful of hits and few runs, it was the rest of the occasion that made this game stand out in the history of the Boston Braves.

On a fair day by most accounts, the game proceeded in fairly usual fashion. Braves starter Dick Rudolph threw a complete game, holding the Cardinals to eight hits and one walk while striking out six. Rudolph wasn't the only one who turned in decent pitching either. While giving up three runs, the Cardinals' Harry "Slim" Sallee held the Braves to five hits while striking out two before being relieved by Lee Meadows in the top of the eighth inning. Were it not for the five walks surrendered by Sallee, the outcome of the game may have been different. As it happened though, the Braves took a three-run lead into the ninth inning before the Cardinals' Tom Long was able to drive in Bob Bescher for a meaningless run.

The Braves, on the other hand, started their scoring early. In the second inning, "[Braves left fielder Sherry] Magee hit a fly, which Bescher came in from deep left for and, after a long run, got his hands on, but could not hold."[1] This Texas Leaguer, combined with a poor throw to the infield, allowed Boston's Magee to advance to second. After a sacrifice by Butch Schmidt advanced Magee to third, Rabbit Maranville used one of his two hits in the game to drive in the Braves' first run. The Braves finished their scoring in the fourth inning when catcher Hank Gowdy plated two by

hitting a double to the right-field gap. This proved to be more than enough scoring, allowing the Braves to emerge victorious. However, neither the pitching of Rudolph nor the offense of Maranville and Gowdy was the star that day. Instead, the star of the day was the field itself –this was the first game played at the new Braves field. The Braves had played the earlier portion of the season at nearby Fenway Park, courtesy of the Boston Red Sox.[2]

Located just off Commonwealth Avenue in Allston, Braves Field was hailed as "the finest baseball park in the world."[3] Construction under owner James E. Gaffney commenced just before the 1915 season, in March.[4] And even though Gaffney built the biggest

The new ballpark's office and front gates.

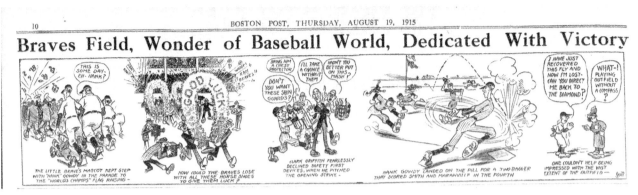

ballpark of the time, the expansive facility turned out not to be big enough to hold all who were interested in attending. With seating for between 43,000 and 45,000, by far the largest in baseball at the time, the Braves still ended up turning away 6,000 fans, even after they exceeded capacity by allowing an estimated 46,000 fans through the gates.[5] Those who were able to get through the turnstiles were not your typical crowd, either. A host of dignitaries were there, including Boston Mayor James Michael Curley, along with 12 other Massachusetts mayors.[6] In addition to political notables, a number of baseball men were present for the opening game. These included Charles Ebbets, president of the Brooklyn Robins; Chicago Cubs president Charles Thomas; National League President John Tener; and National League Secretary John Heydler.[7]

The special guests weren't only in the stands. The first pitch, a strike, was thrown out by Washington manager

Clark Griffith and caught by Braves manager George "The Miracle Man" Stallings.[8] In addition to the baseball and political dignitaries among the 46,000 in attendance were 10,000 children from the Boston area.[9] Also there were 300 members of the Royal Rooters who "as usual, were quick to appreciate the good plays and to encourage anything that looked like a rally."[10] In addition to the Royal Rooter band, who "were out full force with their band and singers and making themselves heard as in the days when 'Tessie' was new,"[11] the 9th Regiment Band was also on hand to add to the cacophony of the day.[12] Finally, according to the *Boston Globe,* "there were fans from every walk, oldtimers galore, and probably not less than 6000 women, the greatest outpouring of the fair sex that the game probably ever has known."[13]

While the game and the crowd were something to see, the field itself was what really took the day. With ceremonies that included the raising of the world's championship pennant, the field itself was massive. Sod from the Braves' former home at the South End Grounds had been transported to help form the infield at the new park. The distance down the foul lines was 375 feet to both poles. Dead center was 440 feet and right center was a monstrous 520 feet.[14] None other than Ty Cobb declared that a ball could not be hit over the fence at the new park.[15] In addition to Cobb, other baseball notables, including Hughie Jennings and Clark Griffith, claimed "that it is all that a modern baseball plant should be."[16] The greatness of the park extended beyond the field as well; the clubhouses under the grandstands were equipped with showers, there was plenty of office space, and there were 22 box

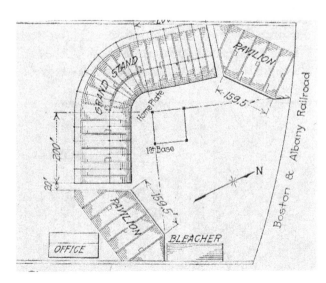

Braves Field layout.

offices and 28 turnstiles to allow for the large crowds to be accommodated.[17]

Even though the afternoon started out in spectacular fashion, with opening ceremonies that included raising the championship flag, followed by a great performance by the Braves, it had to come to an end. With a 3-0 lead in hand heading into the seventh, many of the Braves fans began to leave as quickly as they had arrived.[18] While the splendor of the new park was something to behold, at the end of the day this was another ballgame and another Braves win. As a result, the fans left happy and "the pleasure was due mainly to the fact that the Boston club won from St Louis by a score of 3 to 1; that there was a lot of good playing and very little that was not up to standard."[19]

NOTES

1   J. C. O'Leary, "The Rabbit Sends in the First Run," *Boston Globe,* August 19, 1915.

2   See Bill Nowlin, "The Time(s) the Braves Played Home Games at Fenway Park," in *The Miracle Braves of 1914: Boston's Original Worst-to-First World Series Champions* (Phoenix, Arizona: SABR, 2014), 320-327. The Braves were able to return the favor by allowing the Red Sox to play the 1915 World Series in the larger-capacity Braves Field.

3   J.C. O'Leary, "Braves Field Opening Today," *Boston Globe,* August 18, 1915.

4   "Braves' Field Will be Open Wednesday," *Boston Globe,* August 15, 1915.

5   Melville E. Webb Jr., "Braves Dedicate New Park with Victory Before the Greatest Crowd That Ever Saw a Ball Game," *Boston Globe,* August 19, 1915.

6   "Stallings and Griff Battery," *Boston Globe,* August 17, 1915.

7   Webb, "Braves Dedicate New Park."

8   *Hartford Courant,* August 8, 1915.

9   Webb, "Braves Dedicate New Park."

10 J.C. O'Leary, "The Rabbit Sends in the First Run," *Boston Globe,* August 19, 1915.

11 Webb, "Braves Dedicate New Park."

12 Ibid.

13 Ibid.

14 "Boston's New Ideal Park," *Sporting Life,* August 28, 1915. It should be noted that there were conflicting contemporary reports of the dimensions of the new field. See Philip J. Lowry's *Green Cathedrals* (New York: Walker & Co., 2006) for further discussion.

15 "Braves' Field Will Be Open Wednesday," *Boston Globe,* August 15, 1915.

16 *Sporting Life,* August 28, 1915.

17 Ibid.

18 Webb, "Braves Dedicate New Park."

19 O'Leary, "The Rabbit Sends in the First Run."

WHEN SIZE DID MATTER:
THE RED SOX SQUEEZE BY GROVER CLEVELAND ALEXANDER AND THE PHILLIES IN PIVOTAL GAME THREE OF THE 1915 WORLD SERIES

OCTOBER 11, 1915: BOSTON RED SOX 2, PHILADELPHIA PHILLIES 1 AT BRAVES FIELD (GAME THREE OF THE 1915 WORLD SERIES)

BY C. PAUL ROGERS III

The 1915 World Series featured the upstart Philadelphia Phillies, who had swept to the National League pennant by seven games behind Grover Cleveland Alexander's phenomenal 31 wins (including 12 shutouts, four one-hitters, and three two-hitters),[1] against the heavily favored Boston Red Sox, winners of 101 games in a close pennant race against the Detroit Tigers.[2]

In 1915 baseball still followed the practice of a coin flip to determine which team hosted the opening games of the World Series. Phillies' president William F. Baker won the toss, and the first two games were played in his bandbox ballpark, the Baker Bowl.[3] The Phillies won the October 8 opener, 3-1, behind Alexander's eight-hitter but the Red Sox captured the second game, 2-1, behind a three-hitter by the diminutive Rube Foster, who also knocked in the winning run with a ninth-inning single.[4] President Woodrow Wilson, accompanied by his fiancée, Edith Galt, attended game and threw out the first pitch. He was the first president to attend a World Series game.

The Series then switched to Boston for Games Three and Four. The Red Sox elected, with the consent of the crosstown Braves, to play their home games in brand-new Braves Field, which had a capacity of 42,000, the largest in the big leagues.[5] While the larger seating capacity of Braves Field certainly influenced the Red Sox decision to move, the club was also no doubt seeking a competitive advantage. The Braves Field outfield was expansive, measuring 402 feet down

each foul line and 550 feet to dead center,[6] and would allow the exceedingly fast Red Sox outfield trio of Tris Speaker, Duffy Lewis, and Harry Hooper plenty of room to track down fly balls.

Phillies manager Pat Moran[7] started the redoubtable Alexander on two days' rest.[8] Red Sox manager Bill Carrigan picked Dutch Leonard, one of the top lefties

Grover Cleveland Alexander, 31-game winner for the Phillies in 1915.

in the American League, over the protestations of Babe Ruth, who was arguably the top southpaw in the league and who very much wanted a World Series start.[9] According to one report, Carrigan purposely kept Ruth on the bench to make it clear to the cocky, out-of-control 20-year-old that the Red Sox could win without him.[10]

A World Series record crowd of 42,360 crammed into Braves Field, more than saw the first two games in Philadelphia combined. Among them was a delegation from the Massachusetts Women's Suffrage Association, which gave Red Sox star center fielder Tris Speaker a $10 gold piece for scoring the first Red Sox run of the Series.[11] Once the game started, Speaker promptly lost leadoff hitter Milt Stock's lazy fly ball in the sun. Speaker never moved for the ball, which fell about 15 feet from where he was standing for a gift double. Dave Bancroft sacrificed Stock to third but Leonard pitched himself out of the early hole, retiring Dode Paskert on a foul popup to Larry Gardner at third before striking out Phils slugger Gavvy Cravath to end the inning.

Another taut pitcher's duel quickly developed as Alexander retired the first four Red Sox hitters before allowing a single to left by Duffy Lewis, who was promptly thrown out by catcher Ed Burns trying to steal.[12]

The game was scoreless when Burns led off the Phillies' third with a ground single to right just out of the reach of second baseman Jack Barry. Alexander sacrificed and was safe when first baseman Dick Hoblitzell

muffed Gardner's perfect throw. Stock sacrificed and the Phillies had runners on second and third with one out. Dave Bancroft followed with a single to center to plate Burns with the first run of the game. Alexander took a wide turn at third before Moran, coaching third, put on the brakes. He drew a throw home from Speaker, which enabled Bancroft to scamper down to second. Paskert was next and lofted a ball to short right but Barry made a fine running catch while the runners held.

That again brought up Cravath, the undisputed leading slugger in the game. He'd set a twentieth-century major-league record that year with 24 home runs, his third year in a row to lead the majors. (He also led in runs batted in with 115.)[13] Cravath proceeded to hit the longest ball of the Series, a prodigious blast to deepest left field that sent Lewis racing with his back to the plate. He turned and grabbed the ball just in front of the left-field bleachers, a full 400 feet from home plate, to retire the side. Cravath's blast would have been a three-run homer in Fenway Park or the Baker Bowl, but was just a long out in Braves Field.[14] Thus, two great Red Sox fielding plays in the inning kept the Phillies to a single run.

The Red Sox tied the score in their half of the fourth on Speaker's one-out line triple down the right-field line, quickly followed by Hoblitzell's long sacrifice to Paskert in left to score Tris. Both hurlers then set down the opposition without a baserunner until the bottom of the seventh, when Speaker led off with a single to left. Hoblitzell attempted to sacrifice but Burns pounced on the ball and threw to Bancroft at

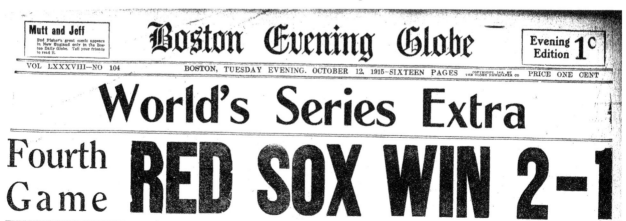

second to force Speaker while Hoblitzell stood at home plate thinking the ball was foul. The Phillies threw to first for the double play and while the Red Sox squawked long and hard to home-plate umpire Silk O'Loughlin, the call stood.[15]

While Alexander held the Red Sox at bay, the Phillies could not even generate a baserunner after the third inning. In the ninth Leonard made it 20 consecutive Phillies retired after two groundouts and a foul pop. In the bottom of the inning Hooper led off with a two-strike single to right field. Everett Scott twice failed to lay down a sacrifice, but with two strikes surprised the Phillies by poking a bunt that got by Alexander. Second baseman Bert Niehoff raced in from second and made a sparkling play, just nipping Scott at first while Hooper advanced to second. Manager Moran then ordered an intentional pass to Speaker to put runners on first and second with one out. As Speaker trotted down to first, he doffed his cap to the Phillies dugout.[16] Hoblitzell was next and slashed a drive that seemed headed to right field. Niehoff, however, made another fine play to get to the ball and threw to first to get the batter by a whisker.

That left runners on second and third with two outs and Duffy Lewis coming to the plate in one of the pivotal and most controversial at-bats in the Series. At that juncture the hot-hitting Lewis was 4-for-7 against Alexander in the Series. The feeling in the press box was that Moran would order Alexander to intentionally walk Lewis to set up a force at any base and bring Larry Gardner to the plate.[17] But after a mound confab, the Phillies decided to pitch to Lewis even with first base open. Lewis laced Alexander's

first pitch to center field to drive in the winning run and end the ballgame. In a happy delirium the Red Sox faithful rushed onto the field, lifted Lewis on their shoulders and carried him off the field. He later lamented that the crowd almost broke his back.[18] The hit proved to be the seminal moment in Lewis' rock-solid 11-year big-league career.[19]

The Phillies couldn't recover from the walkoff loss, which put Boston ahead in the Series two games to one. They proceeded to lose two more one-run games as the Red Sox claimed the world championship in five games.

After the Series, Alexander defended the decision to pitch to Lewis in the ninth inning of Game Three, asserting that in a prior all-star tour Lewis had gotten exactly two hits off him in 12 to 14 games, striking out four times in one game. He wrote, "If there was a player in the world that I should have felt confident in facing on past experiences, that man was Lewis. Every series has its star. I didn't know that Lewis was to be the star of 1915."[20]

Alexander also revealed after the Series that he had strained his pitching shoulder while favoring a blister in a game against Brooklyn on Labor Day and had not been healthy since, even though he had thrown a one-hit shutout against the Braves on September 29 to clinch the pennant. According to Alexander, "[i]t is a very disconcerting experience to find yourself at the critical moment, when every eye is on you, and know that you are not in your best form."[21]

Moran intended to bring Alexander back in Game Five on only one day's rest (after pitching Game Three

Crowd going into Braves Field to see Red Sox play the Phillies in World Series, 1915.

on two days' rest). Alex, however, was forced to tell his manager after warming up that his "arm was not right."[22] To baseball's then greatest pitcher, the 1915 Series was "a peculiar, personal disappointment in that I was unable, through lack of condition to live up to expectations of my friends."[23]

SOURCES

Alexander, Charles C. *Spoke – A Biography of Tris Speaker* (Dallas: Southern Methodist University Press, 2007).

Alexander, Grover Cleveland. "How I Lost the World Series," *Baseball Magazine*, January 1916.

The Baseball Encyclopedia (New York: The Macmillan Company, 1969).

Baseball-reference.com.

Clark, Ellery H., Jr. *Red Sox Forever* (Hicksville, New York: Exposition Press, 1979).

Gay, Timothy M. *Tris Speaker – the Rough-and-Tumble Life of a Baseball Legend* (Lincoln: University of Nebraska Press, 2005).

Golenbock, Peter. *Fenway – An Unexpurgated History of the Boston Red Sox* (New York: G.P. Putnam's Sons, 1992).

Honig, Donald. *The October Heroes* (New York: Simon & Schuster, 1979).

Kavanagh, Jack. *Ol' Pete – The Grover Cleveland Alexander Story* (South Bend, Indiana: Diamond Communications, Inc., 1996).

Krueger, Joseph J. *Baseball's Greatest Drama – World Series History, 1903-1945* (Milwaukee: Joseph J. Krueger, 1946).

Lieb, Frederick G., and Stan Baumgartner. *The Philadelphia Phillies* (Kent, Ohio: Kent University Press, 2009, originally published by A.S. Barnes & Co., Inc., 1948).

Lieb, Frederick. *Baseball As I Have Known It* (New York: Coward, McCann & Geoghegan, 1977).

Lieb, Frederick G. *The Boston Red Sox* (Carbondale: Southern Illinois University Press, 2003, *originally published by* G.P. Putman's Sons, 1947).

Ritter, Lawrence S. *Lost Ballparks – A Celebration of Baseball's Legendary Fields* (New York: Viking, 1992).

Ritter, Lawrence S. *The Glory of Their Times* (New York: Macmillan & Co., 1966).

Skipper, John C. *Wicked Curve – The Life and Troubled Times of Grover Cleveland Alexander* (Jefferson, North Carolina: McFarland & Company, Inc., 2006).

Westcott, Rich, and Frank Bilovsky. *The New Phillies Encyclopedia* (Philadelphia: Temple University Press, 1993).

Zingg, Paul J. *Harry Hooper – An American Baseball Life* (Urbana: University of Illinois Press, 1993).

NOTES

1   After the season *Baseball Magazine* devoted most of an issue to Alexander. One article compared him to Walter Johnson, who had won 28 games in 1915 after seasons of 32, 34, and 28 wins, and concluded that Alexander had surpassed Johnson. "The Greatest Pitcher on the Diamond Today," *Baseball Magazine*, January, 1916, 44.

2   It was the second straight year that Boston and Philadelphia had teams in the World Series as the Miracle Braves had swept the Philadelphia Athletics in 1914. It has not happened since.

3   Baker had made his "bowl" even smaller for the Series by installing 400 temporary bleacher seats on the field in right-center.

4   Foster, a right-hander, was only 5-feet-7-inches tall. He was a good-hitting pitcher and in 1915 had a regular-season batting average of .277.

5   The Red Sox' use of Braves Field was something of a return of a favor since the Red Sox had permitted the Braves to play in Fenway Park during parts of 1914 and 1915 while Braves Field was being built.

6   Lawrence G. Ritter, *Lost Ballparks*, 20.

7   Moran was a rookie manager in 1915 with no previous managerial experience. He had served as a coach and backup catcher for the Phillies previously and later managed the Cincinnati Reds to the 1919 National League pennant and world's championship in the tainted 1919 World Series.

8   The day following Game Two was a Sunday and both Philadelphia and Boston had Blue Laws prohibiting Sunday baseball, so the Series did not resume until Monday, October 11. That offday permitted Phillies manager Moran to go back to Alexander.

9   Frederick G. Lieb, *The Boston Red Sox*, 129. Ruth had gone 18-8 with a 2.44 earned-run average in 1915 while Leonard was

15-7 with a 2.36 ERA. The Babe grounded out as a pinch-hitter against Grover Cleveland Alexander in Game One in what would be his only World Series appearance in 1915.

10   Peter Golenbock, *Fenway – An Unexpurgated History of the Boston Red Sox*, 46. Carrigan also inserted himself as catcher for Game Three, replacing starting catcher Hick Cady, for his only fall classic appearance as a player. Both Carrigan and Moran were former catchers with New England roots. Carrigan was from Lewiston, Maine, while Moran hailed from Fitchburg, Massachusetts.

11   Charles C. Alexander, *Spoke – A Biography of Tris Speaker*, 95. The suffragettes may have been seeking support for the women's suffrage initiative for an upcoming November 2 Massachusetts ballot and to counter opposing forces who were distributing anti-suffrage pocket schedules and negative advertising in ballparks. The initiative was defeated by nearly 2 to 1. Bob Brady, "Pocket Schedule Politicking," *Boston Braves Historical Association Newsletter*, Fall 2014, 4.

12   It was one St. Mary's College alumnus throwing out another. In fact, four players in the 1915 Series had attended St. Mary's College in Oakland, California. In addition to Lewis and Burns, they were Red Sox starter Leonard and outfielder Harry Hooper. A fifth St. Mary's alumnus, pitcher Joe Oeschger, had appeared in six games for the 1915 Phillies while spending most of the season with Providence of the International League. Paul J. Zingg, *Harry Hooper – An American Baseball Life*, 159-60.

13   The Federal League was considered a third major league in 1915 so Cravath actually led three leagues in home runs and runs batted in. In contrast to Cravath's 24 home runs, the Red Sox as a team hit only 14 home runs all season.

14   After the Series, Lewis appeared in a vaudeville show in Los Angeles, Cravath's hometown. Lewis later related that a man in Los Angeles asked him in what park he made that catch off Cravath. When Lewis told him it was Braves Field, the man replied that if Cravath had hit that ball in the Baker Bowl, he (Cravath) would be doing the vaudeville act instead. See Ellery H. Clark, *Red Sox Forever*, 43.

15   Lieb, 131.

16   Charles C. Alexander, 95. After the Series, Speaker was quoted as saying, "Nothing in my career looms up quite so pleasant as that base on balls from Alexander in the pinch." *Cleveland Press*, April 9, 1916, 14.

17   Frederick G. Lieb and Stan Baumgartner, *The Philadelphia Phillies*, 130.

18   Timothy M. Gay, *Tris Speaker – The Rough-and-Tumble Life of a Baseball Legend*, 157.

19   Lewis was the leading hitter in the Series, going 8-for-18 for a .444 batting average.

20   Alexander also thought that Larry Gardner, the next batter, "was a dangerous man in a pinch." Grover Cleveland Alexander, "How I Lost the World Series," *Baseball Magazine*, January, 1916, 37-38.

21   Grover Cleveland Alexander, 36.

22   Grover Cleveland Alexander, 37. Moran and Alexander both assumed that had the Phillies been able to extend the Series by winning Game Five, Alexander would have been ready to toe the rubber a day later in Game Six. Pat Moran, "What I Think About Alexander," *Baseball Magazine*, January, 1916, 53.

23   Eleven years later, in 1926, a 39-year-old Alexander became a World Series hero by winning two games for the St. Louis Cardinals and dramatically coming out of the bullpen to strike out Tony Lazzeri of the New York Yankees with the bases loaded in Game Seven to secure the Cardinals' first world championship.

BRAVES FIELD HOSTS THE TWO-TO-ONE SERIES

OCTOBER 12, 1915: BOSTON RED SOX 2, PHILADELPHIA PHILLIES 1 AT BRAVES FIELD (GAME FOUR OF THE 1915 WORLD SERIES)

BY MARK PESTANA

Game Four of the 1915 World Series was the second home game in the Series for the American League champion Boston Red Sox – but it was not played on their own home field. A year earlier, the National League-pennant-winning Boston Braves had "borrowed" Fenway Park from the Red Sox for the World Series because the two-year-old jewel box stadium provided an upgrade from their own South End Grounds. Now, in an interesting reversal, the Sox accepted the offer of Braves owner James Gaffney to play their World Series games against the Philadelphia Phillies at spanking new Braves Field, opened only two months before and boasting the largest capacity in the major leagues, a little over 42,000.[1]

After a 3-1 opening-game loss in Philadelphia, the Red Sox had gained the upper hand, taking two straight contests by identical 2-1 scores. Their Game Three victory the previous day at Braves Field was especially encouraging, as it came against Phillies ace Grover Cleveland Alexander, upon whom much of Philadelphia's hopes rested.

Although Game Four attendance, reported officially at 41,096, was slightly lower than that of Game Three, it was not through a lack of fans desiring admission. In fact, there was such a crush of prospective ticket-buyers that the fans found themselves somewhat in physical peril as they attempted to muscle through the ballpark gates: "The police were powerless, as apparently no systematic and intelligent arrangements had been made to handle the enormous crowd."[2] Recognizing potential danger, the Red Sox decided to stop selling standing-room tickets, and thus esti-

mated thousands were turned away. Of course, many of these sought out what vantage points were available outside the park and watched from a distance.

The weather was excellent for the 2:00 P.M. start, the "brilliant October sun having in its rays the warmth of early summer."[3] October 12 was Columbus Day, and Boston was celebrating with a number of public activities. Although the usual military parade was canceled due to "conditions in Europe" (the World War was raging), there was a parade of coast artillery from the city's harbor-defense corps, and the third annual Pan-American meeting was held at Faneuil Hall, presided over by Mayor James Michael Curley. Fireworks on the Common were scheduled for 3:00 P.M.[4]

Boston manager Bill Carrigan sent Ernie Shore to the mound on three days' rest. In his second year with the Red Sox, and having enjoyed a career-best season, (19-8, 1.64 ERA), Shore was looking to avenge his Game One loss to Alexander. Today he would face George Chalmers, who, at 27 years old, in the penultimate season of an unspectacular seven-year major-league career, was essentially manager Pat Moran's fifth starter behind Alexander, Erskine Mayer, Al Demaree, and Eppa Rixey. But Chalmers got the call ahead of Demaree and Rixey, and for the most part made Moran look like a genius in choosing him. The two teams together had produced but 10 runs in the first three games, and the huge audience at Braves Field was in for another pitchers' duel.

Third baseman Milt Stock led things off for the Phillies with a single down the left-field line but was erased trying to take an extra base by Duffy Lewis's swift

BOSTON, FRIDAY MORNING, OCTOBER 13, 1916—EIGHTEEN PAGES   PRICE TWO CENTS

SOX TAKE FOURTH WORLD TITLE BEFORE RECORD CROWD OF 42,620

Downhearted Robins Absolutely Helpless Before Sharp Breaking Shoots of Shore, and Outcome
Is Never in Doubt After Home Team Scores Two in Third Inning

By WALLACE GOLDSMITH

peg to shortstop Everett Scott covering second. A walk to future Hall of Famer Dave Bancroft was wasted too, as Shore then fanned Dode Paskert and Cravath. The Red Sox also failed to start well, Harry Hooper and Scott striking out and Tris Speaker getting caught stealing after drawing a base on balls.

Another inning and a half went by without scoring, both pitchers looking strong. Shore was perhaps getting the worst of the pitchers' match, walking a batter in each of the first four innings. He may have been a little wild, or it could have been that Moran's men were finally showing some patience at the plate – as *Boston Globe* columnist (and former nineteenth-century major leaguer) Tim Murnane suggested, consciously "waiting him out."[5]

Boston broke the scoreless tie in the bottom of the third. Second baseman Jack Barry walked and took second on Hick Cady's bunt single. Shore sacrificed Barry to third, and he tallied on Hooper's infield hit.

The Phillies threatened in the fourth, putting two men on, but came up empty when Chalmers hit into an inning-ending force out. Things were quiet on the Red Sox side too until the sixth, when first baseman Dick Hoblitzell stroked his second single of the game and was driven home by Lewis's double into left.

An apparently spontaneous show of patriotism erupted at the outset of the seventh inning, as a brass band struck up "The Star-Spangled Banner." The Braves Field crowd responded en masse, standing and doffing their headwear, and the players and umpires followed suit.[6]

Speaking of crowd demonstrations, Boston's Royal Rooters made their presence in the park well known. Ty Cobb commented in his syndicated column: "It is pretty tough when people have to pay from $1 to $5 for a seat to see a ball game and be pestered to death with the terrible strains of 'Tessie' through an entire world's series."[7]

Meanwhile, Shore had settled down and was picking up steam as the afternoon progressed. In the Philadelphia seventh, Chalmers, aiming to help his own cause, reached on a one-out blooper to center, but the opportunity died on Stock's double-play grounder.

One of the most hotly discussed matters of the Series was the lack of production from Phillies slugger Gavvy Cravath. At age 34 he had enjoyed one of his best seasons, topping the National League in runs, home runs, RBIs, walks, total bases, and slugging percentage. But here in his only postseason series, he was struggling miserably, with just one hit and one RBI to his credit in three games. Many blamed the spacious dimensions of Braves Field, but then again, Cravath did no better in his home park, going 1-for-8 in the Baker Bowl games, the same as in the Boston games. Cravath finally rose somewhat to the occasion in the eighth inning, mashing a two-out, full-count triple past Speaker in center. First baseman Fred Luderus, the one consistent bright spot in Moran's lineup this October, followed with a single that scored Gavvy and cut the Boston lead in half. Oscar Dugey pinch-ran for Luderus and when he stole second, the Phillies had the tying run in scoring position.[8] But Shore got Possum Whitted on an easy grounder back to the mound, and the uprising was quelled.

In the bottom half of the eighth, three men reached base for the Sox, but Larry Gardner's tapper back to

the mound was fired to the plate by Chalmers, forcing Speaker. Catcher Eddie Burns in turn "shot the ball down to Whitted"[9] at first, nipping Gardner. The snappy double play ended Boston's batting for the day. Shore put the Phillies down 1-2-3 in the ninth inning on only four pitches[10] and Game Four went into the books as the third straight 2-1 win for the Red Sox, placing them on the brink of the championship.

Eppa Rixey had been warming up all day, but things never got to the point where he was needed.[11] It was generally agreed that Chalmers had pitched above expectations, perhaps more effectively than either Alexander or Mayer in their games. Tim Murnane, referring to Chalmers as a "moist ball pitcher," said he pitched a "very intelligent game."[12]

The next day, the scene shifted back to Philadelphia for the final act: a 5-4 Red Sox victory in Game Five, giving the city of Boston its second of three consecutive World Series titles from 1914 to 1916.

NOTES

1 *Sporting Life*, October 2, 1915. It is acknowledged that both *Green Cathedrals* (New York: Walker & Co., 2006) and Harold Kaese's book *The Boston Braves* (New York: G.P. Putnam's Sons, 1948) cite the figure of 40,000.

2 *Springfield* (Massachusetts) *Daily Republican*, October 13, 1915.

3 *Springfield Daily Republican*, October 13, 1915.

4 *Boston Journal*, October 12, 1915.

5 *Boston Globe*, October 13, 1915.

6 *Philadelphia Inquirer*, October 13, 1915; *Springfield Daily Republican*, October 13, 1915.

7 *Philadelphia Public Ledger*, October 13, 1915.

8 Frederick G. Lieb, *The Boston Red Sox* (New York: Putnam, 1948), 133.

9 Lieb, 134.

10 Lieb, 134.

11 *Boston Herald*, October 13, 1915.

12 *Boston Globe*, October 13, 1915.

SLIDE, FITZY, SLIDE! BRAVES AND REDS PLAY 16 SCORELESS

JUNE 13, 1916: BOSTON BRAVES 0, CINCINNATI REDS 0 AT BRAVES FIELD

BY MARK S. STERNMAN

Thanks to sterling pitching, no clutch hitting, and two umpiring controversies, the Braves and the Reds settled for a memorable tie featuring a bizarre 2-3-5 double play concluding at home plate that extended the contest so that it ended as the longest scoreless duel in major-league history to date.

Cincinnati's Fred Toney yielded only two hits[1] in 11 innings before giving way to Pete Schneider, who gave up just one hit in five frames. Boston ace Dick Rudolph threw one more inning than Toney but gave up 11 hits. Rudolph made superlative fielding plays to keep the game scoreless; the last such play resulted, however, in a hand injury that required Tom Hughes to pitch after Pete Compton pinch-hit for Rudolph.

With foul weather plaguing the Hub, the Braves had not played since June 7, and the Reds had not taken the diamond since June 6. The game started late to let the field, "a quagmire,"[2] dry, but the delay did not faze Rudolph, who fanned the three Cincinnati batters in the top of the first.

In the second inning, Boston captain Johnny Evers, a record umpire-baiter,[3] could not stay out of the fray even on a day when he was too injured to play. "Dick Egan was called out on strikes, and started to sputter. Johnny Evers … directed his remarks at Pitcher Toney. … Johnny told Pitcher Toney that he, Johnny, had once fired him."[4]

Umpire Ernest Quigley ejected Evers for insulting the visiting pitcher. As Cubs manager in 1913, Evers had sold Toney, owner at the time of a 2-2 record with a 6.00 ERA, to the minors. Three years later, Evers tried to get Toney off his game, but his antics backfired.

"In great measure the laurels of the day swung to Toney[, who] was in rare form."[5]

Toney's 11 innings represented less than his average appearance in his preceding starts, a 16-inning complete-game win on May 31 followed by a 10-inning complete-game win on June 5. In three starts, Toney pitched 37 innings and gave up just 17 hits. "Pitching a team-high 300 innings in 1916, Toney posted a 2.28 ERA but compil[ed] a 14-17 record. In August of that year he stated that he could be a 25-game winner if the Reds would give him the four runs per game he felt he deserved, instead of the 2.5 runs he thought he was receiving."[6]

Boston got its first hit in the bottom of the second inning when Ed Konetchy singled. Konetchy stole second but stayed stranded after Toney struck out two.

In the top of the third, former Brave Buck Herzog, the Reds' player-manager, singled before Rudolph started a 1-6-3 double play via future Hall of Famer Rabbit Maranville.

In the top of the fourth inning, left fielder Greasy Neale singled. Neale, later a starter for the 1919 world champion Reds and coach of the 1948 and 1949 NFL champion Philadelphia Eagles, lit out for second too soon. Rudolph threw to first. Boston tagged out Neale in a rundown, but Neale would stay aggressive.

In the bottom of the sixth, Toney plunked Braves backstop Walt Tragesser. After consecutive fielder's choices, Boston center fielder Joe Connolly walked, but right fielder Joe Wilhoit hit into yet another fielder's choice to strand two mates.

BOSTON POST, WEDNESDAY, JUNE 14, 1916

In the top of the ninth inning, Neale singled again, and Rudolph had him picked off again. But bad throws by Konetchy and Maranville sent Neale to third with two outs. To the plate strode Hal Chase, who would bat a league-leading .339 in 1916. "It was a narrow squeak for Rudolph as Chase all but got an infield single on a slow roller toward third. Only just in time did Rudolph secure the ball and get his man at first while a Red was legging it across the plate."[7]

In the top of the 10th, Cincinnati got two on thanks to a single by first baseman Fritz Mollwitz and an intentional walk to Herzog after a wild pitch, but Baldy Louden hit into a fielder's choice to end the rally.

Boston had major threats in each of the first three extra innings. In the bottom of the 10th, Egan walked. Batting for Tragesser, Zip Collins reached on a fielder's choice/sacrifice when Reds catcher Ivey Wingo threw too late to second to try to cut down the lead runner. Declining to bat for Rudolph with two on and none out, Stallings ordered a bunt. But Wingo "made a beautiful play on what looked like a perfect sacrifice by Rudolph, forcing [Ed] Fitzpatrick, who was sent in to run in place of Egan, at third."[8]

In the 11th, Wilhoit hit a leadoff double, Boston's only extra-base hit, which, "[o]n a dry field ... would have been good for three bases."[9] Sherry Magee popped out to Wingo, then Herzog took Konetchy's grounder and gunned down Wilhoit at third. Facing his final batter, Toney retired Red Smith.

In the top of the 12th, the Reds loaded the bases with two outs after getting multiple hits in an inning for the only time in the game. Herzog replaced Toney with pinch-hitter Tommy Clarke, who "came so close to breaking up the game that there was no fun in it. Clarke hit the ball hard and on a line. It was whistling past Rudolph when the latter stuck out his bare hand and stopped the burning drive dead to toss out the hitter."[10]

The game's great controversy occurred in the bottom of the inning. Fitzpatrick walked. Hank Gowdy, resting to heal a spike injury, had replaced Tragesser behind the plate after Zip Collins pinch-hit, and sacrificed Fitzpatrick to second. With Rudolph already throwing 12 innings and now having a hurting hand, Braves manager George Stallings turned to Compton.

Compton hit a swinging bunt, but "[t]he speedy Ivy Wingo was on the ball like a shadow"[11] and "had gone nearly half way to first to retrieve the ball,"[12] which he threw to Mollwitz at first. With "a good lead off second"[13] and Wingo having vacated the plate, Fitzpatrick never stopped running, trying to end the game by scoring from second base on an infield out.

But Cincinnati third baseman Heinie Groh "beat Fitz to the plate, took Mollwitz's return throw, which was high, and, stooping, made a stab at Fitz, who claimed he touched the rubber with his hand."[14]

The conditions clearly complicated seeing what had actually happened. "In a swirl of mud, Fitzy, Heinie and the ball reached the plate at the same identical moment [as did] Umpire Quigley. As Heinie was doing a back flip-flop and Fitzy was sliding over, Umpire Quigley dropped his arms in the manner generally known to signify 'safe.'"[15]

Quigley's signal seemingly ended the game.

But "before the jubilant Braves or chagrined Reds could say a word, Umpire Quigley … announced … that Fitzy was out because he had failed to touch the rubber."[16]

Opinions differ on whether Fitzpatrick touched home, and whether Groh actually tagged Fitzpatrick at all, much less before he had hit the dish.

"Whether Fitzpatrick was safe or out, Heinie Groh made a great play in covering the plate."[17]

Smith singled for the third and final Boston hit in the 14th. Three newspaper accounts say nothing of what transpired the rest of the game, which "wore along …before descending darkness and hunger called a halt."[18]

Ed Fitzpatrick: hero or goat?

NOTES

1   Braves pitcher Rudolph should have had a hit of his own after "a sharp hit to rightfield … which Tom Griffith, who was playing a shortfield, gathered up and made a quick throw to first. Rudolph would have been out, but Mollwitz muffed the ball." In spite of this error, one reporter wrote that Mollwitz "put up a wonderful game at first." J.C. O'Leary, "Braves and Reds Unable to Score," *Boston Daily Globe*, June 14, 1916, 9.

2   N.J. Flatley, "Braves and Cincy Play 16 Innings to 0-0 Draw," *Boston Herald*, June 14, 1916, 6.

3   Mark S. Sternman, "The Evers Ejection Record," in Bill Nowlin, ed., *The Miracle Braves of 1914: Boston's Original Worst-to-First World Series Champions* (SABR, 2014), 66-67.

4   Flatley.

5   Ed McGrath, "Braves and Reds in 16-Inning Tie," *Boston Post*, June 14, 1916, 18.

6   Brian Marshall, "Fred Toney," sabr.org/bioproj/person/ec97d575 (accessed November 6, 2014).

7   McGrath.

8   O'Leary.

9   Ibid.

10   McGrath.

11   Flatley.

12   O'Leary.

13   Ibid.

14   Ibid.

15   Flatley.

16   Ibid.

17   O'Leary.

18   Flatley. Retrosheet has no play-by-play account, so the game actions described in this article come from the three referenced newspaper stories.

SALIDA TOM NO-HITS THE BUCS

JUNE 16, 1916: BOSTON BRAVES 2, PITTSBURGH PIRATES 0 AT BRAVES FIELD

BY MIKE LYNCH

On paper the game between the Boston Braves and Pittsburgh Pirates at Braves Field on June 16, 1916, looked like nothing special. After jumping out to a decent start and sitting in third place with a 15-11 record on May 22, the Braves hit the skids and lost 12 of their next 18. They sank to fifth place, seven games behind the first-place Brooklyn Robins, and sported a record of 21-23 on June 15.

The Pirates, piloted by James "Nixey" Callahan, were even worse, having gone 21-26, good for seventh place and an 8½-game deficit. Their roster still boasted legendary shortstop Honus Wagner, but he was 42 and in his next-to-last season, and even though he was still productive, he was just a shell of his former self. The rest of the lineup was helmed by 33-year-old right fielder Bill Hinchman, who would lead the National League that season with 16 triples, and speed demon and future Hall of Famer Max Carey, who would lead the league with a career-high 63 stolen bases.

Braves skipper George Stallings sent 32-year-old journeyman hurler Tom Hughes (known as "Salida Tom" for the Colorado town in which he grew up) to the mound to face Pittsburgh's hard-luck lefty, 23-year-old Erv "Peanuts" Kantlehner. Despite pitching to a 2.26 earned-run average in 1915, sixth best in the National League, Kantlehner went only 5-12, and 1916 wasn't much better. Going into the June 16 contest, the southpaw boasted a nifty 1.64 ERA, but was only 2-6. Hughes, on the other hand, had enjoyed his best season in 1915, going 16-14 with a 2.12 ERA, and led the league in games, games finished, and saves.[1] He began the 1916 season with five wins and a save in his first nine appearances and was 5-2 with a 3.05 ERA when he took the slab against the Pirates.

According to the *Boston Post*, a drizzle dampened the field but did not interrupt play, and a chilly east wind blew throughout the contest.[2] Carey led off with a long drive that was hauled in by right fielder Joe Wilhoit, who would be instrumental to Hughes's success on this day. Hughes retired Doc Johnston and Wagner, and the Pirates went down in order in the first, but not before an injury to Boston catcher Walt Tragesser, who was getting a rare start, knocked him out of the game.

The Braves jumped out to an early 1-0 lead in the bottom of the first on a walk, a single, a bunt, and a throwing error. Rabbit Maranville drew the base on balls to start the frame and advanced to second on a Fred Snodgrass base hit. Wilhoit attempted to advance both runners with a bunt, but popped it right to Kantlehner, who snared the ball out of the air, spun

8   BOSTON POST, SATURDAY, JUNE 17, 1916

The Pirates Are Troublesome, but Are Subdued by Thin Tom Hughes

in an effort to double Maranville off second base but heaved the ball into center field. Carey was backing up on the play, but the ball rolled past him and Maranville scored.

Snodgrass moved to third but was erased in a rundown when Sherry Magee grounded to third. Ed Konetchy fouled out to third to end the threat, and Boston held a 1-0 lead. That's all Hughes would need as he continued to mow down Pirates hitters. Hinchman and Joe Schultz went down in the second before Ed Barney lifted what *Boston Post* writer Ed McGrath called an "ominous fly near the [right-field] foul line."[3] Wilhoit raced over and made the catch for the final out of the inning. He would make three more that had McGrath gushing, "Joe Wilhoit had to cover quite a little ground in the pursuit of five hoists that came out to his plot, but managed to get his putouts without any vast trouble."[4]

The Braves fashioned another minor rally in the second when second baseman Dick Egan blooped a single to right and Hank Gowdy, who'd replaced the injured Tragesser, lined a double to left, but Hughes struck out and Maranville grounded out to third and stranded both runners. It would be the only time Maranville failed to reach base in four trips to the plate.

"Beyond that nothing stirred to encourage the Braves until Bob Harmon came in to pitch the last inning for his crew," wrote McGrath.[5] After the second inning, Kantlehner settled down and surrendered only three more hits, all singles, before leaving the game after the seventh inning in favor of Harmon.

But Kantlehner also got an assist from the umpires in the sixth when a controversial call on a steal attempt by the Braves had the *Boston Globe's* James O'Leary suggesting a change in the way arbiters made future calls.[6] With Ed Konetchy at the plate, Sherry Magee attempted to steal second. Konetchy swung at the pitch and fouled it into Walter Schmidt's mitt. Home-plate umpire Bill Klem called "foul" as Schmidt fired a strike to second to nab Magee. Magee insisted he was misled by Klem calling "foul," but the play stood and Kantlehner got out of the inning.

"Umpires will probably evolve some scheme to avoid the confusion which occurred in one play," opined O'Leary. "It would seem … better for the [home-plate] umpire to delay his decision until the play at second is completed, or call it a strike, as are all foul tips if caught."[7]

Meanwhile Hughes had yet to allow a hit, thanks to his command of the strike zone and Wilhoit's glove. "All eyes were centered on the thin Boston pitcher as he cleaved the murky air with his wide curves," waxed McGrath, "compelling the thoroughly helpless hostiles either to lift the ball in the air, where it would drop into the clutches of a waiting Boston fielder, or swing vainly at elusive shoots."[8]

Indeed, only three assists were recorded by Boston's fielders; Hughes fanned seven batters, Gowdy recorded nine putouts and Wilhoit captured everything belted his way, whether short or long. Kantlehner popped a shallow fly to right in the fifth; Johnston poled a "screaming drive" toward the right-field corner in the sixth; and Dan Costello blasted a shot in the eighth that seemed headed for extra bases, yet Wilhoit chased down all of them.[9]

The Braves plated their second tally in the bottom of the eighth when Maranville drew his third free pass of the game, raced to third on another Snodgrass single, and came home on a double steal when catcher Schmidt chucked his throw into center field.

The top of the ninth found Hughes facing Max Carey, Doc Johnston, and Honus Wagner, the first three hitters in Pittsburgh's order. "Every spectator was anxious that Hughes should come through with his 'no-hit game,'" wrote O'Leary.[10]

"Even the Pittsburgh players caught the feeling," O'Leary continued, "and all who could left the bench and lined up on the top step of the dugout. They did not, so far as could be observed, do anything to distract Hughes from his work, which was to their credit."[11]

O'Leary surmised that Carey was the "most dangerous of the bad lot" because of his speed, but the center fielder lofted a popup to second baseman Egan for the first out.[12] Johnston whiffed and Hughes was only one out from something he'd accomplished once before, although this time it would count.

On August 30, 1910, while with the New York Yankees, Hughes tossed 9⅓ innings of no-hit ball against Cleveland only to lose the game in extra innings.[13] His opponent that day was a 20-year-old rookie named George Kahler, who was making only his fourth major-league start and pitched brilliantly, allowing only three hits in 11 innings. Hughes finally gave up a hit in the 10th inning, then fell apart in the 11th and surrendered five runs to lose 5-0.

Now, six years later, he had a chance to capture a no-hitter that would stay in the record books forever.[14] Wagner took the first pitch for a ball, then the second for a strike to even the count at 1-and-1. He "struck wildly at another offering," then took ball two to even the count again.[15] "Hughes took his time," O'Leary wrote, "and finally the count was two and two. Honus took a look at the next ball, which broke over the corner of the plate. Klem raised his hand, indicating

Tom Hughes.

a strike. Gowdy squeezed the ball for all he was worth, and Tommy had reached the goal of all ambitious pitchers."[16]

With the win, Hughes improved his record to 6-2 and began a run that would see him win 10 of his last 11 decisions before a broken wrist suffered on September 7 sidelined him for the rest of the season. He finished at 16-3 and his .842 winning percentage led all of major-league baseball.

NOTES

1   Hughes started 25 games and finished 22 as a reliever in 1915, and became only the third pitcher to start at least 20 and finish 20 as a reliever in the same season. Hall of Famers Mordecai "Three Finger" Brown (27 and 24 in 1911) and Chief Bender (21 and 21 in 1913) were the others.

2   *Boston Post*, June 17, 1916.

3   Ibid.

4   Ibid.

5   Ibid.

6   *Boston Globe*, June 17, 1916.

7   Ibid.

8   *Boston Post*, June 17, 1916.

9   Ibid.

10   *Boston Globe*, June 17, 1916.

11   Ibid.

12 Ibid.

13 Bill Nowlin, ed., *The Miracle Braves of 1914: Boston's Original Worst-to-First World Series Champions* (Phoenix, Arizona: Society for American Baseball Research, 2014), 90.

14 Ibid. Although he didn't throw a complete-game no-hitter against Cleveland, Hughes got credit for one because he threw nine innings of no-hit ball. That made him only the second pitcher after Hall of Famer Cy Young to throw no-hitters in both the American and National Leagues. The definition of what constituted an official no-hitter was changed in 1991, so now Hughes is credited with only one career no-hitter.

15 *Boston Post*, June 17, 1916.

16 *Boston Globe*, June 17, 1916.

THE RED SOX WIN A HOME GAME A MILE AWAY FROM HOME

OCTOBER 7, 1916: BOSTON RED SOX 6, BROOKLYN ROBINS 5 AT BRAVES FIELD (GAME ONE OF THE 1916 WORLD SERIES)

BY BILL NOWLIN

The 1916 season began with the reigning world champion Boston Red Sox featuring much the same roster as the year before. The two major changes were the loss of Tris Speaker and Smoky Joe Wood. Considering their iconic status, one might have expected the losses to have hurt more than they did.

Tillie Walker took over in center field for the holdout Speaker, who had been sold to the Cleveland Indians, but that was really the only significant change in the lineup.

Stout and Johnson write that despite a slow start, "Once the club adjusted to Speaker's absence, they began to respond to [Red Sox manager Bill] Carrigan, a master motivator."[1]

The team as a whole performed as well relative to the other contenders as it had in 1915, finishing two games ahead of second-place Chicago. On September 18 the Red Sox had climbed into first place for good.

They won 91 games, as opposed to 101 in 1915, but it was enough to allow them to hoist another pennant at Fenway Park. For the second year in a row, however, the Red Sox borrowed the larger-capacity Braves Field for their home games. In the World Series, the repeating Red Sox faced the Brooklyn Robins, who had beat out the Phillies by 2½ games.

The Brooklyn team's ERA (2.12) was much better than Boston's 2.48, and the Robins' .261 team batting average was higher as well (the Red Sox hit .248). Brooklyn looked to be a formidable opponent.

The *Boston Globe*'s Tim Murnane expected Brooklyn to break through first, to "start with a rush." He added, "The Red Sox seldom start like winners, but manage to tighten up and show as the game and contests lengthen out."[2]

Neither manager announced his pitcher beforehand. The Robins' Rube Marquard (13-6, 1.58 ERA) was expected to face the unorthodox submariner Carl Mays (18-13, 2.39), according to the newspapers the morning of the first game. Columnist Hugh Fullerton anticipated a Babe Ruth/Marquard matchup in Game Two, and picked the Red Sox to win in five games with Jack Coombs pitching and winning for Brooklyn in the third game of the five. He didn't expect Boston's Rube Foster to be used at all, given that he'd had an off year.

A capacity crowd of 36,117 jammed Braves Field. Interest in the game was such that a "special wire from Braves Field" was hooked up and an estimated 15,000 fans stood in the streets outside the *Boston Herald-Traveler* offices on Tremont Street to hear telegraphed news of each play relayed via megaphone and to see plays reflected on a special scoreboard erected by the newspaper.[3]

Though Boston's Bill Carrigan had Ernie Shore (16-10, 2.63) warming up, the Robins expected Carrigan to call on Babe Ruth (23-12, 1.75) at the last minute, so they took batting practice as though they'd be facing the left-hander. Carrigan chose Shore, however, and Brooklyn manager Wilbert Robinson led with Rube Marquard.

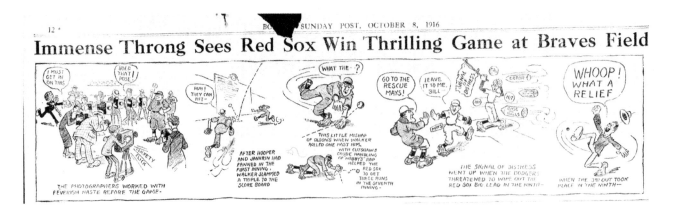

The Robins made a weak showing of it in the top of the first, not getting a ball out of the infield. In the bottom of the first, after two men were out, Tillie Walker tripled to the wall in left, but first baseman Dick Hoblitzell grounded out to end the inning.

The Robins got two men on base in the second, but didn't score. In the bottom of the second the Red Sox put three men on – two on Marquard walks – but didn't score, though only after Harry Hooper's two-out smash to Hi Myers in deep right-center field saw the Brooklyn man "fairly robbing" Hooper of a bases-clearing hit.[4]

Myers singled in Brooklyn's third, but was left stranded. With two outs, the Red Sox put the first run on the board with back-to-back extra-base hits – a triple on a 3-and-2 count by Hoblitzell that went over right fielder Casey Stengel's head and a "fierce liner" of a double down the left-field line by Duffy Lewis. Lewis was then picked off second base when Brooklyn's catcher, Chief Meyers, fired to shortstop Ivy Olson.

Stengel singled to center field to lead off the fourth, and Zack Wheat banged one of Shore's pitches for a triple that hit the right-field wall, evening the score at 1-1. Second baseman George Cutshaw hit into an unusual double play, when Hooper raced in and – as he slipped and fell – caught Cutshaw's shallow fly ball, and then hopped up in time to throw on the fly directly to catcher Hick Cady, who erased Wheat at the plate. The *Washington Post* correspondent termed it "one of the most brilliant plays ever witnessed on a ball field."[5]

With just one out, Meyers tripled in Brooklyn's fifth but again the Robins couldn't get him safely home. The Red Sox re-established the lead, 2-1, in the bottom of the fifth when Hooper led off with a double to center that Myers lost in the sun, took third on second baseman Hal Janvrin's bunt, and scored when Walker singled to left field.

The Red Sox broke the game open in the bottom of the seventh. Janvrin doubled down the left-field line to kick things off. Walker reached safely as Ivy Olson's error allowed Janvrin to get to third; he may have been a bit hasty in anticipating the double play and flubbed the catch. Then it was Cutshaw's turn for an infield error as he tried to scoop up a grounder and throw to home plate, but merely knocked the ball down instead; Hoblitzell reached first and Janvrin scored. After Lewis pushed both runners up a base with a sacrifice, Larry Gardner reached on a fielder's choice and Walker scored. Everett Scott's sacrifice fly brought in Hobby. It was 5-1, Red Sox.

One of the four double plays the Sox turned wiped out another Robins runner in the eighth. It was quite a play, a rocket of a ball that caromed off Shore's glove and then off his ankle directly to Janvrin, who stepped on second and threw to first. With Jeff Pfeffer now pitching in place of Marquard, the Red Sox ran the score to 6-1 in the bottom of the eighth as Hooper walked and Janvrin singled. Stengel committed the Robins' fourth error of the game by throwing the ball so far from any possible fielder that Hooper was able to come all the way home on the single to right.

Red Sox fans jam Braves Field for the World Series contest.

It was a good thing for the Red Sox that they'd built up a five-run lead because the Robins pecked away at Shore in the top of the ninth "as the evening mist was circling in about Braves Field."[6] After walking Brooklyn team captain Jake Daubert on four pitches and giving up a single to Stengel, Shore hit Cutshaw in the ribs, loading the bases with one out. Janvrin's error on Mike Mowrey's drive allowed two runs to score. Olson hit one on a hop to Gardner, who gloved the ball but couldn't make a play. The bases were loaded again. Meyers popped out to Hobby at first for the second out, but Shore walked pinch-hitter Fred Merkle, forcing in a run. Manager Carrigan had seen enough, and changed the whole battery, bringing in "Underhanded Carl Mays"[7] to pitch and Pinch Thomas to catch. The next batter, Hi Myers, bounced a single

over Mays' head to bring the score to 6-5 with the bases still loaded. Daubert hit a hot grounder that got by third baseman Gardner, but shortstop Everett Scott ranged far to his right, snared the ball, and threw a perfect strike to Hoblitzell to just nip Daubert and save the game.

Scoring four runs in the top of the ninth, and leaving the bases full of Robins, had put a scare into the Red Sox and their fans, who left Braves Field somewhat subdued, but relieved that Boston had held on to win.

This account is adapted from Bill Nowlin and Jim Prime, *From The Babe to the Beards* (New York: Sports Publishing, 2014), itself an adaptation of the two authors' *The Red Sox World Series Encyclopedia*, published by Rounder Books in 2008.

NOTES

1   Glenn Stout and Richard A. Johnson, *Red Sox Century* (Boston: Houghton Mifflin, 2000), 110.

2   *Boston Globe*, October 7, 1916.

3   The account of the fans outside their office was printed in the October 8 *Boston Herald*. Traffic was not disrupted, most of the crowd watching from across the street on the Boston Common.

4   All quotations are from the *Boston Globe*, October 8, 1916, except as noted.

5   *Washington Post*, October 8, 1916.

6   *Boston Herald*, October 8, 1916.

7   Ibid.

VICTORY ON A LOANED DIAMOND

OCTOBER 9, 1916: BOSTON BRAVES 1, BROOKLYN ROBINS 0 AT BRAVES FIELD (GAME TWO OF THE 1916 WORLD SERIES)

BY CECILIA TAN AND BILL NOWLIN

For the second year in a row, Boston won the pennant in 1916, by just two games over the Chicago White Sox and four over the Detroit Tigers. As in 1915, the Red Sox' World Series home games were played at Braves Field, but this time Boston faced the Brooklyn Robins (later, Dodgers). The Red Sox presented a similar but not identical team to that of the previous year. Bill Carrigan remained as manager, but Tris Speaker was traded away, and Smoky Joe Wood was injured. George Herman Ruth emerged as the ace on the pitching staff (23-12, 1.75 ERA), while Dutch Leonard and Carl Mays each won 18 games. All in all, the staff ERA was 2.48, slightly worse than the 2.39 of the previous year. Team batting was off marginally, too – the 1915 team average was .260 (.336 OBP) while in 1916 it dipped to .248 (.317 OBP), decent numbers in the era of the dead ball. Run production dropped from 668 runs to 548. Still, the Red Sox had done what they needed to do; they won the pennant.

This was an over-confident team, and there was talk in the papers about the Sox sweeping Brooklyn.

Game One opened in Boston, with Ernie Shore against Rube Marquard (who'd opposed the Red Sox in the 1912 Series for the Giants, but was now pitching for Brooklyn). The game turned into a 6-5 win when the Red Sox managed to shut down a four-run rally in the top of the ninth before the Robins could tie the game.

Game Two pitted Red Sox ace Ruth against Sherry Smith, both southpaws. Ruth's 1.75 ERA had led the American League. Smith was 14-10, with a 2.34 ERA. Brooklyn batted first and didn't wait long to put a run

on the board. After Ruth retired the first two Robins, center fielder Hi Myers drove a ball between Tilly Walker in center and Harry Hooper in right, sparking a Keystone Kops moment. Hooper dove but the ball rolled all the way to the fence and Walker fell trying to field the rebound. Myers legged all the way around the bases for an inside-the-park home run.

Brooklyn's moundsman Smith doubled to right field with one out in the top of the third, and was waved toward third, but Hooper threw the ball to Walker, the cutoff man; the center fielder fired a strike to third and cut down Smith. The score remained 1-0, Brooklyn.

Boston tried to answer in its half of the inning. Everett "Deacon" Scott led off with a triple to the cement wall in right field. He had to hold at third on Pinch Thomas's grounder to George Cutshaw at second. Ruth grounded to Cutshaw, too, but this time the second baseman bobbled the ball. Though Ruth was thrown out on the play, Scott scored to even things at 1-1. After that, both teams put men into scoring position at times but neither brought them home. In the fifth Brooklyn's shortstop Ivy Olson was accused of tripping Pinch Thomas as he rounded second and the umpire awarded Thomas third base on interference. But Thomas languished there when Ruth struck out.

In the eighth Brooklyn again feinted. Harry "Mike" Mowrey singled, moved to second on a sacrifice, and moved up when Otto Miller singled. But Walker fired so fast to the plate that Mowrey had to stop at third, Miller taking second on the throw. With runners at second and third, and just one out, the pitcher Smith grounded to short and Scott luckily caught Mowrey in a rundown between third and home, Ruth making the tag. Jimmy Johnston hit a high bounder and Ruth leapt up to grab it, threw to first, and snuffed the threat.

The score remained tied as Boston came to bat in the bottom of the ninth. Hal Janvrin doubled to lead off for a promising start. Jimmy Walsh, pinch-hitting for Walker, managed only a comebacker. Smith fielded the ball and tossed to Mowrey to cut down the lead runner, but Mowrey dropped the ball and Janny was safe. With runners on first and third and no one out, the crowd was on the edge of their seats. Even a fly ball could score Janvrin. Dick Hoblitzell got that fly to center, but Myers' throw home erased Janvrin, two outs on one play. After an intentional walk to Duffy Lewis, Larry Gardner fouled out to send the game into extra innings, still tied 1-1.

The Red Sox escaped a couple of potential problems in the top of the 10th as a deflected grounder was converted into an out and a walk went for naught, and looked once again to push across that one crucial run. Scott singled to lead off and Thomas moved him up with a sacrifice. Ruth swung hard three times, and missed three times for the second out. Hooper hit a ball down the third-base line; as it went off his glove,

Mowrey knew Hooper had it beat but feigned a throw to first. The decoy worked and Scott overran third. Olson scooted over from shortstop and took Mowrey's throw, nabbing Scott as he tried to get back to the bag. The scorer credited Hooper with a single, but the side was retired.

Neither team had particularly good chances in the 11th or 12th inning, and the sky was growing dark. If the game were called because of darkness, it would go into the scorebook as a tie. Neither team wanted to waste a great pitching performance, but they were running out of time.

So to the 13th. Brooklyn's first batter, Mowrey, reached base when Gardner's throw pulled Hoblitzell off the bag. The Robins sacrificed to move Mowrey to second, but Miller popped up to the catcher for out number two. Smith, still pitching for Brooklyn, almost dropped one into short left but Lewis made a "phenomenal" catch and the Sox were out of the 13th. Tim Murnane of the *Boston Globe* felt sure that Lewis had saved a run: "Tearing along as if it was a case of life or death, he made one final reach while twisting his neck like a seagull and managed to reach and hold the ball."

47,373 fill Braves Field for Game Two.

The game had been characterized throughout by exceptional fielding for both teams. Smith quickly retired all three of Boston's batters, and the game entered the 14th inning.

Babe Ruth had not given up a hit since the eighth inning. He set Brooklyn down again 1-2-3 in the top of the 14th. The Sox came up in the bottom half and Smith walked Hoblitzell, the fourth time in the game that Hobby had worked a walk. Lewis sacrificed the walking man to second, first-pitch bunting. A hit now could win the game. Larry Gardner was due up, but he was 0-for-5 and Carrigan decided to try something different. He put the speedy Mike McNally in to run for Hobby and sent up "Sheriff" Del Gainer (a .254 hitter in 1916) to pinch-hit for Gardner (.308 in the regular season, and 1-for-4 in Game One, and reached on an error). Despite his overall better numbers, Gardner was 1-for-9 in the Series at this point and had struggled against the left-handed Smith. The switch paid off. Gainer singled, a low liner to left, and Wheat had to play it on one hop and hope the throw home could beat McNally. Not a chance. McNally burned around the bases and crossed the plate. The Red Sox had their second run and the game.

No other World Series game before or after has gone to 14 innings. After Myers' freak inside-the-park home run back in the first inning, Babe Ruth had held the National League champions scoreless and earned the complete-game victory.

The Series would be over in five games. Game Three saw Brooklyn take one from the Red Sox 4-3, but the Red Sox handled the Robins by a 6-2 score in Game Four (Larry Gardner's three-run inside-the-park homer in the second inning being the decisive blow). They won the World Series, their fourth, the second in a row, and the third in five years, with a 4-1 triumph the next day, Ernie Shore allowing just three hits and picking up his second win.

A lengthy *Globe* editorial rhapsodized about how the Athens of America followed in the Greek tradition of the Olympics being justly proud of the manly prowess of its sons. Carrigan, who had caught Game Four, gone 2-for-3, and managed the club, was dubbed "another Ivanhoe, less brutal and more civilized, less romantic than Scott's fictional hero, but more skillful." The confidence the Sox had carried into the Series had been justified.

An earlier version of this article was published in *The 50 Greatest Red Sox Games* by Cecilia Tan and Bill Nowlin (Riverdale Avenue Books), and appears here by permission.

A CHAMPIONSHIP CLAIMED ON ADOPTED TURF

OCTOBER 12, 1916: BOSTON 4, BROOKLYN 1 AT BRAVES FIELD
(GAME FIVE OF THE 1916 WORLD SERIES)

BY BILL NOWLIN AND JIM PRIME

It was Columbus Day and the biggest crowd of the 1916 World Series. The Red Sox led the Brooklyn Robins three games to one. Some 43,620 came to Boston's Braves Field to see if the Red Sox could win their second world championship in a row. Brooklyn crowds had been only half the size of Boston's, despite it being their team's first appearance in a World Series. Owner Charles Ebbets charged much higher prices than were customary at the time—all the way up to $5.00. And the weather was very cold. It may be, too, that few in the borough had thought the Brooklyns had much of a chance to win.

The fifth game, in Boston, saw Brooklyn's Jeff Pfeffer start, facing Game One winner Ernie Shore. For Pfeffer, it was his fourth appearance of the Series. He'd thrown the last inning in relief of Rube Marquard in Game One, pitched the last 2⅔ innings saving Game Three for Jack Coombs, and had pinch-hit for Rube Marquard in Game Four (striking out) before Larry Cheney came in to pitch. Pfeffer had been a formidable 25-11 in the 1916 regular season, with a 1.92 ERA.

Red Sox manager Bill Carrigan had already announced that he would retire after the World Series.

For the fourth game in a row, Brooklyn scored first—a single run, without benefit of a hit, in the top of the second. George Cutshaw walked on four pitches and then advanced one base at a time on Mike Mowrey's sacrifice, Irv Olson's high bouncing grounder to third

that Sox third baseman Larry Gardner hauled down, and a passed ball charged to catch Hick Cady.

In no time the Red Sox countered and tied the score in the bottom of the second when Duffy Lewis hit a one-out triple down the left-field line and Gardner flied one just barely deep enough to left that Lewis was able to tag and score when Zack Wheat's throw went wide.

After the Robins (some accounts were already calling them the Dodgers, though they were more frequently termed the Robins in reference to manager Wilbert Robinson) failed to get the ball out of the infield in the top of the third, the Red Sox took advantage of their next opportunity to score as well.

Cady singled to lead off the bottom of the third. Ernie Shore attempted a sacrifice bunt, but fouled out to Brooklyn catcher Chief Meyers. Pfeffer missed with four in a row and walked Harry Hooper. Red Sox second baseman Hal Janvrin hit a ball to shortstop Ivy Olson that looked like a sure double play, but Olson tried to rush the throw and couldn't maintain his grip on it. After he finally corralled it, his only play was to first—but the ball flew out to right field, enabling Cady to score and Hooper to reach third, Janvrin stopping safe on first. Janny was caught stealing, but center fielder Chick Shorten then singled up the middle and into center field, and Hooper trotted home. Shorten was then caught stealing, too, the second aggressive Red Sox baserunner erased in the inning.

Brooklyn finally got its first hit of the game in the fifth, a meaningless single into center field by Chief Meyers, but it came with two outs and Pfeffer was up next. He grounded out, third to first. And, as if to punish the Robins for presuming to get a base hit, the Red Sox added an insurance run when Hooper singled and Janvrin doubled, both of them first-pitch-swinging—a strategy employed by several Sox throughout the game. It was 4-1, Red Sox, after five.

Neither team scored again. Brooklyn added one single in the seventh and one in the ninth. A subsequent error in the seventh resulted in Robins runners on second and third, but there were two outs and Meyers hit one back to Shore, who threw him out at first to retire the side. Casey Stengel singled to lead off the Brooklyn ninth, but Shore buckled down and didn't let the ball out of the infield, striking out Wheat and getting Cutshaw to ground out to second, forcing Stengel. Mowrey was up. While the band was playing "This Is the End of a Perfect Day," Shore induced Mowrey to hit a pop fly to Everett Scott at short for the third and final out.

Shore walked off the mound triumphant as the Red Sox won the game, 4-1, and captured their fourth world championship.

Shore had his famous "down ball" working and allowed just "three measly hits,"[1] with just one base on balls, the only run an unearned one, and won his second game of the Series while the Red Sox won their second Series in succession.

Because they had borrowed Braves Field so they could pack in more fans, the Red Sox had taken the 1916 World Series with ease, despite never once playing on their true home field.

The *New York Times* column on the game said acidly of the 4-1 final that if the score "had been 40 to 1 it would have represented more accurately the respective merits of the two contending teams."[2] The game was said to be so lacking in drama that even the hometown fans didn't get worked up during the competition. The

Times said the contest "resembled a tug of war between an elephant and a gold fish."[3]

Boston fans were so jaded that Wallace Goldsmith's sports-page cartoon of the game in the *Globe* depicted a tradition apparently more longstanding than heretofore appreciated—fans on the first-base side were "so sure of the outcome that it amused itself batting toy balloons about."[4] Not everyone who had wanted to get into Braves Field had, however. The *Boston Herald* observed, "While the game was in progress an army clogged the streets around the park, a disappointed army, because the gates had been closed and the field was filled up."[5]

At the very end, though, there arose such a loud shout from all those present that its effect was all the more startling, given their quiescence throughout. Winning the World Series was apparently still a big thing in Boston, though the Red Sox had now won three of the last five played. The masses flocked to the field and marched around behind the Royal Rooters band. "After the cheering and the marching, the gathered thousands wended out of the vast closure, smiling and happy."[6]

Widely syndicated columnist Hugh Fullerton proposed abolishing the World Series. The American League was superior, he wrote, and the Brooklyn "team was licked, beaten, and dogging before it went to the park. … Brooklyn dogged it." He claimed they'd held a team meeting before the game to decide how to divide the losers' share, a telling and self-fulfilling attitude. Overriding the play of the losers was Fullerton's feeling that "baseball has ceased to be a sport and has become a commercial enterprise." The players were, he felt, more interested in the money than the result on the field. Fullerton closed his column recounting what Christy Mathewson had told him: "I don't know whether the best team won or not, but I am satisfied that the worst team lost. You've got to give it to Brooklyn—they finished the game—and it looked to me as if that was about all they were trying to do."[7]

Postscript on Ernie Shore: Ernie Shore's contract had been purchased by the Red Sox on July 9, 1914, the very same day the Red Sox bought Babe Ruth. The year after the 1916 World Series, Shore pitched as perfect a game as one could ask for—on June 23, 1917. Ruth started the game but became so furious when the home-plate umpire ruled that he'd walked the first batter that Ruth was ejected from the game. Shore came in with the runner on first, and then retired 27 men in order, the first one being the baserunner on first who was picked off. Today Shore's game is considered an "unofficial" perfect game. After a good year in 1917, Shore spent 1918 in the Navy before being traded to the New York Yankees that December, but his better years were behind him.

This account is adapted from Bill Nowlin and Jim Prime, *From the Babe to the Beards* (New York: Sports Publishing, 2014), itself an adaptation of the two authors' *The Red Sox World Series Encyclopedia*, published by Rounder Books in 2008.

NOTES

1 *Boston Herald*, October 13, 1916.

2 *New York Times*, October 13, 1916.

3 Ibid.

4 *Boston Globe*, October 13, 1916.

5 *Boston Herald*, October 13, 1916.

6 Ibid. The *Herald* suggested that one of the happiest might have been Wilbert Robinson, because his Brooklyn team wouldn't have to face the Red Sox again.

7 *New York Times*, October 13, 1996.

BREAKING THE SABBATH

MAY 5, 1918: CHARLESTOWN NAVY YARD ALL-STARS 5, CAMP DEVENS TRAINING BASE 0 AT BRAVES FIELD

BY RICHARD "DIXIE" TOURANGEAU

Though the crowd for the joyous May 7, 1918, Braves Field record 16-0 blowout was rather sparse in comparison, just two days earlier the Wigwam was filled to capacity for what in previous years would have been an illegal Sunday ballgame. Connie Mack's former star shortstop Jack Barry and his Charlestown Navy Yard All Stars were pitted against his old teammate Harold Janvrin's Army squad from the Camp Devens Training Base located near Ayer, Massachusetts. Sunday ball was not allowed, but a quickly enacted city ordinance decreed that games between servicemen were acceptable if no admission was charged. On a beautiful May 5, more than 40,000 "freebie" fans were admitted before the gates had to be closed for safety reasons well before the scheduled 3 P.M. first pitch. Monday's *Boston Post* claimed it was the "largest Sunday crowd ever to witness a sporting event."[1] Meanwhile each city newspaper was filled with World War coverage of various European battlefronts, the sinking of Allied ships, and casualty reports of New Englanders. Six local soldiers were lost in that day's fighting.

The game was intended to benefit sailors and soldiers "help" funds via an expected courtesy "collection" throughout the stands but First Naval District Rear Admiral Spencer S. Wood nixed the idea by citing official Navy Department policy that prohibited its personnel from playing in any contest that involved gate receipts or any form of money exchange, even donations. An innocent compromise was suggested that all proceeds go to the Red Cross but Wood vetoed that, too. Major General Harry Hodges (Camp Devens), Commandant William Rush, and Captain A.L. Key of the Charlestown Navy Yard, many Boston clergymen, and Boston Mayor Andrew J. Peters were seated in prime home-plate boxes for the well-played, 105-minute contest between the friendly rivals. Rear Admiral Wood arrived in the fourth inning.

Former A's "$100,000 Infield" shortstop Barry, who played second base and managed the Red Sox in 1917, was a Navy Yard employee, as were all of his players: pitcher Ernie Shore (of perfect-game fame), shortstop Walter "Rabbit" Maranville (Braves, future Hall of Famer), first baseman Del Gainer (Red Sox/Tigers),

Navy Yard All Stars skipper Jack Barry.

outfielder Ladislaw Whitey Witt (Athletics), outfielder Charles "Chick" Shorten (Red Sox/Tigers), catcher Art Rico (Braves, from the Roxbury neighborhood of Boston),[2] third baseman Marty Killilea (several minor-league teams), and outfielder Jimmy Walsh (Athletics/Red Sox). On the team but not playing that day were future Hall of Fame pitcher Herb Pennock (Red Sox/Yanks) and hurler Lore "King" Bader (Texas League star, Red Sox).

Devens field general Janvrin had no such major-league firepower but made a good showing in losing just 5-1. His locally grown stars were hurler Ralph Waldo "Rube" Cram (Melrose High ace, Brown University), outfielder Billy Mulcahy (Woburn High, Tufts University), outfielder Frank Kane (Weymouth, Providence Grays), catcher Fred "Brick" Wilder (Maynard High, Buffalo, Springfield, Omaha), first baseman William Whalen (East Boston), shortstop Jim Cooney (Red Sox), a kid named Powers from Roxbury who played outfield, and another boy named Glennon who played third base. Veteran National League umpire Charles "Cy" Rigler and rookie ump Charlie Moran donated their time. They were in Boston to oversee the New York Giants sweep that continued on Monday, interrupted only by the scheduled day off on the "Lord's Day." The Braves paid all the policemen and the ushers who directed delighted fans to their priceless seats.

Both of the "military" squads had been assembled less than a week before the game. The local papers followed the practice progress of both and promoted the Sunday contest daily. The likely starting lineups were posted and touted. To fine-tune for the clash, Barry's Navy recruits found Harvard University an easy mark on Saturday, 12-0, behind Bader's four-hitter and his own three safeties at Soldier Field in front of 2,000 fans. Meanwhile Janvrin's Devens boys smacked an all-star team from nearby Somerville, 11-1, in that Boston suburb. Whalen (three runs) and Powers each had four hits. The Somerville hurler, A. Graham, gave up 16 hits but clouted a solo home run. The *Boston Sunday Post* sports page had a prophetic headline: "Big Crowd Expected at Game, Plan for Overflow at Braves Field

Camp Devens field general Hal Janvrin.

Today." The accompanying story declared, "With favoring weather this afternoon it is almost certain that the crowd … will break all baseball attendance records for this city or elsewhere."

Before the Sunday throng, Cram pitched well for Devens against the superb Navy Yard lineup, but two misplayed fly balls, one called an error and one ruled a double by Killilea, led to three Navy runs in the fifth inning. It was claimed that young flychasers Powers and Mulcahy were not ready for the expanse of the Braves Field pasture. Witt singled and scored in the first inning on Gainer's hit while Captain Barry walked and found his way home in the sixth on a Shorten single. Whalen's hit, a groundout, and a single by Wilder got Camp Devens on the board in the seventh. Rabbit Maranville provided entertainment for the huge throng with his "vest pocket" catches, fast play at the keystone sack, and a humorous wrestling match at home plate. Husky Devens catcher Brick Wilder pinned little Rabbit near the plate when an outfielder's throw rolled away from him. He quickly grabbed the ball and tagged Maranville but umpire Rigler ruled that holding the runner down was illegal and allowed Rabbit his score.

The game was such a success that the Army boys played the following Sunday at Braves Field with Cram beating outclassed Fort Strong, 12-2, behind Kane's four singles, Janvrin's two triples (three runs), and Cooney's four scores. The Army team amassed 12 hits, 12 steals, and received 14 walks. This time 20,000 fans showed up and donated $1,100 to the Devens athletic fund.

Navy bragging rights from May 5 were short-lived, however, as on May 8 the flashy Charlestown squad was scuttled by Rear Admiral Wood's decision to transfer many of Barry's stars. He disliked pro players on so-called "Navy" teams even though Barry had assembled possibly the most elite wartime ballclub in the country. Wood staunchly stated: "I have a policy, and a well-defined one, in regard to baseball matters as well as other sports. All athletic contests shall be kept free from professionalism, and in the ranks of amateurism."[3] Maranville, Witt, Gainer, Leo Callahan (Phillies), Mike McNally (Red Sox/Yanks), and Herb Pennock were given over to Boston's 1st Naval District for duty. (Some papers reported it would be "sea duty."[4]) The next Sunday (the 12th) in Worcester, Captain Jack's leftovers and new recruits swamped the 302nd Regiment, 16-1, as the entire lineup got hits (20) and touched home plate.

Boston Herald sports scribe Burt Whitman used the May 5 game's magnificent turnout to write eloquently in favor of Sunday baseball, which was banned in Boston until a 1928 statewide referendum. Monday morning's *Herald* front page included this Whitman observation: "It was the second Sabbath game of ball played in this state under the recently enacted law that teams composed wholly of men in service may play on Sunday, provided there be no admission charged. It was a convincing and human argument for properly regulated sport on Sunday. There was nothing boisterous, nothing loud, nothing hilarious about the gathering. Less than twenty-five percent

were juveniles. Thousands of women not with their escorts, many of the latter unquestionably seeing their first 'big time' ball game in years, because of inability to attend games through the week."[5]

The *Boston American* agreed with its headline: "40,000 Approve Sunday Baseball." Writer Nick Flatly typed, "It was a typical Sunday holiday crowd. Everybody and his best girl was there and enjoyed a real holiday. There was cheering, of course, but not the semblance of anything that could possible raise the least protest against the national pastime on the Sabbath."[6] It didn't take long for one front office to notice the benefits of Sunday ball. The May 20 *Boston Post* had a simple headline for one particular American League game, "First Sunday Ball in East, 15,000 See Senators Beat Indians, 1-0, in 12 Innings. A *Boston Globe* story date-lined May 19 led, "Sunday baseball in the national capital was inaugurated today with a 12-inning game in which Washington defeated Cleveland, 1-0." Senators veteran spitballer Yancey "Doc" Ayers scored the winning run to beat Stan Coveleski. Each team had six errors, while each pitcher walked two, fanned just one, and allowed seven hits.

Nonetheless, it was not until April 1929 that a major-league baseball game was played in Boston on a Sunday.

SOURCES

Baseball-Reference.com

Johnson, Lloyd, and Miles Wolff, *Encyclopedia of Minor League Baseball* (Durham, North Carolina: Baseball America, 2007).

The author also consulted contemporary issues of the *Boston American*, *Boston Globe*, *Boston Herald*, *Boston Post*, *Brooklyn Eagle*, and *New York Times*.

NOTES

1   *Boston Post*, May 6, 1918.

2   Rico died in January 1919 of a burst appendix.

3   *Boston Post*, May 9, 1918.

4   For instance, see the *Boston Herald*, May 9, 1918, 22.

5   *Boston Herald*, May 6, 1918.

6   *Boston American*, May 6, 1918.

A BRAVES FIELD BLOWOUT

MAY 7, 1918: BOSTON BRAVES 16, BROOKLYN ROBINS 0 AT BRAVES FIELD

BY RICHARD "DIXIE" TOURANGEAU

Shortstop Johnny Rawlings had the game of his life leading the cellar-dwelling Boston Braves to their most convincing win in the twentieth century (to that date) by clobbering the visiting Brooklyn Robins, 16-0. It was the 189th game at the huge Wigwam, just off Commonwealth Avenue, and never had the home team won by that wide a margin since a 20-4 crushing of the Phillies in June 1900 at the old South End Grounds. The only thing hotter than Braves bats that day was the abnormal Hub spring weather. Sunday had been pleasantly warm but Monday was blistering and Tuesday topped it, killing three in the city. According to a *Boston American* front-page story the next day, "The official thermometer at the weather bureau reached its maximum height at 3 pm when it registered 89 degrees, thus beating Monday's record of 88 at the same hour, the highest it ever went on May 6 in the 46 years of the weather bureau's existence."[1]

Rawlings, from smallish Bloomfield, Iowa, had a career-high five singles (two RBIs, two runs) in the 17-hit attack. That alone must have shocked the small[2] crowd as Johnny was in a .106 slump, having just five hits and two runs so far for the 3-13 Braves. He doubled those numbers that afternoon. Five other Braves had at least two hits, including two triples by right fielder Al Wickland, while pitcher Don Carlos Pat Ragan contributed a pair and one RBI to serve his own cause. Buck Herzog had three hits. Braves president and part owner Percy Duncan Haughton and manager George T. Stallings were beaming after the game and the next morning when they saw that their neighbors, the first-place Red Sox, had been thrashed 7-2 in Washington by Walter Johnson despite a Babe Ruth

home run for Boston. Of course, those smiles were short-lived.

Victimized in the Teepee slaughter were Brooklyn hurlers veteran Larry Cheney (14 hits) and tryout Rich Durning. Eight walks and three Robins errors gave the Braves even more at-bats, but umpires Bill Klem and Bob Emslie had to work only two hours and the carnage was over. Ex-Cub Cheney and Pat Ragan, who had been traded to Boston from Brooklyn in

Johnny Rawlings.

early 1915, had hooked up five days earlier at Ebbets Field with Cheney winning, 7-4. That had been Ragan's second consecutive day on the slab, after beating Rube Marquard the day before, 4-2. Cheney was in his final full season of 10 in the majors and this was his worst outing ever in terms of the most hits allowed in the fewest innings pitched.

Ragan, born in Blanchard, Iowa (on the Missouri border, population 22 in 2010), split his basic nine-year career between Brooklyn (794 innings) and Boston (775), and played for four other clubs. To that point Ragan had compiled a 6-2 record versus his old team, allowing manager Wilbert Robinson's Flatbush flock more than two runs only twice. He beat ex-Giants star and future Hall of Famer Marquard three times in that stretch. He and Cheney didn't match up again in 1918.

Young Durning pitched for the Portland, Maine, Naval Reserve that year. His entire major-league experience was a mere three innings, one in 1917 and two that day. He gave up three hits and four walks for five runs in the Braves' sudden outburst.

The World War I schedule-shortened season was less than 20 games old (per club). The Giants had just swept the Braves and were 14-1, with Brooklyn's Cheney being the only pitcher who beat them. The Robins and Braves had been trading seventh and eighth place for a week and when Brooklyn arrived in the Hub, host Boston owned the cellar courtesy of the departing New Yorkers.

Manager Stallings juggled his 3-13 Braves lineup that day by benching rookie Roy Massey and Wally Rehg (both of whom had hits in Monday's loss) in favor of Wickland and Ray "Rabbit" Powell. Leadoff man Powell didn't get a hit but walked four times (career high) and scored thrice. Joe "Red" Kelly singled, tripled, had three RBIs, and scored twice. Ex-Federal Leaguer Wickland stroked two triples and knocked home three mates in the first of two straight games. The next day his ninth-inning home run tipped the Robins, 4-3. But Rawlings was the game's Wonder Boy. It was his best day within his worst season (.206). Veteran second baseman Charley "Buck" Herzog (three hits, three scores, and two RBIs), catcher Artie Wilson (a hit, two scores), and third-baseman Jim C. Smith (then hitting .369, had a double, two RBIs, and scored) all had a good day. First sacker Ed Konetchy was 0-for-5 but scored once.

For the vanquished, star left fielder Zack Wheat had a single in his first game of the year after a contract squabble. Sub center fielder Henry "Hi" Myers, first baseman Jake Daubert, and shortstop Ivan "Ivy" Olsen also singled while left fielder Jim Johnston had a double and single. Poor part-time right fielder Jim Hickman fanned a career-high four times and made an error. Future Hall of Famer Wheat eventually won the 1918 NL batting title with a .335 mark. Despite a solid losing record, Stallings' Braves defeated the Robins in eight of 14 games. The Braves' main downfall in 1918 was due to the Giants, as they lost 15 straight to John McGraw before winning the final game of the season.

BOSTON POST, WEDNESDAY, MAY, 8, 1918   11

Boston Nationals Have Regular Picnic With Two Dodger Pitchers

A DOUBLE STEAL BY HERZOG AND SMITH SCORED THE 2ND RUN OF THE 1ST INNING – A BASE ON BALLS, A SINGLE, A SACRIFICE AND AN INFIELD OUT, SCORED POWELL FOR THE 1ST RUN.

THE BASES WERE OVER-POPULATED AND THE LAST HALF OF THE 2ND INNING WAS A DIZZY AFFAIR AND THE CRACKING OF BATS ON BALL WAS REVERBERANT IN BRAVES FIELD, THE HOME TEAM HAMMERING IN FOUR RUNS

AND IT WAS SURE TOUGH ON THE BROOKLYN FIELDERS AS THE "SWATFEST" PROGRESSED –

AND THUS ENDED AN EVENTFUL DAY OF BASEBALL PLAY, FOR THE BRAVES.

Though the usually mild-hitting Braves managed 17 runs (in a home game) in July 1911, September 1940, again in September 1941, and 19 in June 1951, none of those outcomes was a bigger home-park blowout. Before they slipped out of Boston ignominiously before the 1953 campaign began, the Braves could only equal their home-margin record once in more than 2,600 games, when they beat pitiful Pittsburgh 16-0 in late September of 1952. That was just eight games before they would no longer call enormous Braves Field home.

Braves fans were not used to a lot of scoring by their Tribesmen, who had averaged almost exactly three runs per game from when Braves Field opened in late 1915 to that afternoon in 1918.[3] Monday morning's *Boston Post* baseball cartoon illustrated a small Brave being whomped by a husky Giant with a huge bat since the then first-place New Yorkers had won 5-1 and 4-1 on Friday and Saturday. The Monday game was in question but the cartoonist had the disgruntled, tattered Indian get up and thump his Giant tormentor with a larger bat. The hopeful prediction was a day early, as the Giants swept the series by winning 8-4 on Monday—then came Tuesday's record destruction of Brooklyn.

NOTES

1   *Boston American*, May 8, 1918.

2   The *Boston Globe* estimated 2,500 while the *Boston Post* presented the far more conservative figure of only 800 in attendance.

3   During the 38-year history at Braves Field, they scored 10 runs 50 times (45-5) and made even more tallies in 83 games (78-5). Those 16 runs, however, were eclipsed only three times by Tribe batters. The record stood quietly for 22 years when in September 1940 the Braves pounded the Phillies, their favorite target for such mayhem (28), 17-6 and the following September did the same to the Cardinals, 17-7. But on June 30, 1951, the visiting Giants were pummeled 19-7, the high mark that will stand forever. Vern Bickford survived six unearned runs and beat crafty Sal Maglie (12-4). First baseman Earl Torgeson smashed two home runs, one a grand slam, for seven RBIs, and catcher Walker Cooper added three RBIs. Oddly, opposing African-American center fielders Willie Mays and Sam Jethroe were the only batters hit by pitched balls during the slugfest. As for margin of victory, the 16 was finally equaled on September 12, 1952, when in the second game of a doubleheader the Pirates were shut out 16-0 by Ernie Johnson, behind second baseman Jack Dittmer's three RBIs and four runs (career high), catcher Paul Burris's four RBIs (second highest of career), and Torgeson's four scores. Rookie Eddie Mathews (.237) contributed a meaningless single and three whiffs. One-year-Buc wonderbust Ron Necciai lasted eight outs (eight runs) and got the loss. Future Pirate legend Bob Friend won the first game 8-1. For the sake of balance: The Cubs hold the "negative" margin record by embarrassing the Braves 24-2 on July 3, 1945. The Reds are second, running up a 19-2 trouncing at the Wigwam on August 2, 1924, game two.

A SEASON CUT SHORT BY WAR

SEPTEMBER 2, 1918: NEW YORK GIANTS 6, BOSTON BRAVES 2 (FIRST GAME); BOSTON BRAVES 2, NEW YORK GIANTS 1 (SECOND GAME), AT BRAVES FIELD

BY DAN MCCLOSKEY

With baseball nearing the end of its second season of play since the United States declared war on Germany and entered World War I, the game's continued operation was being called into question by high-ranking military officials, particularly the provost marshal of the US Army, General Enoch Crowder, who was in charge of the military draft. With the country fully committed to its involvement in the war, baseball was ruled a non-essential industry and the 1918 season was cut short after Crowder issued a "work-or-fight" order. As a result, the doubleheader scheduled for Monday, September 2 (Labor Day) at Braves Field would be the season's finale.

In lieu of Boston's annual holiday parade, between 4,000 and 5,000 people, mostly military personnel and government workers in the shipbuilding industry, turned out that day to march in the "Win-the-War-for-Freedom" parade. President Woodrow Wilson, in his Labor Day message to the nation, managed to tie the national holiday to the war effort by declaring, "To fail to win (the war) would be to imperil everything that the laborer has striven for and held dear since freedom first had its dawn and his struggle for justice began."[1]

On the field, 1918 was the second consecutive season in which manager George Stallings' Braves were considerably worse than the year before. At 52-70 going into the season's final day, the team retained only a few key players from the team that won the 1914 World Series and posted a .582 winning percentage from 1914 through 1916.

Meanwhile, in another part of town, the Red Sox—with Babe Ruth slated to pitch Game One – were gearing up to travel to Chicago in two days to play in a World Series that would long be remembered as the last one the Red Sox won for 86 years.

As many as 6,000 fans turned out to witness the season-ending doubleheader at Braves Field, more than 1,500 of whom were soldiers and sailors.[2] As had been the case all year, servicemen were admitted free as guests of the management.

The Braves were looking for their first win of the year against the second-place New York Giants, a streak of futility that stretched across 14 games. The defending National League champions had been among the hardest hit by the draft, but you couldn't tell by the way John McGraw's team had dominated Stallings' squad.

The first game of the twin bill did nothing to reverse the Braves' fortunes against McGraw's men. Art Nehf was on the hill for Boston, pitching on one day's rest after twirling an 11-inning complete-game victory in Philadelphia on Saturday for his 15th win of the season.

Nehf had pitched excellently in August, posting a 1.55 ERA over 64 innings in six starts, but with only two wins to show for it. However, the decision to pitch him on short rest on the season's final day proved to be a poor one. The 26-year-old Boston staff ace was tied with Chicago's Hippo Vaughn for the National League lead in complete games, so the season's workload may have been a factor as well.

Opposing Nehf was Red Causey, who was the Giants' second winningest pitcher in 1918 despite not cracking the rotation until mid-June. After weathering some inconsistency immediately after his promotion from the bullpen, Causey had emerged as one of the stalwarts of the Giants' staff, even winning six consecutive complete games from July 13 to August 3. A late-August swoon, in which he'd allowed six earned runs in two of his last three starts, had put a slight damper on his rookie campaign. But on this day, Causey looked more like the pitcher whose ERA was barely above 2.00 less than a month before.

The Giants scored a pair of runs in three of the game's first four innings, leaving the Braves down 6-0 before managing any offense themselves. Heinie Zimmerman—who at 31 was finishing the worst full season of his career, -- was the hitting star with a single, double, triple, sacrifice fly, and two RBIs. Art Fletcher contributed three singles and scored twice.

Ross Youngs started the game by singling to center. Larry Doyle walked and Fletcher beat out a bunt single to load the bases with nobody out. After striking out Jim Thorpe, Nehf yielded a sacrifice fly to Zimmerman and almost worked out of further trouble, but an error by Ed Konetchy on a grounder by Jose Rodriguez scored Doyle with the second run.

In the third, Fletcher reached on an infield hit and scored on Zimmerman's triple. A groundout by Rodriguez scored Zimmerman and gave New York a 4-0 lead.

Youngs led off the fourth with a walk, moved to second as Doyle was retired, and scored on a single by Fletcher. Thorpe walked and Zimmerman followed with a single to load the bases. Rodriguez's fielder's choice brought home Fletcher with the New Yorkers' sixth run of the game.

The Braves scored in their half of the fourth, as singles by Robert Taggert (aka Jim Kelly) and Chet Chadbourne and a walk to Zeb Terry walk loaded the bases with no outs. But Causey managed to limit the damage; a grounder by Red Smith and a single by Konetchy produced Boston's only two runs.

Art Nehf during a later stint with the Giants.

Nehf settled down and pitched scoreless ball the rest of the way, getting his league-leading 28th complete game in the 6-2 defeat.

In the second game, the Braves rode the right arm of 31-year-old ex-Giant Dick Rudolph. Because of arm trouble, Rudolph hadn't performed in 1918 like the pitcher who anchored the Boston staff from 1913 to 1917, winning 94 games and throwing nearly 1,500 innings in his short-lived peak. However, on this day, he was every bit as good as in the past.

The Giants got on the board first, scoring an unearned run in the second inning on a play that nearly resulted in two outs being recorded due to some over-aggressive baserunning.

After Zimmerman drew a one-out walk, Jay Kirke singled to right on a hit-and-run. With Zimmerman advancing to third, Kirke attempted to take second but was thrown out on a close play. Zimmerman

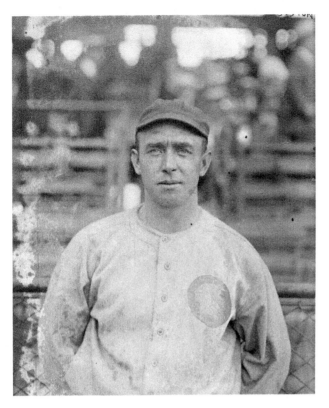

Dick Rudolph.

In the fourth New York left fielder Joe Wilhoit walked to load the bases with one out, but the Boston hurler came back to strike out Bill Rariden and his counterpart Steele to snuff out the rally.

In the fifth Rudolph walked Zimmerman and faced Kirke with two outs and the bases full. Kirke hit one with authority, but Taggert snared it on the run near the left-field line to preserve the tie. Boston scored what proved to be the winning run in the sixth. After one-out singles by Smith and Konetchy, Wagner walked. Johnny Rawlings then lofted a deep fly to left that scored Smith, giving the Braves a 2-1 lead they would not relinquish, and ultimately, their first victory in 16 games against the Giants that season.

With the season over for both the Braves and Giants, players and spectators were left wondering what impact the Great War would have on baseball in 1919.

SOURCES

Neft, David S., and Richard M. Cohen, *The Sports Encyclopedia:Baseball*, 7th ed. (New York: St. Martin's Press, 1987), 84.

Boston Post, September 3, 1918.

Boston Post, September 2, 1918.

Baseball-Reference.com.

Retrosheet.org.

Boston Herald, September 2, 1918.

Boston Herald, September 3, 1918.

Boston Globe, September 3, 1918.

continued through third attempting to score, and Boston shortstop Terry's throw had him dead to rights at the plate, but catcher Bill Wagner dropped the ball while applying the tag.

That was the only run the Giants mustered off Rudolph, although they threatened twice more before the Braves took their first lead of the game. Rudolph helped his own cause in the third, singling off Giants starter Bob Steele and swiping second on a Buck Herzog strikeout. An infield hit by Taggert moved him to third, from where he scored the tying run on a single by Chet Chadbourne.

Rudolph pitched out of bases-loaded jams in back-to-back innings in the game's middle innings.

NOTES

1   "All America in War to Win," *Boston Post*, September 2, 1918, 1.

2   Figures varied. The *Boston Herald* reported 4,000 in attendance and the *Boston Globe* reported 6,000.

HANK GOWDY DAY AT BRAVES FIELD

MAY 24, 1919: BOSTON BRAVES 4, CINCINNATI REDS 1 AT BRAVES FIELD

BY JOHN DIFONZO

Welcoming back their popular soldier-catcher Hank Gowdy after nearly a two-year absence, the Boston Braves held a ceremony in his honor on Saturday afternoon, May 24, 1919, before a game against the Cincinnati Reds.[1] Gowdy had been the first active major leaguer to enlist for military service in World War I. John Heydler, the president of the National League, came, as well as a delegation from Camp Devens, Massachusetts. The first 12 rows of the grandstand behind the Braves dugout were reserved for special guests. Gowdy was admired by fans across the country and "Gowdy Days" were planned in other National League cities, including Cincinnati, Chicago, and St. Louis.[2]

Before his heroics on the battlefield, Gowdy was a hero on the diamond. He was one of the stars as the Miracle Braves swept Connie Mack's heavily-favored Philadelphia Athletics in the 1914 World Series. Gowdy had six hits and five walks in 16 plate appearances. With the Braves down by two runs in the bottom of the 10th inning of Game Three, he started a rally by hitting the Series' only home run.[3] The Braves tied the game later in the inning. In the bottom of the 12th inning Gowdy led off with a double and was replaced for a pinch-runner, who eventually scored the game-winner.[4]

Amid growing tensions, on April 2, 1917, President Wilson asked Congress to declare war on Germany and provide for an initial 500,000 men in military service. War was declared on April 6. On June 1, the Braves game in Cincinnati was rained out, and Gowdy took the opportunity to take the train to his hometown of Columbus, Ohio, and enlist in the Army.[5] (He joined the Ohio National Guard because he wanted to fight alongside men he was raised with.[6]) Gowdy

was 27, in the prime of his career, and he chose not to wait and register for the draft, forgoing his salary.[7]

On June 22 Gowdy played his last game at Braves Field (a 5-3 victory over the eventual pennant-winning New York Giants) before going into the Army. Gowdy played in five more games in Brooklyn before leaving the team.[8]

National League President Tener lobbied for Organized Baseball to honor Gowdy. In an article in *Baseball Magazine,* Tener wrote, "Gowdy was neither a fading veteran nor an untried busher. He was a player in his prime. He occupied a position of great responsibility on an important club. He enjoyed the benefits of a good salary, the protection of a favorable contract. A single season in the army might ruin his subsequent

Gowdy, in military attire, alongside Giants manager John McGraw in 1917.

53

Hank Gowdy: the majors' first WW I veteran.

career as a player. Hank Gowdy knew all this. But he didn't hesitate."[9]

After Gowdy enlisted, Braves teammate Johnny Evers, who waited until he was drafted to go into the service, said Hank's decision not to wait for the draft surprised his teammates and manager George Stallings. "He claimed he was going and he went," Evers said. "Nobody in the club thought he would pull up stakes quite so soon. George Stallings wouldn't believe him when he said he planned to leave last night. But just the same he packed up his things and took the evening train for his home in Columbus. I was in the lobby as he passed out and he waved his hand to us and called out, 'So long boys I'll meet you in Paris.' You would have thought, from the way he acted, that he was going to a party. Now this war is a pretty serious business. I guess my attitude toward it is about that of the majority. If my services are needed on the firing line I am ready to go. But I doubt if I would go the same as Hank Gowdy did, as if I was off for a lark. I don't think I am any more of a coward than the next man. But facing bands and crowds clapping in the galleries is one thing and facing machine guns is another. I would go all right if I was called but I wouldn't feel as if I were off for a matinee show, or act as if I did. So I will have to hand it to Gowdy for having more sand than I have when it comes to a show down."[10] Evers and 13 other 1917 teammates eventually followed Gowdy into military service.[11]

Gowdy himself explained why he had volunteered: "I had no excuse so far as I could see, for not offering my services. The government had shown, by passing the draft law, that they needed several hundred thousand men. I was of the proper age, well and strong, with no physical disabilities that I know of, with no one dependent upon me for support. I have no criticism for those who wait for the draft but I didn't like the idea myself. I could offer my services without hesitation but I didn't like to feel that I was forced to go. This is a matter that everybody has to decide for himself and I decided for myself that I would enlist. I do not know and I don't believe anyone else does, how long this war will last. If it proves to be a longtime contract on my part, why, I want to go to France to do my bit. I wouldn't feel content to stay on this side of the Atlantic in comparative security and know that others were bearing the brunt across the ocean. I don't like to be a target for shrapnel any better than the next man. But that isn't a subject that it does much good to speculate about. Somebody has got to fight and I don't see how I could consistently fail to do my share."[12]

Gowdy served in the 42nd "Rainbow" Division. He saw combat in the Battles of Chateau Thierry, Saint Mihiel, and the Argonne as a color sergeant.[13]

The May 24, 1919, game was Gowdy's first after returning from the service. More than 16,000 fans, turned out to honor him. During the pregame ceremony, he was presented with gifts by Boston Mayor Andrew J. Peters, including: a gold watch and chain, a cigar cutter and $600 in Victory Bonds. Rabbit Maranville and Pat Moran presented Gowdy a trunk full of clothes from his teammates.

A bronze tablet was unveiled that would be placed on the first pillar of the administration building where it would be seen by the fans as they approached Braves Field. At the top of the tablet was the Braves insignia flanked by the years 1917 and 1919. Underneath was a caption reading, "Honor Roll Boston Braves Who Served in the Great War" and below were the names of the 14 Braves who were on the club's roster when they entered the service, including Gowdy; Willard J. McGraw, who died in the service; and Arthur Rico, who died shortly after his discharge from the Navy.[14]

Hank Gowdy wasn't the only person honored that day at Braves Field. Pat Moran, the first-year Cincinnati Reds manager, was from Fitchburg, Massachusetts, and a trainload of his friends came. They sat sit in a section reserved for them behind the Reds bench.

Fittingly enough, Art Nehf, who had pitched in Gowdy's last home appearance before he went to war, was on the mound on the 24th, and, as before, pitched a complete game as the Braves defeated the Reds, 4-1. After Nehf threw the first pitch of the game, Gowdy handed the ball to umpire Cy Rigler. Rigler handed it to Braves pitcher Dick Rudolph, who presented it to Mayor Peters as a souvenir. Gowdy was greeted by cheers when he came to bat for the first time in the second inning, and he delivered a groundball single to right field on the first pitch to him.[15]

When the United States entered World War II, Gowdy enlisted and served as a major and recreation director at Fort Benning, Georgia. He trained soldiers on a baseball field that had been dedicated to him in 1925. He may have been the only active major leaguer to serve in both World Wars, first as a player and then as a coach.[16] Gowdy returned to Braves Field on June 2, 1951, to be honored with his surviving 1914 teammates at a ceremony marking the 75th anniversary of the National League.

NOTES

1 "Hank Gowdy Day Set for May 24," *Boston Globe*, May 11, 1919.

2 "Cards Make Merry on Hank Gowdy Day," *Boston Globe*, June 11, 1919.

3 This was the first extra-inning home run in World Series history.

4 Carol McMains and Frank Ceresi, "Hank Gowdy," *The Miracle Braves of 1914* (Phoenix: SABR 2014), 76-78.

5 "Gowdy Goes Home to Enlist in the Army," *Boston Globe*, June 2, 1917.

6 "Hank Gowdy Quits the Braves to Join His Ohio Regiment," *Brooklyn Daily Eagle*, June 27, 1917.

7 Gowdy's 1917 salary was reported as either $6,000 or $7,000 in newspapers from 1917 to 1919.

8 "Hank Gowdy Quits Braves to Join his Ohio Regiment." Gowdy had originally planned to leave the team on July 1, but he injured his knee sliding into second base in the first game of a double-header on June 25. He played in the second game and caught one inning of the first game of a double header on June 26 after the starting catcher was removed for a pinch-hitter.

9 John K. Tener, "Hank Gowdy—The Man Who Blazed the Trail," *Baseball Magazine*, March 1918.

10 Hank Gowdy, "Why I Enlisted," *Baseball Magazine*, September 1917.

11 baseball-reference.com/bullpen/Category:World_War_I_Veterans. Other 1917 Boston Braves who served in World War I were Fred Bailey, Jesse Barnes, Larry Chappell, Sam Covington, Johnny Evers, Joe Kelly, Rabbit Maranville, Mike Massey, Ray Powell, Johnny Rawlings, Wally Rehg, Art Rico, Hank Schreiber, and Walt Tragesser.

12 "Why I Enlisted."

13 Harold Kaese, "Gowdy Class in Tough Era," *Boston Globe*, August 7, 1966.

14 "Hank Gowdy Day Set for May 24." The 14 Braves names as they appeared on the tablet were Fred M. Bailey, Hugh E. Canavan, Richard D. Conway, Dana Fillingim, Harry M. Gowdy, William L. James, Joseph H. Kelly, Walter J. Maranville, Willard J. McGraw, Ray W. Powell, Walter P. Rehg, Arthur F. Rico, Henry W. Schreiber, and Walter J. Tragesser.

15 James C. O'Leary, "Crowd of 16,000 Out to Honor Hank Gowdy," *Boston Globe*, May 25, 1919.

16 "Hank Gowdy Will Rejoin Reds Next Year as Coach," *Boston Globe*, November 17, 1944.

AN EXTREME EXERCISE IN FUTILITY –
26 INNINGS AND NO DECISION

MAY 1, 1920: BROOKLYN DODGERS 1, BOSTON BRAVES 1 (TIE, 26 INNINGS)
AT BRAVES FIELD

BY WARREN CORBETT

It rained all morning in Boston. Not hard, just a persistent drizzle. When Joe Oeschger and his roommate, Leslie Mann, sat down to breakfast, they figured they were looking at a day off. Their Boston Braves were scheduled to play the Brooklyn Dodgers[1] that Saturday afternoon.

Hearing no word from the ballclub, they reported to Braves Field. That's when Oeschger found out he would be the starting pitcher, if and when.[2]

By game time at 3:00 P.M., the rain had let up, but it was overcast, damp, and raw, not much more than 50 degrees, when Oeschger threw the first pitch in the longest game in major-league history. The game lasted 26 innings. So did Oeschger. So did the Dodgers' pitcher, Leon Cadore. They were both right-handed, both 28 that year, neither a star.

The Dodgers scored in the fifth after Oeschger walked the leadoff batter and bobbled a double-play grounder. With a runner on second, Dodgers second baseman Ivy Olson poked a two-strike, broken-bat flare over shortstop to give Brooklyn a 1-0 lead.

The Braves tied it in the next inning. Walt Cruise tripled to the scoreboard in left and crossed the plate on Tony Boeckel's single up the middle. Rabbit Maranville followed with a double, but Boeckel was thrown out at home.

After that, nothing. The teams played 20 scoreless innings.

Boston missed a chance to win in the bottom of the ninth. Maranville led off with a single. Pinch-hitter Lloyd Christenbury tried to sacrifice him to second, but both were safe when Cadore's throw to first hit Christenbury. After a sacrifice moved the runners up, Dodgers manager Wilbert Robinson ordered an intentional walk to fill the bases with one out. The Braves' Charlie Pick slapped a hard grounder to second baseman Olson, who made a fine stop, tagged the runner coming from first, and threw out Pick for a game-saving double play.

Oeschger during his pre-Braves days with the Phillies.

Leon Cadore's defense had bailed him out, not for the first time. At least one Brave had reached base in each of the first nine innings on 11 hits, two walks, and an error. A writer for the *Sun & New York Herald* commented, "Time and again it looked as if Cadore would fall, but time and again the Brooklyn men behind him rose to heights of superefficiency as they converted seeming hits into outs and lifted their pitcher out of many a tight situation."[3] In addition to Olson's double play, left fielder Zack Wheat had made a shoetop catch and first baseman Ed Konetchy snared a foul popup while teetering on the dugout steps.

Oeschger, throwing fastballs almost exclusively, was just hitting his stride. Beginning in the eighth, he set down 18 consecutive Dodgers. Only six of them got the ball out of the infield.

The Dodgers got to Oeschger in the 17th, when they loaded the bases with one out. Rowdy Elliott grounded back to the mound and Oeschger threw home for the force out. Catcher Hank Gowdy fired to first, going for an easy double play, but his throw was wide and first baseman Walter Holke could only knock it down. The Dodger runner from second, the slow-moving Konetchy, saw Holke scrambling after the ball and lumbered around third, carrying the go-ahead run. Holke's desperate throw pulled Gowdy off the plate, but he sprawled headlong in front of Konetchy's spikes and put on the tag to complete a spectacular double play. Gowdy's dive "saved my neck," Oeschger said.[4]

Oeschger didn't allow another hit for the final nine innings. Cadore, relying on his curveball, had found his groove, retiring 15 straight, allowing a single in the 20th, and then setting down 19 more. A misty rain was falling again. Newspapers estimated that anywhere from 2,000 to 4,500 spectators had been in the stands at the start; there's no telling how many went home as the afternoon grew chillier.

In the 20th inning manager Robinson offered to relieve Cadore, but the pitcher replied, "If that other fellow can go one more inning, I can too."[5] Braves manager George Stallings never asked Oeschger how he was holding up. Oeschger explained, "If a pitcher couldn't go the distance, he soon found himself some other form of occupation."[6]

The 23rd inning set a new National League record; the Dodgers and Pirates had played 22 in 1917. In the 25th it became the longest game in major-league history, surpassing a 24-inning contest between the Philadelphia Athletics and Boston Americans in 1906. Braves second baseman Charlie Pick made the last out in the 25th to finish his own historic day. His batting line for the game, 0-for-11, has not been equaled in at least 100 years.

A quirk of the calendar made the longest game possible. May 1 was the first day of Daylight Saving Time, meaning sunset came an hour later than the day before. The 26th inning ended at 6:50 P.M. EDT, still nearly an hour before official sundown, but the sun was

SOME GAME! THAT 26 INNING BATTLE IN WHICH BRAVES AND DODGERS EACH SCORED ONE LONE RUN

Leon Cadore.

nowhere in sight. The dark clouds and mist made it hard to see. Oeschger said, "The batters were griping to end the game."[7] The umpire in chief, Barry McCormick, talked to both managers and called a halt because of darkness.[8]

The teams played 26 innings, almost three full games, in 3 hours and 50 minutes. Each half-inning, on average, took less than five minutes, even counting the breaks in between. While there has never been another 26-inning game in the majors, the White Sox and Brewers played 25 in 1984; that one, completed over two days because of a curfew, lasted 8 hours and 6 minutes. The 1974 Cardinals and Mets played 25 innings in a brisk 7:04. Obviously players moved at a different pace in 1920.

At the time nobody knew how many pitches Oeschger and Cadore threw. Nobody asked until more than 30 years later. Oeschger guessed his total was about 250. Cadore thought he was close to 300.

"I don't say I wasn't a little tired after those 26 innings," Oeschger said, "but I have been more fatigued in some nine-inning games when I got into a lot of jams. They are what wear a pitcher out. There weren't too many tight situations in this long game."[9] Oeschger went on to win 20 games the next season, the best year of his career.

Cadore finished the 1920 season with the 10th best ERA in the league. He pitched in the majors for four more years, but said his arm was never the same after the marathon game.

Today a 26-inning complete game seems preposterous, not to mention abusive. Even by the standards of 1920, Oeschger and Cadore's feat was recognized as extraordinary. A *Boston Globe* cartoon the next day portrayed them taking their place in the Hall of Fame. (The Hall did not exist, but the idea did.)

Marathon pitching performances were rare, but not unknown. In the previous record-longest game, in 1906, Jack Coombs of Philadelphia and Boston's Joe Harris pitched all 24 innings. With the help of Retrosheet, baseball-reference.com, and researcher Philip J. Lowry, the author has identified 20 times when a starter worked 20 or more innings. The first was in 1892, the last in 1929. Oeschger himself went 20 in 1919, the only man to reach that mark twice. We can wish for a time machine to take us back to July 4, 1905: Cy Young against Rube Waddell for 20 innings.

Mercifully, the Braves had a day off after the longest game, because Sunday ball was not allowed in Boston. But the Dodgers took a train home, where they played 13 innings before losing to the Phillies, 4-3. Then they returned to Boston to wrap up the series there. The two teams played 19 innings on Monday, as the Braves squeaked out a 2-1 win. The Dodgers had fought through 58 innings in three days, without a single victory to show for their labors.

SOURCES

Retrosheet's play-by-play account has not yet been published. David W. Smith of Retrosheet.org provided it.

"Boston and Brooklyn Break Big League Record by Battling for 26 Innings," *New York Times*, May 2, 1920.

"Brooklyn Ties in Record Game of 26 Innings," *Sun & New York Herald*, May 2, 1920.

Corbett, Warren. "Marathon Men." *The Hardball Times Baseball Annual*. Fangraphs and the Hardball Times, 2014.

Cunningham, Ed. "Darkness Finds Longest Game in All Big League History Still Undecided," *Boston Sunday Herald*, May 2, 1920.

"How It Seems to Pitch a 26-Inning Game," *Baseball Magazine*, July 1920.

Lieb, Fred. "Leon Cadore, Who Pitched 26-Inning Duel, Dies at 65," *The Sporting News*, March 26, 1958.

Lowry, Philip J., email, August 23, 2014.

"Major League Record Broken; Score is 1-1," *New York Tribune*, May 2, 1920.

Murphy, Edward T. "Cadore Recalls That 26-Inning Duel with Oeschger," *New York World Telegram and Sun*, April 30, 1955.

Murphy, Edward T. "Cadore Replays Longest Major Game—26-Inning Dodger-Brave Tie in '20," *The Sporting News*, January 18, 1956.

National Weather Service and weatherunderground.com.

O'Leary, James C. "Braves-Dodgers in 26-inning Tie," *Boston Globe*, May 2, 1920.

O'Leary, James C. "Oeschger in Good Trim After His Record Game," *Boston Globe*, May 3, 1920.

Rice, Thomas S. "Superbas in 26 Inning Tie," *Brooklyn Eagle*, May 2, 1920.

Rice, Thomas S. "Bats Not Swinging True for Dodgers," *The Sporting News*, May 13, 1920.

Ruane, Tom. "A Retro Review of the 1920s," Retrosheet.org, retrosheet.org/Research/RuaneT/rev1920_art.htm#A1920, accessed June 18, 2014.

NOTES

1   Histories written later make it appear that the name Brooklyn Robins was universal. It was not. In contemporary game accounts, the hometown *Brooklyn Eagle* called them the Superbas. The *New York Times*, Robins. The *Boston Globe* and the *New York Tribune*, Dodgers. *The Sporting News* used Dodgers in the headline, but the story, by the *Brooklyn Eagle* writer Thomas S. Rice, called them Superbas. "Dodgers" is used here because it is the most familiar.

2   Oeschger said later, "We didn't think the game would be played, but we had to report to the park. It was a Saturday, and I didn't think I would pitch because Manager Stallings usually pitched me on Sundays because I went to church. He always played his hunches. I was happy to get the starting job because Cadore was pitching, and he had beaten me 1-0 in 11 innings earlier in the season. I wanted to even things." Lynwood Carranco, "Joe Oeschger Remembers," *Baseball Research Journal*, Vol. 9 (SABR, 1980).

3   "Boston and Brooklyn Play World's Record Ball Game; Play 26 Innings to a Tie," *Sun & New York Herald*, May 2, 1920.

4   Carranco, "Joe Oeschger Remembers." The *New York Times* wrote that Gowdy "threw himself blindly across the plate to meet Konetchy's spikes with bare fist." *New York Times*, May 2, 1920.

5   "Zach Wheat recalls game of 26 innings," Associated Press-*Washington Post & Times Herald*, June 7, 1962. C2.

6   "Oeschger thinks pitching feat is no longer news," United Press International-*Sarasota Herald-Tribune*, July 17, 1977, 33.

7   Carranco, "Joe Oeschger Remembers."

8   Jerome Holtzman quoted Cadone as saying, "Some of the ballplayers, particularly Ivy Olson, begged the umps to let it go one more inning but they overruled him and called it. Maybe it was just as well. Just what would have happened if they had lights in those days, is hard to tell." Jerome Holtzman, *Baseball Digest*, November 2000.

9   Jack McDonald, "50 Years Ago—Longest Game Ever in Majors," *The Sporting News*, May 16, 1970, 5.

COLLEGE FOOTBALL AT THE WIGWAM

DECEMBER 4, 1920: BOSTON COLLEGE 14, HOLY CROSS 0 AT BRAVES FIELD
BOSTON COLLEGE'S FIRST UNBEATEN SQUAD BRINGS BIG TIME FOOTBALL TO BRAVES FIELD

BY TOM MASON

The 1920 Boston College-Holy Cross football game was an important milestone in New England sports history. Sometimes the most intense rivalries are between family members. The annual game, which began in 1896, always attracted enormous interest among Catholics. Cardinal William O'Connell, the leader of the Archdiocese of Boston, took a personal interest in the annual game. He attended practices and personally awarded an annual trophy named after himself to the winners.[1]

But the hype surrounding the game was unlike any previous contest. Traditional football powers, such as Harvard, Princeton, and Yale, increasingly had to share the stage with other university teams. The football teams' success was a source of Catholic pride in the predominantly Protestant United States. The interest in the BC-Holy Cross game had outstripped their campus playing fields. A supporter of the Eagles was quoted as saying: "The Boston College football has done as much for the cause of Ireland as De Valera himself."[2]

Outscoring its opponents by 181-16, BC was recognized as one of the best college teams in America in 1920.[3] Championships weren't awarded through a playoff or bowl. At stake was its second consecutive Eastern championship, a consensus among fans and the press that it was best Catholic football team in the East.

Both teams had proven themselves against the best. Harvard's ranked team barely survived a too-close-for-comfort 3-0 win over Holy Cross. Boston College was one of the biggest stories in the country. For the second year in a row, the Eagles defeated Yale in New Haven. An eyewitness to BC's upset win at Yale, future Harvard Hall of Famer Charlie Brickley, observed: "They are one of the best football teams I ever saw and the way they played Yale would have beaten any team in the country."[4]

The Eagles were coached by Frank Cavanaugh, who was at BC from 1919 to 1926. The Iron Major was a World War I hero. (In 1927 the College Football Hall of Famer was lured to the bright lights of New York at Fordham. His offensive line, dubbed the Seven Blocks of Granite, brought football fame and fortune to the Jesuit school.) BC's other future Hall of Famer on this day was All-American captain Luke Urban at end. Tony Comerford, the opposite end, was also a significant threat. BC's Jimmy "Fitzy" Fitzpatrick, the starting halfback, was a game-breaker, but was unavailable for this game because of a dislocated shoulder.[5] Besides being the team's leading scorer, Fitzy was a fast runner, an ambidextrous passer, and perhaps the greatest kicker in football. His punting average was over 65 yards and he drop-kicked many long-range field goals. His clutch field goals had defeated Yale, Georgetown, and Holy Cross twice. But star quarterback Phil Corrigan, who had been injured much of the season, was finally healthy enough to return to the starting lineup. It was good timing: Corrigan was also the backup kicker/punter.

Holy Cross, at 5-2, was no slouch. Its signature win was a 3-0 shutout over then-unbeaten Syracuse. The Purple had a stout line and strong defense, boasting a 220-pound left guard. Its main threat was left halfback Chick Gagnon. Practices before the game were used by coach Cleo O'Donnell as open competitions to determine who would start at left tackle, fullback, and end in the finale.

The rivals had split their series, winning eight games apiece. Boston College had won the last three. In 1919 BC, at Fenway Park, upset the heavily favored Crusaders before a record-setting Boston football crowd of 15,000.

But the attendance for the 1920 game shattered that record. Most reports indicated that about 30,000 attended the game. But there were some estimates that as many as 40,000 tickets were sold.[6] According to the *Boston Globe*, the fans were a sight to behold: "It was a magnificent crowd, a typical football crowd. There were the furcoated men and women, the college youth with the greatest thing in style and cover on their overcoats; there were young women and matrons in resplendently bright headdresses."[7] Cardinal O'Connell and VIPs from the Boston Archdiocese presided over the game in a box overlooking the 50-yard line.

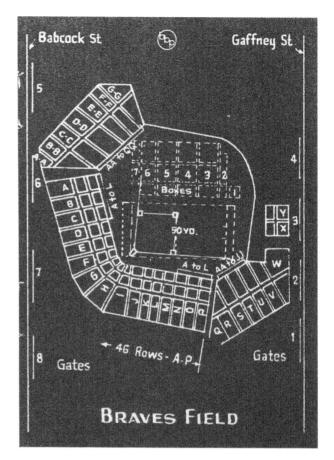

The Wigwam configured for football.

There were many complaints about Braves Field as a setting. The field was never completely football-friendly. Braves Field's shape, designed for baseball, created blind spots for spectators. Harvard Stadium's horseshoe, in comparison, allowed more fans to clearly see how each play developed. At Braves Field, a large number of seats were located in the end zones and many attendees were forced to stand on the sidelines.

On the day of the game, the field was a wet, slippery quagmire of ooze. The game resembled a large mud-wrestling match.

The big difference in the game was kicking. The first crucial sequence of plays occurred midway through the first period. After the Eagles were stopped at their own 44-yard line, a BC punt landed Holy Cross on its own 12-yard line. Two short runs convinced the Purple's coach that the best course of action would be a quick kick. But a fumbled snap cost the Crusaders 10 yards. With fourth and long at the 5, Holy Cross

was forced to punt the ball from its own end zone. The punter slipped and the ball hit the goalpost. Holy Cross won the scrum for the ball and made the recovery in the end zone but BC had the safety and a 2-0 lead.

In the second quarter Boston College had three consecutive opportunities inside its opponent's 20-yard line but came up empty-handed as the Holy Cross defense held. But the kicking game again let the Crusaders down late in the first half. Boston College's substitute punter, Corrigan, placed a perfect coffin-corner kick at Holy Cross's 2½ yard line. Holy Cross's coach decided to punt instead of run and leave the game in the hands of the defense. A shanked punt ruined that strategy and gave BC first and goal at the 5-yard line. Ben Roderick powered the ball over the Eagles' right side for the game's first touchdown. BC missed the point after but held an 8-0 lead at halftime. The Purple had a touchdown disallowed early in the third quarter. A Boston College punt returner fumbled a ball and Chick Gagnon returned it for a touchdown. However, the ball was called dead because a Crusader kicked the ball before taking possession.[8]

The final score of the game came late in the fourth quarter. Holy Cross muffed a punt return and the Eagles recovered it at the Holy Cross 6-yard line. Jimmie Liston ran the ball straight up the middle to give BC a 12-0 victory.

The Eagles had 178 yards rushing and 57 passing yards. They benefited from a 17-yard pass interference penalty. Holy Cross rushed for 130 yards and completed 5 of 15 passes for 57 yards.

The teams made $20,000 apiece for the game which, in today's dollars, translates to $250,000.[9] At the time, it was the largest football crowd in each school's and in Boston's history, but just two years later, the 1922 game at Braves Field attracted 54,000 — a record unbroken as of 2014. The game was a breakthrough for both teams' national ambitions as football powers. Games against national powers replaced local schools on their schedules. Eagles fundraising material featured the football team as a selling point. BC was invited to play Baylor in the Cotton Bowl's inaugural game in 1922. In 1925 Holy Cross finally defeated Harvard. For Holy Cross and Boston College, this game was a beginning of glorious and profitable days in big-time football. And by the way, the 1920 Boston College football team was the first to be referred to as the Eagles.

SOURCES

The *Boston Globe* devoted several pages to coverage of the game. It was a primary source along with the *New York Times* and *The Heights*, Boston College's student newspaper. The Boston College and Holy Cross media guides and websites were consulted for background information. The national weekly AP football poll wasn't started until 1936. But a fan named James Vautravers went through the time and trouble to figure out who the top 25 teams would be if there was a national poll. His site, TipTop25.com, is authoritative as a source for figuring out the strongest pre-1936 college football teams. According to their strength of schedule and wins, BC would have been ranked number 11 and Holy Cross number 23 in TipTop's hypothetical polls. The teams' opponents, Harvard and Yale were respectively ranked 2 and 16.

Boston College's library's virtual exhibit, bc.edu/libraries/about/exhibits/burnsvirtual/teams/3.html, has pictures and information about the 1920 team.

NOTES

1 "Cardinal O'Connell sees B.C. Gridders in Practice," *Boston Daily Globe*, November 30, 1920, 11.

2 "Mr. Daniel J. Coakley Makes Donation of $1,000 to the Athletic Association," *The Heights*, Volume II, Number 3, October 15, 1920, 1.

3 "College Football Teams of the Eastern Section as Ranked for the 1920 Season by The New York Times," *New York Times*, December 5, 1920, 114.

4 "B.C. Team One of the Best Says Charley Brickley," *Boston Daily Globe*, December 4, 1920, 6.

5 Melville E. Webb Jr., "Rivals Ready for the Big Game: Fitzpatrick out of the Boston College Lineup," *Boston Daily Globe*, December 4, 1920, 1 and 6.

6 "Cardinal O'Connell Sees B.C. Gridders in Practice," *Boston Daily Globe*, November 30, 1920, 11.

7 "Wonder Crowd Throngs Field: Battle in Mud is Seen by at Least 30,000," *Boston Daily Globe*, December 5, 1920, 18.

8 Melville E. Webb Jr., "Boston College Winds Up With 14-0 Victory," *Boston Daily Globe*, December 3, 1920, 1, 18-19.

9 "B.C.-Holy Cross Contract for Three Years Signed," *Boston Daily Globe*, December 15, 1920, 17.

COLLEGIANS VERSUS THE PROS

MAY 9, 1921: BOSTON BRAVES 4, BOSTON COLLEGE 0 AT BRAVES FIELD

BY BOB LEMOINE

Jimmy "Fitz" Fitzpatrick was already known as one of the best athletes in the history of Boston College when he stepped onto the mound at Braves Field on May 9, 1921. His coach, Frank Cavanaugh, called Fitz "the greatest athlete Boston College has ever had," and added, "I doubt that any has ever done more for his college in athletics than Fitzy has done for Boston College."[1] The Braves were playing the Boston College Eagles to benefit the $2 million BC Building Fund.[2] While this exhibition game has been long forgotten, if you are traveling on Interstate 295 in Portland, Maine, you will pass Fitzpatrick Stadium, named in honor of the legendary football coach. Fitzpatrick's 45-year career at Portland High School as teacher, coach, and athletic director would begin later in 1921. On this day, the young left-hander showed the Boston Braves, "the old story of 'What a wonder that Fitz is!'" in the words of Burt Whitman of the *Boston Herald*.[3]

Fitzpatrick held the Braves to one hit through six innings, a feat made even more amazing by the fact that he was pitching on a Monday after a nine-inning start on Saturday against Fordham. Yet the Braves were "utterly helpless before the crafty fork slants of Boston College's sterling athlete," wrote the Boston College weekly paper, *The Heights*.[4] That one hit was controversial: Billy Southworth hit a ball to deep shortstop that Ted Palmer played slowly, then made a wide throw. Nevertheless, it was scored a base hit.

In the seventh inning, however, the Braves scored all four of their runs. Al Nixon doubled to left field and scored on a single by Tony Boeckel, who made it to second base on a bobble in the outfield. Fitzpatrick quickly fielded a Walter Holke bunt, but his throw was wild, and the runners were safe. Hod Ford singled

to left field, scoring Boeckel, and then both Ford and Holke scored on a double by Frank Gibson. Edward Mullowney pitched the ninth inning for the Eagles, retiring the Braves in order, with one strikeout.

Johnny Cooney started for the Braves and allowed two hits over five innings. Cy Morgan pitched the final four innings, allowing only one hit.

Fitzpatrick, a native of Meriden, Connecticut, was a remarkable athlete who lettered in four varsity sports at Boston College: baseball, football, basketball, and hockey. He played center and guard for the basketball team, and goalie for the hockey team. Fitzpatrick had

Jimmy "Fitz" Fitzpatrick.

63

a punting average of 65 yards per kick, and in his
sophomore year he faced the legendary Jim Thorpe
in a punting competition in Canton, Ohio. "I don't
really remember if he beat me or I beat him. I know
we got off some pretty good shots," Fitzpatrick recalled.[5] Fitzpatrick's football career ended when he
broke a shoulder in 1920.

After graduation from BC in 1921, Fitzpatrick joined
the faculty at Portland High School, where he remained until he retired in 1966. He stayed active as a
player in semipro baseball, and once faced Babe Ruth
at Bayside Park in Portland. Ruth had come to Portland
to do batting exhibitions. "I pitched the whole game,"
Fitzpatrick recalled. "Ruth popped twice to the infield
and the other two times, I struck him out, and when
Babe didn't speak to me after the game I knew he was
mad and I was some shook up."[6]

Fitzpatrick coached the Portland High School football,
baseball, basketball, and golf teams. In 1947 he became
the athletic director, a post he held until he retired.
He was inducted into the Boston College Hall of
Fame in 1970. The Fitzpatrick Trophy, nicknamed the
"Fitzy," recognizes the best high-school football players
in Maine each year.[7]

"In the early years of the fast-moving 20th century,
Jimmy Fitzpatrick put Boston College athletics on
the map. His football exploits made headlines in the
Boston papers. He was the Doug Flutie of his era,"
wrote Tom Chard of the *Portland Press Herald*.[8]

Boston College third baseman Luke Urban, from Fall
River, Massachusetts, made some sparkling defensive
plays in this game. Urban played 50 games for the
Braves in 1927-1928. He compiled a .273 batting average
in 128 at-bats. Frank "Squash" Wilson, from Malden,
Massachusetts, was the Eagles' right fielder that day.
Wilson played for the Braves from 1924 to 1926 and
for the St. Louis Browns and Cleveland Indians in
1928. He batted .246 in 168 major-league games.

No specific information was found on how much
money was raised for the fund. However, rain before
the game began kept the crowd sparse. James C.

O'Leary of the *Boston Daily Globe* reported an attendance of only 70 spectators.[9]

SOURCES

In addition to the Sources cited in the text, the author was assisted
by the following Sources:

Barker, Matthew Jude, "Fitzpatrick Stadium," Maine Irish Heritage
Trail. maineirishheritagetrail.org/fitzpatrickstadium_053.shtml.
Accessed November 16, 2014.

"Doug Flutie," Boston College Eagles. bceagles.com/genrel/flutie_
doug00.html. Accessed November 26, 2014.

Gilley, Chad (2005), "Fitzy," Gilley Media, gilleymedia.com/05/
fitzpatrick/default.asp. Accessed November 16, 2014.

"Jim Fitzpatrick," Boston College Varsity Club Hall of
Fame: bceagles.com/genrel/fitzpatrick_jim00.html. Accessed
November 16, 2014.

Pro-football-reference.com

Sports-reference.com/cfb

NOTES

1   "Teams of Destiny," Burns Library Virtual Exhibit Fall 2001.
    bc.edu/libraries/about/exhibits/burnsvirtual/teams/3.html.
    Accessed November 16, 2014.

2   James C. O'Leary, "Braves to Play Boston College to Help
    Fund," *Boston Daily Globe*, May 9, 1921, 7.

3   Burt Whitman, "Boston College Plays Remarkable Ball Until
    Braves Open in Seventh," *Boston Herald*, May 10, 1921, 11.

4   "College Loses to Braves in Game for Drive," *The Heights*
    (Boston College), May 12, 1921, 1.

5   Bud Leavitt, "Jimmy Fitzpatrick: The Maine Sports Legend,"
    Bangor (Maine) *Daily News*, November 13, 1981, 10.

6   Ibid.

7   Every Thanksgiving Day through at least 2014, one can
    watch the Portland Bulldogs-Deering Rams football game at
    Fitzpatrick Stadium.

8   Tom Chard, "The Man Behind the Trophy: James J. Fitzpatrick
    was a class act as an athlete, coach—and man," *Portland* (Maine)
    Press Herald, January 14, 2001, 1D. Doug Flutie was a quarter-
    back for Boston College from 1981 through 1984. Flutie won
    the 1984 Heisman Trophy, presented to the outstanding college
    football player of the year. He had a 22-year professional foot-
    ball career in the Canadian Football League and the National
    Football League. He was elected to the College Football Hall of
    Fame in 2007.

9   James C. O'Leary, "One Bad Inning Knocks Out B.C.," *Boston
    Daily Globe*, May 10, 1921, 10.

ONE FIELDER – ONE PLAY – THREE OUTS

OCTOBER 6, 1923: BOSTON BRAVES 4, PHILADELPHIA PHILLIES 1, AT BRAVES FIELD

BY MARK PESTANA

In 1923, the National League Braves and the American League Red Sox, besides sharing the city of Boston, had a couple of other notable things in common. One was that they both had truly awful seasons. With a record of 61-91, the Red Sox finished at the bottom of the junior circuit, 37 games behind the pennant-winning Yankees. The Braves sported an even worse record, 54-100, winding up 42 games off the pace, but were spared the ignominy of a last-place finish by defeating their rivals for the NL cellar, the Philadelphia Phillies, on the final day of the season.

The other noteworthy commonality was that both teams, in the final weeks of the campaign, turned a defensive trick that had happened only twice previously in the twentieth century.

More rare than a perfect game or a four-strikeout inning, the unassisted triple play requires not only a particular set of game situation circumstances (no outs and at least two runners on base), but also a serendipitous combination of luck and lightning reflexes. On the infield dirt of Braves Field, in the 155th game of the 1923 baseball season, a 24-year-old rookie shortstop found himself in the right place at the right time, and made the most of his opportunity.

Ernest Padgett, born March 1, 1899, in Philadelphia, had already played 122 games, batting at a .317 clip, for the Memphis Chicks of the Southern Association when he was summoned to "The Show" at the end of September 1923.[1] He debuted October 3 with a late-inning pinch-hit appearance against the Brooklyn Robins, and then got the nod from manager Fred Mitchell to start the final three-game series against the Phillies.

On October 4 Padgett played second base and collected his first major-league hit, but the Braves were crushed, 10-2, by the Quaker City nine. Friday the 5th was an offday, and the season was scheduled to wrap with a Saturday doubleheader. Boston at this point was two games ahead in the standings, but a closing-day sweep by the Phillies would lock the teams in a tie for the cellar.

Weather conditions were less than favorable as a much smaller than normal crowd of Braves Field patrons took their seats for the twin bill. Ed Cunningham in the *Boston Herald* referred to "about 1000 frost-bitten customers,"[2] and the *Boston Globe* noted, "The weather was cold and with an overcast sky most of the time...."[3]

The fans got their money's worth in the opener alone, as the two teams battled into extra innings, the veteran first-sacker Stuffy McInnis finally driving in the winning run for the Braves on a triple in the bottom of the 14th. Winning pitcher Jesse Barnes went the distance, while Padgett, playing shortstop, walked, scored a run, and participated in three double plays.

Because of the lengthy first game, the approaching darkness, and, no doubt, the unpleasant weather, an agreement was made between games that the second contest would go only five innings.[4]

Manager Mitchell, at the tail-end of a second straight 100-loss season at the Braves' helm, but now assured of avoiding eighth place, let his regulars sit; McInnis and left fielder Gus Felix were the sole representatives of the Braves' first-stringers in the finale. Padgett started again at shortstop.

Rookie left-hander Joe Batchelder pitched for the Braves; it was to be his only major-league start.

Another southpaw, Lefty Weinert, took his dismal 4-16 record to the mound for Art Fletcher's Phillies.

In the bottom of the first, McInnis's second triple of the day scored Felix, who had reached on a force out. Boston's lead ballooned an inning later, Padgett and second baseman Jocko Conlon each singling and then scoring on a base hit by catcher Dee Cousineau. Cousineau himself came home two outs later on Felix's safety.

Batchelder, meanwhile, kept Philadelphia off the board until the third inning, when Ralph Head, relieving Weinert, singled, went to third on Heinie Sand's double, and then notched the Phillies' only run on a sacrifice fly by Johnny Mokan.

The scoring in this abbreviated game was now over … but one flashing moment of incomparable brilliance remained.

Cotton Tierney led off the fourth for the Phillies. A fair slugger for a second baseman (top 10 in homers and extra bases in 1923), he singled to left and moved to second on Cliff Lee's drive to right.

The potential tying run came to the plate in the guise of switch-hitting Walter Holke, who had been purchased by the Phillies from the Braves after the 1922 season and won the first-base job. Batting righty against Batchelder, Holke cracked a low liner in the direction of left field. The ball was snared "a few inches from the ground"[5] by Padgett at short. Tierney, already racing for third, was easily doubled up as Ernie stepped on second base. "Without faltering an instant in his stride,"[6] Padgett set his sights on Lee coming down from first. The startled runner attempted a quick retreat but Padgett ran him down in just "a couple of strides,"[7] applying the tag, killing the Quaker rally, and completing the fourth unassisted major-league triple play of the twentieth century.

This was not the only instance of a miraculous defensive feat in Boston's 1923 baseball season. Three weeks earlier, first baseman George Burns of the Red Sox had retired three Cleveland Indians single-handedly in the second frame of a 12-inning tilt at Fenway Park.

Ernie Padgett with the 1923 Memphis Chickasaws prior to his late September big-league promotion.

Of course, as Paul Shannon pointed out in the *Boston Post*, Burns was "a seasoned veteran of a wealth of experience and perhaps might have had similar chances in his big league career before"—while the "recruit" Padgett was "entitled to even more credit for showing the quickness of thought and the lightning execution that this play developed."[8]

The *Boston Herald* of October 7 reported that Padgett was the first shortstop to pull off such a play, but in fact, Neal Ball had been playing shortstop for Cleveland when he did it in 1909. Second baseman Bill Wambsganss, also of the Indians, in 1920 became the only man (as of 2014) to achieve the play in a World Series.

In 1925 another 24-year-old shortstop, Glenn Wright of the Pirates, accomplished the singular feat, and two years after that, the Tigers' Johnny Neun and the Cubs' Jimmy Cooney[9] followed in the footsteps of the Burns-Padgett tandem—pulling off solo triple killings in the same season (in fact, on *consecutive* days, May 30 and 31, 1927). After these dazzling deeds of the '20s, a drought of four decades ensued, not another unassisted triple play occurring in the major leagues until 1968, when Ron Hansen performed the feat for the Washington Senators.

As for the raw rookie who wrote his page in baseball history October 6, 1923, Ernie Padgett never lived up to his early promise. He took over as starting third baseman in 1924 after Tony Boeckel died in a preseason auto accident. He logged 138 games, second highest on the Braves, who unfortunately could not escape a last-place finish this time around. But the man who led all Southern Association hitters in 1922 with a .333 mark batted a disappointing .255 in his only full major-league season, although he did boast the third best fielding percentage among NL hot-corner men.

Never again a regular, Padgett assumed the role of utility infielder in 1925, toiling usually at second base when he did play. Whatever magic attached itself to the Pennsylvania native as a result of his wondrous rookie play, it had worn off by 1926 and Padgett was peddled to the Cleveland Indians, with whom he closed out his short major-league career on July 30, 1927.

SOURCES

In addition to the Sources listed, the author relied on Retrosheet.org and Baseball-Reference.com.

NOTES

1   *Boston Globe*, October 7, 1923.

2   *Boston Herald*, October 7, 1923.

3   *Boston Globe*, October 7, 1923.

4   *Boston Post*, October 7, 1923.

5   *Boston Herald*, October 7, 1923.

6   *Boston Globe*, October 7, 1923.

7   *Boston Globe*, October 7, 1923.

8   *Boston Sunday Post*, October 7, 1923.

9   Jimmy Cooney was the older brother of pitcher-outfielder Johnny Cooney, a teammate of Padgett's on the 1923 Braves. The elder Cooney wrapped up his big-league playing career with the Braves in 1928, a teammate of his younger brother.

THE RESUMPTION OF THE CITY SERIES

APRIL 11, 1925: BOSTON BRAVES 4, BOSTON RED SOX 3 AT BRAVES FIELD

BY MIKE RICHARD

As *Boston Herald* sportswriter Burton Whitman saw the preseason matchup, "It was the first time in 18 years that Boston teams engaged in Civil War."

However, as *Boston Globe* sportswriter James C. O'Leary averred, "It will be the first time these two clubs have come together since the days of Old Cy Young and Young Cy Young, the latter having been with the National League club when it was playing at the Walpole St. grounds."

For the record, postseason City Championship Series took place in October of both 1905 and 1907 between the American and National League franchises of Boston.

In the 1905 game, Denton True "Cy" Young pitched one of his best games, striking out 15 batters while allowing only two hits, both singles, in a 3-1 victory over Irv "Little Cy" Young of the Nationals. The 15 strikeouts were the most that the future Hall of Famer ever had in one game throughout his long career.

The 1907 series ran from October 7 to October 12 and the Boston Americans clinched the championship series with a doubleheader sweep to take the series, four games to none. Cy Young won two games, while Irv Young suffered a complete-game loss for the Nationals.

Altogether, the two Boston teams had played 14 games from the 1905 and 1907 series with the Boston Americans winning 12, losing one and tying one against the Nationals.

Needless to say, the resumption of the city series was something that Boston baseball enthusiasts looked upon with great delight.

From a fan's perspective, the exhibition opener of the home-and-home series at Braves Field between Boston's two professional baseball teams was a purist's delight rather than a battle for bragging rights.

The home-team Braves came back from a 2-0 deficit with four runs in the seventh to win the exhibition game over their crosstown rival Red Sox, 4-3.

"It was a new sensation for the fans who refused to take the rivalry too seriously. They tell us that the divided fans of Chicago are willing to do bodily harm to each other when the Cubs and the White Sox engage in diamond warfare," wrote Whitman, "but the splendid crowd yesterday merely seemed anxious to see the new men on each team, wanted to pay tribute to their old favorites, and did not seem to give too much attention to the outcome of the contest."

Braves manager Dave Bancroft approached the game like the baseball exhibition it was meant to be.

"We will certainly try to win that game Saturday, because it will make us feel good and add to our confidence," he said. "I do not want to belittle the Sox's two-game series, but the championship games come first."

The Red Sox had just returned from a Southern swing through Louisville, while the Braves had made a Florida spring-training trip in St. Petersburg.

A bipartisan crowd of perhaps more than 18,000 turned out for the exhibition game that saw both teams combine for a whopping total of 23 hits but not many

runs. However, most were on hand to see the new players who were making their debuts for both teams.

Chief among the newcomers was left fielder Bernie Neis, who had been acquired by the Braves in a trade sending Cotton Tierney to the Brooklyn Robins. In addition, rookie Jimmy Walsh and Dave Harris also comprised the new Braves outfield.

Meanwhile, the Red Sox had rookie Bill Rogell at second base and, while he went on to play 15 seasons in the major leagues, it was his seventh-inning error that proved costly and led to the Braves' win.

Starter Jesse Barnes of the Braves pitched four scoreless innings, while Red Sox starter Alex Ferguson hurled three and Jack Quinn added a shutout inning in the fourth.

Braves reliever Joe Genewich came on in the top of the fifth and the first batter he faced, Val Picinich, reached when his fly ball was misjudged by Walsh for a two-base error. The center fielder lost the ball in the tough sun and never saw it until it dropped at his feet.

It appeared that the Braves might get out of further trouble, though, when Jack Quinn lined to shortstop Dave Bancroft and Picinich was doubled up off second.

However, Genewich lost his control on the mound as he walked Ira Flagstead and then hit Doc Prothro with a pitch. Ike Boone singled to left, scoring Flagstead for a 1-0 Red Sox lead.

The Red Sox added a run in the top of the seventh when Flagstead singled to center with two out and scored on Prothro's double to deep left. Bernie Neis, who had made a one-handed catch earlier in the game, tried to do the same on Prothro's gap shot, but failed.

In their half of the seventh, the Braves took the lead for good when Johnny Cooney reached on the error by second baseman Rogell. Neis singled to center, sending Cooney to third, and Bancroft lined a double past first baseman Joe Harris, scoring Cooney.

A groundout to first by Bill Marriott scored Neis, tying the game, then Dave "Sheriff" Harris drove a sharp single between third and short to plate Bancroft with the go-ahead run.

The inning continued when Walsh beat out a bunt and Dick Burrus drove in Harris with a single, his third hit of the afternoon.

Buster Ross relieved Quinn and struck out Red Lucas, but the damage had been done and the four runs were enough to win.

The Red Sox scored a run in the eighth, when Tex Vache singled and Harris dropped a Texas Leaguer to center. Vache came around to score on Gross's second bunt hit of the day for the 4-3 final

There were a few highlights in the game, perhaps the most spectacular being the one-handed catch by Neis on a ball hit by Flagstead. Neis turned his back on the ball two or three times while it was still high in the air and after some short sprints snared it close to the fence in left-center field.

"The fans were fair in their treatment for players on both teams and they stayed until the finish," the *Boston Post* reported. "Both clubs showed plenty of pep, considering the weather. The grounds were heavy after the rain which made fast base running impossible."

It was also noted that Red Sox president Bob Quinn called the Braves office after the game to offer congratulations to Judge Emil Fuchs, owner of the Braves.

"They're close friends and wished each other all kinds of luck. That is, after Monday next when the clubs meet at Fenway Park in the second game of the series. Both were particular to qualify their felicitations in that regard after Monday."

As it turned out, that second game, scheduled for April 13, was canceled because of cold weather.

A decade later Quinn reversed his roles and in 1936 replaced Fuchs as the principal owner and president of the Braves, renaming the Boston ball club the Bees and Braves Field National League Baseball Field.

SOURCES

Boston Globe, April 11 and 12, 1925.

Boston Herald, April 10-12, 1925.

Boston Post, April 11 and 12, 1925.

Williams, Frank J. *The Battle for Baseball Supremacy in Boston: A Chronicle of the Annual City "Championship Series" Between the Boston Red Sox and Boston Braves* (Boston Braves Historical Association Press, 1998).

FIRST RADIO BROADCAST FROM BRAVES FIELD

APRIL 14, 1925: BOSTON BRAVES 5, NEW YORK GIANTS 4 AT BRAVES FIELD

BY BOB LEMOINE

The first radio broadcast at Braves Field took place on April 14, 1925. The WBZ broadcast was believed to be the "First Time Radio Fans Have Been Given Such a Treat, Other Than During the World's Series," wrote the *Springfield* (Massachusetts) *Republican*.[1] Both the pregame ceremony and the game would be broadcast in their entirety, "courtesy of the Western Union Company and the Crosscup-Pishon post of the American Legion, Members of the 40 American Legion posts in Boston, and veterans from the government hospitals near Boston will be guests at the game."[2]

"A capable announcer will be before the WBZ microphone and fans who are unable to attend this game in person should enjoy the broadcast," the *Republican* advised its readers.[3] Who was that "capable announcer"? The author could not find any reference to who announced this game. In July of 1925, WNAC was given permission to broadcast five games from Braves Field, with Benjamin H. Alexander and Charles Donelan doing the announcing.[4]

This was Opening Day with all its glamour and familiar pageantry. The "first pitch" was thrown by Massachusetts Governor Alvan T. Fuller, with Boston Mayor James Michael Curley catching, National League President John Heydler at bat, and Massachusetts Lieutenant Governor Frank Allen umpiring. Much was made of the mayor muffing the pitch. Soldiers, sailors, and members of the Legion marched, and 150 veterans of the West Roxbury (Boston) Hospital glee club sang selections during the game. A stiff wind blew through the field on that chilly April day in Boston, and many topcoats and shawls were seen in the crowd. The *Boston Herald* noted, "Some far seeing fans in the boxes brought along their automobile robes, and after the sun hid behind those cloud banks and the east wind began sweeping in off the river late in the game, the extra protection came in handy."[5]

Player-manager Dave Bancroft of the Braves and players Hank Gowdy and Hugh Jennings of the Giants took advantage of the "temporary sending station that WBZ had installed in a box behind home plate."[6] Bancroft asked Jennings if the Giants were going to win the pennant, to which Jennings replied, "Why, of course."[7] Not exactly an engaging interview, but definitely an historic one. The *Boston Globe* even included a picture of the interview with the caption, "Telling it to Radio Audience Before Teams Begin Battle."[8]

Jesse Barnes took the hill for the Braves, and was opposed by his former Braves teammate, Art Nehf of the Giants. The Giants were defending National League champions for the fourth consecutive season.

With two out in the first inning, the Giants' Ross Youngs reached second on a throwing error by

A contemporary radio's operation demonstrated by Babe Ruth.

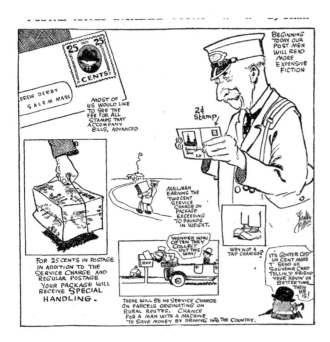

Bancroft. George "High Pockets" Kelly walked and scored with Youngs on a triple lined off the center-field fence by Bill Terry that James C. O'Leary of the *Globe* called "undoubtedly the longest hit ever made in a game at Braves Field."[9] Burton Whitman of the *Herald* remarked, "Had the barrier in centre been made of middle aged pine, that smash would have penetrated said fence like a bullet boring through cheese."[10] The Giants led, 2-0.

The Braves came back with four runs in the third inning. Red Lucas led off with a walk, and Frank Gibson singled. Lucas was thrown out at third on an attempted sacrifice bunt by Barnes. A fly ball by Bernie Neis to right-center fell between Youngs and Hack Wilson, allowing Gibson to score. A single by Bancroft scoring Barnes was followed by a single by William Marriott that scored Neis. Bancroft scored when Terry dropped a throw to first base from Frankie Frisch. The Braves led 4-2. They added an insurance run in the seventh inning on a sacrifice fly by Bancroft.

Nehf had allowed only one single since the third inning, but in the eighth inning Heinie Groh led off with a double and scored on a groundout, making the score 5-3 Braves. In the Giants' ninth inning, Wilson drew a walk and scored on a triple by Emil "Irish" Meusel, who could have scored on a better set of wheels. Frank Walker was sent in to run for Meusel,

representing the tying run with only one out. Jack Bentley pinch-hit for the pitcher and hit a wicked grounder to first base. Dick Burrus raced in and cut down Walker with a sweeping tag by Gibson at the plate. Groh next hit a foul popup into the wind. Third baseman Marriott struggled with it but made a one-handed catch to preserve the 5-4 win for the Braves, their shivering fans in the stands, and all of the first-time listeners on Boston radio. The Braves "convinced the 10,000 fans who turned out that they are a fighting bunch," wrote O'Leary, despite the fact that "the weather was more suitable for football than baseball."[11]

Not everyone was thrilled about baseball broadcasting, and one writer even saw doom for the future. In his column "The Once Over," The *Globe's* H.I. Phillips spoke of news that "Radio Movies" would soon become a reality through the invention of Charles Francis Jenkins, who would one day become one of the inventors of television. Phillips dreaded the day when "people will soon be able to sit at home and see the World Series, Olympic Games, Missouri cyclones, fires, floods, riots and murder trials without putting on their shoes. Folks can see everything there is to see and hear everything there is to hear merely by twisting a knob. Thus is the prospect of the dishes getting washed in the Great American home rendered more remote than ever.... All that remains to be perfected is a device to broadcast fresh roasted peanuts, ice cold cones and 'hot dogs' to every home."[12]

SOURCES

In addition to the Sources cited in the text, the author used retrosheet.org and baseball-reference.com for game information.

NOTES

1   "WBZ Will Put Major League Game On Air Today, New Departure," *Springfield* (Massachusetts) *Republican,* April 14, 1925, 1.

2   Ibid.

3   Ibid.

4   "Baseball Broadcasts," *Boston Globe,* July 7, 1925, 17; Curt Smith, *Mercy!: A Celebration of Fenway Park's Centennial Told Through Red Sox Radio and TV* (Dulles, Virginia: Potomac Books, 2012), 24.

5 "Fuller and Curley Were Battery Mates for a Day; His Honor Muffed Again," *Boston Herald*, April 15, 1925, 20.

6 "Fuller and Curley Were Battery Mates."

7 Ibid.

8 *Boston Globe*, April 15, 1925, 13.

9 Ibid.

10 Burton Whitman, "Braves Top Giants, 5-4, In Thrilling Opening Of Big League Season," *Boston Herald*, April 15, 1925, 1.

11 James C. O'Leary, "Revamped Braves Start By Beating Giants, 5-4," *Boston Globe*, April 15, 1925, 13. Retrosheet.org lists the attendance as 15,000, not the 10,000 cited by O'Leary.

12 H.I. Phillips, "The Once Over: Home, Static Disturbance, There UIs No Place Like Home," *Boston Globe*, April 14, 1925, 16.

Boston Herald advertisements which includes the radio broadcast of the Braves game.

GOLDEN JUBILEE GAME

MAY 8, 1925: BOSTON BRAVES 5, CHICAGO CUBS 2 AT BRAVES FIELD

BY BOB LEMOINE

"By gory," blurted Jack Manning to former teammate George Wright at Braves Field. "They say these fellows are faster than we were, George, but they make as many mistakes. See that, now, he's pitching outside to him, when it's a cinch he could not hit a ball in close."[1]

A trip to Braves Field in Boston on that brisk day, May 8, 1925, was a stroll down memory lane. The occasion was the "Golden Jubilee" game, which celebrated the 50th anniversary of the National League and the genesis of Organized Baseball as we know it today. The National League began on April 22, 1876, after Alexander Graham Bell received a patent for the telephone and before General Custer's demise at the Battle of Little Bighorn. As America's Founding Fathers began a new country in Philadelphia, so baseball became a "national" game there a century later, about three miles across town at the Jefferson Street Grounds.[2] Ford Sawyer of the *Boston Daily Globe* recalled "the days when baseball playing was a rather precarious undertaking and one didn't know whether or not financial adversity would cause the league to toss up the sponge."[3]

The league survived but only two charter teams of the original eight remained, Boston and Chicago, and they would play the first Jubilee Game. Each National League team would host its own celebration later in the season. This would be a moment unlike any other in baseball history. Hundreds of living legends from a bygone era stepped from the pages of the 19th century and onto the field as a great cloud of witnesses. Braves Field provided one of the last glimpses of baseball's early National League pioneers, where past met present in the cool Boston air. "Old timers, grayed and stooped, came to the game today despite a chilly wind and clouds that alternated with the sunshine," reported the Associated Press.[4]

They stood at the center-field flagpole and helped raise the Golden Jubilee pennant, followed by the 101st Regiment Band playing the "Star Spangled Banner." Then in front of the Boston dugout they acknowledged the applauding fans while the band played "Auld Lang Syne."

"We hobnobbed with royalty out at Braves Field yesterday afternoon, meeting the grand old baseball veterans, now silvery haired and rapidly ageing … old in years, but young in spirit," wrote Ford Sawyer of the *Boston Daily Globe*.[5]

Three players from the 1876 Boston opener were present: shortstop George Wright, first baseman Jack Manning, and second baseman John Morrill. Actually, Morrill didn't play in the opener because, as James O'Leary of the *Daily Boston Globe* remembered, "In the old days the regular players on a team alternated as gatekeepers."[6]

Also present was Billy McLean, the 92-year-old who umpired the first National League game. McLean was ribbed for his failing eyesight, but gladly recalled that in his day he would read distant signs that players couldn't, to prove his keen eyesight. "The chill in the atmosphere had a depressing effect on the spectators, but Billy McLean … did a jig step to show how young he felt," wrote O'Leary.[7]

Joining them were 92-year-old William H. Conant, Boston Nationals team owner from 1877 to 1907, Baseball Commissioner Kenesaw Mountain Landis, National League President John A. Heydler,

MEMORABLE MOMENTS AT BOSTON'S LOST DIAMOND 75

Massachusetts Governor Alvan T. Fuller, "and hundreds of others who played the game in later years."[8]

Joe Genewich was the starting pitcher for the Braves, opposing future Hall of Famer Grover Cleveland Alexander. Genewich was making his fourth start of the season, bringing a 2-1 record with a 1.12 ERA. Alexander was 2-2 with a 3.44 ERA.

The game was scoreless until the bottom of the third inning, when the Braves' Dave Bancroft doubled to left field and scored on a single by William Marriott. In the fourth inning, Bob Smith doubled home Jimmy Welsh. Welsh had been recently purchased for $50,000, and as he batted, Conant recalled signing 1870s star Mike Kelly for $10,000. "One could buy a whole club for $50,000 in the 70's," joked Wright.[9]

In the fifth inning, Bancroft tripled home Genewich, and the Braves had a 3-0 lead. The numerous foul balls hit into the stands conjured up a memory for Wright. "We didn't have so many balls in those days," he recalled, "and when a ball went over a fence or into the crowd we would often halt the game for a few minutes until the ball was returned, then the ball would be put back into the game."[10]

In the sixth inning, the Cubs got on the scoreboard as Sparky Adams singled home Jigger Statz. A double steal followed by a walk to Gabby Hartnett loaded the bases. Bob Barrett's sacrifice fly cut the Braves' lead to 3-2. The Braves answered with two runs of their own after two were out in their half of the sixth inning. Mickey O'Neil doubled home Bob Smith and later scored on a single by Genewich to give the Braves a 5-2 lead.

Guest's Ticket

BOSTON BRAVES vs. CHICAGO CUBS

Golden Jubilee Celebration

BRAVES FIELD, BOSTON, MASS.

FRIDAY, MAY 8TH, 1925

COMMEMORATIVE   GAME AT
EXERCISES 2.45 P.M.   3.00 P.M.

PLEASE PRESENT THIS TICKET AT GATE NO. 7

Alexander lasted only six innings, surrendering 12 hits. He would one day join the ranks of the legends … but not today. "As he swung along towards the exit with his sweater over a shoulder and slightly stooped, he was a memory-stirring picture for those old time players of 50 or less years ago. In his day Alexander had been a wonderful pitcher, one of the best of all time, but those old boys in the front box seats out there know from experience, as does Alec, that the time inevitably comes when the arm loses its strength and the wrist its cunning swerve," wrote Burton Whitman of the *Boston Herald*.[11]

Genewich allowed only two hits through the first five innings. There was a scary moment in the ninth inning as a sharp line drive by Ike McAuley hit him in the shin and "for a few moments it was thought his leg was broken, as it would not support him. It was only numbed, however," wrote James C. O'Leary.[12] Genewich struck out the last two batters to finish the complete-game 5-2 victory.

McLean reminisced. "They have much better facilities. When Wright was at short, he might have had his chest broken any time by a bad bounding ball. The diamond was not as smooth then as it is now … and what an easy time the umpires have. There are three out there. I used to work all alone, without a mask or protector in between the catcher and batter. I had to watch bases and batters. I had my jaw broken twice by foul tips, but I'm 92 and still going."[13]

That evening the legends were treated to a dinner at Boston's Copley Plaza. Commissioner Landis praised Manning and Morrill, who "played baseball before it was professionalized. … They and their companions were the foundation of the present national game. … [T]oday they live to see baseball played throughout the country, in every place that is commercially active, and in places that have not so advanced."[14]

McLean was introduced by Landis as the man "who was 27 years old when Lincoln was inaugurated."[15]

"Their stories were of rough diamonds, of 'games every day, but with exhibitions in various places,' and of pitching that at first started from the knee and finally developed into the overhand delivery," the *Boston Daily Globe* reflected on the evening affair.[16]

One man at the dinner had almost literally seen it all. John "Tony" Marsh of Boston attended the first National League game in 1876 and attended nearly every Boston game, even traveling to away games, until his death in 1940. Marsh was hailed as the "No. 1 major league baseball fan in New England," and "his circle of friends resembled baseball's hall of fame."[17]

SOURCES

Game information was supplied by the Sources listed in the notes as well as retrosheet.org and baseball-reference.com.

NOTES

1   "Little Change in Fifty Years, Old Brave And Ump Opine," *Boston Herald*, May 9, 1925, 6.

2   "The Bostons Get Away With the Athletics, 6 to 5—The Hartfords Defeat the Yales," *Boston Daily Globe*, April 24, 1876, 3.

3   Ford Sawyer, "Veterans of Boston Teams of 70's At Golden Jubilee Celebration," *Boston Daily Globe*, May 9, 1925, 8.

4   "Boston Braves Down Chicago Cubs in National League Golden Jubilee Game," *Charlotte* (North Carolina) *Observer*, May 9, 1925, 13.

5   Sawyer.

6   James C. O'Leary, "Observe Golden Jubilee Today," *Boston Daily Globe*, May 8, 1925, 25. Even during the 1903 World Series, one finds mention of Cy Young serving as a ticket taker at Boston's Huntington Avenue Grounds. O'Leary also mentioned that the terms of Morrill's contract placed him at the team's disposal year-round. "Morrill had a five-year contract with the Boston club, probably the longest contract in the history of baseball," O'Leary noted.

7   James C. O'Leary, "Stars of Days of Old See Braves Drub Cubs 5 To 2," *Boston Daily Globe*, May 9, 1925, 1.

8   O'Leary, "Stars of Days of Old," 8.

9   Sawyer.

10 Ibid.

11 Burton Whitman, "Young Braves Defeat Cubs, 5 To 2, in First Golden Jubilee Game," *Boston Herald*, May 9, 1925, 6.

12 O'Leary, "Stars Of Days of Old."

13 "Little Change in 50 Years."

14 "Dinner Ends Celebration," *Boston Daily Globe*, May 9, 1925, 9.

15 Ibid.

16 Ibid.

17 "'Tony' Marsh, Noted Baseball Fan, Dies," *Boston Herald*, June 20, 1940; 19; "Heydler Host At Baseball Dinner," *Boston Herald*, June 9, 1925, 6.

NEIS'S HISTORIC CLOUT LEAVES BRAVES FIELD

JULY 7, 1925: BOSTON BRAVES 7, ST. LOUIS CARDINALS 3 AT BRAVES FIELD

BY MIKE RICHARD

An ordinary doubleheader on a lazy Tuesday afternoon turned extraordinary on one swing of the bat by Braves center fielder Bernie Neis.

In his second at-bat of the first game, the 29-year-old Neis became only the second major-league player—and the first member of the Braves—to hit a home run over the left-field wall at Braves Field. Neis's mighty blast cleared the concrete barrier and landed on the nearby railroad tracks.

With one out, Neis teed off on a 3-and-0 pitch from Cardinals starter Art Reinhart, tying the game at 1-1. The Braves went on to win the first game, 7-4, and then captured the second, 8-2.

However, the talk of the day concerned the memorable blast off the bat of the 5-foot-7, 160-pound switch-hitting Neis.

Since Braves Field opened in August of 1915, members of the Braves, as well as opposing players, wondered just how long it would take for someone to drive a ball over the left-field wall.

Several times the wall had been hit on a line, and then, a few days before the start of the 1925 season, Neis drove one over it during batting practice.

As Burton Whitman reported in the *Boston Herald* on April 11, 1915, "Bernie Neis, the new and tremendously powerful outfielder from Brooklyn, slammed the ball over the left field wall on the fly and fair during a practice session. So far as I can learn the stunt never had been accomplished before. It is a titanic smash and someday will be done in a game."

Boston Globe reporter James C. O'Leary noted that the preseason blast by Neis was "one of the longest drives ever made at the park, either in a game or in practice."

In his book *The Boston Braves*, Harold Kaese wrote that after Neis's smash, "Players rubbed their eyes, and asked, 'Was that a baseball or a golf ball you hit, Bernie?' Neis, a rugged little 165-pounder who was a switch hitter, nonchalantly replied, 'I must have muscles in my hair.'"[1]

O'Leary recalled that "Ty Cobb, on a visit to Braves Field, once stood on home plate and took a survey of the park. 'Nobody will ever knock a ball fair over the fences here,' said he. This hit of Neis's yesterday cleared the fence to the left of the scoreboard."

According to Bob Ruzzo's *Braves Field: An Imperfect History of the Perfect Ballpark*, when Braves Field was

Neis performing pre-game batting practice.

being designed, team owner James Gaffney sought a stadium that was wide open and allowed more inside-the-park home runs than over-the-fence clouts.

The configuration was rectangular with the expansive fences far from home plate. The concrete wall in left field was 430 feet from home plate; the distance to the extreme center-field corner was 550 feet and the fence to the right of the bleachers in right field known as the Jury Box was 375 feet away. With the east wind frequently blowing in from the nearby Charles River and causing a stiff breeze, Braves Field became a pitcher's dream but a long-ball hitter's nightmare. Nobody was able to clear the fence for nine years, and then it was done twice within six weeks.

The first player to hit a ball over the left-field wall was New York Giants catcher Frank "Pancho" Snyder, who did it earlier in the 1925 season, on May 28. Snyder broke an eighth-inning tie with a 430-foot drive over the wall at the left-field corner off Braves hurler Larry Benton, to lead the Giants to an 8-6 victory.

However Neis's home run had a greater elevation, according to the *Boston Post*, "the ball carrying farther beyond the fence than the one hit by Snyder. Neis' ball cleared the top of the fence by 50 feet midway between the scoreboard and the left field foul line."

Snyder's ball was 50 feet nearer the left-field corner, making a longer distance inside the grounds, but it cleared the fence by 10 or 12 feet. The wind conditions were said to be nearly identical and favored both hitters.

Whitman's description in the *Boston Herald* noted, "(Snyder's) ball just barely struggled over the top of the cement wall. Neis' cleared it by 50 feet. The Snyder drive landed on the B&M passenger tracks not far from the park, but Neis' blast went well over those four tracks and in the midst of the freight and shifting tracks near the banks of the Charles."

Neis's clout was also drawing comparisons with the blasts by another favorite former Boston slugger.

"This prodigious wallop compares favorably with Babe Ruth's longest clout made in 1919 in Tampa, Florida,

Bernie Neis.

when the Bambino was with the Red Sox and they were playing an exhibition game with Washington," the *Post* related.

Neis was not known for his power. The home run was the second and final one he would hit that season at Braves Field. The first had been an inside-the-park homer off St. Louis pitcher Johnny Stuart on May 21.

While it was the 21st home run of Neis's career to that time, it was his fifth and last of the 1925 season.

The Braves went on to score three runs in the sixth and added three more in the eighth to post the 7-4 victory.

Dick Burrus opened the sixth with a walk, went to third on a single by Neis and scored on a Gus Felix sacrifice fly. Ernie Padgett tripled to the scoreboard to drive in Neis and came home on a sacrifice fly by Mickey O'Neill.

The Cardinals answered with three in the seventh to tie the game, 4-4. Specs Toporcer tripled to left and scored on Les Bell's triple to center. Bob O'Farrell followed with a single to plate Bell, and scored the tying run on an infield error and a wild pitch.

Boston grabbed three in the eighth to win the game. Padgett led off with his second triple of the game and Johnny Cooney ran for him. O'Neill's double to left scored Cooney. Winning pitcher Jess Barnes then drove a liner to center on which Ralph Shinners tried

Braves Field's distant left-field wall.

to make a shoestring catch, but the ball bounded away and went to the scoreboard for an inside-the-park home run.

To say that the Braves had the number of St. Louis at that point of the season would be an understatement. The doubleheader sweep gave Boston four straight victories over the Cardinals; the Braves had won two straight on their recent trip to St. Louis.

The next season Neis was sold by the Braves to Buffalo of the International League, and wound up playing for their parent Cleveland Indians during the 1927 season.

He wound up hitting a mere 25 home runs during an eight-year career that featured stints with the Brooklyn Robins (1920-24), the Braves (1925-26), and the Indians and Chicago White Sox, both in 1927.

A lifetime .272 hitter, Neis drove in 210 runs with his best season at the bat in 1924, when he hit .303 in a season in which the National League as a whole hit .283.

However, it was one swing of the bat and a towering home run over the concrete wall at Braves Field for which he would be forever remembered.

SOURCES

Boston Globe, April 11, 1925.

Boston Herald, April 11 and July 8, 1925.

Boston Post, July 8, 1925.

Caruso, Gary. *The Braves Encyclopedia* (Philadelphia: Temple University Press, 1955).

Kaese, Harold. *The Boston Braves, 1871-1953* (Boston: Northeastern University Press, 2004).

Ruzzo, Bob. *Braves Field: An Imperfect History of the Perfect Ballpark* (Boston Baseball History.com, 2013).

NOTES

1 Harold Kaese, *The Boston Braves, 1871-1953* (Boston: Northeastern University Press, 2004), 197.

BOSTON'S FIRST PRO FOOTBALL GAME

DECEMBER 9, 1925: PROVIDENCE STEAM ROLLER 9, CHICAGO BEARS 6 AT BRAVES FIELD

BY CHIP GREENE

From the birth of the National Football League, in 1922, it took three years for Boston to host a professional football game. At the time, collegiate football reigned supreme, and with Boston area universities like Harvard, Boston College, Tufts, and Holy Cross all fielding powerful amateur teams, the professional variety held little allure for Beantown's sports fans. In fact they, like fans of most other cities, generally looked down upon men who accepted money for play.

That began to change on December 9, 1925. It was perhaps fitting, given their affinity for the collegiate game, that the first time Boston's football fans witnessed professionals clashing, they had the opportunity to watch one of the most electrifying players ever to set foot on a college gridiron. By the time Harold "Red" Grange completed his three-year football career at the University of Illinois, he had permanently etched his name as one of the greatest players in the annals of his sport. From 1923 through '25, over 21 collegiate games, Grange rushed for 2,071 yards, averaging 5.3 yards per carry; passed for 575 yards, in an era when the forward pass was used sparingly; and tallied 34 touchdowns; additionally, in era of two-way football, Grange totaled six interceptions as a defensive back, and was also a sensational kick returner.[1] Unquestionably his greatest single performance occurred on October 18, 1924, when, in a legendary effort before an estimated crowd of 67,000 at home versus the University of Michigan, the Galloping Ghost tallied 402 rushing yards, 78 passing yards, and five touchdowns (four on the ground and one through the air), in a 39-14 dismantling of the Wolverines.

It was his style of play that made the Illinois back so exciting. Grange, wrote famed sportswriter Grantland Rice, runs "with almost no effort, as a shadow flits and drifts and darts." Indeed, there was no wasted motion in his running, "only the effortless, ghostlike weave and glide upon effortless legs with a body that can detach itself from the hips—with a change of pace that can come to a dead stop and pick up instant speed, so perfect is the coordination of brain and sinew."[2] Such divine skill had left many a college defender gasping for air when Grange ran by.

At first Grange had no intention of playing professional football; once graduated, he would apply himself to some profession with the same intensity he brought to the playing field. But when an entrepreneur named Charlie Pyle convinced Grange that he could one day become a millionaire by joining the fledgling NFL, Grange found Pyle's entreaties hard to resist, and signed a contract to join the professional ranks. Pyle, with Grange's consent, immediately sold Grange's contract to the Chicago Bears, who promised Grange a 50-50 split of all gate receipts; and in November 1925, Grange joined the NFL.

It didn't take long for Grange or his fans to realize that the professional brand of football was entirely different from its collegiate counterpart. For Grange, it was to be a painful reality; and for the fans at Braves Field who came that day to see the rushing king, a bitter disappointment. Seeking to quickly cash in on the fame of their new star, the Bears, with their co-owner George Halas, began a barnstorming tour that soon took a physical toll on Grange, "The Wheaton Ice Man."[3] After his professional debut on November

The "Galloping Ghost" at Braves Field.

26, at Wrigley Field versus the Chicago Cardinals, the Bears ranged across the country and played as many as three to four games a week, an unmerciful schedule that left the team battered and bruised. As their train pulled into Boston on the morning of December 9, "the Bears were in a pitiful condition," Grange later recalled, "with many of us bandaged from head to foot. I was in particularly bad shape. I had hurt my left arm in New York and it was still badly swollen. Andy Lotshaw, the Bears trainer, worked feverishly all night on the train to help ease our miseries and prepare for the next assault. ... Under such conditions it was to be expected the Bears would not fare well against the Providence eleven."[4]

In fact, they did not, and by the time Grange's day ended, he lamented years later, "I was booed for the first time in my football career."[5]

The day was miserable from the start; it was a frigid afternoon, and the "cruelly cold" weather had left the field as "hard as a board."[6] An estimated 18,000 fans were in attendance. The Bears' opponents, the Providence Steam Roller, were in their first season in the NFL; yet, if the Bears, a charter member of the league, were "as big and powerful a set of men as ever stepped on a football field,"[7] the game ultimately belonged to Providence, which "throughout the game ... kept the Bears jammed back against their own goal line. Providence did not have enough power to slam through the massive western defense to a touchdown, but they took advantage of two breaks, one of which they forced."[8]

Grange's only highlights occurred early in the game. In the first two minutes he caught a punt on his own 10-yard line and, using his customary zig-zag running style to elude tacklers, returned the ball to near the Bears' own 25. A few plays later, the Bears having punted and Grange now on defense, Providence's diminutive tailback, from nearby Salem, Massachusetts, Cy Wentworth, just 5-feet-8 inches tall and 160 pounds, broke through the center of the Bears' line and ran 40 yards to Chicago's 21, before Grange tackled him and forced a fumble, saving a sure Providence touchdown.

Several times on offense Grange made rushing attempts, trying to burst around the end, but each time the Bears protection broke down and Grange "came down like a log when tacklers hit him."[9] He also attempted several passes, but each time the ball fell incomplete. As the game wore on, every time Grange touched the ball the fans jeered and offered him mock applause, leaving the Galloping Ghost standing forlornly on the sidelines, aloof from his teammates and for all intents as if he wanted to be anywhere else at that moment than Braves Field. With his painful forearm exacerbating Grange's sour disposition, he left the game for good after the third quarter.

Grange's teammates fared little better. On a day when both teams' defenses ruled, Chicago's most productive player was Hunk Anderson, its punter. With the brutal conditions, scores were hard to come by. Providence was first to get on the board. In the opening quarter, with Chicago pinned deep in its own territory, Anderson attempted to punt the Bears out of trouble. However, smashing through from his right end position, the Steam Roller's Red Maloney blocked the ball, and it bounded into the end zone, where Maloney fell on it. As it turned out, though, the ball had first struck a fence behind the end zone and, by the rules of the day, was automatically ruled dead, resulting in a safety rather than a touchdown. So Providence led 2-0.

The second quarter score again involved Anderson. Near the end of the second period, with the score still 2-0, he dropped back to punt from his own 45-yard line. This time, though, the center snap soared past him and Providence's Franny Garvey, a Holy Cross graduate, from Worcester, Massachusetts, scooped up the ball and ran untouched into the end zone for a touchdown. When Maloney drop-kicked the extra point, Providence led, 9-0.

With no scoring in the third quarter, the Bears finally got on the board in the fourth. In their most productive drive of the day, again from deep in their own end, quarterback Joey Sternaman,[10] all of 5-feet-6 inches and 152 pounds, tossed a pass to tailback Johnny Bryan, who caught the ball at his own 25-yard line and raced 75 yards into the end zone. When Sternaman missed the point after touchdown, the score stood Providence 9, Chicago 6.

And that was the score when the gun sounded to end the game.

For Red Grange the day brought one more humiliation. As he made his way towards the tunnel to leave Braves Field, a small crowd gathered and blocked his exit. In short order, the fans became unruly. Shielding his good friend, Hunk Anderson struck one of the spectators who tried to get at Grange, and two bystanders began a fight that soon found them rolling around and choking each other, before the police were able to restore order.

That night, Grange and his teammates boarded a train for Pittsburgh, where, worn out, nervous, and bruised, they were to play another game the next day.

In all, Chicago played 18 games in 66 days, with Grange scoring 17 touchdowns. The Galloping Ghost played eight more seasons in the NFL, retiring in 1935 at age 32.

In 1963 Grange was elected as a charter member to the National Football League Hall of Fame.

SOURCES

Morton, Ira, *The Red Grange Story: An Autobiography*, as told to Ira Morton (Urbana and Chicago: University of Illinois Press, 1957 and 1981).

Pegler, Westbrook, *Sioux City* (Iowa) *Journal*, December 10, 1925, via NewsPaperArchive.com.

Boston Herald

Boston Globe

pro-football-reference.com

fightingillini.com/sports/m-footbl/grange-stats.html

NOTES

1   The University of Illinois official statistics were used for these totals. They can be found at fightingillini.com/sports/m-footbl/grange-stats.html.

2   Ira Morton, *The Red Grange Story: An Autobiography*, as told to Ira Morton, (Urbana and Chicago: University of Illinois Press, 1957 and 1981), Kindle edition, 9.

3   Raised in Wheaton, Illinois, Grange spent seven consecutive summers in the town working on an ice truck, carrying heavy blocks of ice to customers.

4   Morton, Kindle edition, 66.

5   Ibid.

6   *Boston Herald,* December 10, 1925.

7   Ibid.

8   Ibid.

9   Ibid.

10 In researching this game, the author consulted several periodicals of the day. It should be noted that due to the inaccuracy of reporting during the period, multiple Sources differed in their accounts of the game. Not only were attendance and yardage figures different, but also different players were often credited with results. For example, the Associated Press credited the Bears' Lawrence Walquist with throwing the pass to Bryan, but the *Boston Herald* credited Sternaman, as does pro-football-refrence.com. Here, an attempt was made to select the most accurate account of the game.

THE "WIGWAM" BECOMES A "KENNEL"

**OCTOBER 9, 1926: NEW YORK YANKEES, 13, BOSTON BULLDOGS 0 AT BRAVES FIELD
AMERICAN PROFESSIONAL FOOTBALL LEAGUE**

BY CHIP GREENE

Less than a year after Red Grange and the Chicago Bears debuted professional football in Boston, Beantown had its own professional franchise. Once again Grange was on the gridiron at Braves Field for one of the city's singular sporting events.

Credit for Boston's entry into the professional ranks belonged to Grange's business partner, Charlie Pyle. After the 1925 season, which had proved wildly successful financially not only for Grange and Pyle, but also for the Bears, Pyle had approached the Bears' co-owners, George Halas and George Sternaman,[1] and asked for an ownership stake in the team. Without Grange, Pyle reasoned, the Bears would be hard pressed to repeat that financial success; and without a greater share of the financial bonanza, Grange wouldn't play for the Bears. Halas and Sternaman said no.

Next, Pyle approached the National Football League and asked the league to allow him to put a team in New York, build it around Grange, and call the team the Yankees. The NFL, too, said no.[2]

So Pyle decided to launch his own league, to compete head-to-head with the NFL. He called it the American Professional Football League (more commonly referred to as the AFL). The 1926 season would be the league's inaugural and, as it turned out, its only season in existence.

As president of the new league, Pyle hired, for a yearly salary of $25,000, former Princeton All-American Big Bill Edwards. Pyle retained controlling interest in the AFL, and placed teams in eight cities: the Los Angeles Wildcats, a traveling team in which Pyle retained a

50-50 split; the Chicago Bulls; the Rock Island (Illinois) Independents,[3] the Cleveland Panthers; the Brooklyn Horsemen; the New York Yankees, which Pyle and Grange each held equally; the Newark (New Jersey) Bears; the Philadelphia Quakers; and the Boston Bulldogs. The Bulldogs would play their home games at Braves Field.

The Bulldogs' coach was Charles Herbert "Herb" Treat. He came to his position with a significant scholastic pedigree. Treat had been a member of the 1922 Princeton team dubbed by sportswriter Grantland Rice as a "team of destiny"[4] when, on October 28, 1922, in Chicago, Princeton's defense had staged a gritty fourth-quarter, fourth-down goal-line stand to defeat the powerful University of Chicago Maroons, and their legendary head coach, Amos Alonzo Stagg, 21-18, thereby preserving what became an undefeated 8-0 season (accomplished when the Tigers later beat Harvard and Yale to win the Big Three championship). At the conclusion of that season, Treat was named a consensus All-American.[5]

That Treat's body of work encompassed one of the most renowned defensive plays in Princeton history was significant, because four years after that thrilling defensive stand at Chicago, the new Bulldogs coach helmed a professional team strong on defense but woefully inadequate on the opposite side of the ball. On September 22 Boston began its competitive season with an impressive 22-0 exhibition victory over the semipro Abington Old Town squad; but only once over the course of their regular season would the Bulldogs again come remotely close to such an offensive output.

The Bulldogs' regular season began on October 3, 1926, at Newark's David's Stadium. In what was a harbinger of things to come for the league, only an estimated 1,000 fans were in attendance as the Bulldogs defeated the Bears, 3–0. Six days later Boston opened its home schedule, as the powerful New York Yankees and their superstar, Red Grange, visited Braves Field. This time, both the size of the crowd and the result were decidedly different.

Saturday, October 9, 1926, marked the inaugural home game by a Boston professional football team. As the Bulldogs warmed up on the Braves Field gridiron before a crowd estimated at between 10,000 and 12,000,[6] the players undoubtedly must have been aware of the level of competition they were up against that day. Indeed, the following day the *Boston Globe* said it was "doubtful if a more powerful football team than the New York Yankees ever came to Boston. The line, composed of the biggest men playing football, was utterly impregnable, hard charging and savage in both attack and defense"; their "teamwork was precise," their "interference fast-moving and solid." In contrast, the *Herald* said of the home team, "Boston showed good condition and admirable gameness everywhere."[7] In truth, if Boston was not the equal in talent of the football Yankees that day, neither were they vastly inferior. As it turned out, the Bulldogs more than held their own.

With AFL President Edwards in attendance (he sat on the Boston side during the first half, and the New York side in the second), as well as future light-heavyweight boxing champion Slapsie Maxie Rosenbloom,[8] in town to fight Tiger Flowers, the blueprint for the game was drawn right from the start. At the outset a Boston fumble was recovered by the Yankees at the Bulldogs' 26, and for the rest of the afternoon Boston dug in their heels and tried to withstand the superior Yankees attack. Although there was no scoring in the first quarter, New York several times drove deep into Boston territory, only to have the Bulldogs stop the vaunted Yankees backfield. Finally, as the clock ran down and the period ended, New York was poised for the first score of the afternoon.

If Grange was the Yankees' biggest star, on this day it was his running mate who stole the show. In 1979 Eddie Tryon, from Medford, Massachusetts, just five miles northwest of Boston, was inducted into the Colgate University athletics Hall of Honor. From 1922 to 1925 Tryon had starred as a runner for the Maroon (now the Raiders); in his freshman season Tryon finished second in the East in scoring, and in his senior season led the nation and was named an All-American. Now, at Braves Field, as Grange and Tryon led New York down the field with crafty running, they advanced the ball to the Boston 21, as the first quarter ended.

In Tryon's Hall of Honor biography on the Colgate website is written: Tryon "once piled up five touchdowns in a gorgeous exhibition of broken field running against Ohio State in 1923."[9] As the second quarter began this day at Braves Field, Tryon likely harkened back to that earlier day, for on the first play of the quarter he took a handoff and, as reported the next

N. Y. Football Yankees
vs.
Boston Bulldogs

SATURDAY, OCTOBER 9, 1926
BRAVE'S FIELD, BOSTON   Price, 10 Cents

Game day program.

day by the *Boston Herald*, "shot through a quick opening inside of tackle and was under full headway before anyone could lay a hand on him. … He traveled like a veering bullet as he cut through the secondary defense … was hit on the three yard line [which] carried his feet out from under him, but threw himself over the line for the first touchdown."[10] In an alternate and perhaps even more descriptive account of the touchdown, the *Globe* reported that, Tryon "banged through the line, reversed field, shook off several tacklers and dove across the line with several tacklers hanging on." Tryon then kicked the extra point. The Yankees led, 7-0.

There would be one final Yankees score before the game was through, but none for Boston. Try as they might, the Bulldogs failed to mount any semblance of an offense, missing their lone field-goal try and not generating even a single first down the entire game.[11] They almost scored on a kickoff return in the third quarter, but runner Joe McGlone slipped on the baseball basepath and fell short of the goal. Of the Bulldogs defense, though, Boston fans could be proud. Indicative of the kind of intensity Boston's defenders brought to the field was this effort: As New York's Pooley Hubert "was bowling up the field like an express freight," Boston's Al Pierotti,[12] who eventually spent nine years in the NFL, "met him with one of the most jarring tackles we ever saw. The shock was like that of a train wreck, but both boys got up unhurt and Pooley held onto the ball."[13] So it went on this day for Boston.

In the fourth quarter, the Yankees scored on a two-yard pass from George Pease to Roy Baker. When the point-after kick was missed, the score was 13-0, and that's how the game ended. In the end, opined the *Globe,* the "difference between the two teams was the greater speed and offensive power of the Yankees beating back an eleven that was entirely a defensive aggregation."[14]

It was an apt description of the Bulldogs' season. With a final record of 2-4, Boston was outscored 81-20 in league play[15] and finished sixth among nine teams.[16] (With poor attendance throughout the league, three of their road games were canceled.[17]) The following

season, Pyle took his Yankees to the NFL and folded his league. It wasn't until 1929 that Boston again hosted a professional team, when the NFL's Pottsville (Pennsylvania) Maroons relocated to Boston for the 1929 season.

They played that lone NFL season as the Boston Bulldogs.

SOURCES

Morton, Ira, *The Red Grange Story: An Autobiography*, as told to Ira Morton (Urbana and Chicago: University of Illinois Press, 1957 and 1981), Kindle edition, 72-75.

Boston Globe

Boston Herald

profootballarchives.com

pro-football-reference.com

princeton.edu

gocolgateraiders.com

NOTES

1   In Grange's first game at Braves Field, with the Bears, the previous December, one of his Chicago teammates was quarterback, Joey Sternaman. Joey was the brother of Chicago Bears co-owner George "Dutch" Sternaman and was the owner, coach, and quarterback of the APFL's Chicago Bulls.

2   Pyle had already taken out a *five-year* lease on Yankee Stadium when he made his demand for a New York franchise in the NFL. New York Giants owner Tim Mara, who personally disliked Pyle, opposed the request because Pyle and Grange were muscling in on his territory. See David S. Neft and Richard M. Cohen, *The Football Encyclopedia: The Complete History of Professional Football from 1892 to the Present* (New York: St. Martin's Press, 1994), 60.

3   Rock Island had jumped from the NFL to the AFL.

4   princeton.edu/paw/archive_new/PAW07-08/03-1024/sports.html.

5   princeton.edu/~football/pfball.html.

6   Football reporting of this period was often inaccurate with respect to attendance figures, as well as the play on the field and even the players themselves. While the *Boston Herald* reported the day after this game an estimated crowd of 10,000, the credible research website profootballarcnives.com lists that estimate at 12,000.

7   *Boston Herald*, October 10, 1926.

8   The Rosenbloom-Flowers fight took place on October 15 and Flowers lost by being disqualified on a foul in the ninth round

at Mechanics Hall in Boston. Flowers was the reigning world middleweight champion at the time of the game (the first African American to capture that division's crown). Rosenbloom and Flowers are both members of the International Boxing Hall of Fame.

9 gocolgateraiders.com/hof.aspx?hof=20&path=&kiosk=.

10 *Boston Herald*, October 10, 1926.

11 *Boston Globe*, October 10, 1926.

12 Al Pierotti, the Bulldogs' center, was familiar with Braves Field. As a right-handed pitcher, he had made brief appearances on the mound for the Braves in 1920-21. As a football player, Pierotti had a nine-year NFL career, playing 48 games with seven teams.

13 *Boston Herald*, October 10, 1926.

14 *Boston Globe*, October 10, 1926.

15 Bulldogs tailback Bill "Crungy" Cronin of Boston College scored the team's only offensive touchdown ever during a 17-0 defeat of the Brooklyn Horsemen on October 17. He played for the 1927-29 Providence Steam Roller. Cronin played baseball for the Boston Braves during the 1928-31 seasons as a backup backstop.

16 The Bulldogs played only one other game at Braves Field. On October 16 they lost to the Los Angeles Wildcats, 21-0, before 2,000 fans. The Bulldogs never scored a point at Braves Field during the regular AFL season and were shut out in four of their six games overall (Neft and Cohen).

17 At the end of October, Newark and Cleveland folded. Brooklyn folded in early November, followed by Boston. Rock Island gave up in mid-November. At the end of the schedule in December, only New York, Philadelphia, Chicago, and the traveling Los Angeles squad were still playing.

LES IS MORE

BY LEN LEVIN

No ballpark was more suited to the Deadball Era in which it was built than cavernous Braves Field. Modern-day estimates of the former ballpark's outfield distances vary, but they were all huge. In the 12-plus seasons from August 8, 1915, the day Braves Field was opened, through the end of the 1927 campaign, when the distances were shortened—only 235 home runs were hit there, and all but 17 were inside the park.[1]

Left and center fields were enclosed by a 10-foot concrete fence.[2] But the Deadball Era was over and fans clamored for home runs. The most that had ever been hit in Braves Field was 38, in 1921.

After the 1927 season the Braves announced that stands would be built in front of the fence to shorten the home-run distance, especially for promising young catcher Shanty Hogan. In January 1928 Hogan was sent to the New York Giants in a deal for Rogers Hornsby, but the project remained on track, now aimed at benefiting Hornsby. Bleachers seating 6,500 were erected in front of the fence.

Opening Day for the Braves in 1928 was April 11. By June 2 they had played only five games at Braves Field, with long stretches away (including a 21-game road trip from April 29 to May 20). In the Braves' five games, their opponents had hit 10 homers, and the Braves had hit only two (by Hornsby and backup outfielder Eddie Moore). Judge Emil Fuchs, the Braves' owner, decided that the imbalance warranted having the bleachers removed. While the dismantling was in progress, Boston's new third baseman, Les Bell, gave Braves fans a game to remember, walloping three home runs and a triple and driving in six runs as the Braves lost a 20-12 slugfest to the Cincinnati Reds.

Bell, the St. Louis Cardinals' regular third baseman from 1925 through 1927, had been one of the heroes in the Cardinals' march to the world championship in 1926. In that season he batted .325 with career highs in home runs (17) and RBIs (100). In the Cardinals' World Series victory in seven games over the New York Yankees, he hit a home run and drove in six runs. His batting in that pennant year "made him a thorn in the side of the greatest pitchers,"[3] and in the field, "(O)pposing batters made it a point never to hit the ball near third base if they could help it."[4] But in 1927,

Bell batting.

"(It) was a different story with Bell. (He) was a complete flop. ... He couldn't hit, couldn't field and was finally benched in favor of Specs Toporcer."[5] Some observers attributed Bell's reversal of form — a .259 batting average in 1927 with just 9 home runs, and 24 errors in 100 games at third base — to the absence of Hornsby, who had been traded to the Giants; the pair had formed a close bond in the Cardinals' infield, and manager Hornsby cut Bell far more slack than some of the other players. Frederick G. Lieb, in his history of the Cardinals recalled that in the spring of 1926, when a stretch of poor play at third base by Bell made him the target of unhappy Cardinals fans, Hornsby told him, "Don't you mind; I'm sticking with you."[6] But Bill McKechnie, Hornsby's successor as manager, was reportedly down on Bell in 1927 "because the infielder had shown a desire to fight shy of hard hit balls."[7] Whatever the reason, late in 1928 spring training Bell was sent to the Braves in a trade for infielder Andy High and $25,000. In Boston he would be reunited with Hornsby.

Hitting three home runs in a game, a feat we take for granted in the twenty-first century, was something rare in the first half of the twentieth. Indeed, during the 1900-1920 Deadball Era, not a single batter drove three pitches out of the ballpark in a single game. With the advent of the livelier ball and the Babe Ruth era, batters began flexing their muscles, but until Bell's feat, only 13 batters had hit three home runs in a game in the 1920s.

The Braves had returned from a road trip on Friday, June 1, and lost that day to Cincinnati, 7-6 in 10 innings. After that game they were in seventh place with a 16-24 record, 11 games behind the first-place Reds (31-17, leading the second-place Giants by 2½ games). Braves manager Jack Slattery had been fired a week and a half earlier and Hornsby was the new skipper. Bell was batting .299 going into Saturday's game with 10 doubles, 1 triple, and 1 home run, a three-run shot against the Phillies at Philadelphia's bandbox Baker Bowl on April 30.

On June 14 the Reds slipped out of first place and finished the season in fifth place with a 78-74 record.

(Six of the eight National League teams, all but the Braves and Philadelphia Phillies, finished over .500.) (This seems an out of place paragraph. Shouldn't it go toward the end of the article — sort of a follow up on the Reds season?) Maybe, "After their victory Cincinnati was riding high with a 31-17 record, leading the second-place Giants by 2 ½ games. Less than two weeks later they slipped out of first, destined to finish the season in fifth place with a 78-74 record. (Six of the eight...)

Few of the eight pitchers who toiled for the two teams distinguished himself in the 20-12 slugfest. (One sportswriter described the game as "one prolonged batting orgy."[8]) The Reds' starter and winner, Pete Donohue, gave up 14 hits and 11 runs in his 6⅓-inning stint. Carl Mays, who relieved Donohue in the seventh, gave up the third of Bell's three home runs, but allowed no other damage. The Braves' starter, Kent Greenfield (3-11, 5.32 that season), made an error on the first play of the game, a bunt by Hughie Critz, and things went downhill from there. After seven batters, the error, four hits, two wild pitches, and a passed ball,[9] Greenfield was out of the game and the Reds had four unearned runs.

The Braves came back with four runs in the bottom of the first, two of them on Bell's blast into the new left-field stands. But the Reds continued their on-

Les Bell.

slaught, and by the time Bell batted in the bottom of the fifth, they were leading 13-4. With George Sisler (in the first of the Hall of Famer's three seasons with the Braves) and Hornsby on base, Bell ripped his second homer into the left-field stands. The Braves made it closer (15-11) in the bottom of the seventh with four runs highlighted by Hornsby's two-run homer into the right-field grandstand and Bell's triple off the high screen that had been erected in front of the center-field stands to cut down on home runs by the opposition. The triple was the longest of Bell's four hits, the *Boston Herald* said, but "it was straight out to center and, hitting high on the screen, bounced back into the field of play and he was held at third."[10] Said the *Globe*, "Two or three more inches to the right(,) the ball would have cleared the screen in the left center bleachers and passed through a break in the outfield bleacher stands. Instead it struck the upright to which the screen is attached at its eastern extremity and bounded back into the field."[11]

Had the ball reached the stands, Bell would have become only the third major leaguer to hit four home runs in a game, joining Bobby Lowe of the Boston Beaneaters, the Braves' predecessors, who clouted four homers in 1894 at the old Congress Street Grounds, and Ed Delahanty of the Philadelphia Nationals, who did it in 1896 at the West Side Grounds in Chicago. (Two of Delahanty's homers were inside-the-park.)

The next time Bell batted after his triple, it was the bottom of the ninth inning and the Reds had tacked on five more runs in the top of the inning for a 20-11 lead. Carl Mays, who was in the next-to-last of his 15 major-league seasons, was wrapping the game up for the Reds. Bell drove his third home run into the left-field stands. A few minutes later the game was over. The Braves' third-sacker was now hitting .314 with 10 doubles, 2 triples, and 4 home runs. He ended the season with a .277 batting average, 36 doubles, 7 triples, 10 home runs, and 91 RBIs.

The Rajah's tenure as the Braves' manager was brief and unsuccessful. After he succeeded Jack Slattery, he could do no better than guide the team to 39 victories and 83 defeats and a seventh-place finish (50-103),

44½ games behind the first-place Cardinals. By the end of the season, 86 home runs had been hit at the ballpark, more than in the previous four seasons combined. But only 24 of the 86 had been hit by the Braves. The four hit by Bell and Hornsby on June 2 were 16.7 percent of the Braves' total.

The Reds also had problems. On June 14 they slipped out of first place and finished the season in fifth place with a 78-74 record. (Six of the eight National League teams, all but the Braves and Philadelphia Phillies, finished over .500.)

After another season as the Braves' main man at third base, Bell was sent to the Chicago Cubs, where he was again reunited with Hornsby.[12] After two seasons as a part-timer with the Cubs, he was sold to Louisville in April of 1932. Later he spent 12 seasons as a minor-league manager, eight of them with his hometown Harrisburg club. In 1941 and 1946, Bell's Harrisburg Senators won the championship of the Inter-State League.

SOURCES

Besides the Sources mentioned below, the writer accessed Les Bell's file at the Baseball Hall of Fame. Thanks for research assistance to Cassidy Lent at the Hall of Fame library; Ron Selter, David Vincent, Bob Brady, Greg Erion, and Bill Nowlin.

NOTES

1   Bill Nowlin, "The First Homers Over the Fence at Braves Field," in *Braves Field: Memorable Moments at Boston's Lost Diamond*, writes that when the ballpark opened, the left-field and right-field fences were 375 feet from home plate, center field was 440 feet, and the deepest part of right-center field was 542 feet. Ron Selter, in "Braves Field Boston NL: 1928" (unpublished), gives the outfield dimensions from 1921 to 1927 as: left field 402 feet; left-center 402 feet; center field 461 feet; right-center 542 feet; right field 365 feet. Harold Kaese, in *The Boston Braves* (New York: G.P. Putnam's Sons, 1948), 205, mentions that before the distances were shortened for the 1928 season, the left-field fence was 402 feet from the plate and the center-field distance was 550 feet. Philip J. Lowry, in *Green Cathedrals* (New York: Walker & Co., 2006), 32, says the left- and right-field distances were 402.5 feet.

2   Lowry, *Green Cathedrals*, 33.

3   Article in unidentified newspaper in Bell's file at the Baseball Hall of Fame library.

4 Ibid.

5 Ibid.

6 Frederick G. Lieb, *The St. Louis Cardinals: The Story of a Great Baseball Club* (New York: G.P. Putnam's Sons, 1947), 112.

7 Ibid.

8 James C. O'Leary, "Three Homers for Bell as Reds Triumph, 20-12," *Boston Globe,* June 3, 1928.

9 The box score at Retrosheet.org lists Taylor's passed ball, but the box score at baseball-reference.com does not.

10 Tom McCabe, "Bell Hits Three Homers and Triple, but Cinci Reds Beat Braves in Batting Orgy, 20-12," *Boston Herald,* June 3, 1928.

11 O'Leary, "Three Homers for Bell."

12 In a deal linked to the Bell transaction, the Braves acquired slugger Wally Berger from the Cubs' Los Angeles Angels farm team. See *The Sporting News,* November 21, 1929, 7.

A NINE-STRAIGHT-DOUBLEHEADER STREAK ENDS AT BRAVES FIELD

SEPTEMBER 15, 1928: BOSTON BRAVES 5, CHICAGO CUBS 2 (FIRST GAME); CHICAGO CUBS 6, BOSTON BRAVES 1 (SECOND GAME), AT BRAVES FIELD

BY HARVEY SOOLMAN

When Ben Cantwell took the mound for the Boston Braves at Braves Field on Saturday, September 15, 1928, it was the start of what would become his team's major-league record ninth consecutive doubleheader played.

The first eight had not gone so well for the seventh-place Braves, who would go 50-103 for the season and finish 44½ games out of first—a period in their existence that sportswriter Harold Kaese would later call "The Boston Punching Bag."[1] The consecutive doubleheader streak began on September 4 and continued through the 15th. The Braves dropped both ends of the first doubleheader to the Brooklyn Robins, then took both games from Brooklyn the next day. Then they split a doubleheader in Philadelphia, but proceeded to drop both ends of the next five, one more in Philadelphia and four at home against New York.[2]

It was far from what the schedule maker had laid out for the Braves in the Official National League Schedule. The two weeks were supposed to have gone as follows:

- Monday, September 3 (Labor Day), two games versus Brooklyn at home followed by single contests on the 4th and 5th.

- A doubleheader on Thursday, September 6, in Philadelphia and single games on Friday the 7th and Saturday the 8th.

- An offday on Sunday, September 9 [both Massachusetts and Pennsylvania still prohibited Sunday sports].[3]

- Single games at home against New York, September 10-13.

- A four-game set at home against Chicago beginning Friday, September 14, with no doubleheaders slated for the series.[4]

Nevertheless, the Labor Day twin bill was rained out, and those games were made up one each on the next two days; the doubleheader on the 6th was also postponed and those games also were made up one each on the next two game days; and four rainouts from April 23-25 and June 20 were pegged to be made up in four doubleheaders over four days, September 10-13, at home versus New York. And when the two games on September 12 were postponed due to rainy weather, they were pushed to another two-game day on Friday, September 14, since the single Chicago-Boston game originally scheduled for that date had already been moved to a Saturday doubleheader, doubleheader number 9, to free up the date in anticipation of the cold, wet weather forecast and to enable the Cubs to stay in Chicago one more day to make up a crucial game in the pennant race against St. Louis on Thursday before heading east by train on Friday.[5]

Boston had also played doubleheaders involving makeups at home against Philadelphia on the previous Friday and Saturday, and only a one-day jaunt to New York on Sunday to squeeze in a makeup game there (before coming back home for the scheduled holiday doubleheader on Monday) prevented the doubleheader streak from having been extended to 11 game days in a row. It was ironic that Sundays would one day become

Ben Cantwell.

synonymous with doubleheaders, but for now in Boston Sunday baseball was illegal.

New York had used the eight-game surge to move from 4½ games back, past Chicago and into second place only one game behind St Louis in a pennant race the Cards eventually won by two games. Boston, on the other hand, had already been eliminated from the pennant race by the end of August. Despite having a rarely seen combination of two of the game's greatest all-time hitters, future Hall of Famers George Sisler and Rogers Hornsby, hitting third and cleanup, and right fielder Lance Richbourg, who would hit .337 with a career best 206 base hits in the leadoff spot, Boston had nonetheless scored the fewest runs in the league and was floundering toward the finish line. Sisler, whom many thought to be finished, batted .340 for the Braves, finishing fourth in the batting race;

and Hornsby in his lone season with Boston led the league at .387.[6] At the onset of the Cubs-Braves series, the *Chicago Tribune* opined, "After their four double bills with the Giants, the Braves are in such state that almost anybody is liable to pitch for them."[7] Actually, the Braves had utilized eight different starting pitchers over the first 16 games in the streak, including their ace, Bobby Smith, in both ends of Friday's double-header. After getting knocked out in the first inning of game one, player-manager Hornsby brought him right back to start game two only to have Smith take the loss in both outings.[8]

Cantwell, still a rookie, brought a 2-3 record with a 5.26 ERA on four days' rest into the contest to try to put a halt to his team's sudden 10-game plummet. He escaped the first inning unscathed despite singles by Boston native Freddie Maguire and Hack Wilson. Then he received a most unexpected bonus: a four-run offensive explosion in the bottom of the first off 14-game winner Charlie Root. Jack Smith doubled down the right-field line with one out, Sisler grounded a single and Hornsby walked to load the bases. Then 37-year-old Eddie Brown tripled to right-center to clear the bases. He scored on a sacrifice fly hit by third baseman Les Bell that sent Wilson to the recently moved-in center-field fence.

Charlie Grimm and Gabby Hartnett opened the second with singles. But with one out, Johnny Moore, who had joined the team on the train east in New York and was making his major-league debut, batted for Root and hit into an inning-ending double play.

Cantwell cruised over the next three innings with Ben Tincup matching him zero for zero until the bottom of the eighth.[9] Sisler opened with his third single; and Hornsby, now hitting .383, bunted him to second. Whereupon Brown singled and picked up his fourth run batted in of the game.

So Cantwell took a 5-0 lead into the ninth against a team scrapping to stay in the pennant race. Riggs Stephenson singled to start the frame. Grimm grounded to Hornsby, who forced Stephenson. But Farrell dropped the ball before he could complete the relay to first. "Cantwell pitched a whale of a game," wrote the *Boston Globe*, "and really should have had a shutout."[10] Hartnett struck out. Then Beck singled through the box. Veteran Cliff Heathcote pinch-hit and singled. English also singled, scoring Grimm, and Earl Webb, batting for Maguire, walked to force home Beck and make the score 5-2. Norm McMillan ran for Webb as the potential tying run; finally Kiki Cuyler tapped one back to Cantwell, who retired him at first to end the game.

The opening-game loss by the Cubs to "the local comedians,"[11] as *Chicago Tribune* writer Irving Vaughan derisively referred to the Boston nine, dropped the Cubs to 3½ games back of St Louis. Despite taking the next three from Boston, they never got back any closer.[12]

Game two pitted Chicago's Guy Bush (12-6) and the Braves' rookie left-hander Ed Brandt (9-18). This game would be a totally different story before the estimated crowd of 4,500 and a return to the Cubs' "customary machinelike effectiveness," according to the reporter Vaughan.[13]

English led off the game with a single. Maguire pushed a bunt single past Brandt. Cuyler also dropped down a bunt; Brandt threw late to third to get English, and the bases were loaded. Wilson spanked a single past short, good for two runs; and though he had hardly been tattooed, that was it for Brandt in favor of Foster Edwards. True to the Cubs' "machinelike effectiveness," Stephenson also laid down a sacrifice bunt to move both runners along, and Grimm hit a sacrifice fly to score the third run of the inning.

The Braves bounced right back to a degree in the bottom of the first. Richbourg opened with a double to right-center past Wilson, and Jack Smith, a five-time .300 hitter, promptly singled him home. However, Sisler grounded into a double play. Hornsby followed with a single, but the Tribe would muster only more single for the duration of the contest.

The Braves' one last threat came in the third. Smith walked, Sisler singled, and Hornsby walked to load

Guy Bush.

the bases. Brown flied to center, and Smith, who had apparently scored on the play, was called out on appeal for having left third base early.

In the fourth English, who would gather four hits in the game, singled. With Joe McCarthy's bunch still playing small ball, Maguire laid down a sacrifice bunt, and Cuyler stroked an RBI single to center.

The Cubs closed out the scoring in the sixth against three Braves relievers. With Bill Clarkson on the hill, Cuyler walked, Wilson singled him to third, Stephenson's single scored Cuyler and sent Wilson to third, and Grimm's single scored Wilson. Virgil Barnes, who had started twice in the doubleheader streak, entered the game with a sore arm and bounced a ball well in front of the plate. Hornsby appealed to the umpires to be able to remove Barnes, but he was forced to finish the at-bat and walked Hartnett on four tosses.[14] Finally, Kent Greenfield came on and got out of the inning with no further damage, but this ballgame belonged to Bush.

The Braves still had four more doubleheaders to play in September, making a total of 32 doubleheaders for the year, but Braves fans were glad to see this day's first-game win after the team had dropped 10 games in a row.[15]

SOURCES

Retrosheet.org

Boston American, September 3-15, 1928.

Boston Sunday Advertiser, September 16, 1928.

Boston Globe, September 3-16, 1928.

New York Times, September 13, 1928.

Chicago Tribune, September 14-16, 1928.

Boston Herald, November 5, 1928.

Kaese, Harold. *The Boston Braves* (New York: Putnam Publishers, 1948).

NOTES

1   Harold Kaese, *The Boston Braves* (New York: Putnam Publishers, 1948), 203.

2   The Giants blew away the Braves with eight wins in four days, winning 4-1, 11-0; 11-6, 7-6; 12-2, 7-6; and 6-2, 5-1. The Braves only briefly led in two of those games and only once after the fourth inning. The Giants outscored them 65-24—not outrageous for an eight-game stretch, but an average score of 8-3, plenty big enough game after game.

3   In a highly contentious referendum in the fall of 1928 that included charges of bribery directed at the Braves owner, Judge

Emil Fuchs, Massachusetts voters chose to allow Sunday sporting events. *Boston Herald*, November 5, 1928. For more on the story, see Chapter 8, "The Sunday Baseball Flap," in Robert S. Fuchs and Wayne Soini, *Judge Fuchs and the Boston Braves, 1923-1935* (Jefferson, North Carolina: McFarland & Co., Inc., 1998), 63-67.

4   "Official National League Schedule, 1928" as supplied by the National Baseball Hall of Fame,

5   *New York Times*, September 13, 1928.

6   To further taint the Braves' steady slide to obscurity, stories appeared in the Boston newspapers on Friday, September 14, linking Braves player-manager Rogers Hornsby along with Giants manager John McGraw to an insider horse racing tipping probe by the Illinois Turf Association. See the *Boston American* and *Boston Globe*, September 14, 1928. Sisler had been sold by the St. Louis Browns to Washington in December 1927 for $25,000, but had hit a paltry .245 for the Senators and was dumped off to the Braves for a discounted $7,500 on May 27.

7   *Chicago Tribune*, September 15, 1928.

8   Hornsby replaced Jack Slattery, who resigned early in the season after just 31 games at the helm. Some opine that Hornsby undercut Slattery's authority, prompting his departure. *See* Fuchs and Soini, 58-59, and Kaese, *The Boston Braves*, 204-05.

9   The 35-year-old Tincup, a Cherokee Indian who was making only his second appearance of the season, had last pitched in the major leagues in 1918, when his career was interrupted to serve in the military during World War I. This became his final big-league game—seven innings, allowing just the one run in the eighth and seven hits.

10   *Boston Globe*, September 16, 1928. The Braves' lone shutout of the season was thrown by Brandt on April 26.

11   *Chicago Tribune*, September 15, 1928.

12   The Cubs played their final 14 games on the road, going 9-5. However, they still dropped two games further back from the pennant-winning Cardinals.

13   *Chicago Tribune*, September 15, 1928.

14   The game was Barnes' final big-league appearance.

15   The major-league record for doubleheaders in one season (44) is held by the 1943 Chicago White Sox.

A LORD'S DAY BOSTON FIRST

APRIL 14, 1929: BOSTON BRAVES 4, BOSTON RED SOX 0 AT BRAVES FIELD

BY DONNA L. HALPER

The weather turned unseasonably cold, rainy, and windy in Boston during the second week of April 1929, and that was bad news for baseball fans. The Boston Braves and the Boston Red Sox were scheduled to play back-to-back exhibition games on April 13 and 14, with one game at Fenway Park and the other at Braves Field. Sportswriters wondered if either game would be played, given the unpleasant conditions, and the players, who had just returned to Boston after spring training in warm and sunny Florida, were shocked to encounter near-freezing temperatures.[1] To make matters worse, the bad weather not only played havoc with Boston, but it also affected Worcester, 35 miles away, where the Braves had agreed to play an exhibition game against the Holy Cross Crusaders on Friday the 12th. That game had to be postponed, much to the disappointment of the fans, who were eager to see the collegians take on the major leaguers.[2] And the next day's weather wasn't much better: Rain and cold caused the Saturday game in Boston to be postponed too.

In addition to the weather, local baseball writers had one other story line to discuss: Assuming conditions improved, the April 14 game at the Wigwam would be the first time major-league baseball had been played in Boston on a Sunday. It had been a long and hard-fought battle to persuade opponents of Sunday baseball to relent. In fact, clergy, politicians, team owners, and fans had debated the issue for decades; but finally it was legal to attend a Sunday ballgame in Boston.

To modern readers there is nothing unusual about Sunday as a day to watch the local teams in action. But in the early 1900s, playing professional sports on "the Lord's Day" was extremely controversial. Influenced by its Puritan founders, the Massachusetts Legislature had passed "Sunday laws," promoting strict observance of Sunday as the day of rest. And it was not just in Boston that Christian clergy insisted upon keeping the Sabbath holy: In many other cities, religious leaders stressed that Sunday was a day for going to church, not a day for going shopping or seeing a ballgame. There were occasional exceptions, however. In Rocky Point, an amusement park in Warwick, Rhode Island, minor-league baseball (as well as some exhibition games with major-league teams) was played on Sunday from 1891 through 1917. The games were especially popular with working-class fans, who could not get time off from their jobs Monday through Saturday, but had leisure time on Sunday; attendance was often between 5,000 and 7,000, and Sunday baseball proved quite lucrative for Colonel Randall A. Harrington, who owned the resort property where the games were played.[3]

But despite the growing number of people who wanted to go to a Sunday game, most legislators were reluctant to have a confrontation with the clergy. In Massachusetts, repeated attempts to change the Sunday laws were stymied by opposition from Cardinal William O'Connell[4] and organizations like the Lord's Day League and the Christian Endeavor Union.[5] It was not until November 1928, when a voter referendum to permit Sunday sporting events passed decisively, that the future of Sunday baseball looked brighter. Some legislators tried to delay or even stop the referendum from becoming law, but by the end of the year the Boston City Council had agreed to let it be implemented, much to the delight of not just the fans, but the owners of both the Braves and the Red Sox. Most other major-league teams had already begun playing on Sunday, and the Boston teams could now

TRIBE WINS 4-0 TO START SUNDAY BALL IN BOSTON

Half-Frozen Crowd of 5000 Sees Gaston Force In Three Runs in Third to Settle Game

have a chance at the profits Sunday baseball brought to them.[6] Sportswriters also noted that Sunday games would give a boost to the state's minor-league, semipro, and town teams; players could now be paid, and clubs could charge admission.[7]

Despite the fact that the Braves-Red Sox game was just an exhibition, excitement was in the air; the bad weather reduced the size of the crowd, but still about 5,000 diehard fans were in attendance at Braves Field. They huddled together, shivering in the near-freezing temperatures and biting wind. Many wore heavy coats and boots or wrapped themselves in thick blankets, as if at a football game. (*Boston Globe* cartoonist Gene Mack, illustrating the game for an article by Jim O'Leary, had two characters jokingly referring to football expressions, and then correcting themselves: "That was a nice forward pass, I mean single, that Dugan hit." Mack's cartoon also noted that WNAC radio play-by-play announcer Fred Hoey looked as if he were trapped in an igloo.) The players too struggled to keep warm. The Braves management brought a portable oil stove to the dugout, and players on both teams were seen wearing sweaters. But for one celebrity, the bad weather was no reason to stay home: Humorist and film star Will Rogers, a friend of the Braves' president, Judge Emil Fuchs, "laughed off" the cold, as he sat in a box seat behind the Braves dugout.[8] Fuchs was about to begin his first, and only, year managing the Braves; he hoped to improve upon their dismal 1928 record of 50-103.

As for the game itself, the Braves won, 4-0. It was surprisingly well-played, given the poor conditions. Reporters commented that neither team treated it as just an exhibition. Paul Shannon noted that it was as hard-fought a game as fans might see during the

regular season.[9] Burt Whitman of the *Boston Herald* even described it "brilliant, air-tight baseball"; he was impressed with the Red Sox new shortstop, Hal Rhyne, who made a "miracle short-hop stab" of a hard-hit groundball from Braves left fielder George Harper, robbing him of a hit.[10] Jim O'Leary's report also praised several Braves players for good fielding, including first baseman George Sisler, second baseman Freddie Maguire, and Rabbit Maranville, who had returned to playing shortstop. (Maranville delighted the crowd by making one of his famed "vest pocket" catches, fielding a fly ball at his belt-line with ease.)

Maguire, who was playing his first game as a member of the Braves, also had a good day at the plate, with three hits. Each team used three pitchers. For the Braves, it was Harry "Socks" Seibold, Art Delaney, and Bruce Cunningham, while the Red Sox used Milt Gaston, Danny MacFayden, and Ed Carroll. Gaston, whom Red Sox manager Bill Carrigan believed to be a good cold-weather pitcher, failed to live up to expectations; he pitched two uneventful innings, but he lost his good control in the third. Maguire, Sisler, and center fielder Earl Clark singled, loading the bases, and then Gaston walked three consecutive batters, forcing in three runs. The Braves then scored a fourth run in the eighth inning. Catcher Al Spohrer singled, stole second, and came home on a hit by right fielder Lance Richbourg.

The Braves outhit the Red Sox. Interestingly, some box scores and game summaries said the Braves had nine hits and the Red Sox had six; but others said the Red Sox had seven. In the field, the Sox made two errors, while the Braves did not make any. (Reporters observed that most fans had avoided taking sides; they cheered the good plays of both teams, enthusiastically applauded the new members of the Red Sox and Braves, and seemed happy to be in the stands for this historic Sunday game.[11])

The Braves then traveled to Worcester on Monday to make up the game against Holy Cross. The weather was still cold and windy, but the Braves had no trouble defeating the Crusaders, 6-1, before 3,000 shivering fans.[12]

Boston Fans to See Major League Teams In Action on Sunday For First Time Today If Weather Permits

SOX AND TRIBE EAGER FOR GAME

First Sunday Clash in Boston Between Big League Teams
On Program at Wigwam Today

Having completed their exhibition schedule on a positive note, the Braves prepared for Opening Day, on April 18 at the Wigwam. The weather still did not cooperate: Rain and chilly winds were in the forecast. But the Braves sent their fans home happy, beating the Brooklyn Robins, 13-12.

SOURCES

Bevis, Charles. "Rocky Point: A Lone Outpost of Sunday Baseball in Sabbatarian New England," *NINE: A Journal of Baseball History and Culture*, Volume 14, Number 1, Fall 2005, 78-97.

"Fight on Sunday Baseball Begins in Hearing," *Springfield* (Massachusetts) *Union*, February 4, 1915, 4.

"First Baseball Game Saturday," *Boston Herald*, April 7, 1929, 38.

Mumpton, Leroy J. "Braves Tally 6-1 Win Over Holy Cross," *Worcester Telegram*, April 16, 1929, 15.

Mumpton, Leroy J. "Either Ray Dobens or Nekola to Pitch," *Worcester Telegram*, April 12, 1929, 30.

O'Leary, James C. "Tribe Wins 4-0 to Start Sunday Ball in Boston," *Boston Globe*, April 15, 1929, 1, 8.

Sawyer, Ford. "Baseball's Plans for Sunday Sports," *Boston Globe*, March 24, 1929, B14.

Shannon, Paul H. "Braves Defeat Red Sox 4 to 0," *Boston Post*, April 15, 1929, 1, 21.

Shannon, Paul H. "First Sunday Baseball in Boston Today," *Boston Post*, April 14, 1929, 1, 34.

"Sunday Baseball Ratified in Boston," *New York Times*, December 28, 1928, 26.

"Sunday Sports Rules Adopted," *Boston Globe*, January 29, 1929, 1, 26.

"Take Sides on Sunday Ball," *Boston Globe*, February 18, 1913, 15.

Whitman, Burt. "Braves Win in Boston's First Sunday Game," *Boston Herald*, April 15, 1929, 1, 16.

Whitman, Burt. "Sunday Baseball Opens in Boston Today," *Boston Herald*, April 14, 1929, 13.

"Will Rogers to See Sox and Braves Today," *Boston Herald*, April 14, 1929, 14.

NOTES

1   Paul H. Shannon, "First Sunday Baseball in Boston Today," *Boston Post*, April 14, 1929, 34.

2   Leroy J. Mumpton, "Either Ray Dobens or Nekola to Pitch," *Worcester Telegram*, April 12, 1929, 30.

3   Charles Bevis, "Rocky Point: A Lone Outpost of Sunday Baseball in Sabbatarian New England," *NINE: A Journal of Baseball History and Culture*, Fall 2005, 79.

4   "Takes Sides on Sunday Baseball," *Boston Globe*, February 18, 1913, 15.

5   "Fight on Sunday Baseball Issue Begins in Hearing," *Springfield Union*, February 4, 1915, 4.

6   "Sunday Baseball Ratified in Boston," *New York Times*, December 28, 1928, 26.

7   Ford Sawyer, "Baseball's Plans for Sunday Sports," *Boston Globe*, March 24, 1929, B14.

8   James C. O'Leary, "Tribe Wins 4-0 to Start Sunday Ball in Boston," *Boston Globe*, April 15, 1929, 1, 8.

9   Paul H. Shannon, "Braves Defeat Red Sox 4-0," *Boston Post*, April 15, 1929, 21.

10 Burt Whitman, "Braves Win in Boston's First Sunday Game," *Boston Herald*, April 15, 1929, 1.

11 Whitman, 16.

12 Leroy J. Mumpton, "Braves Tally 6-1 Win Over Holy Cross," *Worcester Telegram*, April 16, 1929, 15.

A Braves Field streetcar at the Kenmore Square tunnel.

NEVER (BEFORE) ON SUNDAY

SUNDAY, APRIL 28, 1929: PHILADELPHIA ATHLETICS 7, BOSTON RED SOX 3 AT BRAVES FIELD

BY BOB RUZZO

By the late 1920s, the longstanding prohibition against playing baseball on the Sabbath had largely evaporated. Not surprisingly, Puritan Boston was one of the last major-league locales to sanction attendance at Sunday rites in the Green Cathedrals of the national pastime.[1] By order of the people, as expressed through a November 1928 statewide ballot question, Sunday baseball would thenceforth be permitted throughout the state, provided that no regular place of worship was located within 1,000 feet of the playing field.[2]

The Unitarian Church of the Disciples was located at the corner of Peterborough and Jersey Streets, within the shadow of the American League park in the eponymous Fenway section of Boston.[3] Arrangements were therefore made to have the Red Sox make use of Braves Field for their Sunday games, as it was conveniently located a mere mile to the west along Commonwealth Avenue.

THE DEVIL FOOLS WITH THE BEST LAID PLANS

The original plan called for the American League upstarts to wait their turn. Boston's Braves were to introduce Sunday baseball in a game scheduled for April 21. One final protest from the heavens was registered in what was proving to be the extraordinarily wet spring of 1929,[4] and the scheduled game between the unbeaten Braves and the Giants was rained out.[5] Thus, the Red Sox and the Philadelphia Athletics stumbled into history one week later.

Unbeknownst to the Red Sox and their fans, Athletics shortstop Jimmy Dykes had apparently made a deal of sorts with the devil, and sent Boston fans home disappointed after garnering a pair of doubles, a home run, and two runs batted in, all while scoring a pair.

The day had started with brighter forecasts, as the *Boston Post* predicted that "the Red Sox may get away with it today as the weather man calls for fair weather." Plans were "being made to handle an enormous crowd of baseball fans at Braves Field."[6] The box office opened at 9 A.M. to accommodate those not inclined to attend church, and the gates were opened at 12:30 for the 2:30 start, so that those having partaken of religious services could immediately refocus their faithful prayers.

Ed Morris was slated to pitch for the hometown nine, against either George "Rube" Walberg or Eddie Rommel, one of the pioneers of the modern knuckleball. Morris, however, was felled by a bad cold and Red Sox manager Bill Carrigan tapped Charlie "Red" Ruffing in his stead. The weather forecast was equally unreliable: "(T)he game was played under a gray, watery looking sky which threatened rain at any moment. If the weather had been bright and sunny, it is safe to say that at least 35,000 clients would have crowded into the big ball yard."[7]

BISHOP TAKES ADVANTAGE OF SACRIFICE

American League President E.S. Barnard was on hand to witness history and had barely settled into his seat when Philadelphia's Max Bishop, the first batter of the game, doubled to right field. Catcher Mickey Cochrane, a local favorite because he was a native of Bridgewater, Massachusetts, followed, smashing a ball at Red Sox third baseman Bob Reeves that proved too hot to handle. Philadelphia left fielder Al Simmons

23,000 SEE SOX BEATEN, 7 TO 3

Athletics Win First Official
Sunday Ball Game
In Boston

RUFFING WEAKENS
IN SIXTH INNING

then poetically brought home Bishop with a sacrifice to deep center, a fitting first score in the annals of Boston Sunday baseball.[8]

Thereafter, the baseball gods remained quiet until the bottom of the third inning, when the Red Sox scratched out two runs against Rommel after there was one out. Philadelphia right fielder Bing Miller lost the ball in the clouds and made "an inglorious two base muff of Ruffing's fly to right."[9] Red Sox center fielder Jack Rothrock singled, advancing Ruffing to third. Shortstop Hal Rhyne singled to left, scoring Ruffing, and Russ Scarritt followed with a bloop single to center that brought home the second run. Right fielder Doug Taitt killed the rally, blazing one back to Rommel, who threw to Dykes, who then fired to Jimmie Foxx for a double play.

THE SKY IS FALLING

Ruffing, the Red Sox' starter, had not yet blossomed into the Hall of Fame hurler he became for the New York Yankees and, according to one observer, seemed "to pitch better when his team is trailing than he does when it is out front."[10] On this first Boston baseball Sunday, Ruffing began to unravel with one out in the sixth inning.

Simmons doubled, then went to third on a sacrifice by third baseman Sammy Hale. Foxx drove him home with a single to center.[11] Miller gained some redemp-

tion for his earlier fielding transgression by blasting the first pitch he saw for a home run to left field. Dykes followed with the same result, having at least had the decency to hold off until Ruffing's second offering.

The Sunday crowd had been boisterous in its support of the Red Sox, particularly after they "pulled off two lightning double plays";[12] but heading into the home half of the sixth, the carnival atmosphere had dissipated as there "was almost a cathedral quiet in the huge park." It became so quiet "you could almost hear the Sabbath stillness so intense did it become."[13] The Red Sox pushed back modestly in the bottom half of the inning when left fielder Russ Scarritt doubled and second baseman Bill Reagan tripled him home.

ONE LAST GASP, THEN OBLIVION

The Red Sox still had some life in them in the seventh. First baseman Phil Todt led off with a single and after pinch-hitter Kenny Williams fell victim to a fine play by Bishop at second, Elliot Bigelow pinch-hit for Milt Gaston and blasted a ball into the teeth of the wind to the base of the center-field wall. Todt, concerned that the ball might be caught, advanced only to second on the double.[14] Bill Narleski, a speed merchant, ran for Bigelow, but Rothrock struck out and Rhyne grounded out, and "Boston's chances went up the spout."[15]

Rookie Eddie Durham came on to pitch the last two innings for the Red Sox and "was touched up fairly heavily."[16] With one out, he made a wild throw to first base that allowed Foxx to reach base. After Durham righted his ways and threw out Miller, Jimmy Dykes doubled again and pitcher Rommel singled, bringing home the final two runs of the contest. The defensive play of note was a spectacular one-handed grab for the second out in the ninth by favorite son Cochrane, who reached into the third-base dugout to snare the foul pop of pinch-hitter Bob Barrett.

PRAYERS ANSWERED, VISIONS, SAINTS, AND MIRACLES

As anticipated, the arrival of Sunday baseball in Boston had a discernible impact upon attendance. Total attendance for the 1929 last-place edition of the Red Sox was 394,620. More than 100,000, or 25-plus percent of those attendees, were accounted for in four Sunday games: the inaugural contest against the Athletics, and May, June, and September contests against the New York Yankees.[17] The notion of giving fans the opportunity to attend a game on what was for many their only day of leisure, made both sense and dollars and cents. It also made the schedulers' job much easier.[18]

Woven into all of this success, however, was the vision of a challenge that lay ahead. Game accounts, particularly one by Burt Whitman, noted not only the large numbers in attendance, but also the large numbers attending by auto. "A remarkably large part of the crowd—a much bigger percentage than on week days—evidently motored in from various outlying points for the contest. … The neighborhood streets on which parking was permitted were congested with more cars than we've seen since the B.A.A. marathon run."[19] This pattern would be repeated with the advent of night baseball (which arrived some 18 years later in Boston), and the increase in the use of automobiles for commuting to games would accentuate the inadequacy of parking facilities around a number of the jewel box ballparks, ultimately leading to the demise of many.

If members of the Baseball Hall of Fame are the patron saints of the national pastime, there were more than a few apparitions on the day of this first Sunday contest in Boston. Foxx, Simmons, Cochrane, and Ruffing all took the field and of course Connie Mack himself was in the dugout, opining after the game that "I like the looks of my own club."[20] He was right. The Athletics would win the World Series that year.

One final note from this history-making contest: Early in the game, public-address announcer Stonewall Jackson (undoubtedly a Yankee hater) announced that no inning would start after 5:40 P.M., in order to assure compliance with the 6 o'clock closing law. He need not have bothered. The elapsed time for the game? One hour and 40 minutes.[21] Amen!

NOTES

1 Pennsylvania was the last jurisdiction with a contingent of major-league teams to allow Sunday baseball.

2 The text of the referendum question may be found at "Questions of Interest on the Ballot this Fall," *Boston Globe*, October 30, 1928, 13. After more than a modest amount of controversy, the Boston City Council voted to exercise the local option afforded to it by the referendum question, thereby permitting professional baseball to be played within the city limits on Sunday for the first time. The City Council's vote (and associated allegations of attempted extortion) afforded yet another opportunity for the tensions between old-line Boston Brahmins and the ruling Irish political class to play themselves out, this time with Braves owner Judge Emil Fuchs in the middle. This particular debacle is recounted in Robert S. Fuchs and Wayne Soini, *Judge Fuchs and the Boston Braves* (Jefferson, North Carolina: McFarland & Company, 1998), 63-67.

3 Bill Nowlin, *Red Sox Threads* (Burlington, Massachusetts: Rounder Books, 2008), 399-401.

4 "More Rain Adds To April Total," *Boston Herald*, April 29, 1929, 1.

5 James C. O'Leary, "Disappointed by Weather So Far—Rain Prevents Sunday Clash at Wigwam," *Boston Globe*, April 22, 1929, 16.

6 "Red Sox and A's in Game at Braves Today," *Boston Post*, April 28, 1929, 21.

7 David F. Egan, "Crowd Law Abiding Except On Balls Knocked Into Stands," *Boston Globe*, April 29, 1929, 16. Retrosheet shows 23,000 attended the game, and the *Boston Globe* shows 22,000.

8 Jack Malaney, "23,000 At Game Lost by Red Sox," *Boston Post* April 29, 1929, 1.

9 Burt Whitman, "23,000 See Sox Beaten, 7 to 3," *Boston Herald* April 29, 1929, 1.

10 James C. O'Leary, "Athletics Victors in Sunday Clash," *Boston Globe* April 29, 1929, 1.

11 Whitman, "23,000 See Sox Beaten, 7 to 3."

12 O'Leary, "Athletics Victors in Sunday Clash."

13 Whitman, "23,000 See Sox Beaten, 7 to 3."

14 Malaney, "23,000 At Game Lost By Red Sox."

15 O'Leary, "Athletics Victors in Sunday Clash." Although the newspaper account spelled it Narlesky, the player was Bill Narleski, who was the father of future major-league pitcher Ray Narleski.

16 Malaney, "23,000 At Game Lost By Red Sox."

17 baseball-reference.com/teams/BOS/1929-schedule-scores.shtml. Retrieved December 15, 2014.

18 Nor did it have the negative impact on the Brooklyn franchise predicted by some. Brooklyn for years had enjoyed 20 to 23 Sunday home dates in a typical 25-week season. Now for the first time, Brooklyn would have to play on Sunday in Boston and would also lose the opportunity to play one-game series against teams that would did not wish to linger in Beantown. Brooklyn's 1929 attendance actually increased by almost 70,000 over 1928 totals. For details, see "Clergyman Clears Name of Baseball," *The Sporting News*, November 15,1928, 1, and baseball-reference. com/teams/BRO/1929-schedule-scores.shtml. Retrieved December 15, 2014.

19 Whitman, "23,000 See Sox Beaten, 7 to 3."

20 John Drohan, "A's Look Like Club to Keep Yanks from Title," *Boston Traveler* April 29,1929, 1.

21 Whitman, "23,000 See Sox Beaten, 7 to 3."

SENIOR CIRCUIT SUNDAY BASEBALL DEBUTS AT THE WIGWAM

MAY 5, 1929: PITTSBURGH PIRATES 7, BOSTON BRAVES 2 AT BRAVES FIELD

BY ERIC ARON

Playing the national pastime on a Sunday was officially illegal in the United States until the early twentieth century. Players could be and were arrested for picking up a bat and ball on the day of the Christian Sabbath. Many brave souls were even put in handcuffs for just playing chess or checkers outdoors on a Sunday.[1]

Boston was among the last major-league cities where it became legal, with Midwest cities St. Louis, Chicago, and Cincinnati leading the way (1902). Philadelphia was the last (1934).[2] A 1928 Massachusetts referendum (earning 63 percent approval) made Sunday baseball legal as of February 1929.

Judge Emil Fuchs purchased the Boston Braves in 1923. An attorney for the New York Giants, Fuchs saw firsthand how profitable Sunday baseball games could be and he became a proponent of Sunday games.[3] The 1929 Braves were managed by their owner, Fuchs, aided by Johnny Evers as assistant manager.

Fuchs and the Braves led the crusade for Sunday baseball, though it was a bitter battle in which he alleged that Boston politicians solicited bribes and suffered personal slurs from those he had rebuffed. Fuchs spent an estimated $200,000 on the campaign, printing 5 million booklets and sample ballots. He was forced to plead nolo contendere in court to charges of spending money to influence the vote.[4]

The Tribe were scheduled to host the first major-league Sunday game in Boston. A purported hex put on by the dissenting Lord's Day League, however, seemed to work like magic when the Braves' first scheduled Sunday game (against the New York Giants on April 21) was postponed by rain.[5] A week later, the Boston Red Sox played the city's first Sunday game.[6]

The Braves played their first Sunday game on May 5. The home team took on spitballer Burleigh Grimes, a future Hall of Famer, and the Pittsburgh Pirates.[7]

Starting for the Braves was right-hander Bobby Smith, who logged a team-leading 231 innings pitched in 1929. The converted infielder finished the 1929 campaign with a record of 11-17 and a 4.68 ERA, and won 106 games with the Braves, Cubs, and Reds.

The gates to Braves Field opened at 12:30 P.M. and there was such a rush that "(r)eserved seats were all gone, except those in the inevitable hands of speculators, by noon."[8] "The grandstand, with its capacity of 17,000 was filled to the brim, while the fans in the right field seats were packed in like sardines, but there was plenty of room in the left and right field pavilions."[9]

Just as fans were getting into their seats, Smith got the Tribe into an early 3-0 hole, one that they never recovered from. Bucs second baseman Dick Bartell, who played mostly shortstop in his 18-year major-league career, smashed a single past the Braves' first baseman, future Hall of Famer George Sisler.

Center fielder Lloyd Waner drove in Bartell on a "long, wind-carried triple to the far right center field corner."[10] On the very next pitch, Lloyd's older brother, right fielder Paul Waner, hit a fly to Braves center fielder Earl Clark, who tried to trap the ball with "the sad result that it went through his legs to the barrier as a triple, and his brother Lloyd tallied."[11] The first out of the inning came next when Pirates third

Judge Emil E. Fuchs.

baseman Pie Traynor grounded to his counterpart at the hot corner, Les Bell, who was holding Waner at third.

The third run of the inning came home when George Grantham hit a fly ball that dropped into short center, scoring Paul Waner. Smith then threw a wild pitch, advancing Grantham, and walked first baseman Earl Sheely. The inning ended when shortstop Harry Riconda grounded into a short-to-second-to-first double play.

Several players on the field were local to Massachusetts. Traynor hailed from Framingham, Braves second baseman Freddie Maguire was from Roxbury, and shortstop Rabbit Maranville was from Springfield. When Maranville came to the plate in the second, the crowd showed its appreciation for one of its locals. "One of the biggest yells from the gang was when the Braves first raced out to take the field at the start," a sportswriter reported. "But when the Rabbit tucked in his great one-handed play at (catcher Charlie) Hargreaves' expense in the second and when he came to bat in the second, there were enthusiastic uproars.

He's Boston's white-haired kid, and he will stay that way for so long as his marvelous play continues."[12]

Maguire had played college ball at Holy Cross in Worcester. When he "pranced up to the plate for the first time, he got a big boisterous hand."[13]

The Braves picked up their only two runs of the game in the third. The rally started with a double off the left-field screen by backstop Al Spohrer. It was the only extra-base hit off Grimes all day. Spohrer "went to third when Traynor made a brilliant play on Smith, a stop in front of the shortstop and a throw that just nipped the runner."[14] Clark then hit a ball to Sheely, who made a throw home that Hargreaves dropped, allowing Spohrer to score. Maguire singled and Sisler hit another ball to Sheely, who again threw to Hargreaves, but the Bucs catcher was unable to apply the tag to Clark, whose score cut the Pirates' lead to 3-2.

The Braves were victims of three double plays and one triple play. The triple killing, one of 12 in Braves Field history, occurred in the fourth inning, with the Pirates leading 4-1. Right fielder Heinie Mueller led off with a single and raced to third on a single to right by Maranville, who just beat out a throw by Paul Waner. With runners on the corners, the Tepee got noisy, but the excitement didn't last long. On the very next pitch, Al Spohrer hit a topspin ball that rolled right to Grimes. Grimes threw to catcher Charlie Hargeaves and the catcher threw the ball to Traynor, who tagged out Mueller between third and home. The second out came when Spohrer headed to second base. Traynor fired to Bartell, who applied the tag. Meanwhile, Maranville, perhaps being overly aggressive amid the confusion, tried to go all the way around and score. Second baseman Bartell threw home and Maranville was nailed at the plate for the inning-ending third out. Score that play 1-2-5-4-2.

The visitors scored runs in the fifth and sixth on sacrifice flies to George Harper in left by Paul Waner and shortstop Harry Riconda. The Bucs scored their seventh and last run in the eighth. With two outs, Riconda doubled to left over Harper's head and scored on a single to left off the bat of Hargreaves.

The last chance for the Braves came in the eighth. Pinch-hitter Jack Smith walked and Sisler reached on a throwing error by Riconda, his second of the game. Next up was slugging left fielder Harper, who had hit 17 home runs the previous season with the St. Louis Cardinals and led the Braves in homers in 1929 with 10. There would be no dramatic blast from Harper, however, as he grounded to Bartell to end the inning.

Bob Smith lasted eight innings before being pinch-hit for by Jack Smith. His pitching line was 8 innings, 11 hits, 7 runs (6 earned), 2 walks, and a strikeout. Smith gave up two triples and two doubles. Reliever Bunny Hearn pitched the ninth, allowing just a hit by Bartell.

Grimes went the distance, allowing seven hits and two earned runs. He walked two and had zero strike-outs. "(Grimes) held the Tribe to seven hits, had the luck commonly associated with the devil, and at any rate hung up a 7 to 2 verdict for the Buccaneers against the still first place (8-3) Braves."[15] The game took a brisk 1:45 to complete.

Official records showed a paid attendance of 29,462, while the *Boston Daily Record* said that "more than 3,000 nonchalantly crashed the Annie Oakley gate without a detaining finger."[16]

After the game, injured Braves right fielder Lance Richbourg, who was in the press box along with Tribe pitcher Ben Cantwell, said, "Well, the boys had won five in a row and were due for a tumble. But it's tough they could not have had a few more of the breaks today, before such a great crowd."[17]

The Braves concluded the season with a 5-6 Sunday record on their home turf (nine regularly scheduled games, and two makeup doubleheaders).

With two teams in Boston, Braves Field was in use every Sunday of the 1929 season. Unfortunately, the Sox and the Braves had otherwise forgettable last-place finishes.

NOTES

1   Charles W. Bevis, *Sunday Baseball: The Major Leagues' Struggle to Play Baseball on the Lord's Day, 1876-1934* (Jefferson, North Carolina: McFarland & Company, 2003), 219. On February 3, 1922, a bill failed to pass the Massachusetts House of Representatives to "legalize the playing of checkers and chess outdoors on Sunday."

2   In Boston one of the most ardent and passionate leaders in the fight to legalize Sunday baseball was Eugene J. O'Connor. The Dorchester resident was arrested for what today would be considered an act of civil disobedience." On October 12, 1912, the *Boston Globe* reported that O'Connor "began batting a ball to several youngsters at 3:40 and was arrested by patrolman Gallop of Division 4." When O'Connor died, the *Globe* ran a brief appreciation entitled "Father of Sunday Baseball." See Bill Nowlin, *Red Sox Threads: Odds & Ends from Red Sox History* (Burlington, Massachusetts: Rounder Books, 2008), 400-401.

3   The Giants' John McGraw encouraged Fuchs to purchase a controlling interest in the Braves and facilitated a meeting with Christy Mathewson to enable Fuchs to hire the esteemed pitcher, disabled by a World War I gas attack, as the club president. See Harold Kaese, *The Boston Braves* (New York: Putnam Press, 1948), 190-91.

4   Fuchs' fight for Sunday baseball is detailed in Robert S. Fuchs and Wayne Soini, *Judge Fuchs and the Boston Braves, 1923-1935* (Jefferson, North Carolina: McFarland & Co., Inc., 1998), 63-66, and in Kaese, 207.

5   Bevis, 240.

6   "Major league Sunday baseball became a reality in Boston yesterday afternoon (April 28)," reported the *Boston Globe*, "when upwards of 22,000 fans defied discouraging weather conditions to see the (Philadelphia) Athletics defeat the Red Sox 7 to 3 at Braves Field in the first scheduled Sunday game between two major league teams ever played in this city."

7   Grimes ended up with the Braves in 1930.

8   Burt Whitman, "Tribesman Checked By Burleigh Grimes," *Boston Herald*, May 6, 1929.

9   Eddie Hurley, "Bobby Smith Wilts Before Record Crowd," *Boston Daily Record*, May 6, 1929, 20.

10   Whitman.

11   Ibid.

12   Ibid.

13   Ibid.

14   Hurley.

15   Whitman.

16   Hurley.

17   Whitman.

THOU SHALT NOT... CUBS RALLY SCRUBBED BY SUNDAY LAW

JULY 13, 1930: BOSTON BRAVES 3, CHICAGO CUBS 0 AT BRAVES FIELD

BY MIKE RICHARD

The clock didn't exactly strike midnight for the Chicago Cubs, but when it did strike 6:00 P.M. it was good enough to negate a potential 4-3 win and hand the Boston Braves a 3-0 victory in the second game of a Sunday doubleheader at Braves Field. The Braves won the earlier game as well, 2-1.

Boston's Sunday law, which limited baseball games on those afternoons to 6 o'clock, worked in favor of the Braves in the second game. A big four-run ninth-inning rally for the Cubs went for naught and the score reverted to the end of the eighth inning, when Boston led, 3-0.

"Though this decision is not definitely settled and it may take (National League) President John Heydler to straighten out a tangle which probably saved the Tribe from a reverse that sent the Cubs back to their hotel last evening raving at puritanical Boston and the law which beat them out of a likely chance to divide the honors for the day," wrote Paul H. Shannon of the *Boston Post*.

At promptly 6 o'clock, Boston police Lieutenant Charles B. McCloskey of Station 14 came onto the field and ordered home-plate umpire Jim Scott to call the game. The Cubs entered rigorous protests, but the lieutenant and the umpire remained adamant.

Since umpires in the past had ruled that no inning should start after 5:40 P.M. on a Sunday, this game was proceeding ever so close to that bewitching time when the ninth inning began at 5:38.

The umpires may have had an inkling that Boston, ever aware of the rule, was stalling for time to drag out the eighth inning.

With one out in the bottom of the eighth, Braves captain Rabbit Maranville began to purposely foul off pitch after pitch trying to prolong the inning, before finally striking out on a fouled-off bunt.

Then Wally Berger, hoping to wait it out at the plate, took three quick strikes poured over the plate by Cubs reliever Lynn Nelson. It was two minutes ahead of the 5:40 deadline and the game was ordered continued.

With the Cubs three runs down and having done little damage against Braves starting pitcher Bob Smith, the umpires likely believed that Boston would make quick work of the visitors. There would be no need to play the bottom of the ninth.

However, Chicago had other plans. Hack Wilson led off the top of the ninth with double off Smith and Riggs Stevenson reached safely on a bunt. Charlie Grimm then drove a single that got past Wally Berger in left field, scoring a run and moving runners to second and third.

Pinch-hitter Chick Tolson struck out but Doc Farrell singled home a run and then Gabby Hartnett gave Chicago a 4-3 lead when he doubled in a pair of runs.

Then, realizing they needed to speed things up in order for the runs to count, the Cubs engaged in a bit of chicanery to quickly bring the top of the ninth to a close.

106

After Braves manager Bill McKechnie summoned reliever Bill Sherdel from the bullpen, Hartnett began to hurry up matters by nonchalantly strolling from second to third, where he was easily caught stealing. Then Clarence "Footsie" Blair purposely fanned for the third out.

Leading 4-3, the Cubs quickly took the field at 5:55 P.M., but the Braves refused to go quietly, all the while checking the big clock positioned atop the jury box in right field that loomed toward 6 o'clock.

George Sisler opened the bottom of the ninth with a clean single off reliever Charlie Root, the third pitcher of the game for the Cubs. Johnny Neun ran for him and Buster Chatham, repeating Maranville's stunt by attempting to stall for time by bunting, was finally called out on a fouled third strike.

Jim Welsh then bounced a double over the head of first baseman Charlie Grimm, and the Braves now had the tying and winning runs in scoring position. With pinch-hitter Randy Moore, who came on in favor of Bill Cronin at bat, the scoreboard clock read exactly 6 o'clock.

Players in the Boston dugout, as well as members of the press corps, were quick to alert the umpires and the Cubs that further play would render the teams liable for an infraction of the Sunday law.

The umpires seemed inclined to let the game go on but Lieutenant McCloskey walked out upon the field toward third-base umpire Ernie Quigley and warned them again. Quigley and McCloskey went to the plate and spoke with home-plate umpire Scott, who ordered the game called. The final score reverted to the end of the eighth inning with Boston leading, 3-0.

Manager Joe McCarthy left the field quite irate, with the Cubs making threats of a protest.

However, while the Cubs did not file an official protest, McCarthy felt that the umpires, in their report to league President Heydler, would explain what the teams were up against regarding the Boston Sunday baseball law.

Walter "Rabbit" Maranville.

Edward Burns of the *Chicago Tribune* reported that McCarthy would lodge the protest "on the stalling tactics of the Boston club," yet made no reference to the similar tactics carried out by the Cubs in the game.

"McCarthy thinks a good solution would be to call the game incomplete as of 6 o'clock, then play it to a conclusion with the same personnel," Burns wrote.

"At the time the game actually was halted the Braves were in their ninth inning. Sisler had singled, Chatham had struck out, and Welsh had doubled, Sisler stopping at third. According to the Chicago calculation Sisler is entitled to his single and Chatham his strikeout, but Welsh doubled at 6:01 o'clock, making the blow utterly sinful and null and void.

"A more equitable solution would be to play the game over, perhaps."

Bill McKechnie.

After the field had been cleared, the umpires admitted they knew that Sunday baseball in Boston was legal only between the hours of 2 and 6 but figured 20 minutes would be ample time to play the last inning. On days when teams were forced to make early trains, 12 minutes were allowed for the playing the last inning.

The controversial ending sent the reported 31,160 Boston fans home happy, but many fans listening to the game at home over Boston radio station WNAC were left in the dark.

Because a show on the station began promptly at 6:00 P.M. on Sundays, the studio left the contest with announcer Fred Hoey in the middle of a detailed explanation of what was going on.

Many callers besieged the radio station as well Boston as newspaper offices to get the final word on what had just happened.

Four days later, Heydler after a hearing with Veeck and Emil Fuchs, president of the Braves, disallowed the protest, and the 3–0 Boston victory held up.

As things turned out, the victory-turned-defeat may have played a part in the 1930 National League pennant race, which ended with the Cubs in second place, two games behind the St. Louis Cardinals.

Had the Cubs won the Braves game, the final days of that pennant race might have taken on a different complexion and perhaps manager McCarthy—who was fired with four games left in the season—would not have lost his job to Rogers Hornsby.

SOURCES

Boston Herald, July 14, 1930.

Boston Post, July 14, 1930.

Boston Record, July 14, 1930.

Chicago Tribune, July 15 and 18, 1930.

ANCIENTS MAKING HISTORY

SEPTEMBER 8, 1930: BOSTON OLD-TIMERS 8, "ALL-STAR" OLD-TIMERS 4 AT BRAVES FIELD

BY BOB LEMOINE

"The romantic affection which Boston always has for the players who have made big league history throbbed into thunderous beat." — Burt Whitman, Boston Herald.[1]

The band began to play some old familiar favorites, including "Silver Threads Among the Gold" and "Love's Old Sweet Song," a grand beginning on that picturesque Boston day. Then, like a portal to the past, the right-field gates clanged open and in "came rolling the old green tallyho[2] with old Pat Daley in his venerable stove pipe hat, proudly 'driving the Boston team to the ball game,'" observed Bill Cunningham of the *Boston Post*.[3] Older Boston fans would have recalled the days when they heard the "clop, clop, clop" of horse hooves approaching the Walpole Street Grounds, transporting the visiting team from the Quincy House or the United States Hotel, where they had dressed for the game.[4] This was a day to reminisce on memories such as these and many more, as Braves Field was host to an Old-Timers Game, featuring future Hall of Famers from the 1880s to the 1920s.

Some 22,000 fans came to Braves Field on this day, September 8, 1930, to see these "tottering heroes of a bygone day, the passing veterans of a later generation," as Paul H. Shannon of the *Boston Post* put it.[5] This Old-Timers Game was between old-timers from both Boston teams and an "all-star" team of old-timers. The players had Braves Field all to themselves, as the current-day Braves had this Monday off. Unlike modern old-timers games immediately preceding a "regular" game, this game could stand on its own by the presence of these legends. It was sponsored by the

Post, with proceeds being given to the Children's Hospital of Boston and the Professional Baseball Players of America Charity Fund. Over 50 old-timers were present.[6]

Before the tallyho began its trip to the ballpark, Joe Conway and crew of the Horace Partridge Company[7] were on hand with extra pants, shirts, socks, and shoes, as some uniforms were "a little tight" on these legends. Honus Wagner needed socks because his dog had chewed his while he was packing his suitcase.[8]

Candy LaChance's famous mustache "has withstood the attack of the years. It's still in place and going strong," wrote Cunningham.[9]

As the tallyho rolled in, "The years rolled back for them as its creaking wheels turned, and the ovation … thundered and quivered as it came up the first base line,"[10] Cunningham wrote. The players stepped off the carriage to great applause. "Baseball games may

The Partridge Company was an annual advertiser on Braves Field's outfield wall.

Fun-loving Rabbit Maranville with the ballplayer/comedian Nick Altrock, September 1934.

come and go, but probably never again will lovers of baseball see a more illustrious assemblage of diamond heroes," wrote Ford Sawyer of the *Boston Globe*.[11]

Fred Hoey, the radio broadcaster for Braves and Red Sox home games, called the game on WNAC alongside Bill Cunningham. The game was also carried by CBS radio, the first such national baseball broadcast to emanate from Boston.[12] Jake Morse and Walter Barnes were the official scorers, as they were 30 years prior, and Jim Shannon was again working the telegraph wires.[13] He had "sent his first baseball box score over the country in 1886 from the Walpole Street Grounds."[14]

Fans became teary-eyed when the old-timers gathered for a group photo, as the band played "Auld Lang Syne." Many removed their caps "exactly as if the band had begun the National Anthem. … It was a simple thing, but a memorable one. …"[15] A fan brought his baby to be photographed with Honus Wagner. As the legend cradled the infant, wrote Cunningham, "you'd have got a new slant on that celebrated and soft-hearted old Dutchman and seen something never duplicated on any baseball field."[16]

Cy Young (age 63), took his place on the mound for Boston again. After he pitched a scoreless first inning, the Boston Old-Timers scored two runs in their half of the inning. Jimmy Collins singled, Duffy Lewis doubled, and they both scored on Freddie Parent's double, which was misplayed by Ty Cobb. The All-

Stars scored a run in the second inning as a single by Ed Walsh scored Edd Roush. They took a 3-2 lead in the third inning on hits by Fred Clarke, Eddie Collins, and Roush. Boston countered in its half of the third inning with a barrage of hits that scored Tris Speaker, Duffy Lewis, and Bill Sweeney to give Boston a 5-3 lead. The All-Stars cut the lead to 5-4 in the top of the fifth inning as Stuffy McInnis reached on a muffed fly ball by Harry Hooper and scored on a single by Jack Barry. Boston scored three more runs in the seventh inning for the final tally of an 8-4 win.

Jimmy Coughlin's 10th Infantry Band, famous for traveling with Boston's "Royal Rooters" when Boston was in the World Series,[17] resurrected "the strains of 'Tessie,' the inspiring song which spurred on the 1903 Boston champions," reported Sawyer.[18]

Nick Altrock provided the comedy by running the bases in reverse and attempting to score from first base. He was called out at home plate by umpire Beans Reardon, whom Altrock jokingly put into a headlock that brought the house down. Eddie Collins delighted the crowd by chewing bubble gum he peeled off the bill of his cap.[19] Harry Hooper thrilled the Fenway fans just as in old times with a beautiful catch to rob Rube Oldring of a hit.[20] Hugh Duffy and a young 43-year-old Ty Cobb, who both had illustrious seasons of batting over .400, went hitless. Cobb was 0-for-3

Cy Young reminiscing with an unknown gentleman in a Boston hotel lobby.

for the All-Stars and 0-for-1 when he decided to bat for Boston in the eighth inning. Sixty-five-year-old Patsy Donovan, who had played for Boston in 1890, got a pinch-hit single in his only at-bat. Born a month before Abraham Lincoln was assassinated, Donovan would later coach baseball at Phillips Academy in Andover, Massachusetts, where one of his young players was future President George H.W. Bush.[21]

I doubt many would concur with the exuberant comments of the *Post's* Arthur Duffey that "it was the greatest day in Boston's baseball history,"[22] but it was a shining moment in the history of Braves Field, and a special moment for players and fans alike.[23] Still, time marched on.

"Baseball has taken its sentimental journey. The tallyho has gone back to the museum and the players to less strenuous tasks."[24]

SOURCES

Baseball-reference.com

O'Leary, James C. "Old Timers Again on Diamond Before 20,000," *Boston Globe*, September 12, 1922, 1.

"Old-Time Ball Players and Fans in Reunion," *Boston Globe*, July 22, 1909, 6.

"Old-Time Ball Players' Festal Day," *Boston Globe*, August 11, 1910, 7.

"Old-Time Players Had the Time of Their Lives," *Boston Globe*, August 10, 1906, 4.

"Old Timers Have Right Good Time," *Boston Herald*, August 13, 1908, 5.

Retrosheet.org.

Thorn, John. *Baseball in the Garden of Eden: The Secret History of the Early Game* (New York: Simon & Shuster, 2011).

Thorn, John. "Tim Murnane: Heart of the Game," Our Game, May 8, 2013. Accessed December 6, 2014. ourgame.mlblogs.com/2013/05/08/tim-murnane-heart-of-the-game/#comments.

Special thanks to Bill Nowlin and Bob Brady for research assistance in writing this article.

NOTES

1   Burt Whitman, "22,000 See All-Boston Stars Set Back All-Team, 8 to 4, Harry Hooper Fielding Star," *Boston Herald*, September 9, 1930, 30.

2   A tallyho was similar to a stagecoach in that it was a "four-in-hand" coach: four horses controlled by a single driver.

3   Bill Cunningham, "More Like Huge Revival Session," *Boston Post*, September 9, 1930, 25. Pat Daley had a long history of transporting baseball players and equipment, beginning with the Boston Braves in 1876. In 1901 he also began the same duties for the modern-day Red Sox, which he continued to perform into the 1930s. J.G. Taylor Spink's column in *The Sporting News*, November 9, 1933, mentions Daley having just upgraded from the horse and carriage a couple of years prior. Melville E. Webb in the *Boston* Globe, April 9, 1933, said that Daley had been replaced by the Braves but was still working for the Red Sox. See *Opening Fenway Park With Style: The 1912 Champion Red Sox*, ed. Bill Nowlin (Phoenix: SABR, 2012), 27. The company itself still transports equipment for the Red Sox through the 2014 season. See also *Fenway Lives: The Team Behind the Team: The People Who Work in and Around Fenway Park*. (Cambridge, Massachusetts: Rounder Books, 2004).

4   Paul H. Shannon, "Heroes Of Other Days Thrill Mighty Throng," *Boston Post*, September 9, 1930, 24. The Walpole Street Grounds in Boston was a stadium with a double-decked grandstand built in 1871. It served as the home of the Boston National League team until it was destroyed by fire in 1894. Also known as the South End Grounds, it was rebuilt, and was home to the Braves until Braves Field was built in 1915. Quincy House was a prominent hotel in Boston in the 19th and early 20th centuries.

5   Paul H. Shannon, "Heroes Of Other Days," 1.

6   As best as the author can determine, this is the complete list of players and umpires present that day. Not all of the players played in the game. Nick Altrock, Jimmy Archer, Frank "Home Run" Baker, Dave Bancroft, Jack Barry, Hugh Bedient, Chief Bender, Bill Bradley, Kitty Bransfield, Roger Bresnahan, Max Carey, Bill Carrigan, Fred Clarke, Ty Cobb, Eddie Collins, Jimmy Collins, Ray Collins, Jack Coombs, Bill Dinneen, Patsy Donovan, Larry Doyle, Hugh Duffy, Clyde Engle, Johnny Evers, Hobe Ferris, Buck Freeman, Larry Gardner, Hank Gowdy, Billy Hamilton, Bob Hart (umpire), Olaf Henricksen, Dick Hoblitzell, Harry Hooper, Harold Janvrin, Candy LaChance, Duffy Lewis, Hans Lobert, Les Mann, Bunny Madden, Leslie Mann, Rabbit Maranville, Stuffy McInnis, Fred Mitchell, Charlie Moran (umpire), Rube Oldring, Freddy Parent, Dode Paskert, Beans Reardon (umpire), Edd Roush, Dick Rudolph, Dave Shean, Tris Speaker, Amos Strunk, Bill Sweeney, Fred Tenney, Jeff Tesreau, George Tyler, Honus Wagner, Big Ed Walsh, Smoky Joe Wood, Steve Yerkes, Cy Young.

7   Joseph F. "Joe" Conway was the president of the Horace Partridge Company and later served as the Braves' treasurer at the beginning of the Quinn syndicate regime in 1936. The Horace Partridge Company was called the "Athletic Outfitter to the Braves." See Bob Brady's blog entry "The Braves Left a Trail in Boston," retrieved from bostonbaseballhistory.com/braves-left-a-trail-in-boston/.

8   Bill Cunningham, "Old-Timers' Game Is Here At Last," *Boston Post* September 8, 1930.

9   Ibid.

10   Cunningham, "More Like Huge Revival Session," 25.

11   Ford Sawyer, "Old Timers Flash on Diamond Today," *Boston Globe*, September 8, 1930, 8.

12   "Old-Timers Day Game Broadcast," *Boston Herald*, August 31, 1930, 27.

13   Walter S. Barnes Jr. was a *Boston Globe* sports editor. Jacob C. Morse had worked for the *Herald*. At one time, a Walter Barnes Memorial Trophy was given by the Boston baseball writers to the outstanding Boston player.

14   "Batt'ries for Today: Walsh-Archer; Cy Young and Carrigan. Play Ball!" *Boston Herald*, September 8, 1930, 13.

15   Cunningham, "More Like Huge Revival Session."

16   Cunningham, "Old-Timers' Game Is Here," 24.

17   Ibid.; For more on the history of the Royal Rooters, see Peter Nash, *Boston's Royal Rooters* (Charleston, South Carolina: Arcadia, 2005).

18   Ford Sawyer, "Old Timers Play Before 22,000 Fans," *Boston Globe*, September 9, 1930, 28.

19   For more information on Collins' superstitions, see his SABR biography written by Paul Mittermeyer: sabr.org/bioproj/person/c480756d.

20   "Old Timers Play Before 22,000," 28.

21   David Jones, "Patsy Donovan," SABR BioProject. Retrieved from sabr.org/bioproj/person/753652af.

22   Arthur Duffey, "Arthur Duffey's Sport Comment," *Boston Post*, September 9, 1930, 24.

23   The author attempted to trace the history of old-timers baseball games in Boston and beyond. The first discovered game could have been one among members of the New Metropolitans, considered the first organized baseball team. An old-timers game was played on September 27, 1875, according to the *New York Clipper* ("The Knickerbocker Club. Baseball in the Olden Time," October 9, 1875, 221). The vets of 1850, referred to as the "Old Duffers," played against the vets of 1860, referred to as the "youngsters." A Metropolitans Old-Timers' Game against Washington was played and included "the majority of the oldest men who played on the diamond in the sixties," ("Some of the Old Timers," *Boston* Herald, July 14, 1886, 8). A "Harry Wright Memorial Day" game was held in Rockford, Illinois, on April 13, 1896, and included the pitching of A.G. Spalding. An Old-Timers' Game was held at the South End Grounds in Boston against a touring Australian team on June 20, 1897. "Father" Henry Chadwick, as he was called, served as a host for the Australians and lectured on the history of baseball. George Wright and A.G. Spalding played, the latter remarking "We're not as spry as we used to be." ("Vets in Armor," *Boston Globe*, June 22, 1897, 4). Former player John Irwin owned a hotel on Peddocks Island, located in Boston Harbor, and each year from 1906 to 1910 (or possibly continuing until World War I), he hosted a yearly "Ye Old Timers' Gambol" Game. Candy Cummings, credited with inventing the curveball, was one of the attendees. Braves Field had also previously hosted an Old-Timers' Game on September 11, 1922, which also featured Cy Young.

24   N.B. Belth, "Diamond Stars of Long Ago Ride the Tallyho," *Brooklyn Daily Eagle*, September 12, 1930, 24.

A BIG DAY FOR BERGER

SEPTEMBER 17, 1930: BOSTON BRAVES 6, CINCINNATI REDS 3 (FIRST GAME) AND CINCINNATI REDS 6, BRAVES 4 (SECOND GAME) AT BRAVES FIELD

BY JACK ZERBY

Today's ballplayers and their union would be aghast, but Great-Depression-era club owners responded to the new economic reality with doubleheaders — lots of them. On Wednesday, September 17, 1930, the Boston Braves were playing their 30th twin bill of the season and sixth in an extended Wigwam stand that had begun on September 1. They'd played one the prior Sunday and would play their final one 10 days later as part of a season-closing series in Brooklyn.[1]

At this point in the season, the outcome of the games didn't mean much to either the Braves or the visiting Cincinnati Reds. Boston was 67-78 and sixth in the eight-team National League; Cincinnati stood seventh, 9½ games behind the Braves. But with their 67 wins, the Braves had already surpassed the 56 the 1929 club had managed to win under the quirky guidance of principal owner Judge Emil Fuchs. Casting himself as manager to save salary but in practice "frequently out of town or at least out of the dugout on other business,"[2] Fuchs customarily had "assistant manager" Johnny Evers run the team. Recognizing that the dugout was not his realm, Fuchs brought in Bill "Deacon" McKechnie for 1930. McKechnie had won the 1925 World Series managing the Pittsburgh Pirates and the 1928 National League pennant with the St. Louis Cardinals.[3]

A rookie, Wally Berger,[4] was responsible for a great deal of that improvement. In his definitive history, *The Boston Braves*, Harold Kaese styled the righty-hitting Berger a "lanky, raw-boned blond, a free-swinging young giant ... the frosting on the [McKechnie Braves'] cake."[5] McKechnie, whose keen

managerial instincts carried him to the Hall of Fame, saw potential,[6] and installed Berger in left field,[7] batting fifth, on Opening Day. He stayed there, slotted in the heart of the order, and had played in all but three of Boston's 146 games up to September 17. The frosting he added was remarkable for a rookie: He entered the day's play batting .307 and slugging .607, with 34 home runs and 109 RBIs. He'd already broken the major-league rookie home-run record back on July 20 in another game against Cincinnati at Braves Field.[8]

Berger summed up his rookie outlook later in a memoir: "Before I went to spring training the first year with Boston, I got myself in pretty good shape. I was going to a big-league club from the minors, and I knew that the first impression was going to count. I had to battle for position with the other outfielders. I wanted to get off to a good start — and I did."[9]

Thirty thousand had seen the Braves and Cardinals split a Sunday twin bill on September 14; a reported 5,000 ventured out to Braves Field for this midweek action, which followed two offdays but competed with a parade also taking place in downtown Boston.[10] Even in the middle of the week and with a free parade, fans with limited spare dollars were getting another doubleheader, and knew that their prize rookie's steady production was still solid late in the season — Berger had reached base by hit or walk in 16 of the 17 games in the extended homestand. To boot, Cincinnati, "Porkopolis" to *Boston Post* writer Paul Shannon,[11] came to town dragging a 12-game losing streak.

Right-hander Socks Seibold, out of the majors for 10 years before resurfacing with the Braves in 1929, started

Walter Antone Berger.

the opener for the locals and spun a complete game, shutting out Cincinnati in all but the seventh inning, when the Reds touched him up for three runs. By then the Braves already had five of their own. Berger had gotten things started with an RBI single off Benny Frey in the first inning, then drilled a two-run homer in the third that ended Frey's day. McKechnie gave Seibold enough leash to finish what he started and Lance Richbourg's great defensive work in right field helped, too. The Braves tacked on an insurance run in the eighth to win, 6-3. Berger was 2-for-4 with a run scored on the home run, his 35th of the year. He'd moved his RBI total to 112.

He wasn't finished. Although the scoring in the second game was essentially a turnabout from the first, with Cincinnati's Red Lucas[12] staked to a 5-0 lead through five innings,[13] Berger got to work in the sixth. He

broke up Lucas's shutout bid with a two-out solo homer, then victimized the right-hander again with a three-run shot, number 37, in the eighth. Before these pyrotechnics, both "full-blooded" and "smashed" to left field,[14] he'd added his 27th double of the season. The Berger barrage drove in all four Boston runs, but the one-man offense wasn't enough as Cincinnati finally snapped its losing streak at 13 with a 6-4 win. Despite his difficulties with Berger, Lucas managed a complete game and helped his own cause with a two-run single and a run scored.

This late-season day at cavernous Braves Field, notorious as a pitchers' park where home runs were hard to come by,[15] clearly belonged to Wally Berger. He'd given the Depression-pinched fans the two-for-one heroics they'd looked for. For the day he was 5-for-8 with three home runs, a double, seven RBIs, and three runs scored. With 11 days left in the season Boston's rising star, already likened to the Red Sox' departed Babe Ruth,[16] had 37 home runs and 116 RBIs.[17] The day nicely exemplified his exceptional rookie year, giving long-suffering Braves fans a slugger to cheer—and, with an experienced manager also in place, hope for the seasons to come.[18]

And Berger was glad to oblige: "Playing baseball was the only job in my life that I liked. By the time I came along, professional ballplayers—especially in the major leagues—had prestige. You got a lot of attention. People looked up to you, wanted to be around you."[19]

SOURCES

Berger, Walter Anton, and George Morris Snyder. *Freshly Remember'd* (Redondo Beach, California: Schneider/McGuirk Press, 1993).

Bevis, Charlie. *Doubleheaders, A Major League History* (Jefferson, North Carolina: McFarland& Company, Inc., 2010).

Caruso, Gary. *The Braves Encyclopedia* (Philadelphia: Temple University Press, 1995).

Fuchs, Robert S., and Wayne Soini. *Judge Fuchs and the Boston Braves, 1923-1935* (Jefferson, North Carolina: McFarland & Co., Inc., 1998).

James, Bill. *The Bill James Guide to Baseball Managers from 1870 to Today* (New York: Simon and Schuster, Inc., Scribner, 1997).

Johnson, Richard A. *Images of Sports: Boston Braves* (Mount Pleasant, South Carolina: Arcadia Publishing, 2001).

Kaese, Harold. *The Boston Braves* (New York: G.P. Putnam's Sons, 1948).

Reichler, Joseph L. *The Great All-Time Baseball Record Book* (New York: Macmillan Publishing Co., Inc., 1981).

Vincent, David W., ed. *Home Runs in the Old Ballparks* (Cleveland: Society for American Baseball Research, 1995).

Brattain, John. "Blast From The Past: Wally Berger," The Hardball Times.com, April 22, 2005 (accessed November 1, 2014).

O'Leary, James C. "Berger Has Three Homers in Braves Double-Header," *Boston Globe*, September 18, 1930.

Shannon, Paul H. "Berger Makes Three Homers," *Boston Post*, September 18, 1930.

Whitman, Burt. "Braves Split with Reds, 6-3, 4-6, as Berger Knocks Three Homers and Smashes in Seven Runs," *Boston Herald*, September 18, 1930, 36.

BallparksofBaseball.com, Braves Field (accessed October 7, 2014).

Baseball-Almanac.com, Single-Season Rookie RBI Records (accessed November 1, 2014).

Baseball-Reference.com

Braves.com, All-Time Statistics Totals (accessed October 30, 2014).

Retrosheet.org

NOTES

1   The 62 games in those 31 doubleheaders comprised slightly more than 40 percent of the Braves' 154-game schedule. Retrosheet.com.

2   Caruso, *The Braves Encyclopedia*, 297.

3   When St. Louis was swept in the 1928 World Series by the Yankees, owner Sam Breadon demoted McKechnie to managing the Cardinals' farm team in Rochester and brought Rochester manager Billy Southworth to St. Louis for 1929. By July McKechnie was back. He left St. Louis with Breadon's blessing when the Cardinals were unwilling to offer a contract in excess of two years; Judge Fuchs, who had talked to Breadon about McKechnie's possible availability, signed him for three years. Kaese, *The Boston Braves*, 212-213.

4   Berger was 24 when he debuted with the Braves on April 15, 1930. After two failed tryouts with his hometown San Francisco Seals, he was already 21 and playing company-team baseball in Montana when friends secured him a spot with Pocatello in in the Class-C Utah-Idaho League during the 1927 season. He quickly advanced to the Pacific Coast League Los Angeles Angels for 1928, and had a breakout season there with 40 home runs in 1929. Fuchs gave the Angels two players and cash for the rights to Berger and signed him to a $4,000 contract for 1930. Kaese, 215; Fuchs and Soini, *Judge Fuchs and the Boston Braves*, 100.

5   Kaese, 215.

6   Bill James ranks Berger as the best center fielder to play for McKechnie, whose managerial career began in the Federal League in 1915 and spanned 24 major-league seasons, with four pennants and two World Series titles. James, *The Bill James Guide to Baseball Managers*, 107.

7   McKechnie moved Berger to center field for 1931. He remained there for the remainder of his Boston career, which ended with a trade to the Giants on June 15, 1937. Jimmy Welsh played 110 games in center for the 1930 Braves. He was traded to the Cubs during the 1930-31 offseason, opening center field for Berger, who combined good range and a strong arm with his slugging.

8   Del Bissonette of the Brooklyn Robins had hit 25 home runs as a rookie in 1928. Baseball-Reference.com.

9   Berger and Snyder, *Freshly Remember'd*, 120.

10   Whitman, "Braves Split with Reds," *Boston Herald*, September 18, 1930.

11   Shannon, "Berger Makes Three Homers," *Boston Post*, September 18, 1930.

12   Lucas is remembered as one of the best-hitting pitchers in baseball history, often used as a pinch-hitter in his career with four NL teams. He had a .423 on-base percentage in 137 plate appearances in 1930 and hit .281 over 16 seasons.

13   The Braves had clinched sixth place over Cincinnati with the win in the first game. McKechnie started rookie Ken Jones in the second game. It was the only start in his major-league career; he lasted only into the fourth inning. Despite pitching only 21⅔ innings over nine games in the majors, Jones managed to get himself a nickname, "Broadway." Shannon.

14   Whitman.

15   "Not only did [Wally Berger] hit home runs in quantity, but he was also forced to hit most of his home runs the proverbial 'country mile,' the large expanse of Braves Field, against a prevailing north wind." Johnson, *Boston Braves*, 52.

16   "A new Babe Ruth seemed to be coming to life in Boston." Fuchs and Soini, 84-85.

17   The final RBI on September 17 tied Jimmy Williams's (Pittsburgh, 1899) rookie RBI record. Berger broke it with No. 117 on September 21. He finished the 1930 season at .309/.375/.614 with 38 home runs and 119 RBIs. His 38 home runs upped the then-existing major-league rookie record by 13 and is still the National League rookie standard, tied in 1956 by Frank Robinson of Cincinnati. Berger's 119 rookie RBIs were the major-league record until Ted Williams drove in 145 in 1939. His NL rookie RBIs record lasted longer—until Albert Pujols (St. Louis) drove in 130 in 2001. Reichler, *The Great All-Time Baseball Record Book*, 281, 284; Brattain, *Blast From The Past: Wally Berger*. Berger was certainly the top National League rookie in 1930, but not "Rookie of the Year." The ROY award wasn't instituted until 1947.

18 Berger led the Braves in home runs and RBIs every season from 1930 through 1936. He was selected to the first National League All-Star team, in 1933, and again in 1934 through 1936. He stands second (.533) to only Henry Aaron (.567) in career slugging percentage for the combined Boston-Milwaukee-Atlanta franchises. Braves.com. Berger won two-thirds of the National League Triple Crown in 1935 with 34 home runs and 130 RBIs. Baseball-Reference.com. His 103 home runs in Braves Field are the most by a Braves hitter, and he added two more there while playing with other teams. Vincent, *Home Runs in the Old Ballparks*.

19 Berger and Snyder, 185-186.

FRED HOEY DAY

JUNE 20, 1931: BOSTON BRAVES 5, ST. LOUIS CARDINALS 1 (FIRST GAME) AND BOSTON BRAVES 3, ST. LOUIS CARDINALS 2 (SECOND GAME) AT BRAVES FIELD

BY BOB LEMOINE

My dear Mr. Whitman,

While "days" for baseball players are in vogue, I would like to suggest some sort of a testimonial of appreciation to Fred Hoey for the splendid service he has rendered to baseball and to the thousands of fans who cannot always be at the game. I am sure that great numbers of people would welcome an opportunity to contribute to such a testimonial.

I don't know how such a thing is started, but I offer the suggestion and I hope I may have the opportunity to contribute.

Sincerely yours,
Palmer York[1]

A crowd of 30,000 filed into Braves Field in Boston on a hot Saturday, June 20, 1931, as the Braves faced the St. Louis Cardinals in a doubleheader. Many of those fans were anxiously anticipating not the games themselves, but the ceremony between them. They came to show appreciation for popular Braves radio broadcaster Fred Hoey, the first regular baseball announcer in Boston.[2] He had been a long-time sportswriter for several Boston newspapers, beginning with the *Boston Journal* in 1909, then on to the *Boston Herald* and *Boston American*. He began broadcasting Braves and Red Sox games on the radio in 1927, when radio was still in its infancy.[3] Fans who could not have attended a game experienced it through the voice of Hoey, and now many came to say thanks.

"If all this did not constitute a perfect day," wrote James C. O'Leary of the *Boston Globe*, "it certainly ought to stand until the perfect day comes along."[4]

The Braves announced that "hundreds of fans have signified their wish to help make a Hoey day a success. Stay-ins and shut-ins will have a chance to show their appreciation."[5] Fans had sent in gifts, and Harry Faunce, who worked the turnstiles at Braves Field, wrote a song for the occasion, entitled "It's a Great Game."[6]

"From all parts of New England the fans and those who seldom attend games, but often listen to them, are sending in their requests for tickets. Probably some of the outlying fans will not be able to attend, and those who will find themselves up against that obstacle are sending donations," wrote Burt Whitman of the *Boston Herald.*[7]

Ken Coleman, a young listener to Hoey who would one day himself become a Red Sox broadcaster, said Hoey "wasn't polished. He wasn't a professional. … There was an electricity to him — not in *how* he used the language, particularly, but in the feeling he gave

Hoey posing for a publicity photo for one of his sponsors.

Ad publicizing Hoey's role as announcer for both of Boston's baseball clubs.

Being emotionally affected, Hoey "did his talking into the mike and modestly and with well-chosen words, as usual, thanked his friends. He received a tumultuous ovation when he first walked to the plate," wrote Burt Whitman.[10]

The Waltham (Massachusetts) High School band "gave a splendid exhibition of marching, and the baton swinging of the girl drum major was a very interesting feature," the *Boston Globe* reported. Music was also provided by Jimmy Coughlin's 101st Regiment Veterans band.[11] Being so inspired, Rabbit Maranville of the Braves was seen practicing twirling a bat in the dugout, in case he was needed to perform.

To make the day even more satisfying, the Braves won both games of the doubleheader.

Tom Zachary pitched an outstanding game one for the Braves, allowing one unearned run on only four hits and no walks. Zachary zipped through the first two innings, throwing only 10 pitches. James C. O'Leary remarked, "A fan who says he kept track of them thereafter says he never pitched more than two balls to any one batter during the game, which probably would be a record if there were any way of determining the fact absolutely."[12]

that this mattered, that baseball counted, that it meant something special in our lives."[8]

Hoey received a bank certificate of deposit for $3,000 from the fans, money from the Red Sox and Braves, a wristwatch, gold, a pipe, and even a check from the visiting Cardinals. A box of silk shirts came from Boys of Quincy, and flowers came from relatives. Fans sent gifts of cakes, socks, and neckties. Burt Whitman concluded (considering it was Father's Day), that "some of the fans had robbed dad of the things they were planning to give him today."[9]

Speeches were made by Suffolk County District Attorney William J. Foley; the Braves owner, Judge Emil Fuchs; *Boston Post* sportswriter Jack Malaney; and Johnny Igoe, a druggist and local sports figure..

Flint Rhem pitched for the Cardinals. The Braves scored a run in the third inning when Zachary doubled to right field, moved to third base on a wild pickoff throw from catcher Gus Mancuso, and scored on a wild pitch.

The Cardinals tied the score with an unearned run in the fourth inning. Frankie Frisch reached on a fielder's choice, stole second base and reached third base as catcher Al Spohrer made a wild throw. Frisch scored on a groundout.

In the fourth inning the Braves had back-to-back singles by Red Worthington and Earl Sheely. Wes Schulmerich drove a line drive to deep center field, just over the glove of a leaping Pepper Martin. Worthington scored, giving the Braves a 2-1 lead.

Hoey in Red Sox garb during 1913 spring training.

In the bottom of the seventh inning, after two were out, Worthington and Sheely singled, and Frisch lost a fly by Schulmerich in the sun. It went for a double and Worthington scored. Spohrer was walked intentionally, then Freddie Maguire doubled, scoring Sheely and Schulmerich, making it 5-1 Braves.

Frisch of the Cardinals made the fielding play of the game. In the eighth inning he made a diving catch "then turned three or four somersaults before he came to a stop and came up with the ball. The big crowd applauded him all the way to the bench," observed James C. O'Leary.[13]

Zachary finished the complete-game 5-1 victory for the Braves, who outhit the Cardinals 14 to 4 and left 11 runners on base.

In game two, the Braves scored in the first inning off Cardinals starter Jim Lindsey as Bill Dreesen doubled and scored on a Worthington single. The Braves added a run in the fourth inning when Schulmerich tripled and scored on Bill Cronin's single.

The Cardinals rallied in the fifth and sixth innings. Consecutive singles by Martin, Jimmie Wilson, and Jake Flowers produced a run in the fifth inning, then Chick Hafey scored on a passed ball to tie the score, 2-2, in the sixth.

In the bottom of the ninth, with the score still 2-2, Maguire doubled off Tony Kaufmann on a ball that took a funny hop and bounded away from third baseman Sparky Adams. Maguire moved to third on a sacrifice bunt, and then scored on a walk-off single by Dreesen. Bruce Cunningham went the distance for the Braves, allowing one earned run.

"So far as the Braves and the fans are concerned, Freddy Hoey can have a day every day provided he can guarantee of two games for the Braves against tough first division competition," concluded Burt Whitman.[14]

In later years, Hoey's WNAC producer, Jack Moakley, summed up his influence by saying, "In the old days we had our ears and our imaginations and Fred made that ballpark just as big and as little, as green or as brown as he desired. We depended on Fred to tell us why the crowd was hollering and where the ball went. In that era I don't think there was anyone better than Fred Hoey."[15]

Boston fans would long remember Hoey's voice in those early years on the radio. In this day of instant communication, it is hard for us to imagine what that voice meant to Boston fans listening to him describe the game for them. "On the air, Fred *was* Boston baseball," Ken Coleman remarked.[16] One fan, Bill Ahearn of Everett, Massachusetts, wrote to the *Boston Herald Travele*r 40 years later:

"I started following baseball in 1930, and any real baseball fan that remembers Fred Hoey will tell you that he was the best ball announcer that Boston ever had. He had the voice and every fan liked his delivery. In those days, dozens of fans walking the streets of Boston would stop at candy stands and stores that aired the game to listen to Fred Hoey. He was good, believe me."[17]

SOURCES

In addition to the Sources cited in the text, the author used baseball-reference.com and retrosheet.org for accounts of the games.

NOTES

1   Burt Whitman, "Baseball Fan Writes Urging Fred Hoey Be Given 'Day' for His Baseball Broadcasting," *Boston Herald*, August 27, 1930, 28.

2   Fred Hoey was born in Boston (1884 is the date written on his draft cards, while other records list 1885) and raised in Saxonville, Massachusetts, a section of the town of Framingham. Hoey's got his first experience with baseball when his father took him to Boston's South End Grounds to see the Boston Beaneaters play Baltimore for the 1897 Temple Cup. Hoey was a semipro athlete, and became a hockey and football referee as well as a baseball umpire. He was the head usher at the Red Sox' Huntington Avenue Grounds in Boston, then wrote for three Boston newspapers, the *Journal*, the *Herald*, and the *American*. Hoey covered numerous sporting events, but mostly covered school athletics, even picking his own all-scholastic teams. He later became the Braves' official scorer. Hoey became the publicity director for the Boston Arena and was a major factor in the spread of hockey in the Boston area.

Hoey was already a well-known Boston sports celebrity when he became the first regular baseball radio announcer. He broadcast Braves and Red Sox home games for WNAC, which was owned by John Shepard. Shepard created a regional radio network, the Yankee Network, which had a listening audience of 5 million, according to Edgar G. Brands of *The Sporting News* (May 7, 1936).

Hoey kept a chart with details of each player in the game so as not to trust any details to memory. Boston fans campaigned for Hoey to be a World Series announcer, and got their wish in 1933, when the New York Giants played the Washington Senators. But in Game One Hoey lost his voice and had to be replaced. He had been suffering from a cold but refused to stop smoking his pipe, making his voice garbled and inaudible. Hoey always kept throat lozenges. Rumors circulated, however, that Hoey's well-known drinking problem was to blame, and that he came to the radio booth drunk. Hoey did have another chance at a national broadcast, however, as he announced the 1936 All-Star Game from Boston. There was constant friction between Hoey and Yankee Network owner Shepard, and Shepard attempted to fire him in 1936. Public protests, including one by President Franklin D. Roosevelt, won Hoey his job back. After 1938, however, Hoey asked for a raise and was fired. This time the public couldn't save him, and his broadcasting career ended. Hoey began a new sports show evenings on WBZ in 1939 and wrote for the *Boston American* into the 1940s. He died in 1949 after an accident at his home in Winthrop, Massachusetts, a Boston suburb.

3   Some accounts list Hoey as beginning his broadcasting career in 1925, the first year of radio broadcasts from Braves Field. Newspaper accounts from the era list Hoey as having a 12-year broadcasting career in Boston from 1927-1938. He is first mentioned as a broadcaster in 1927.

4   James C. O'Leary, "Braves Take Two Games From Cards," *Boston Globe*, June 21, 1931, A1.

5   "Fuchs Plans Day for Fred Hoey in June," *Boston Herald*, January 8, 1931, 31.

6   "Fans Turn Out to Pay Tribute to Fred Hoey at Wigwam Today," *Boston Herald*, June 20, 1931, 5. You can find a copy of the score to "It's a Grand Old Game," with words and music by Harry Smith Faunce, at the Giamatti Research Center Library at the Baseball Hall of Fame in Cooperstown, New York.

7   Burt Whitman, "Fighting Braves Return Home Today to Open Six-Game Series With League-Leading Cardinals," *Boston Herald*, June 18, 1931, 21.

8   Curt Smith, *Voices of the Game* (New York: Fireside, 1987), 24.

9   Burt Whitman, "Fred Hoey Day Proves Lucky One for Tribe," *Boston Herald*, June 21, 1932, 22.

10 Ibid.

11 "Fred Hoey Day at Wigwam Great Tribute to Radio Announcer," *Boston Globe*, June 21, 1931, 25.

12 O'Leary, "Braves Take Two Games From Cards," 25.

13 Ibid.

14 Whitman, "Fred Hoey Day Proves Lucky," 19.

15 Ted Patterson, *Golden Voices of Baseball* (Champaign, Illinois: Sports Pub LLC, 2002), 103.

16 *Voices of the Game*, 24.

17 "Mailbag—Our Readers Write on Hunters' Day, Fred Hoey," *Boston Herald Traveler*, September 20, 1972, 28.

CHARITY BEGINS AT HOME PLATE

SEPTEMBER 23, 1931 — BOSTON BRAVES 4, BOSTON RED SOX 3 AT BRAVES FIELD
BOSTON CITY UNEMPLOYMENT FUND BENEFIT GAME

BY TOM HUFFORD

In 1931 the United States was two years into the Great Depression, with an unemployment rate of 15.8 percent, nearly double the previous year. Jobs were hard to find, and what jobs there were generally came with lower salaries than before. Breadlines, soup kitchens, and the number of homeless persons were on the rise.

Baseball was one thing that could provide a diversion. Boston Red Sox faithful had been optimistic about the club's chances, after six straight last-place finishes (1925-30). Going into the season's final week, the *Boston Herald* even reported that "the Red Sox … have staged a surge which has carried them to the top of the second division."[1] Even though the Red Sox were improving on the field, home attendance had dropped over 20 percent, from 444,000 in 1930 to just under 351,000. The Braves, who had looked forward to the season after a 14-game improvement in 1930 had moved them from last to sixth in the standings, instead took a step backwards. Buoyed by a surge in interest in the early part of the season, though, the Braves actually showed an increase in attendance of about 10 percent.

Throughout the majors, teams were looking for ways to help fans who had fallen onto hard times. As the season entered September, teams began looking for open dates in their schedules to stage benefit games for the local charities and unemployment funds. On September 9 the Cubs and White Sox met at Chicago's Comiskey Park and the New York Giants and Yankees faced off at Yankee Stadium. In late September the Cardinals-Browns game was the big attraction in St. Louis, as was the Athletics-Phillies tilt in the City of Brotherly Love. The Reds and Indians staged an Ohio

showdown. The planned New York City Series was canceled and replaced by a charity doubleheader on September 24 at the Polo Grounds. The National League Giants and Robins paired off in the opening game, followed an hour later by a game between the Robins and Yankees — with players from all three teams participating in a field meet during the intermission.

In Boston, Mayor James Michael Curley spearheaded a charity game, proposing that all funds raised should be donated to the Boston City Unemployment Fund. The Braves and Red Sox wanted to cooperate, of course, but had a hard time finding a date to schedule the game. The Braves were scheduled for a 20-day road trip, September 3-22, ending with a Tuesday game in Cincinnati, and returning home for a season-ending series against the Phillies September 25-27. (which ended up as a doubleheader on the 27th). The Red Sox had gotten to enjoy home cooking for a 23-game, 19-day stretch from September 4-22. They then were

Boston mayor James Michael Curley throws out first pitch.

to play games in Philadelphia on September 23-26 and a season finale in Washington on September 27. The only way the hoped-for charity game could be scheduled was to wait until the Braves were back in Boston, and then to postpone the Red Sox' road trip by a day. The Athletics agreed to eliminate the opening game of their series, allowing the Red Sox to remain in Boston for the charity game on September 23. Braves Field, the larger of the two Boston ballparks, was chosen as the site for the game, since it would allow more spectators to attend.

Once arranged, the game would actually be the third time the teams had met in Boston that season. The Red Sox had won the first two exhibition contests, played in the early spring, so the Braves were bent on revenge. In truth, they were looking for some way to end their season on a positive note. Since September 1, the Braves had been in a tailspin, winning only 4 of 25 games, and falling from fifth place to sixth in the National League. The Red Sox were also below .500 for the month, being victorious in 12 of 25 decisions, but had moved up from last place to fifth during that stretch.

The benefit game and associated activities were judged to be both artistically and financially successful. Crowd estimates ranged from 20,000 to 25,000.[2] Considering that the Red Sox had drawn an average crowd of about 5,750 per home game and the Braves averaged about 8,700, all parties had to be very pleased with the outpouring of fans.

In pregame festivities, Mayor Curley gave a touching and eloquent speech, in which he thanked team presidents Emil Fuchs of the Braves and Bob Quinn, of the Red Sox, for the cooperation of the players of both teams, the four umpires, ticket sellers, ticket takers, the musicians' union and members of the band, ushers, other team employees, volunteers, everyone in attendance, and most anyone else he could think of.

A relay race was held by four-man teams from each club, who raced each other around the bases. For the Braves, Ed Brandt led off, running from home plate to first base, Johnny Neun ran the leg from first to

second, Ben Cantwell covered the distance from second to third base, and Wally Berger from third to home. The Red Sox players covering the same respective legs were Bill Sweeney, Jack Rothrock, Bobby Reeves, and Rabbit Warstler. The Red Sox team won the event by one-fifth of a second over the Braves quartet.

Next up on the program was an auction of autographed baseballs. Four balls went on the auction block—one each bearing the signatures of Mayor Curley, Babe Ruth, and Earl Webb (in the midst of his record-setting 67-doubles season), and a final ball signed by the entire Philadelphia Athletics team. The Athletics team ball netted $225 from Boston sportsman V. Bruce Wetmore. He had purchased stock in the Braves in 1927, and from time to time liked to fill in as an umpire in spring-training games. The autographed Philadelphia Athletics ball is probably as close as he ever got to a championship team.

There was vocal and instrumental musical entertainment throughout the game, and a baby elephant amused the crowd by fishing for peanuts from the pockets of on-field participants.

The benefit game itself was not played like a typical exhibition game, which would normally be rife with numerous player substitutions and rookie tryouts. Both teams fielded starting lineups that were almost identical to those used in their previous regular season games. The only changes, except for the starting pitchers and catchers on both teams, were in the Red Sox outfield, where an injury to Tom Oliver the previous day necessitated a substitution. In a highly unusual move for an exhibition game, each club started its best pitcher—Danny MacFayden (16-12) for the Red Sox against the Braves' Ed Brandt (18-11).

Red Sox center fielder Jack Rothrock led off the game with a high fly to his counterpart, Wally Berger, who camped under the ball, lost it in the sun, and then sidestepped to assure that he wouldn't be hit in the head. Rothrock ended up on second base. Otto Miller scored Rothrock with a single to right, and advanced to third on Marv Olson's hit. Olson was then caught trying to steal second, and Earl Webb's single to left scored Miller. Four straight hits. Braves hurler Ed Brandt began to think that adding participation in a relay race to his pregame warmup routine may not have been of much help.

MacFayden held the National Leaguers hitless through the first two innings, but the Braves broke through in the third when Al Spohrer walked, stole second, and was driven home on a double by newcomer Wolters/Walters.[3] Wally Berger's hit to center tied the score at 2-2.

The score remained knotted until the sixth inning, when the teams switched from using the National League ball to the American League ball. The Braves found the AL ball to their liking. With one out, Earl Sheely walked and was replaced by pinch-runner/auctioneer Johnny Neun. Wes Schulmerich, wondering why he was not on the relay team, legged out an infield single. Neun and Schulmerich pulled off a double steal, then watched as Bill Urbanski struck out. Red Worthington then stroked a single to right-center, plating two runs, for a 4-2 Braves lead.

The Red Sox mounted a threat in the seventh inning as Bill Sweeney singled and advanced to third on Hal Rhyne's Texas Leaguer. Sweeney scored as Howie Storie grounded into a double play, bringing the score to 4-3. Neither team tallied again, and both starting pitchers closed out their work for the 1931 season with complete games.

The Braves-Red Sox event raised over $22,000 for the Unemployment Fund, the equivalent of nearly $350,000 in 2014 dollars. In each of these charity games, held across the major-league map, everything was contributed by the team management and players, with everyone entering the park paying admission, and all proceeds being turned over to the designated beneficiaries. It was believed to have been the first time that charities had received 100 percent of the receipts from any sporting event.[4]

SOURCES

Boston Globe, September 24, 1931

Boston Herald, September 23-24-25, 1931

Boston Post, September 24, 1931

Hartford Courant, September 24, 1931

New York Times, September 24, 1931

Springfield Republican, September 24, 1931

The Sporting News, October 1, 1931

Baseball-Reference.com

Bizofbaseball.com

History.com

Retrosheet.org

NOTES

1   The Red Sox were in fifth place in the American League on September 23, and they slipped one spot to finish the season in sixth place.

2   The *Boston Herald*, in its September 25 edition, reported that 19,369 tickets were sold, with 276 unused. Ticket sales amounted to $21,241, with an additional $547.50 in contributions, and $380 in the autographed-baseball auction (the actual amount was $395).

3   Fans of both teams could be forgiven if they had no idea who was playing third base for the Braves in this game. The press covering the game had problems with him, too. Most of the local papers called him "Walters," while the *Boston Daily Globe* referred to him as "Wolters." Perhaps the *Globe's* scribes thought him to be the reincarnation of former big leaguer Harry Wolter, who as a member of the New York Highlanders had played in the inaugural game at Fenway Park on Opening Day 1912. This was, in fact, Bill "Bucky" Walters, who had joined the Braves on the road a week earlier, after a stellar season at Williamsport in the New York-Penn League. He would spend several seasons, including 1933 and 1934 with the Red Sox, as an infielder, before switching to the mound and becoming one of the premier pitchers in the National League over the next decade. This September 23 benefit game was his first appearance before the Boston fans.

4   *The Sporting News*, September 24, 1931.

THE BEARDS VERSUS THE BRAVES

AUGUST 1, 1932: BOSTON BRAVES 2, HOUSE OF DAVID 1 AT BRAVES FIELD

BY BILL NOWLIN

"You shall not round off the hair on your temples or mar the edges of your beard"
—Leviticus 19:27 [1]

The House of David touring baseball team let their beards and long hair grow, because of biblical stricture and just because it made them look more like the way many have imagined Jesus and the disciples to look.

What has been described as "a minor apocalyptic cult," the House of David was a Christian commune founded in Michigan in 1903 which "sought to reunite the 12 tribes of Israel in preparation for the return of Jesus Christ at the onset of the new millennium. Members gave all their worldly possessions to the commune and were required to refrain from sex, alcohol, tobacco, and meat." Its founder, Benjamin Franklin Purnell, a "self-proclaimed messenger of God," also realized that a traveling baseball team would help spread the Word as he saw it.[2] The team barnstormed around the country into the 1940s, and proved quite successful. They even carried portable lighting with them, enabling them to play night baseball in the years well before any major-league team played under lights.

The House of David team set up their lights at Braves Field on August 1, 1932, to play an exhibition game against the Boston Braves.

The first night baseball game ever played had in fact been more than 50 years earlier—in Hull, Massachusetts, on September 2, 1880, on the grounds of the Sea Foam House at Nantasket Beach. That newfangled invention of the day, the Weston light bulb, was but three years old at the time. (Edison's first incandescent bulb was invented in 1879.) Three 100-foot-tall wooden towers were built, supporting 12 Weston lamps.[3]

By the 1930s, the House of David team would also retain advertised "ringers" such as future Hall of Famers Grover Cleveland "Pete" Alexander and Satchel Paige (years before the major leagues were desegregated). Alexander pitched for the visitors in this game at Braves Field.[4] Game time was 8:30 P.M. on August 1. It was to be, noted the *Boston Globe* in advance, "the first game ever played in artificial light at a Boston big league park."[5]

Some 2,500 came out to see Pete Alexander pitch for the House of David nine (he was the only beardless member of the team, and was quite unlikely to have abjured alcohol) against Braves right-hander Fred Frankhouse. It was about the same size crowd as had turned out for the day's afternoon regulation National League game, which had seen the St. Louis Cardinals beat the Braves, 4-2.

The lighting came from several locations—two big trucks in foul territory near first and third bases to illuminate the infield, and 80-foot poles farther down both foul lines as well as in deep right and deep center. There were 36 lights in all, in clusters, which "made things almost as bright as some days."

Umpiring were first baseman Art Shires of the Braves and a man named Lewis.

The game was one that ended with drama, though, all in all, the *Boston Herald* allowed that the game was "listless and eventless, except for the bits of comedy." The House of David team specialized in pregame Harlem Globetrotter-style stunts and acrobatics with ball, bat, and glove. The Braves' Rabbit Maranville

The Braves' Rabbit Maranville and Art Shires imitate their opponents' grooming style.

wasn't without some vaudevillian flair of his own.[6] Predictably, the comedy centered on the Rabbit as well. Before the game, he'd put on an exhibition of infielding with an imaginary ball, performing all manner of tricks. And in the third inning, Braves Wally Berger and Wes Schulmerich both came out of the dugout sporting "big, luxurious beards" while Maranville "had a towel hanging down from the side of his cap, like an Arab of the desert."

The Braves put the first run on the board, in the bottom of the first. Maranville led off and doubled to right field. With one out, he scampered to third base when Billy Urbanski hit into a fielder's choice, and then scored on Berger's fly to center.

The House of David team tied it up with one in the top of the third, when Alexander doubled and center fielder Henry LaFleur walked. An attempted sacrifice by second baseman Ralph Williams backfired and the 45-year-old Alexander was erased at third, but Frankhouse then walked the bases loaded. He struck out the next two batters, but not before LaFleur scored on a wild pitch.

A reliever named Grant (and dubbed "General" Grant or "Ulysses S." by the Boston papers for his resemblance to the former US president) took over from "Old Pete" Alexander in the bottom of the third and

held the Braves hitless until the seventh, though he'd doled out three bases on balls in the fifth, spared a run thanks to a caught stealing and a subsequent double play. Bruce Cunningham took over pitching from Frankhouse after six full. The Braves starter had given up four hits; Cunningham allowed only one hit in the final three frames.

The Braves collected only six hits; getting base hits had apparently not been easy for them in regular-season games at the time. They were robbed of one hit by House of David shortstop Gus "Buster" Blakeney, who "earned a big, generous hand" with his fielding of a ball hit by the Braves' Earl Clark.

Blakeney later committed two errors, however, which set up the winning run. In the bottom of the ninth (and let's recall this would not be a game called due to darkness), Schulmerich drove the ball to deep short; Blakeney's throw was wide of the first-base bag as "Schul" slid in safely. Randy Moore tried to sacrifice, but pitcher Grant pounced quickly and threw to second—whereupon Blakeney dropped the ball. Then it was Fritz Knothe's turn to put down a bunt. Grant grabbed that one, too, and again tried to cut down the lead runner. There was no error; his throw to third just didn't arrive in time.

The bases were loaded with nobody out, and "the obscure Johnny Benson of Whitman" came to the plate. He was a "practice catcher" who, as it happens, never did play in the major leagues (and put in only two seasons of minor-league ball, with the Ogdensburg (New York) Colts of the Canadian-American League, in 1936-37). Benson had a big night on August 1, however. Grant delivered a pitch and Benson singled to short center field, driving in the go-ahead run: a walk-off 2-1 win for the Boston Braves.[7]

The game had lasted less than two hours.

The columnist "Sportsman" of the *Boston Globe* concluded, "As a novelty, night baseball is all right. As a permanent diet its value is at least doubtful."[8] The *Boston Post* saw less prospect: "The bright lights may attract in some cases, but not for those used to big league baseball. … (T)he nocturnal sport in this neck of the woods will hardly become popular."[9]

SOURCES

The Boston daily newspapers were the source of game play information. All of the direct quotations come from the *Boston Herald* of August 2, 1932, except as noted. Thanks also to Bob LeMoine for assistance in preparing materials for this article.

NOTES

1 Leviticus, 19:27, *The Bible*. An illustrated history of the team is presented in Joel Hawkins and Terry Bertolino, *The House of David Baseball Team* (Columbia, South Carolina: Arcadia, 2000).

2 *Boston Globe*, October 27, 2013. In 1927 "Purnell stood trial for sexual assault against young girls in the commune, and for embezzlement. Five weeks after being convicted of fraud, the charismatic preacher died." The religious colony failed, but the baseball team lived on.

3 For a more complete story of this 1880 game, see Bill Nowlin, *Red Sox Threads* (Burlington, Massachusetts: Rounder Books, 2008), 364.

4 Alexander should have been a major draw. He was a 20-year major-league veteran with a record of 373-208, his wins total tying him with Christy Mathewson for the most in National League history.

5 *Boston Globe*, August 1, 1932.

6 Indeed, Maranville actually took to the stage on the Keith Circuit at one time. See Walter "Rabbit" Maranville,"Rabbit's Stage Career," in *Run, Rabbit, Run* (Phoenix: Society for American Baseball Research, 2012), 34.

7 Bob Brady of the Boston Braves Historical Association writes, "Johnny Benson was a member of the BBHA and attended a couple of our reunions. He indicated that he spent the entire 1932 season in the bullpen, never getting into a game. A shoulder injury in the minors ended his pro career, although he played semipro ball in the area. One of his semipro teams' batboys was Rocky Marciano. Benson met Ted Williams while making deliveries to Ted's baseball camp in Lakeville." E-mail from Bob Brady, October 22, 2014. Benson himself said, "I'm always embarrassed when I'm introduced as Johnny Benson, a catcher for the Braves, because I never even got into a major league game. All I did was warm up the pitchers." When he was introduced to Ted Williams as a former Brave, he said, "I was only a bullpen catcher." "Don't put yourself down," Williams said, with that blustery good will he was known for, then turning to the other people in the room he added, "this man was in the big leagues at a time when there were only 16 major league teams. You had to be good to just get there." *The Patriot Ledger* (Quincy, Massachusetts), April 29/30, 2000.

8 *Boston Globe*, August 2, 1932.

9 *Boston Post*, August 2, 1932.

NFL BOSTON BRAVES VERSUS NFL NEW YORK GIANTS

OCTOBER 9, 1932: BOSTON BRAVES 14, NEW YORK GIANTS 6, AT BRAVES FIELD

BY CHIP GREENE

As the 1932 National Football League season began, there was reason for excitement among Boston's sports fans. Since the Boston Bulldogs folded after their lone season in 1929,[1] Boston had been without an entry in the 12-year-old NFL. However, in July 1932, a syndicate headed by George Preston Marshall, a laundry tycoon from Washington, D.C., was awarded a team in Boston, and they joined the Chicago Cardinals, Chicago Bears, Staten Island Stapletons, Green Bay Packers, Brooklyn Dodgers, New York Giants, and Portsmouth Spartans to form a revamped league.[2]

The new team cost the Marshall syndicate nothing; all the owners had to do was pay the operating expenses. (Seventy years later, *Forbes* magazine estimated the team's value at $1.55 billion.[3]) As Marshall made marketing plans, he contracted with Boston's National League baseball team, the Braves, for the use of their ballpark, Braves Field; and he also borrowed their name. In 1932 the Boston Braves joined the NFL.

To coach, Marshall hired J.R. Ludlow "Lud" Wray, a former University of Pennsylvania center who had played in the NFL during the early 1920s; and to sign players, the laundry king searched far and wide, sparing no expense. From Washington State University, he obtained for the lavish sum of $1,500 All-American tackle Albert Glen "Turk" Edwards, who had been sought by several NFL teams; from the University of Southern California, Marshall signed running backs Ernie Pinckert and Jim Musick; and from little-known West Virginia Wesleyan College, he recruited a dynamic runner named Cliff Battles. Both Edwards

and Battles were later enshrined in the NFL Hall of Fame.

As the Braves roster began to take shape, the team held training camp in Lynn, Massachusetts, a couple of towns away from Boston, and played exhibition games around Boston; they defeated teams from Quincy and Beverly, but lost to the Providence Steam Roller, a former NFL entry, which featured several players previously cut by the Braves. Throughout, Marshall hyped the team, promising in Boston's local dailies to provide quality football at bargain prices. He was true to his word, too, as ticket prices were 55 cents for the Braves Field bleachers, $1.10 for the grandstands, and $1.65 for box seats. A man of fabulous wealth, Marshall knew how to give the fans what they wanted.

On October 2, 1932, the Braves, adorned in blue and gold uniforms, the colors of Marshall's Palace Laundry empire, played their inaugural game, at home, versus the Brooklyn Dodgers. The previous season, Brooklyn had finished ninth in the league, with a record of 2-12-0. Behind their new coach, future NFL Hall of Famer Benny Friedman, the Dodgers shut out the Braves, 14-0, the first of just three wins the Dodgers garnered that year. A week later, the Braves were scheduled to play the New York Giants, who promised to be even more challenging. Much to Marshall's pleasure, though, this time his team produced a much different outcome.

October 9 was a sickly hot day in Boston. At Braves Field an estimated 10,000 fans endured the heat to watch the Braves take on the Giants. If those fans

"Red" Grange of the Chicago Bears practices his placekicking before a game against the Braves at the Wigwam.

hoped for a change in their team's fortunes, they must have been aghast when Pinckert fumbled the opening kickoff and the Giants recovered, beginning their first drive at the Boston 35-yard line.[4] Shortly, though, the Giants, too, fumbled, and Jim Musick recovered, giving the ball right back to Boston. Thus began a back-and-forth first quarter during which both teams moved the ball with hard running and timely passing, only to encounter staunch defenses that brought about a flurry of punts.

As the clock wound down in the first quarter, the Braves finally found creases in the Giants' defensive line. Beginning at their own 40-yard line, Musick, Pinckert, and Henry "Honolulu" Hughes, the Braves' bruising fullback and kicker from Oregon State, via the Hawaiian Islands, alternately ran hard and moved the ball for a first down at the New York 26-yard line. As time expired in the quarter, with the two teams in a scoreless tie, the Braves seemed poised to capitalize on their first scoring opportunity of the afternoon.

With the teams reversing direction in the second quarter, the Braves continued their march to the end zone. Beginning the period, Musick carried twice to the Giants' 17 yard-line. Over the next three plays, wingback Oren Pape, Pinckert, and Hughes each carried, but amassed only five more yards. Then, on a rare pass, Pape hit Pinckert, who advanced to the

6-yard line for a first down and goal to go. From there, Musick again crashed the line, fumbled, but recovered, resulting in a yard gain. Next, Pape drove forward to the 2, and finally, Musick sliced over the line for a touchdown. Hughes kicked the extra point, and the Braves led, 7-0.

The Giants quickly answered; after returning the kickoff to their own 43, New York proceeded to amass four first downs that delivered them to the Braves' goal line. First, 5-foot-11-inch, 200-pound Giants end Glenn Campbell hauled in a pass and advanced nine yards, before he was leveled by the Braves' diminutive Tony Siano; the Waltham (Massachusetts) High School and Fordham graduate stood just 5-feet-8-inches tall and weighed 172 pounds. Next, Boston's own Jack Hagerty, from nearby Dorchester High School, and Georgetown University, maneuvered the Giants to the Braves' 35-yard line. From there, John "Shipwreck" Kelly, Dale Burnett, and Elwin "Tiny" Feather, who was anything but, at 6-feet tall and 197 pounds, carried the ball to Boston's 7-yard line.

Here, a rare substitution cost the Braves five yards. With one of his players tiring, coach Wray inserted second-string lineman Russell Peterson. In those days, such a move was a penalty, so the ball was placed at the 2. Impressively, the Braves held, as Peterson led the defensive line to stiffen, stopping Shipwreck Kelly on three successive carries which resulted in a gain of just one yard.

It was fourth down and one yard to go for the Giants.

In 1981 Morris "Red" Badgro, then 78 years old, was elected to the NFL Hall of Fame. A two-way end, in 1934 Badgro would lead the league in receptions, with 16. On this day, Badgro lined up at the 1 for the Giants, and immediately ran along the goal line. Deep in the Giants' backfield, Jack Hagerty spotted the tall receiver, rifled a pass diagonally across the goal line, and Badgro snared it for a touchdown. However, Boston's Oren Pape blocked Hagerty's extra-point attempt, and the Giants trailed, 7-6. With time running out in the quarter, "Honolulu" Hughes later attempted a field goal for the Braves, but it sailed wide of the goal posts.

So the Braves took their one point lead to the locker room.

Despite the powerful running of Giants' fullback and former Army runner Chris "Red" Cagle, who three times led New York's advance deep into Boston territory, the third quarter produced no scoring: twice the Giants fumbled, and the third time the Braves stopped them at Boston's 5-yard line. With the score still 7-6, Braves, the fourth quarter ensued.

Again, the Giants' ground attack proved lethal. As the Braves continually failed to advance the ball, Hughes punted them out of trouble, only to have New York drive the ball down the field. Finally, though, the Giants' offense made a mistake. After yet another Hughes punt, the Giants started deep in their own territory. Quickly, they moved the ball to midfield. Then disaster struck. At the 50-yard line, Hagerty threw a two-yard toss to end Ray Flaherty, who four years later joined Boston and began a Hall of Fame coaching career. Immediately, Flaherty attempted to lateral the ball to Cagle, sprinting around the end, but the Braves' Myers "Algy" Clark stepped in front of Cagle, intercepted the ball, and returned it untouched 55 yards for a score. Hughes's point after kick was good, and the Braves led, 14-6. Shipwreck Kelly and Red Cagle continued the Giants' attack, leading New York to five first downs, but couldn't advance beyond Boston's 17-yard line. On the Giants' final drive of the day, Hughes intercepted a pass, and time expired.

The Braves had scored the franchise's first victory.

The next season Marshall's partners relinquished their ownership stakes, leaving him fully in charge of the team. After the exit of coach Wray, Marshall hired a Native American named William "Lone Star" Dietz as his replacement. In recognition, Marshall changed the team's name to the Redskins and their colors to burgundy and gold. He also moved the Redskins to Fenway Park, where they played through the 1936 season. Throughout, Marshall was never able to cultivate a fan base, and attendance suffered. When the Redskins won the NFL's Eastern Division in 1936, the championship game against the Western Division champion Packers was held at the Polo Grounds, in New York City.

In 1937 Marshall moved the Redskins to his hometown of Washington, D.C.

Seventy-seven years later, they were still there.

SOURCES

Smith, Thomas W., *Showdown: JFK and the Integration of the Washington Redskins*, (Boston: Beacon Press, 2011).

Boston Herald

Boston Globe

Boston Post

pro-football-reference.com

NOTES

1   From 1925-28, the Bulldogs had been the Pottsville Maroons. Following the '28 season, the Maroons were purchased by a Boston syndicate and relocated to Boston for 1929, but had folded after that lone abbreviated season, the only one in which the city had been represented since the NFL's formation in 1920.

2   Among the 10 teams who competed in 1931, the Providence Steam Roller, Cleveland Indians, and Frankford Yellow Jackets were no longer members of the NFL. Boston's addition restored the league to eight teams.

3   Thomas W. Smith. *Showdown: JFK and the Integration of the Washington Redskins*, (Boston: Beacon Press, 2011), ebook version, 12.

4   In researching this article, the author utilized multiple daily periodicals. With few exceptions, each periodical differed with respect to attendance figures, yardages and sometimes, even the identify of players. Such was the novelty of football reporting at time. Where possible, the figure most often quoted is used as the primary source.

BERGER'S BASH MEANS CASH

OCTOBER 1, 1933: BOSTON BRAVES 4, PHILADELPHIA PHILLIES 1 AT BRAVES FIELD

BY SAUL WISNIA

It didn't have nearly the impact of Bobby Thomson's pennant-winning home run or the World Series-winning blasts of Bill Mazeroski and Joe Carter, but for the perennially weak Boston Braves of the 1920s and '30s, Wally Berger's pinch-hit grand slam on the final day of the 1933 season was worthy of bold-face headlines and its own nickname: "The $10,000 homer."

The monetary significance was a sign of the times. While "finishing in the first division" is not a term familiar to most baseball fans born in the era of four- and six-division baseball, for many years this goal was an important one for major-league teams. Before the American and National Leagues were broken into East and West divisions in 1969, clubs finishing in the first division — the upper half (or top five) of the 10-team AL and NL — received a portion of the "Players Pool" money funded by gate receipts of that year's World Series. From 1901 to 1960, when both leagues had eight teams, the upper half corresponded to the top *four* clubs in each circuit.

Logically, the higher you finished in the first division, the greater a percentage of the World Series loot your team collected. Since players then almost all had offseason jobs to make ends meet, this extra cash meant a lot — and thus the difference between fourth and fifth place did as well. Strong teams like the Yankees and Cardinals routinely got a piece of the pie, but from 1922 to 1932 the Braves received nether a sliver with 11 consecutive seasons in fifth place or lower.[1]

In 1933, however, Boston made a spirited late-season run not only for the first division, but for the NL championship. Under .500 as late as July 30, the Tribe used a 22-6 August to climb to second place heading into a huge six-game series at home against the league-leading New York Giants. Nearly 160,000 fans packed Braves Field for the contests — more than one quarter of the team's total attendance for their 77 home dates — but the Giants won four of five (with one tie) to drop Boston nine games back.

That started a tailspin that soon had the Braves in fifth place, and a bout of pneumonia that knocked their leading hitter (Berger) out of the lineup for three weeks down the stretch kept them from rebounding. Boston remained in fifth heading into the season finale at Braves Field against the Philadelphia Phillies on October 1, and although a still-weak Berger had emerged from a Pittsburgh hospital bed to rejoin the club, he was in street clothes on the bench at game's start.

Berger, however, was itching to get back into uniform. The starting pitcher for Philadelphia was Reggie Grabowski; two weeks before, after being discharged from the hospital, Berger had spent his last afternoon in Pittsburgh watching the young right-hander pitch a complete game against the Pirates at Forbes Field. "I sat right behind home plate to see what kind of stuff he had," Berger told author and SABR member Richard "Dick" Beverage during a July 1988 video interview, conducted five months before Berger died at 83. "I saw a little curve and I said, 'Yup, that's what he's got.'"[2]

The slugger-turned-spectator stored away the knowledge, and looked forward to hitting against Grabowski in the future. He assumed that would be next season, but suddenly the future was now. Boston was just a half-game behind the fourth-place St. Louis Cardinals, and a Braves win coupled with a Cardinals loss to the Chicago Cubs would clinch fourth place—and the first-division money that came with it—for Boston. Braves manager Bill McKechnie likely would not have thought of letting Berger play if this were not the case, but in the fourth inning he allowed his slugger to suit up. Berger, after all, had 26 of the team's 53 home runs and 102 of its 507 RBIs to go along with his .311 batting average, and a fourth-place finish would mean hundreds of dollars for each player—a good chunk of the average major leaguer's salary at the time—as well as a hefty $5,000 bonus for McKechnie.

While the manager waited for the perfect opportunity to get Berger in, the game stayed tight most of the day. The Phillies scored a run in the third off Braves starter Ed Brandt, and still led 1-0 behind Grabowski heading into the bottom of the seventh. Boston started the frame strong, as Baxter Jordan and Randy Moore both singled, but Pinky Whitney struck out and Hal Lee grounded to first, advancing the runners to second and third. Grabowski now intentionally walked catcher Shanty Hogan, a logical move in that it set up an out at any base and brought shortstop Walter "Rabbit" Maranville to the plate.

Maranville was a .218 hitter near the end of his Hall of Fame career, and McKechnie figured this might be his best chance to use Berger. He called Rabbit back, sent Berger up to pinch-hit, and put Ben Cantwell in at first base to run for Hogan. Berger's broad back flashed his familiar number 3 as he carried several bats to the plate, and then flung all but one aside. "They came out to talk with him [Grabowski]," Berger told Beverage, "and I just *know* he's going to come in with that dinky little curve."

Berger swung and missed on Grabowski's first pitch, losing his grip and sending his bat flying, but managed to work the count to 2-and-2. Then, according to Gerry Hern of the *Boston Post*, Grabowski "tried to push an inside pitch through the slot for the third strike"[3] and Berger met the anticipated dinky little curve dead on. The ball sailed into the left-field stands for a grand slam, and the crowd and bench erupted. Maranville

Braves slugger Wally Berger.

greeted the still-sick hero at home plate with a hug and a kiss on each cheek, and the rest of the team joined in the on-field celebration—a very unusual scene in this era for a game not yet completed. "It certainly was the most dramatic incident seen in a game in Boston in years," wrote James O'Leary in the *Boston Globe*, "and the tumult lasted for five minutes or more."[4]

That was it for the Braves offense, but it was enough. Bob Smith, who had come on in relief in the sixth when Brandt hurt his leg fielding a bunt, held Philadelphia scoreless the rest of the way. The Cardinals still had to lose for fourth place to be Boston's, so many of the 4,000 fans at Braves Field stayed in the ballpark until news of the final score (7-1, Cubs) came in from St. Louis. The reaction by the crowd, especially since there would be no postseason games coming for the home club, underscored just how lean a period

An after-game chat between Berger and Manager
McKechnie.

the previous 15 years had been for Hub baseball fans
saddled with awful Braves and Red Sox teams.

Along with the pride that came with helping the club
to its best record (83-71) in 12 years, each Braves player
now also knew he had a check coming. Front-page
headlines the next day in Boston's several daily newspapers varied in predicting exactly how much the
homer would be worth in bonus money, since the total
amount was predicated on attendance in the World
Series yet to be played. The *Post* called it "the $10,000
HOMER," the *Boston Herald* deemed it a "$15,000
HOME RUN," and the *Globe* noted it worthy of
"$10,000 of Series Spoils." In the end, it would actually
be worth $7,100 to the players—or $242.82 for
each—along with $5,000 for future Hall of Fame
skipper McKechnie out of the Braves' coffers.

Over the years, the aura around Berger's blast grew.
Later accounts claimed that he had announced to
McKechnie in front of the entire dugout earlier in
the game that he wanted just one at-bat against
Grabowski. "If he throws that curveball over the plate,"
Berger supposedly stated, "I'll hit it out of the park."[5]
He never mentioned such a boast in his interview
with Beverage, but Berger clearly delighted in retelling
the story.

So did the guy whom Berger's shot hurt the most.
The Braves would later field better teams in Boston
than this one, including the 1948 National League
champions. But for Judge Emil Fuchs, who owned
the Braves from 1923 to 1935, the '33 finale would remain
his favorite all-time game—albeit in expensive one.
"One of the biggest thrills I ever got out of baseball
cost the Braves $5,000, but I always regarded it as well
worth it," Fuchs later wrote in one of a series of guest
columns he did for the *Globe,* referring to the bonus
he paid his manager. "I recall having a hat and cane.
The first thing I knew [when Berger homered] both
were flying high in the air. I tossed them as high as I
could. I never paid out $5,000 more readily or received
so much happiness than when I gave that check
to Bill!"[6]

SOURCES

Beverage, Dick. Video interview with Wally Berger at Berger's
Redondo Beach, California, home, July 27, 1988.

Boston Globe, "Babe Ruth and Berger Heroes on Final Day,"
October 2, 1933.

Boston Herald, "Berger Wallops $15,000 Home Run With Bases
Full," October 2, 1933.

Boston Post, "Berger Slams $10,000 Homer," October 2, 1933.

Caruso, Gary. *The Braves Encyclopedia* (Philadelphia: Temple
University Press, 1995).

Fuchs, Judge Emil. "Berger 'Earns' $5000 for Boss," *Boston Globe,*
December 22, 1942.

Kaese, Harold. *The Boston Braves* (New York: Putnam Press, 1948).

Klapisch, Bob, and Pete Van Wieren. *The World Champion Braves: 125
Years of America's Team* (Atlanta: Turner Publishing, 1995).

NOTES

1   According to Robert S. Fuchs (the Judge's son) and Wayne Soini
    in *Judge Fuchs and the Boston Braves*, the players had an additional
    incentive for striving for the players' pool money. "Everyone on
    the team, including the owner, the Judge, took a pay cut in 1933
    down 10 or 20 percent. Berger dropped from $10,000 to $9,000.
    The cuts, justified or not, were inflicted with the stated proposi-
    tion that they would be made up for if attendance at Braves
    Field in 1933 was as good as 1932. It was not, but the Judge wrote
    Berger before the end of August: 'I believe your spirit and the
    spirit of the club has done so much for Boston and the Braves
    that irrespective of whether or not [the 1932 level] is reached, I
    feel it is justly due to you for me to reinstate the amount of your

1932 contract, and you will receive the proportionate amount of your cut in your salary check on the various pay days left this year. The first check to have the added share will be your salary check of September 1st." (See Robert S. Fuchs and Wayne Soini, *Judge Fuchs and the Boston Braves, 1923-1935* (Jefferson, North Carolina: McFarland & Co., Inc., 1998), 100. According to the authors, Berger constantly felt that he was being underpaid and engaged management accordingly in negotiations. "In 1933, when everybody was taking cuts, he argued that he had expected a raise: 'I will sign for the same salary as last year and consider that I have received a pay cut.'" Correspondence relating to these negotiations can be found in Appendix B of the book at 139-152.

2   Dick Beverage video interview with Wally Berger at Berger's Redondo Beach, California, home, July 27, 1988.

3   Gerry Hern, "Berger Slams $10,000 Homer," *Boston Post*, October 2, 1933.

4   James O'Leary, "Babe Ruth and Berger Heroes on Final Day," *Boston Globe*, October 2, 1933. Former Knot Hole Gang member Philip Gates retained his membership card into adulthood as one of his most prized possessions. Fuchs and Soini wrote, "With the card and a nickel, a Knot Hole Gang member would have a seat over in the third base pavilion near left field, where the bullpen crews warmed up before and during the games. The cards were passports for thousands of youngsters at a time of tight family budgets. For one nickel Philip Gates saw something he remembered the rest of his life. 'I remember Wally Berger,' he said, 'hitting the grand slam in the final game of the 1933 season, which lifted the Braves into the First Division! Unheard of heights!'" Fuchs and Soini, 92.

5   Harold Kaese, *The Boston Braves* (New York: Putnam Press, 1948, republished by Northeastern University Press, 2004), 222-223.

6   Judge Emil Fuchs, "Berger 'Earns' $5000 for Boss," *Boston Globe*, December 22, 1942. Fuchs recalled, "I was sitting in the bleachers with Sidney Rabb, who headed the Stop & Shop supermarket chain. Sidney was not only a stockholder of the Braves but a close personal friend. In the last part of the game, the Braves were behind. With bases loaded, McKechnie called upon Wally Berger. Berger, though one of our great hitters, had had a severe cold but that day put on his uniform and an overcoat, suffering from a fever with a temperature of 102. Nonetheless, he took the first pitch and hit it into the bleachers for a home run. I was among many who cheered without restraint, taking my cane and hat and waving them around with enthusiasm. Afterward, Sidney said to me, 'Judge, you are a baseball fan but a bad business man. Don't you know that hit will cost you $5,000?' He knew, of course, about a clause in our contract with McKechnie, providing him with a nice bonus if the team finished in the first division." Fuchs and Soini, 87-88.

THE BABE RETURNS TO BOSTON AS A BRAVE

APRIL 16, 1935: BOSTON BRAVES 4, NEW YORK GIANTS 2

BY SCOTT FERKOVICH

The uniform seemed strange.

Gone were the Yankee pinstripes and the interlocking "NY" on the left breast. The jersey that Babe Ruth buttoned over his considerable paunch was that of the Boston Braves, his new team. "Trimmed with red piping, (it) looked comical and cheap after the sober Yankee garb he had worn for so long," Robert Creamer wrote decades later.[1] It was April 16, 1935. The setting was Braves Field. Opening Day was always a festive occasion, but this one was extra-special. After 15 seasons with the Bronx Bombers, The Babe was once again calling Boston home, albeit this time as a National Leaguer.

A lot had happened since Ruth had been traded from the Red Sox to New York after the 1919 campaign. Back then, Wilson was in the White House, and the nation was on the cusp of the economic prosperity and good times of the Roaring Twenties. And a young Ruth was primed to lead a Yankee dynasty to four World Series championships, as the most dominant slugger the game had ever seen.

Things were different now. The party was over, as the nation was in the middle of the throes of the Great Depression. Franklin Delano Roosevelt was commander-in-chief. As for Ruth, he had recently turned 40, and tipped the scales at 245 pounds. He was coming off a season in the Bronx that had seen his numbers decline precipitously (22 home runs, 84 RBIs, and a .288 batting average). After that, it was clear the Yankees were no longer interested in his services.

The acquisition of Ruth by the Braves in February was a sentimental one by the locals. The Braves (and the Red Sox as well) had suffered on the field and at the gate for over a decade. If nothing else, the return of the Bambino to Beantown would give baseball fans a reason to come out to the ballpark. For how long was anybody's guess. The Braves owner, Judge Emil Fuchs, along with Yankees owner Jacob Ruppert, arranged for Ruth's release from the Yankees. Fuchs then signed Ruth, with the carrot that he could one day become manager of the Braves, not to mention part-owner. Ruth, who had managerial aspirations, jumped at the opportunity. The Sultan of Swat was also named a Braves executive, largely in a goodwill-ambassador capacity.

Despite the near-freezing April weather, a crowd of almost 22,000 made their way to the Wigwam. "There was little doubt," wrote Hy Hurwitz in the *Boston Globe*, "that every man, woman, and child in the gathering was on hand to see the Babe."[2] With game time approaching and snow falling, a band played "Jingle Bells." "Presentations were made, speeches were de-

Fuchs, Ruth, and Ruppert announce the Bambino's Braves signing.

livered, (and) cannon fired their resounding salute," noted the *Boston Post*.[3] Manager Bill McKechnie, filling out his lineup card, wrote Ruth's name in the third slot, playing left field, behind second baseman Les Mallon and ahead of center fielder Wally Berger. (Berger, the Braves' own "Babe Ruth," had deferred to the Bambino and gave him his uniform number 3, which Ruth had worn with New York. Berger chose number 4 as his replacement.) Opposing the Braves were Bill Terry's New York Giants, who started left-hander Carl Hubbell, winner of 44 games the previous two seasons. Boston sent southpaw Ed Brandt, who had gone 68-55 for the Braves since becoming a full-time starter in 1931.

The big moment arrived in the bottom of the first. With Billy Urbanski on second base with one out, the Babe strode to the plate "amid a storm of applause."[4] On a one-ball count, Ruth sent Hubbell's next offering on a line through the legs of Terry at first base, as Urbanski raced home with the first run of the season for the Braves. "The multitude lifted a hymn of praise for the Babe," wrote Burt Whitman in the *Boston Herald*.[5]

In the top of the fifth, Ruth showed that he could still work magic with his glove as well. With two outs and Mark Koenig on first, Hubbell came up to bat. King Carl popped a ball to short left field, near the line, that seemed certain to land as a Texas Leaguer. Ruth, "chugging along like a coasting truck," reached out and down with his glove hand to snare the ball, to the delirious cheers of the crowd.[6]

The Bambino, who had fanned in the second frame, faced Hubbell again in the fifth, "with the crowd begging for a home run."[7] Having run the count to 2-and-2, Ruth swung at a Hubbell screwball, launching a towering drive to right field. Mel Ott sprinted back to the wall, but to no avail. The ball landed a dozen feet up the concrete runway between the pavilion and the Jury Box, caught by a policeman on one bounce. It was the 709th home run of Ruth's career, his first in the National League, and made the score 4-0. The Braves Field faithful erupted in pandemonium.

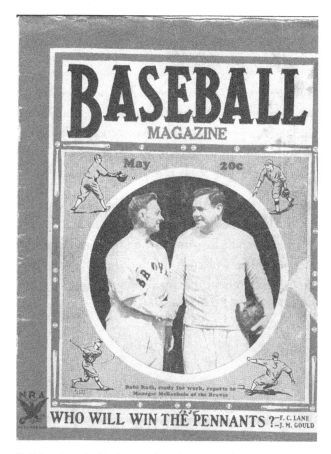

Ruth's return to Boston worthy of a cover story.

"As (Ruth) trotted happily around third base," wrote Whitman, "McKechnie chased him and wrung his hand. (Ruth's) wide boyish grin was on his face as he crossed the plate and doffed his cap to his new subjects. He may not be the man he once was, but he still totes around enough punch to help the Braves."[8]

Enthusiastically watching from a box seat were Ruth's wife, Claire, and his stepdaughter, Julia. The Bambino's home run was an early gift to Claire for their sixth wedding anniversary, which was to be the next day. "This one's for the old lady," he shouted as he trotted back to the dugout.[9]

Ruth's final at-bat of the game came in the seventh, against lefty Al Smith. He struck out on three pitches, and was taken out of the game in the top of the eighth, Tommy Thompson taking over in left. The final score was Braves 4, Giants 2.

"Naturally I was greatly thrilled at his first game in the National League," Mrs. Ruth gushed after the contest. "And especially here in Boston, the city he has always loved. The applause was wonderful and he loved it."[10]

Bill Carrigan, Ruth's manager when he broke in with the Red Sox back in 1914, was at the game. "You'd think it was part of a story," he commented, referring to Ruth's home run. "Babe never hit the ball any harder during the height of his career than he did today."[11]

Ruth held court with reporters at his locker after the game. "I didn't even dream I'd get off to such a start. (It) sure overshadows my first game as an American Leaguer when I pitched the Red Sox to a 3 to 2 win over the Cleveland Indians."[12] Actually, the Red Sox beat Cleveland by the score of 4-3.

The day had belonged to Ruth, who went 2-for-4 with three RBIs and two runs scored. He had figured in all four of Boston's runs. Brandt was the winning pitcher, surrendering only five hits in a complete game. It was one of the few bright spots of Brandt's summer, as he finished at 5-19, with an ERA of 5.00. Hubbell took the loss, but he went on to his third straight 20-win season in 1935.

For Ruth, there simply was not much left in the tank. He hit only five more home runs for the Braves. In June, after realizing that Judge Fuchs only wanted him around to put fannies in the seats, and had no plans to make him manager, Boston's prodigal son announced his retirement, having hit .181 in 28 games.

NOTES

1   Robert Creamer, *Babe: The Legend Comes to Life* (New York: Fireside, 1992), 392.

2   Hy Hurwitz, "Ruth Gets Homer to Delight Fans," *Boston Globe*, April 17, 1935, 28.

3   "Ruth Wins Game for Braves, 4-2," *Boston Post*, April 17, 1935, 18.

4   "Babe Ruth Makes Great Debut as a Boston Brave," *Christian Science Monitor*, April 17, 1935, 13.

5   Burt Whitman, "Ruth's Homer Gives Braves 4-2 Victory," *Boston Herald*, April 17, 1935, 1.

6   Ibid.

7   Ibid.

8   Ibid.

9   Ibid.

10 "Babe Provides His Wife With Plenty of Thrills," *Boston Post*, April 17, 1935, 18.

11 Hurwitz

12 Ibid.

Ruth in his Opening Day apparel.

THE AFTERNOON THE STARS CAME OUT IN BOSTON: THE 1936 ALL-STAR GAME

JULY 7, 1936: NATIONAL LEAGUE 4, AMERICAN LEAGUE 3 AT NATIONAL LEAGUE PARK

BY LYLE SPATZ

Brilliant pitching by Dizzy Dean, Carl Hubbell, and Lon Warneke led the National League to its first All-Star win. The 4-3 triumph was played in 89-degree weather, Boston's hottest July 7 since 1883. However, while thousands of Bostonians chose to spend the day at nearby beaches, it was not the weather that was responsible for the disappointingly small crowd of 25,534. Nor was it, as some said, that because baseball people had treated the last two games as meaningless exhibitions, the fans just weren't interested.

The reason for the poor turnout—it remains the lowest-ever attendance at an All-Star game—was poor planning. The Bees had announced that they'd sold 17,000 reserved seats and would put the remaining 25,000 unreserved seats on sale the morning of the game. (During the winter the Boston club had changed its name from Braves to Bees. Braves Field was now officially called National League Park, although informally it was known as Bees Field or just the Beehive.)

Club president Bob Quinn had said he expected a crowd of about 42,000. Boston club officials notified the public that to reduce congestion on game day, the Babcock Street entrances to the park would be open for the first time. Nevertheless, fans purchased fewer than 9,000 of those unreserved seats. Evidently, Bostonians had decided they didn't want to wait in what they assumed would be long ticket lines on such a hot day. Of course those lines never materialized, and large portions of the left- and right-field bleachers remained unoccupied. The real victim of the low turnout was the Association of Professional Baseball Players of America, which received 83½ percent of the proceeds from the game.

Although Boston was a two-team city, the crowd was decidedly rooting for the National Leaguers, who as usual were the underdogs. "We admit the American League power at bat, but we're going to combat it by great pitching, by speed, and by generally tight defense," said National League manager Charlie Grimm. "And we are not sparing our horses in our effort to win this game."[1] That last sentiment was in line with National League President Ford Frick's position. Frick, stung by three straight losses, felt that in the last two games his league had not always put its best players on the field.

Grimm named two starters strictly because of their superior defensive abilities. He started St. Louis's Leo Durocher at shortstop ahead of Pittsburgh's Arky Vaughan, the league's defending batting champion and the fans' choice, and his own Augie Galan in center, over many other outfielders who received more votes. The leagues had increased the size of the roster from 20 to 21, still, the National League had some surprising omissions. Neither Philadelphia's Dolph Camilli nor Boston's Buck Jordan, the top two in the National League batting race, made the team; nor did the eventual batting champion, Pittsburgh's Paul Waner.[2]

True to his word not to "spare the horses," Grimm made only two nonpitching substitutions in the game. Both were in the eighth inning, when Mel Ott batted for right fielder Frank Demaree, and Lew Riggs batted for third baseman Pinky Whitney.

Press pass to Boston's first All-Star Game.

American League manager Joe McCarthy took a different approach. He said he would try to start the lineup that the fans favored and to play as many men as possible. While Grimm's strategy worked, it left many Bees fans disgruntled. Wally Berger, their only representative and the starting center fielder in the three previous All-Star games, didn't get to play. In addition to Galan, Grimm had three more of his Cubs in the starting lineup, along with four players from the Cardinals and one from the Phillies.

Not surprising for a team that entered the break with a 10-game lead, McCarthy had seven of his Yankees on the squad and easily could have had nine. Red Rolfe, generally considered the league's best third baseman, wasn't chosen, and Washington outfielder Ben Chapman had been a Yankee before they'd traded him to the Senators three weeks earlier. McCarthy chose to put just two of his Yankees in the starting lineup: first baseman Lou Gehrig, the league's leading hitter, and 21-year-old Joe DiMaggio, the first rookie ever to start an All-Star Game. In fact, DiMaggio was the first rookie ever named by either league to its All-Star squad. McCarthy's selection of Lefty Grove of Boston, the fans' choice, as his starting pitcher, ended the run of three consecutive starts by his own ace, Lefty Gomez.

Detroit had repeated as American League pennant-winners in 1935, which would have given the Tigers' manager, Mickey Cochrane, winner of the 1935 game, the privilege of again managing his league's entry. However, Cochrane was in Wyoming recuperating from a nervous breakdown, and because the Yankees were in first place and had finished second to the

Tigers in 1935, the league named McCarthy to take his place. It was the first All-Star appearance for both McCarthy and Grimm, although they had each led their teams to pennants in 1932. Had it not been for the sentimental choices of Connie Mack and John McGraw, McCarthy and Grimm might have been the managers in the first All-Star Game.

Grimm picked Dean, the majors' winningest pitcher at 14-4, to start. Dean responded with an overpowering performance, pitching three hitless innings and not allowing a ball out of the infield. He did walk two batters, but faced just the minimum nine batters as both runners were erased on the basepaths.

Dean got two quick strikes on Luke Appling, the game's first batter, before walking him. He was retired when DiMaggio bounced into a double play. The crowd had given DiMaggio a big hand when he stepped in, but it would be a very disappointing day for the Yankees' rookie sensation. He batted five times in this game, each time with one or more runners on base, and failed to get a hit or drive in a run. He also had his problems in the field. His error on a single by Billy Herman in the fifth allowed Herman to take second, drawing some boos from the crowd. Three innings earlier, he'd misplayed into a triple Gabby Hartnett's low line drive that most observers felt he should have caught, or at worst held to a single. Red Sox manager Joe Cronin, a spectator at the game, said afterwards that DiMaggio had played the ball "a trifle nonchalantly."[3] DiMaggio made no excuses, saying the ball just sunk on him. He also, no doubt, never forgot the criticism.

Hartnett's second-inning triple, following a leadoff single by Demaree and preceding Whitney's scoring fly ball, gave the National League an early two-run lead against Grove. The Nationals added two more in the fifth against Detroit's Schoolboy Rowe. With one out, Galan, now turned around to bat left-handed, homered off the flagpole in right field. After hitting the pole, which separated fair and foul territory, the ball caromed into foul ground. The American Leaguers protested, claiming it should be a grounds-rule double, the ruling for such hits in many AL parks. The umpires (coincidentally three of whom, Bill Stewart, Beans Reardon, and Bill Summers, were Massachusetts natives) correctly stayed with their ruling of a home run. Herman's single and advancement to second on DiMaggio's error followed, and after Collins walked, Joe Medwick scored Herman with a single to left.

Meanwhile, Hubbell, the Giants' great left-hander, replaced Dean in the fourth and continued the mastery over the American Leaguers he'd shown at the Polo Grounds in 1934. He pitched three more scoreless innings, allowing just two singles and a walk. In the seventh, still leading 4-0, Grimm called on Cubs right-hander Curt Davis to wind it up. Gehrig, hitless in 10 previous All-Star at-bats, greeted him with a long home run to right. Two outs later the Americans loaded the bases on singles by Goose Goslin and Jimmie Foxx and a walk to George Selkirk. Appling's single to right scored Goslin and Foxx, making the score 4-3 and finishing Davis.

Grimm brought in Lon Warneke, another of his Cubs pitchers, who walked Charlie Gehringer to reload the bases. That brought DiMaggio to the plate with a chance to redeem himself. He didn't, but only because

Durocher was standing in the right place and managed to hold on to a scorching line drive that appeared headed safely to left field. The American Leaguers mounted another rally in the eighth. They had runners at first and third with two out and Foxx at the plate. But Foxx, already immensely popular in his first season in Boston, struck out. A final chance came in the ninth when Gehringer doubled with two outs. Once again DiMaggio came up with a chance to tie the score, but Joe popped weakly to Herman to end the game.

SOURCES

This game account largely comes from Vincent, David, Lyle Spatz, and David W. Smith, *The Midsummer Classic: The Complete History of Baseball's All-Star Game* (Lincoln: University of Nebraska Press, 2001).

NOTES

1   *Boston Herald*, July 7, 1936, 12.

2   The 21-man rosters consisted of 16 players chosen by the fans and five chosen by the managers. The fans' 16 comprised included four pitchers, two catchers, five infielders, and five outfielders. The managers could not have more than two pitchers in their five selections.

3   *Boston Herald*, July 8, 1936, 18.

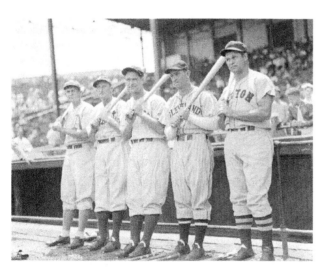

AL All-Stars Higgins, Goslin, Gehrig, Averill, and Foxx at the Beehive.

THE HIVE HOSTS INTEGRATED BASEBALL

JULY 6, 1938: BOSTON ROYAL GIANTS 4, HOUSE OF DAVID 3 AT NATIONAL LEAGUE BASEBALL FIELD

BY BILL NOWLIN

Bob Quinn owned the Boston Red Sox from 1923 into 1933. In 1936 he became president of the Boston Braves and renamed them the Bees, changing the name of the ballpark from Braves Field to National League Baseball Park. More imaginative locals called the place the Beehive. Some continued to call it Braves Field. African American journalist Doc Kountze paid Quinn a visit in 1938, and Quinn foresaw the end of segregation in baseball. The two, wrote Kountze later, "talked about bringing Colored teams to Braves Field in order to help break the color line and make Boston take the lead, as the Cradle of Liberty should."[1]

In Kountze's March 12, 1938, column in the *Boston Chronicle*, he wrote, "Negro major league baseball stars will cut capers on the green sodded diamond of a Boston ball park this coming season of 1938 and against Boston's own popular Royal Giants, probably featuring for the last time the Eastern famous battery of Jackman and White."[2] It was the Giants' catcher/manager Burlin White who told Kountze of the plan, which was expected to feature his batterymate Will "Cannonball" Jackman playing against Satchel Paige and the Pittsburgh Crawfords; alternatively, teams under consideration as opponents included the Homestead Grays and the New York Black Yankees.

One way or the other, Kountze said, the proposed game "will be a test and a challenge for the colored Baseball fan of New England. If well supported it will mean the debut of a new era in colored baseball and will establish here in Boston a definite proof of our numbers in regards to impressing our two major league club managers, one of whom has said that the Negro baseball attendance in Boston is far too low to impress club owners here. ... The entire success of the proposed venture will largely depend on the loyalty of New England's colored baseball following. It will be a test case of national significance; it will put Bronze Boston on the spot."[3]

Arranging an opponent for White's team proved difficult. At the end of April, as the Royal Giants' season was getting under way, Kountze wrote of White's background in the game, a catcher who'd played black ball even before Rube Foster and C.I. Taylor organized Negro League Baseball. "Here in the Hub," he wrote, "we have a veteran still carrying on their great Spirit. We hope you fans will support Burlin this year—especially at Braves Field."[4] As late as the end of June, the game scheduled with the Crawfords was canceled when Satchel Paige's contract was reportedly sold.[5]

Instead of facing the Homestead Grays or another Negro Leagues team, the bearded barnstorming House of David team was welcomed as an opponent and the game set for 3 P.M. on July 6. The Benton Harbor, Michigan, House of David team had been to Braves Field before, in August 1932, to play the Braves themselves. The House of David was a religion-based ballclub and they frequently toured at the time in tandem with Negro League teams, sometimes showing up in communities without letting those communities know of their traveling companions until it was pretty much too late for local hosts who might wish to cancel, and then telling them, "After the games, they're going to eat in the restaurant with us and then stay in the same hotel as us."[6]

A view from the Hive's grandstand.

When Burlin White's team played at National League Park, it was "the first time a Negro nine has ever played in a Boston major league park."[7]

The game was a good one, not decided until the bottom of the ninth. Pitching for the Boston team (called the "Royal Giants" in Boston's black newspaper, the *Chronicle*, but called the "Colored Giants" in the *Boston Globe* and the "Royal Colored Giants" in the *Boston Post*) was Will Jackman. The House of David featured left-hander Remo Cicone. None of the newspapers provided the attendance, but the *Chronicle* wrote that "the play of the colored boys incited ovations of appreciation."[8]

The Giants scored first, in the bottom of the third. Jackman reached on an error by the second baseman. Shortstop Bud Tyrance rolled out, but then first baseman King Tut "smashed a hit to left scoring Jackman after catcher Henville dropped a perfect peg to home by Lokey in a close and thrilling play."[9] Burlin White's single to left-center let Tut take second and then Rabbit Tucker, the Giants' second baseman, "scored the King on a clean blow to right."

The House of David team took the lead in the top of the fifth, with Cicone doubling off the right-field wall to lead off. Mittman walked and both Rea and Vann made hits, Vann's a double. It was 3-2 in the visitors' favor.

In the bottom of the sixth, Burlin White "looped one into left" but two outs followed. Spike Corbin, from Cambridge's Rindge Teach and West Virginia State,

hit a "screaming double down the third base line" that scored White to tie the game. The *Globe* called center fielder Corbin's hit a "wicked single."[10]

It was 2-2 in the bottom of the ninth. Giants left fielder Babe Robinson beat out an infield grounder and Jackman sacrificed him to second. Tyrance was walked intentionally. King Tut flied to center field—but Mittleman dropped the ball. Robinson had to hold at third. The bases were loaded and Burlin White came to bat. He "hit a sharp grounder to shortstop Pierce, who booted the ball, permitting the winning run to cross the plate."[11] Jackman hadn't walked a batter, struck out four, and held the House of David team to nine hits.[12] Cicone struck out seven, but allowed 12 hits and, of course, the winning run.

In a look back a week later, Kountze quoted a "white veteran fan who saw Jackman pitch" as saying his underhand slants were better than Elden Auker of the Detroit Tigers. "Jackman looked like a major leaguer out there on the same hill used by Lou Fette, Jim Turner and Danny McFayden."[13] He also mentioned pitcher Johnny Taylor, who'd once squared off for 22 innings in a game against Jackman in Hartford, as believing Jackman "a smarter pitcher than Satchel Paige."[14]

Gerry Hern of the *Boston Post* gave Kountze a ride to the El after the game and praised both Jackman and Burlin White, "who are both popular with Hub daily writers." Kountze wrote, "I can still hear Burlin's bull frog war chant that was audible all over Braves Field for nine full innings. Few catchers work as hard as does Burlin and he almost outplayed himself at Braves Field."[15]

SOURCES

In preparing this book for the 100th anniversary of Braves Field, many understood there had been a game in 1938 featuring a Negro League team, but no one was able to track it down until the book was mostly completed. Thanks to Bob LeMoine, who located the game.

NOTES

1   Doc Kountze, *Fifty Sports Years Along Memory Lane* (Medford, Massachusetts: Mystic Valley Press, 1979), 24. Quinn said he knew that major-league owners would have voted him down at the time if he had desegregated his own ballclub, but he predicted the change would happen first with the National League Braves (or Bees) before it did with the Red Sox.

2   *Boston Chronicle*, March 12, 1938.

3   Ibid.

4   *Boston Chronicle*, April 30, 1938. A good overview of Black baseball in Boston during its heyday is provided by Bijan C. Bayne, "Black baseball in Boston: recovering a lost legacy," *Bay State Banner*, April 27, 2006.

5   *Boston Chronicle*, June 25, 1938. He had actually suffered an injury during a game in Mexico and did not play in the Negro Leagues in either 1938 or 1939. See Larry Tye, *Satchel: The Life and Times of an American Legend* (New York: Random House, 2009), 120-126,

6   Chris Siriano, curator of the House of David Museum in Addison, Michigan, quoted by Mike Pryson, *Jackson Citizen Patriot*, October 1, 2011. The Jackson Citizen Patriot

7   *Boston Chronicle,* July 9, 1938.

8   Ibid.

9   Ibid. Tut was described by the *Chronicle* as "the colorful first baseman … of the famed Zulu Cannibal Giants." His real name was Richard King and he also played for the Ethiopian Clowns. "He often appeared with an oversize mitt," writes Bijan C. Bayne, adding, "He and 'Spec Bebop,' and 'Goose' Tatum, were the Meadowlark Lemons, Curly Neals, and … Goose Tatums of the diamond." Email from Bijan C. Bayne on December 20, 2014.

10   There were a couple of relatively minor variances between accounts in the Boston newspapers.

11   *Boston Globe*, July 7, 1938.

12   The *Post* box score showed seven hits, but listed none for Cicone and only one for Pierce.

13   *Boston Chronicle*, July 16, 1938. The correct spelling of the last-named pitcher is MacFayden. It's been written that "Jackman's fastball was described as being faster than either Paige's or [Bob] Feller's and Will had big hands that completely wrapped around the ball, making his fastball seemingly explode out of nowhere." James A. Riley, *The Biographical Encyclopedia of The Negro Baseball Leagues* (New York: Carroll & Graf, 1994), 411. After their playing days, both White and Jackman remained residents of Boston.

14   Ibid. Paige finally appeared in uniform at Braves Field during the 1948 World Series, wearing a Cleveland Indians uniform. His only pitching against the Braves was two-thirds of an inning in Game Five, at Cleveland Stadium. Jackman was honored in July 1971 when Governor Francis Sargent declared "Will Jackman Day" in the Commonwealth of Massachusetts.

15   Ibid.

STORM OF THE CENTURY HITS THE "HIVE"

SEPTEMBER 21, 1938: ST. LOUIS CARDINALS 4, BOSTON BEES 0 - THE HURRICANE GAME AT NATIONAL LEAGUE PARK

BY GERALD E. BEIRNE

"Peace in our time" dominated international headlines everywhere on September 21, 1938. The words were spoken by British Prime Minister Neville Chamberlain after he signed a pact with Hitler giving Nazi Germany control over the German-speaking Sudetenland section of Czechoslovakia. In the Northeastern United States, a more immediate disaster was headed its way—the worst hurricane in New England history, one for which residents were totally unprepared.

One survivor of the storm recalled 50 years later "(W)e had no warning whatsoever." Earlier in the day a Coast Guardsman had commented, "Gee, it's a strange day."[1] Typically these storms would come up the Atlantic seaboard and then veer out to sea. Not this one; it slammed into land with a triple punch—100-plus-mph winds, Noah's Ark-type rain and abnormally high tides.[2] "Hurricanes are tropical children, the off-spring of ocean and atmosphere, powered by heat from the sea. They are driven by their own fierce energy," a government publication noted.[3]

One survivor of the hurricane reminisced that he was sent home early from grammar school, simply being warned "to be careful."[4] No one knew of the danger from fallen wires and downed trees. Movie star Katharine Hepburn spent the morning in Old Saybrook, Connecticut, "swimming and playing nine holes of golf."[5] She nearly drowned as the venerable family home, Fenwick, was carried away.

Meanwhile, in Boston, Paul Shannon wondered that morning in the *Boston Post* "if the Bees and Cards may play two today at the Bee-hive (aka National League Park) if the weatherman relents. The outfield looks like a swamp."[6] In fact, because of rainouts, the entire National League schedule that Wednesday afternoon was for doubleheaders, all in the four Northeast cities. (American League teams that day were playing in what was then called "the West"—Cleveland, Detroit, Chicago, and St. Louis—where conditions were drier.) Hank Greenberg led the majors with 53 home runs and Mel Ott paced the senior circuit with 33. Jimmie Foxx had an amazing

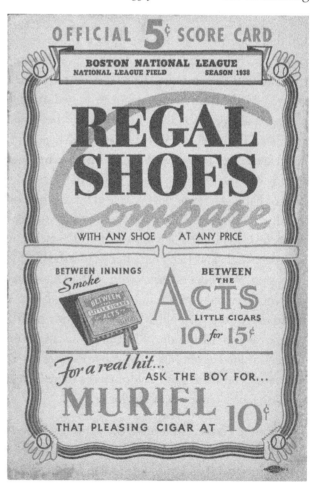

Nondescript typical program of the Bees era.

143

A sample of the Hurricane of '38's devastation.

161 RBIs in just 141 games. The first-place Yankees lost their fifth straight, to Monty Stratton and the White Sox. The Boston Bees were in fifth place in the National League, 12 games behind the first-place Pittsburgh Pirates, and the St. Louis Cardinals were 2½ games behind the Bees.

On that fateful Wednesday, September 21, Bees president Bob Quinn opened the ballpark gates with some reluctance to accommodate the few fans who had shown up.[7] The Bees were 69-69 in an annual struggle to finish above .500. Their lineup could be called "modest." Only Al Lopez (2), Vince DiMaggio (2) and Lou Fette (1) ever made an All-Star game, and then it was mostly in wartime. Lopez did make the Hall of Fame but it was not because of his .241 batting average in Boston. Nor were these still the once-powerful Gas House Gang Cardinals—Dizzy Dean, Frankie Frisch, and Leo Durocher were gone but Joe Medwick and Pepper Martin were still on hand and Johnny Mize and Enos Slaughter had arrived. In the first game of the twin bill, Medwick's eighth-inning homer off Jim Turner drove in three runs and Paul Dean scattered seven hits to shut out the Bees, 4-0. Shannon's comment was: "Seldom has a more listless performance been given by the locals."[8]

By the time Game Two began, the storm and winds (and even snow) were much stronger. Boston hurler Lou Fette (10-13) and St. Louis rookie Mort Cooper (1-0) were the starters. Each gave up a single and no runs. Hal Epps led off for the Birds by beating out an infield roller, which was followed by a Boston error, but Fette pitched out of the jam. Third baseman Joe Stripp "connected for the home team"[9] in the second, but by now "the elements were doing weird things with balls hit into the air."[10] Bees rookie Ralph McLeod, who had gotten his first big-league base hit in the first game as a pinch-hitter, remembered in a 1995 interview, "Part of the fence blew down. They had to stop the game and make up new ground rules. Balls hit to center ended up foul in left. The hurricane game was cut short at Braves Field (sic), the umps called it when Fletch's pop fly was blown into the right field stands."[11]

Boston first baseman Elbie Fletcher's recollections, while vivid, also do not seem entirely accurate. "In a September 1938 afternoon game against the Cubs (sic), Fletcher noticed that the wind was whipping up stronger than usual and the sky was getting dark, but they kept on playing. Then a big billboard behind the left field fence blew down and infield dirt was whirling around pretty good. Occasionally someone's hat would blow off, but they still kept at it. Then a Cub hitter

Ralph McLeod, who often talked about his experience in 1938 at BBHA reunions.

lifted a pop fly over first base that Fletcher called for, then the shortstop was calling for it, then the left fielder and finally it blew right out of the park, an infield fly home run. At that point the umpires called the game, and it wasn't until Fletcher left the ballpark that he realized the enormity of the storm."[12] Both of these versions, told decades after the game, smack of the anecdotal, told in an old boys' way of storytelling, more for humorous hyperbole than for accuracy. So not even first-person accounts are always entirely reliable. (The "billboard behind the left field fence" presumably was the "part of the fence" mentioned by McLeod.)

Baseball Digest also rendered an inaccurate report, writing that "the game was called when Elbie Fletcher hit a popup that was blown wildly into the stands."[13] A more reliable description came from Herb Davis of Douglas, Massachusetts, who wrote that the game was called "when Bees second baseman Tony Cuccinello called for a popup behind second base only to have catcher Al Lopez make the catch at the backstop."[14] Three Boston dailies, the *Globe, Herald,* and *Post* reported unanimously that "the game was called with one out in the top of the third" by umpire Beans Reardon, which means that the Cardinals were batting, not the Bees. All records were erased so there is no definitive account of the game. *The Herald* featured a picture of four nattily dressed Cardinals, Piere *(sic)* Lanier, Paul Dean, Morton Cooper, and Max Macon, "taking refuge under Beehive on day of big wind," as "storm interrupts finale."

The Bees did win the next day's makeup game; in fact they won both tilts that day, 6-5 and 4-1. The Cardinals made major-league history by leaving Boston right after the game—by chartered airplane. This was the first time that a major league club chose to fly during the season.[15] Interestingly, the Giants than arrived in The Hub by overnight boat, arriving early Friday morning—for two more doubleheaders, on both Saturday and Sunday. The voyage was necessitated because the New York, New Haven, and Hartford Railroad was out of commission after the hurricane.

Aftermath of the storm: Almost 700 lives were lost. Property damage was estimated at $306 million, the equivalent of $4.6 billion in 2014 dollars. In 1938 the minimum wage was 25 cents an hour.[16] War did start, in September 1939, but life and baseball went on, and the Cubs, not the Pirates, won the pennant after Gabby Hartnett's "Homer in the Gloamin'."

NOTES

1   James Nestor, quoted in the *Providence Journal-Bulletin,* September 21, 1988, 1.

2   *The Storm,* a publication of the Blue Hill Observatory (Green Hill Books, Randolph Center, Vermont, 1988).

3   *Hurricane, the Greatest Storm on Earth,* US Department of Commerce, 1973, 3.

4   Recollection of Leonard Levin, mentioned to author.

5   Jennifer Steadman, "Katharine Hepburn, Fenwick and the Hurricane of 1938," WNPR News, June 27, 2014.

6   Paul Shannon, *Boston Post,* September 21, 1938, 14. According to the *Globe,* the Braves reported the attendance as 1,356, "but that must have indicated ushers, players, press et al."

7   Shannon.

8   Shannon.

9   Gerry Moore, *Boston Globe,* September 22, 1938, 22. Despite the inference, Stripp's hit was a single, not a home run.

10 Moore.

11 Dick Thompson, "An Afternoon With Ralph McLeod," *The National Pastime,* Volume 16, 1996. McLeod did not elaborate on "new ground rules."

12 Steve Wallace blog, "Boston Blow-Up."

13 *Baseball Digest,* January-February 2007, 10.

14 Herb Davis, letter to *Baseball Digest,* January-February 2007, 10.

15 Burt Whitman, *Boston Herald,* September 23, 1938.

16 *The Storm,* Blue Hill Observatory.

DARKNESS DESCENDS AFTER 23 FULL

JUNE 27, 1939: BOSTON BEES 2, BROOKLYN DODGERS 2 (TIE, 23 INNINGS) AT NATIONAL LEAGUE BASEBALL FIELD

BY HERB CREHAN

The Boston Bees and the Brooklyn Dodgers raced the sun for 23 innings, over 5 hours and 15 minutes, on June 27, 1939, at the Beehive in Allston, and the sun won. Despite 179 plate appearances and 33 base hits,[1] the two second-division teams ended tied 2-2 when plate umpire Babe Pinelli called the game on account of darkness at exactly 8:15 P.M.[2]

As the game continued into extra innings, longtime baseball observers recalled the 26-inning game at Braves Field between these same two teams on May 1, 1920, which ended in a 1-1 tie. The June 27, 1939, game fell three innings short of this major-league record, but the 5 hours and 15 minutes time of game did establish a new major-league standard for length of game.[3]

Only 2,457 fans paid to see this marathon contest, played under mostly cloudy skies with temperatures in the mid-60s, but as most fans stayed until the very end they certainly got their money's worth.[4] At least an equal number of youngsters crowded the left-field pavilion as members of the Knot Hole Gang.[5]

PITCHER'S DUEL

The afternoon contest between the seventh-place Bees and the fifth-place Dodgers shaped up as a pitchers' duel with Boston's Lou Fette (8-3) matched against Brooklyn's Whit Wyatt (7-0.)[6] Fette had won 31 games for the Bees during the two prior seasons and Wyatt had been the MVP of the American Association in 1938, winning 23 games with the Milwaukee Brewers.

The Bees got to Wyatt early, pushing two runs across the plate in the second inning to take a 2-0 lead. Max

West, Tony Cuccinello, and Hank Majeski singled consecutively with Majeski's single scoring West for the game's first run. Boston shortstop Eddie Miller then lifted a fly ball to left field, plating Majeski.

The Dodgers struck right back when Pete Coscarart doubled to right in the top of the third inning and advanced to third on pitcher Wyatt's bloop single. Coscarart scored when Mel Almada's groundball forced Wyatt at second, while Almada beat the throw to first.

Both pitchers held the line through the seventh inning. In the top of the eighth, with one out, Brooklyn rookie Art Parks started things off with a single to right field.

Dodgers first baseman Dolph Camilli followed with another single into right, advancing Parks to third base. With two gone, Dodgers left fielder Ernie Koy grounded yet another single to right field and Parks scored to knot the score at 2 each.

Stengel monitors the action from the Bees' dugout, 1938.

Boston pitcher Fette held Brooklyn scoreless in the ninth, but left the game for pinch-hitter Al Simmons in the bottom of the inning. Fette left with a pitching line of eight hits, six walks, and two earned runs.

HUBER HUMBLED

Brooklyn pitcher Wyatt pitched into extra innings, holding the Bees at bay until the 13th. Wyatt retired the first hitter in that inning but Majeski reached on an error by Dodgers second baseman Pete Coscarart. Majeski, who was hobbling as he ran hard to first, was replaced by pinch-runner Otto Huber.

Huber, who was appearing in his sixth big-league game, advanced to second base on Eddie Miller's fourth single of the game. Boston catcher Al Lopez then sent a routine groundball in the direction of Brooklyn's third baseman, Harry "Cookie" Lavagetto. What appeared to be an easy chance went right between Lavagetto's legs and rolled slowly into left field.[7]

With the play in front of him, pinch-runner Huber took off from second on pace to score the winning run. But as he rounded third, Huber tripped over the bag and sprawled face-first along the third-base line. Huber jumped to his feet, feinted briefly towards home, and then scrambled back safely to third.[8]

In his story for the *New York Times*, Roscoe McGowen described Boston manager Casey Stengel as apoplectic at Huber's pratfall: "Professor Stengel threw his cap high in the air, sprang at least four feet in the same direction and came down screaming in anguish. Casey didn't know then how anguished he was really going to be, for Whit Wyatt struck out Stan Andrews, a pinch-hitter, and got Debs Garms on a grounder to Coscarart to end the frame."[9]

HEADING FOR HOME

With the score still tied in the top of the 14th inning, Bees pitcher Fred Frankhouse replaced John Lanning, who had pitched four scoreless innings in relief of starter Fette. Meanwhile, Dodgers starter Wyatt was

Casey's "goat," Otto Huber.

still on the mound and would continue there through 16 innings.

Wyatt, whose left leg was heavily taped because of an early-season injury, was finally relieved after he had retired three Bees on four pitches in the 16th inning. Over 16 innings Wyatt had given up 15 hits, walked only two batters, and limited the Bees to those two earned runs.

The last seven innings of this marathon game were relatively uneventful. Boston's Milt Shoffner, who had replaced Frankhouse in the 16th inning following his two scoreless innings, pitched the final eight frames for the Bees, holding the Dodgers to six hits, two walks, and no runs.

Brooklyn's Ira Hutchinson pitched a scoreless 17th inning and he was replaced by Tot Presnell, who

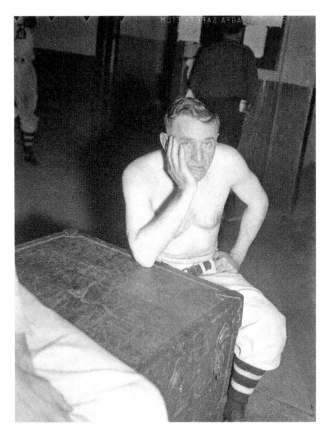

Frustrating times in Boston for the "Perfessor."

Bees Facts: Otto Huber, who was "the goat" of the game, played in five more games before his major-league career came to an end. Al Simmons, who pitch-hit for Lou Fette in the ninth inning, was on the downside of a distinguished career. He was inducted into the Baseball Hall of Fame in 1953. Bees catcher Al Lopez played for eight more seasons in the majors and went on to manage the Cleveland Indians and Chicago White Sox for 17 seasons, earning induction into the Baseball Hall of Fame in 1977. Tony Cuccinello, uncle of Red Sox player and executive Sam Mele, played five more seasons and coached for 20 years in the majors, including stints under Al Lopez in Cleveland and Chicago.[12] Debs Garms won the batting title in 1940, for the Pirates.

Dodgers Data: Manager Leo Durocher continued as an active player through 1945, managed 24 seasons in big-league ball and was inducted into the Baseball Hall of Fame in 1994. Third baseman Cookie Lavagetto played his last game for the Dodgers in the 1947 World Series, coached for many years in the majors, and managed the Washington Senators/Minnesota Twins from 1957 to 1961. Starting pitcher John "Whit" Wyatt went 78-39 for the Dodgers between 1939 and 1943, and he was the pitching coach for the Milwaukee/Atlanta Braves from 1958 to 1967.[13]

pitched five scoreless innings for the Dodgers. Hugh Casey retired three straight Boston hitters in the bottom of the 23rd inning to bring the game to a merciful conclusion.[10]

When the sun set at 8:20 P.M., 50 batters had reached safely—33 on base hits, 12 on walks, and five on errors—and the two teams had left 37 runners on base. Only four of the 50 runners had managed to score and five were erased by double plays.

The 23-inning marathon fell short of the 26-inning Braves-Dodgers record-setter played in 1920. It was not the second longest game in major-league history and it wasn't even the second longest game in Boston baseball history. The Philadelphia Athletics had defeated the Boston Americans, 4-1, in a 24-inning game played at the Huntington Avenue Grounds on September 1, 1906.[11]

The Bees and Dodgers had to comfort themselves with the dubious consolation prize of taking the then-record 5 hours and 15 minutes to finish their tie game.

NOTES

1 Box score, *Boston Herald*, June 28, 1939, 22.

2 Gerry Moore, *Boston Globe*, June 28, 1939, 1.

3 Edwin Rumill, *Christian Science Monitor*, June 28, 1939, 12.

4 Gerry Moore, *Boston Globe*, June 28, 1939, 1.

5 Gerry Moore of the *Boston Globe* estimated that there were as many Knot Hole Gang members as paid attendees, while Burt Whitman of the *Boston Herald* estimated that were twice as many Knot Hole Gang members there.

6 Boston Averages, *Boston Globe*, June 26, 1939, 7.

7 Burt Whitman, *Boston Herald*, June 28, 1939, 22.

8 Ibid.

9 Roscoe McGowen, *New York Times*, June 28, 1939, 29.

10 Ibid.

11 Ibid. Jack Coombs pitched for the Athletics and Joe Harris pitched for the Boston Americans, and both of them went the distance—all 24 innings!

12 baseball-reference.com.

13 baseball-reference.com.

AN ABSOLUTE CLUBBING

SEPTEMBER 7, 1941: BOSTON BRAVES 17, PHILADELPHIA PHILLIES 6 (FIRST GAME) AND BOSTON BRAVES 10, PHILADELPHIA PHILLIES 1 (SECOND GAME) AT BRAVES FIELD

BY TIM GOEHLERT

Doubleheaders were common in 1941, but not like this day. For the second time in eight days, and the fourth time in the season, the Boston Braves and Philadelphia Phillies treated their fans to two games on one day. The teams previously squared off against each other for doubleheaders on May 30 in Philadelphia, July 4 in Boston, and August 31 in Philadelphia. The results of the two games on August 31 were typical, as the contests were split, with the Braves winning the first game, 8-3, and the Phillies winning the second, 8-5. Splitting doubleheaders was typical for the Braves that season; they had played 24 doubleheaders already in 1941 and split 14 of them.

Boston had swept three doubleheaders, June 22 at Chicago, July 4 at home against the Phillies, and August 3 at Cincinnati. In the July 4 matchup against Philadelphia, the Braves won both games, with relatively low scores of 4-3 and 2-0. Interestingly enough, the Braves won both games of a doubleheader on the same date the previous season, with low scores of 3-2 and 3-1.

Low scoring had been common for the Braves in doubleheaders. In the doubleheaders in 1941 before September 7, they scored 179 runs in 48 games, an average of 3.72 runs per game or 7.45 runs per day. But this September 7 was special. It would be the Braves last day at home before they headed out on a 19-game road trip, and it was their last scheduled home doubleheader of the season. But most importantly, it was a day in which the Braves scored 27 runs in an absolute clubbing of the Phillies in both games, with scores of

17-6 and 10-1. The day was historically significant because of the level of offensive output the Braves displayed in comparison to how they had played until this day during the season.[1]

Casey Stengel's Braves had not had a great season. They entered the day 52-77, and had been in seventh place since late May. The only team with a worse record was Doc Prothro's Phillies, being run this day by Hans Lobert. The Braves' last win had been one week before, an 8-3 victory on August 31 in the first game of a doubleheader against the Phillies. The Braves had scored 27 runs in the previous seven games. The team and the fans were ready to see something special happen in what had been a disappointing season.

As with the Braves, the Phillies' season was a lost cause. They entered the day 38-92, in eighth place, where they had been since May 8. The weekend series against Boston was their first stop on a five-city, 13-game road trip. The Phillies had won their last two games and had given up 26 runs in their previous six games (4.33 runs per game). They were prone to giving up lots of runs; they had already let teams score 10 or more runs against them 12 times in the season.

The first game of the doubleheader produced the most runs scored by the Braves all season long. They had scored 10 runs or more in only five previous games, and this day they did it twice. The last time they'd scored as many runs was September 12, 1940, when they tallied 23 runs in sweeping a doubleheader from the St. Louis Cardinals. Being home games, the Braves only needed eight innings per game to score all 27 runs.

West rests between games.

Stengel started Manny Salvo (5-14) in the first game. Lobert countered with right-hander Cy Blanton (6-11). The Phillies scored the first two runs in the top of the second inning in the first game. But the Braves then scored 13 unanswered runs in innings two through six on their way to the 17-6 victory. From the second through seventh innings, the Braves scored multiple runs in each frame.

The Braves leadoff hitter, second baseman Skippy Roberge, had four RBIs. Their sixth batter, shortstop Eddie Miller, scored four runs. Johnny Cooney, who finished second in the league in batting (.319), Eddie Miller, and Paul Waner each had four hits. The Braves had 20 hits in all and struck out only three times. They had seven two-out RBIs and went 7-for-19 with runners in scoring position. Yet the Braves had only four extra-base hits—two doubles, one triple, and one home run, Max West's two-run shot in the third inning. The triple was also West's.

Even pitcher Manny Salvo contributed to the batting onslaught as he walked twice, and had one hit, one run, and one RBI. Right-hander Salvo pitched a complete game, walking two and striking out one.

The Phillies went through four pitchers: Blanton lasted 2⅓ innings, with Lee Grissom pitching one and Dale Jones (in the first of his only two major-league games) and Paul Masterson each working 2⅓. Even with all the scoring and pitching changes, the game lasted just

2 hours and 15 minutes. After a short break, the teams matched up once more and the Phillies had to hope for a split.

The second game had its own share of highlights. Braves pitcher Tom Earley (4-5) and the Phils' Lefty Hoerst (2-7) started. Neither team scored in the first inning. The Braves retired the Phillies without a run in the top of the second, despite loading the bases, and the Braves pushed three runs across in the bottom of the inning on a three-run inside-the-park homer by catcher Ray Berres (one of only three home runs in his 11 years in the big leagues).[2] The team was off to the races, as they scored two more runs in the third and three in the fourth. The day also included a pinch-hit two-run home run into the right-field pavilion by Bama Rowell.

Tom Earley pitched a complete game and gave up six hits, one earned run, four walks, and no home runs. He struck out two and faced 36 batters in all. The only run the Phillies scored came in the eighth, on a double play that followed back-to-back singles. The Braves had 15 hits of their own and five players had two or more hits. They had four extra-base hits, two doubles, and two home runs, including Berres' inside-the-park home run. Three players scored two or more runs and the Braves went 5-for-8 with runners in scoring position.

Max West, who'd produced so well in the first game, was involved in two bizarre incidents in the second. The first could have resulted in his being given a fielding "assist" while his own team was at bat. In the Braves fourth, after grounding out to first, West trudged back to the dugout, head down, but the game had continued. A passed ball eluded Phillies catcher Mickey Livingston. West saw the ball rolling toward the backstop but he didn't see Braves teammate Frank Demaree break for home plate. "Very nonchalantly, West picked up the ball, flipped it to [Livingston], who relayed it to Tom Hughes, the Phils pitcher who was covering the plate" for the third out.[3] In the fifth inning, West had to leave when he suffered a cut lower lip when a Paul Waner liner knocked him unconscious in the dugout.

West meets West: Mae and Max get acquainted.

For the day the Braves had 27 runs and 35 hits, and 17 of their runs occurred in innings two, three, and four. Four Braves batters had four or more hits for the day. Eddie Miller went 6-for-10 and scored five runs. Ray Berres had five RBIs in the two games. The Braves struck out only six times all day (three in each game).

The team batting average for the day was .432, which compared well to the team's season average of .251. Safe to say, the Braves accomplished a lot in one day in comparison to what they had achieved this season, and they truly gave their 7,161 fans something to remember forever.

SOURCES

Boston Globe, September 8, 1941.

Boston Herald, September 8, 1941.

Retrosheet.org.

Thanks to Tom Ruane and Dave Smith of Retrosheet.

NOTES

1   The Phillies were far from formidable opponents. For five years in a row (1938-1942), they lost more than 100 games each season, averaging over 106 losses each year.

2   It was officially Stan Benjamin Day in honor of Framingham, Massachusetts, native Stan Benjamin, the Phillies' right fielder. He had achieved all-state status in baseball, basketball, and football while attending high school in Framingham. The home run came as a result of Benjamin's attempt at a shoestring catch, which eluded him as "the ball shot past him to the jury-box partition" (*Boston Globe*, September 8, 1941). It was a tough day for Benjamin, who was 0-for-9 at the plate, lost another ball in the sun, and twice came close to collisions with teammates.

3   *Boston Globe*, September 8, 1941. The *Globe* mistakenly had Ben Warren as the catcher; we have placed Livingston's name in brackets in place of Warren's.

THE PITCHER IS A SLUGGER

MAY 13, 1942: BOSTON BRAVES 6, CHICAGO CUBS 5 AT BRAVES FIELD

BY GREGORY H. WOLF

The Boston media had a veritable field day when the Braves' affable right-hander, Jim Tobin, belted three consecutive home runs while pitching a complete game to defeat the Chicago Cubs, 6-5, at Braves Field on May 13, 1942. "One of the most astounding feats of baseball history," exclaimed Howell Stevens of the *Boston Post*.[1] An "adjective-exhausting feat," opined Fred Knight of the *Boston Traveler*.[2] Not to be outdone, Jerry Nason of the *Boston Daily Globe* wrote that Tobin "went absolutely berserk with the bat and with piledriving power" to become the first big-league pitcher to clout three round-trippers in one game since Guy Hecker of the Louisville Colonels in the American Association in 1886.[3] Even

Tobin practicing his swing.

Irving Vaughan of the *Chicago Tribune* was impressed. "[Tobin's] bat was nothing short of terrifying," he wrote.[4]

The Braves were brimming with confidence as they headed to their ballpark, affectionately called the Wigwam, on a Wednesday afternoon to play the second of a two-game series with the Cubs as part of an 11-game homestand. Casey Stengel, in his fifth season as pilot of the Tribe, had led his club to 11 victories in the last 16 games to move into third place, just 3½ games behind the front-running Brooklyn Dodgers. The Cubs had defeated the Braves the day before, in the first of a grueling 12-game Eastern road swing, but manager Jimmie Wilson's squad was mired in sixth place at 12-14.

The Braves treated the 3,443 fans who ventured to Gaffney Street or Babcock Street, off Boston's Commonwealth Avenue, to a season-high five round-trippers, but some shoddy defense made for what Howell Stevens called a "nerve-shattering contest."[5] With two outs in the top of the third and the Cubs' Clyde McCullough on second base courtesy of a single and stolen base, Lennie Merullo hit a routine grounder to third baseman Nanny Fernandez. Instead of throwing to first for an easy out, Fernandez attempted to tag McCullough who had run on contact, but missed. After Merullo stole second, shortstop Eddie Miller, a seven-time All-Star, committed the Braves' second error of the inning, as well as his second in two frames, when he fumbled Stan Hack's roller, permitting McCullough to score.[6] Bill Nicholson followed with a single to right to drive in Merullo and give the Cubs a 2-0 lead.

In Tobin's first at-bat, in the third inning, he sent a pitch from the Cubs starter, right-hander Jake Mooty, deep to right field, missing a "haymaker by inches," before Nicholson snared it as he brushed up against the fence. The near-miss didn't surprise the Cubs. The day before, Tobin had smacked a pinch-hit home run in the eighth inning for his second home run of the season and the fourth in his six-year career. The Braves narrowly avoided disaster in the fourth inning when the Cubs' Lou Stringer, who had walked, scampered to second on a short passed ball. Instead of throwing to second base, catcher Ernie Lombardi threw the ball back to Tobin, who reflexively whirled around and heaved the ball, but his throw was off target and the ball rolled into the outfield. As Stringer rounded third, second baseman Sibby Sisti took a relay throw from center fielder Tommy Holmes and threw a strike to Lombardi, who tagged Stringer out at home plate. In the bottom half of the frame, Lombardi put the Braves on the board with a solo shot, his third home run in three days, before departing the game with an injured finger suffered an inning earlier from catching Tobin's knuckleballs. In his only season with the Braves, the 34-year-old backstop and seven-time All-Star won his second of two batting crowns (.330).

Tobin led off the fifth inning with a prodigious blast to tie the score, 2-2. "It was a mighty swat," wrote Gerry Hern of the *Boston Post*, "clearing both the billboard fence and the park's outer boundaries and landing in the freight yards that fringe the Charles River."[7] The Cubs responded immediately, taking the lead, 4-2, in the sixth inning on Nicholson's two-run homer. "Old Ironsides," as Tobin was affectionately known, led off the seventh and sent Mooty's first pitch, according to the *Boston Globe*, "screaming 10 feet inside the foul pole over the left field wall" to pull the Braves to within one.[8] Three batters later, Miller atoned for his two miscues by belting a home run to tie the score, 4-4.

"Pandemonium raged," wrote Howell Stevens, when Tobin came to the plate with two outs in the eighth and Paul Waner on base.[9] After McCullough and skipper Williams conferred with pitcher Hi Bithorn,

who had relieved Mooty the previous inning, the rookie from Puerto Rico decided to challenge the Braves pitcher. "All I knew was that I had to keep swinging," said Tobin after the game. "I didn't think about the record books."[10] Defying all odds, Tobin connected for his third home run of the game, launching one over the advertising section in left field. A "deafening ovation" erupted, reported the *Boston Post*, as Waner and Tobin circled the bases to give Boston the lead, 6-4.[11] Tobin joined Les Bell (1928) as the only Braves players to hit three home runs in one game in the history of Braves Field (1915-1952).

The Cubs tacked on a run in the final inning when pinch-hitter Rip Russell doubled to drive in Phil Cavaretta, who had drawn Tobin's third walk of the game. When Charlie Gilbert popped up to Sisti to end the game, Tobin was mobbed and congratulated by his teammates for a memorable victory, completed in under two hours. "That was the best individual effort I ever saw," said Casey Stengel to the throng of reporters surrounding his pitcher in the clubhouse after the game.[12]

Described by Gerry Hern of the *Boston Post* as the "big man with the Lakes of Killarney in his eyes and a smile as wide as the River Shannon," Tobin, with his Irish humor and sometimes temper, had no answer when asked to explain his home run outburst.[13] "I just swing the same as ever," the ever-modest Oakland native told Gerry Moore of the *Globe*, and recounted a story about driving in seven runs on a grand slam and a bases-loaded double in one inning as a member of the Oakland Oaks in 1935.[14]

Ed Rumill of the *Christian Science Monitor* surmised that Tobin's offensive heroics would once again ignite the discussion among fans about whether Tobin should be moved to first base to take advantage of his hitting.[15] But most of the sportswriters knew that the Braves needed Tobin on the mound. "He isn't glamorous with a dazzling fast ball and nothing else," wrote Gerry Hern of Tobin, who relied on his knuckleball, a curve, and an assortment of off-speed pitches for his success.[16] "Give me the knuckler breaking right and the proper weather conditions and I'll bet you the American

League All-Stars won't score more than three runs off me," said Tobin confidently after the game.[17]

Tobin's strong pitching performance may not have been reflected in the final score, but it was not lost on the cadre of sportswriters following the team. "His famous butterfly was fluttering away from the fat part of the Cubs' bats all afternoon," wrote Arthur Sampson of the *Boston Herald*. "That [the Cubs] didn't throw out their sacroiliacs swishing at Tobin's elusive knuckler was a miracle."[18] In limiting Cubs to just five hits, Tobin overcame four errors resulting in two unearned runs to complete his seventh of eight starts for the season and improve his record to 5-3 with an impressive 2.32 ERA.[19] Coincidentally, he did not record a strikeout.

SOURCES

In addition to the Sources listed in the notes, the author consulted:

Baseball-Reference.com

Retrosheet.org

SABR.org

NOTES

1   Howell Stevens, "Jim Tobin Slams Three Home Runs," *Boston Post*, May 14, 1942, 16.

2   Fred Knight, "Probing Reveals Tobin, Lombardi on Home Run Diet," *Boston Traveler*, May 14, 1945, 24.

3   Jerry Nason, "Tobin Hits 3 Homers, New Pitchers' Mark," *Daily Boston Globe*, May 14, 1942, 1.

4   Irving Vaughan, "Tobin Blasts 3 Circuit Drives," *Chicago Tribune*, May 14, 1942, 23.

5   Stevens.

6   Miller made only 13 errors in 142 games in 1942 and according to Harold Kaese in *The Boston Braves*, set an all-time fielding record of .983 for big-league shortstops. See Kaese, *The Boston Braves* (Boston: Northeastern University Press, 2004), 250.

7   Gerry Hern, "Tobin Content To Remain Pitcher," *Boston Post*, May 14, 1942, 16.

8   Nason.

9   Stevens.

10 Hern.

11 Stevens.

12 Knight.

13 Hern.

14 Gerry Moore, "Tobe Is 'Swinging the Same,'" Let's Talk Pitching," *Daily Boston Globe*, May 14, 1942, 23.

15 Ed Rumill, "Jim Tobin Showered With Congratulations in Clubhouse After Three Homers," *Christian Science Monitor*, May 14, 1942, 14.

16 Hern.

17 Moore.

18 Arthur Sampson, "Pitcher Tobin Hits 3 Homers For Braves," *Boston Herald*, May 14, 1942, 20.

19 By season's end, Tobin's record was not as good. The Braves finished in seventh place and his record was 12-21, leading the league in losses but also in complete games (28).

PAUL "BIG POISON" WANER JOINS 3,000-HIT CLUB AGAINST FORMER TEAM

JUNE 19, 1942: PITTSBURGH PIRATES 7, BOSTON BRAVES 6 AT BRAVES FIELD

BY TYLER ASH

Boston Braves outfielder Paul Waner collected his 3,000th career hit on June 19, 1942, a fifth-inning single off Pittsburgh Pirates starter and ex-teammate Rip Sewell. Playing against the team for whom he had labored for 15 seasons, Waner became just the seventh player to reach the 3,000-hit milestone—the first National Leaguer since Honus Wagner achieved the feat in 1914 and the first major leaguer since Eddie Collins made his 3,000th hit in 1925. The RBI single by the left-handed-swinging Waner came in Boston's 11-inning loss to the Pirates at Braves Field.

Home-plate umpire Tom Dunn stopped the game briefly after Waner's hit so that the future Hall of Fame right fielder could soak in the historic moment.[1] Waner's former Pittsburgh teammates and his current Boston teammates gave him a standing ovation after the ball he mashed for his 3,000th hit was presented to him. According to the *Boston Globe*, the game was stopped for three minutes while members of the Braves and Pirates congratulated Waner.

Waner's single to center plated Tommy Holmes to cut the Braves' deficit to 4-2 in the fifth. The Braves added a run in the sixth, then tied the score, 4-4, in the bottom of the ninth against Sewell.

Bob Elliott's 10th-inning home run—his second of the game—off Boston's Johnny Sain gave the Pirates a 7-4 edge. In the bottom of the inning Nanny Fernandez, who went 3-for-6 in the contest, pulled the Braves within one, smacking a two-run homer off Pirates reliever Dutch Dietz. Then Dietz closed out

the 7-6 victory for the Pirates in the game that would be remembered for the single that put Waner in rare company in baseball history.

With his hit off Sewell, Waner joined Ty Cobb, Tris Speaker, Honus Wagner, Eddie Collins, Nap Lajoie, and Cap Anson as the only players at the time to reach the 3,000-hit plateau. It was only fitting that Waner connected on the momentous hit against the Pirates, the team with which he had spent a decade and a half (1926-1940) tearing the cover off the ball.

"Big Poison" sharpens his batting eye during spring training.

Waner contemplating his next at-bat.

Waner was the National League Most Valuable Player in 1927, his sophomore year in the big leagues, recording a .380 average and his first of three batting titles as a member of the Pirates. Waner also led the NL in RBIs (131) and hits (237) that season, spearheading the Pirates to a pennant before they were swept by the New York Yankees in the World Series.

During his 15-year tenure in Pittsburgh, Waner batted .340 and led all players with 2,868 hits, 558 doubles, and 187 triples. Despite his small stature (5-feet-8), Waner was known as "Big Poison" when he played for the Pirates. Big Poison patrolled right field for Pirates, while his younger brother Lloyd — nicknamed Little Poison — took the center-field duties. Paul and Lloyd dominated baseball in Pittsburgh for 14 years together. (Lloyd broke into the big leagues in 1927, a year after his older brother.)

Legend has it that the Waner brothers attained their "Poison" nicknames in a game against the Dodgers at Brooklyn's Ebbets Field. A Dodgers fan who had a deep Brooklyn accent told other people in the stadium that he was there to see the "big person and little person" from Pittsburgh (Paul and Lloyd) but because of his accent, "person" sounded like "poison."[2]

Paul and Lloyd were also referred to by many as the "Waner Wonders." They combined to record 5,611 hits — the most by two brothers in the major leagues.[3]

The Waner tandem — the only brother duo to be elected to the Baseball Hall of Fame[4] -- was broken up when Paul was cut by the Pirates at the age of 37 after a disappointing 1940 season. He signed with the Brooklyn Dodgers, but was released a month into the 1941 season and signed with the Braves. There he rejoined Lloyd, whom the Pirates had traded to the Braves in May for right-handed pitcher Nick Strincevich. The reunion was brief; in June Lloyd was traded to the Cincinnati Reds for Johnny Hutchings, a right-handed reliever.

It had appeared that Paul Waner got his historic 3,000th hit in a home contest against the Cincinnati Reds on June 17. Waner knocked a sharp grounder to Reds shortstop Eddie Joost in the fifth inning. Moving to his left, Joost knocked the ball down with his backhand near second base, but was unable to make a throw to first, and Waner was rewarded with a hit by the official scorer, Jerry Moore. Fearing that some would view the play as an error rather than a hit (thus tainting the moment), Waner waved furiously at the press box to get Moore's attention so that he could change the call to an E-6.[5]

"No, no. Don't give me a hit on that. I won't take it," screamed Waner, who eventually convinced Moore to charge Joost with an error.[6]

"I don't want it to be a questionable hit. I want number three thousand to be a good clean hit that I can remember," Waner said.

Waner recorded his "clean" hit two days later at Braves Field with his single off Sewell.

It took almost 16 years (May 13, 1958) for another hitter—the St. Louis Cardinals' Stan Musial –to join Waner in the 3,000-hit club.

Before leaving the major leagues in 1945, Waner collected another 152 hits, for a career total of 3,152.

SOURCES

Parker, Clifton Blue. *Big and Little Poison: Paul and Lloyd Waner, Baseball Brothers* (Jefferson, North Carolina: McFarland, 2003).

Okrent, Daniel, ed. *The Very Best of Red Smith* (New York: Library of America, 2013).

Kavanagh, Jack. "Players Profiles: Paul Waner." BaseballLibrary.com. baseballlibrary.com/ballplayers/player.php?name=Paul_Waner_1903

Smith, Red. "Red Smith on Baseball: Big Poison." BaseballLibrary.com baseballlibrary.com/excerpts/excerpt.php?book=red_smith&page=10

baseballhall.org/hof/waner-paul

baseball-reference.com/players/w/wanerpa01.shtml

digital.library.okstate.edu/encyclopedia/entries/W/WA016.html

baseball-reference.com/boxes/BSN/BSN194206190.shtml

exhibits.baseballhalloffame.org/3000_hit_club/waner_paul.htm

pabook.libraries.psu.edu/palitmap/bios/Waner__Paul.html

NOTES

1   exhibits.baseballhalloffame.org/3000_hit_club/waner_paul.htm.

2   Red Smith, "Red Smith on Baseball: Big Poison," BaseballLibrary.com.

3   baseballhall.org/hof/waner-paul.

4   digital.library.okstate.edu/encyclopedia/entries/W/WA016.html.

5   digital.library.okstate.edu/encyclopedia/entries/W/WA016.html.

6   Clifton Blue Parker, *Big and Little Poison: Paul and Lloyd Waner, Baseball Brothers* (Jefferson, North Carolina: McFarland, 2003).

"OLD IRONSIDES" TOBIN TOSSES NO-HITTER AND WALLOPS A HOME RUN

APRIL 27, 1944: BOSTON BRAVES 2, BROOKLYN DODGERS 0 AT BRAVES FIELD

BY GREGORY H. WOLF

During the war years (1942-1945), the fans of the Boston Braves didn't have a whole lot to cheer about as the club averaged 87 losses per season. Only the dreadful Philadelphia Phillies lost more often. One exception was fan favorite, right-handed knuckleballer, Jim "Old Ironsides" Tobin who provided the Tribe faithful with some of the most memorable games of that era. He belted three home runs on May 13, 1942 against the Chicago Cubs to become the first big-league pitcher since Guy Hecker of the Louisville Colonels in the American Association in 1886 to connect for three long balls in one game. On April 27, 1944, Tobin hurled a sparkling no-hitter against the Brooklyn Dodgers, and also smashed a home run, to record Boston's first no-hitter at Braves Field since Tom Hughes on June 16, 1916. It was a "brilliant pitching performance" wrote Jack Malaney of the *Boston Post* about Tobin's gem. "Seldom again even under hall of fame settings will a better game be pitched by anybody."[1]

Manager Bob Coleman's Braves limped to the Wigwam, as Braves Field was often called, in last place with a miserable 1-6 record to play the latter contest of a two-game set with the Dodgers. Only 1,236 spectators showed up for the first game, an 11-3 shellacking, two days earlier. The Dodgers, skippered by Leo Durocher, were 3-3, but were a shell of the club that won the 1941 pennant and recorded a franchise-best 104 victories the following season. They had lost a number of pivotal players to the war effort, including All-Stars Billy Herman, Kirby Higbe, Pee Wee Reese, and Pete Reiser.

Since his acquisition by the Braves prior to the 1940 season, Tobin unexpectedly emerged as the most durable hurler in the NL. He had suffered a career-threatening injury as a member of the Pittsburgh Pirates in 1939 when he slid into second base and injured his right arm, but resurrected his career as a knuckleballer with Boston. "[Tobin controls] the peculiar type of pitches he throws by digging his nails into the hide of the baseball rather than fingering the ball," explained Jack Malaney about Tobin's mastery of the dastardly pitch.[2] Though Tobin posted a pedestrian record of 38-47 from 1941 to 1943, he completed

Tobin honing his skill with the bat.

159

72 of 89 starts, averaged 259 innings per season, and paced the NL with 28 complete games and 287 2/3 innings in 1942. The colorful Californian was off to an impressive start in 1944. Following a tough-luck, three-hit loss, 2-1, in his debut, Tobin fashioned his first and only one-hitter, blanking the Phillies on April 23.

"The murky gloom and cold of Braves Field," suggested Henry McKenna of the *Boston Herald*, portended a low-scoring game for the 2,034 spectators, including the 578 servicemen in uniform.[3] "Tobes" began the game by walking 41-year-old Paul "Big Poison" Waner, his former roommate when the right fielder played with the Braves in 1941 and 1942. Waner advanced to second base on Dixie Walker's grounder to second baseman Steve Shemo, but that was the closest the Dodgers came to home plate all afternoon.

The light-hitting Braves (they finished last in batting average and sixth in runs scored in 1944) came out slugging against the Dodgers starter, 35-year-old lefty, Fritz Ostermueller, whose career was given second chance with so many big-league pitchers serving in the military. Leadoff hitter Connie Ryan belted a double. With two outs, Ryan on third and clean-up hitter Chet Ross on first courtesy of a walk, Phil Masi smacked a fly to deep right field. According to the *Boston Herald*, Waner made a "running-back-to-the-fence stab" to rob Masi of a sure extra-base hit.[4] The Braves got on the board in the third when Ryan led off with another double, moved to third on Tommy Holmes's long fly to Waner,[5] and later scored on Chuck Workman's single. Ostermueller, an 11-year veteran, surrendered only one more hit the rest of the game. Tobin led off the eighth with what Henry McKenna described as "a tremendous home run over the left field wall" to give the Braves a 2-0 lead while the crowd "went into ecstasy."[6]

"Tobin was the absolute master of the game," wrote Jack Malaney. "[He is a] purveyor of the fluttering knuckle ball pitch which is so elusive that not even his catcher knows what the ball is do."[7] After walking Waner to lead off the game, Tobin "breezed along in nonchalant fashion," retiring 26 consecutive batters

Tobin loosens up before a starting appearance.

and did not yield a hard-hit ball.[8] "The nearest thing to a Brooklyn hit," continued Malaney, "was a Bill Hart bunt in the third that rolled foul just before reaching the bag."[9] Jerry Nason of the *Daily Boston Globe* noted that "there wasn't a real spectacular defensive play of the game."[10]

"Tension thick enough to cut with a knife hung over the field," wrote McKenna, as the ruggedly built, 31-year-old Tobin began the ninth inning three outs away from one of baseball's most cherished feats.[11] Tobin punched out catcher Mickey Owen for the first out. Frenchy Bordagaray, pinch-hitting for Ostermueller, grounded to Ryan at third base. The 24-year-old infielder, who earned his first and only All-Star selection in 1944, tossed a strike to first base in a "fast, close play."[12] Facing his old pal, Waner, and just an out from a no-hitter, Tobin was cautious. He fired in three consecutive low pitches, and walked the future Hall of Famer on five pitches. "Waner didn't get a deliberate base on balls," wrote Malaney, "but it was the next thing."[13] The game ended when Dixie Walker hit a "nasty hopping grounder" to Shemo's right side, but the keystone sacker fielded the ball cleanly and tossed to first for an easy out.[14] As Tobin threw his arms in the air in celebration, his teammates rushed the mound, as did some fans, to congratulate him.

Tobin needed only 98 pitches and 90 minutes to pitch the big-leagues' first no-hitter since the St. Louis Cardinals' Lon Warneke's on August 30, 1941.[15] "[Tobin] threw nothing but knucklers in the seventh, eighth, and ninth innings," batterymate Masi told Ed Rumill of the *Christian Science Monitor*. "He wouldn't take a chance with his fastball."[16] The Dodgers hit only six balls out of the infield; 15 batters were retired on ground balls, and six whiffed. "At no time did Tobin appear to feel the pressure," quipped Jerry Nason, who also noted that Tobin sent a "torrent of 'butterfly' pitches dipping, fluttering, and staggering across the plate" to mesmerize Dodgers hitters.[17] Braves president and part-owner, Bob Quinn, was as excited as his players were. "It was one of the most intelligent games I ever saw pitched," he told Rumill. "[Tobin] had good hitters like Dixie Walker, Augie Galan, and Mickey Owen looking foolish, waving their bats wildly and missing by two feet."[18] The highly respected Rumill, who covered major-league baseball in Boston for 45 years before his retirement in 1972, voiced his frustrations with Leo Durocher who "proved himself to be a rather poor sport by not coming into the Braves clubhouse to offer congratulations."[19]

"I had good stuff all the way, but I was afraid of Waner," said Tobin after the game. "I didn't want to give him anything to hit" and refuted accusations that he walked him on purpose.[20] "Abba Dabba" as Tobin's teammates and sportswriters liked to call him, extended his hitless streak to 12 2/3 innings and his scoreless streak to 25

innings with his no-hitter. In what proved to be his most productive season his relatively short nine-year career, Tobin was named to his first and only All-Star squad, set personal highs in wins (18) and innings (299 1/3), and led the NL with 28 complete games.

SOURCES

In addition to the Sources listed in the notes, the author consulted BaseballReference.com, Retrosheet.org, and SABR.org.

NOTES

1 Jack Malaney, "Tobin Tosses Up No-Hitter, 2 to 0," *Boston Post*, April 28, 1944, 1.
2 Ibid.
3 Henry McKenna, "Tobin Hurls No-Hit Win," *Boston Herald*," April 28, 1944, 36.
4 McKenna.
5 Contemporary newspaper accounts, such as those from the *Boston Herald*, reported that Ryan tagged up on Holmes' fly out. However, play-by-play accounts on BaseballReference.com and Retrosheet.org have Ryan remaining on second.
6 McKenna.
7 Malaney.
8 Ibid.
9 Ibid.
10 Jerry Nason, "Tobin Hurls No-Hitter, Homers Against Brooklyn," *Daily Boston Globe*, April 28, 1944, 1.
11 McKenna.
12 Ibid.
13 Malaney,
14 McKenna.
15 Ed Rumill, "Tobin Great Pitcher For 90 Minutes," *Christian Science Monitor*, April 28, 1944, 9.
16 Rumill.
17 Nason.
18 Rumill.
19 Ibid.
20 McKenna.

ABBA DABBA DOES IT AGAIN!

JUNE 22, 1944: BOSTON BRAVES 7, PHILADELPHIA PHILLIES 0 (SECOND GAME)

BY GREGORY H. WOLF

"The record books recognize only those no-hitters that go nine innings or longer," wrote *The Sporting News*, "but [this] feat nevertheless deserves high recommendation."[1] Less than two months after tossing a no-hitter against the Brooklyn Dodgers, Boston Braves knuckleballer Jim Tobin held the Philadelphia Phillies hitless in the second game of a doubleheader that was called after five innings due to darkness.

The Braves players were well rested and looking for answers when they arrived at Braves Field on Thursday, June 22, 1944, to play their fifth doubleheader in 12 days. After a scheduled day off on Monday, their first two games of a four-game series with the Phillies had been rained out. The weak-hitting club was reeling, having lost 11 of its last 14 games. Skipper Bob Coleman's Tribe was in sixth place (24-34), 16½ games behind the St. Louis Cardinals, who were running away with their third consecutive NL pennant. Philadelphia, managed by former big-league hurler and 217-game winner Freddie Fitzsimmons, was one of the early-season feel-good stories in baseball after an offseason filled with controversy. The previous November, club owner William Cox had been suspended by Commissioner Kenesaw Mountain Landis when it was discovered that he had bet on Phillies games, and he was later forced to sell the club. Robert R.M. Carpenter, of the wealthy DuPont family, purchased the team and promised a new era. The upshot Phillies moved into second place on May 10 with a record of 14-10, but had since won just 9 of 29 games and had fallen to sixth place with a record of 21-30.[2] They arrived in Boston to begin a grueling 20-game road trip.

"The Braves were trying a new idea for Boston," wrote Jack Malaney of the *Boston Post*, "a double header starting at 3:15, the second game to be a twilighter."[3] The game was scheduled at a time when daylight savings ran year round. The War Time Act of 1942 instituted this policy, which ran from 1942 through 1945, to conserve energy reSources during World War II. Nonetheless, it was a calculated gamble as Braves Field did not yet have lights (they were installed before

Braves program cover art incorporates WW II servicemen's interest in the National Pastime.

Tobin hurls an abbreviated masterpiece.

the 1946 season). Nonetheless, in an era when games routinely lasted two hours, it was a reasonable plan, provided the games did not go into extra innings and the weather cooperated. Boston went 0-for-2 in this regard.

The opening contest of the doubleheader was a nail-biter for the 2,556 spectators who braved the ominous clouds on this summer afternoon. Boston's 26-year-old All-Star righty, Al "Bear Tracks" Javery, who had led the major leagues with 303 innings pitched in 1943, tossed a career-best 15-inning complete game. In a scoreless pitchers' duel, the Massachusetts native yielded a home run with one out in the 15th inning to Ron Northey, but that was the only run the Blue Jays, as the Phillies were often called in 1943 and 1944, needed. Philadelphia rookie Charley Schanz relieved starter Bill Lee after a 41-minute rain delay and blanked the Braves on two hits over the final nine innings to pick up the victory, 1-0. The tough-luck loss dropped Javery's record to 3-9.

Boston's Jim "Abba Dabba" Tobin got the second game under way at 7:05. The easy-going 31-year-old hurler, in his eighth season, had been the Braves' most consistent hurler since the club acquired him from the Pittsburgh Pirates before the 1940 season. He averaged 13 wins and 259 innings per season from 1941 through 1943 while completing 72 of 89 starts. He entered this game with a 7-7 record, including, eight weeks earlier on April 22, the Braves' first no-hitter since Tom Hughes in 1916. Tobin owned a robust 2.48 ERA. By tossing a hitless first frame, he erased the lingering bad memories of his last outing, when he surrendered five hits and four runs in just one-third of an inning in a loss to the New York Giants.

"After a dearth of power hits in the first game," wrote Jack Malaney, "the Braves started the second game like a bunch of Bronx Bombers."[4] Center fielder Tommy Holmes led off the game with what Arthur Sampson of the *Boston Herald* called a "gigantic poke" into the bullpen in right-center field off 37-year-old starter Dick Barrett.[5] Out of majors since 1934, Barrett got a second chance on the big stage in 1943 when he was drafted by the Chicago Cubs and traded during the season to the Phillies. After Chuck Workman's one-out single, cleanup hitter Butch Nieman connected for his eighth homer, which sailed "over the screen in right" field, to give the Braves a 3-0 lead.[6] Nieman knocked in Boston's fourth run when he connected for a single to drive in Holmes, who had reached on an error by third baseman Ted Cieslak in the third frame.

While the Braves resuscitated their offense after collecting just six hits in the first game, Tobin continued his early-season mastery of the Phillies. In two starts against them thus far, he had not yielded an earned run and beaten them twice, including a stellar one-hit shutout in April.[7] Tobin kept the Phillies, the NL's lowest-scoring team, off balance with his mesmerizing, self-described "butterfly" ball. "Tobin's knuckleball is one of the most amazing pitches of all time," gushed Ed Rumill of the *Christian Science Monitor*. "It dances and slides and flutters and does a few more tricks en route to the catcher."[8] Through five innings Tobin had struck out one and issued two walks, but "nothing approaching a hit was made off Tobe," wrote Malaney.[9]

According to *The Sporting News*, it was approaching 8:00 P.M. when the Braves came to bat in the bottom of the fifth and darkness had settled over the field. "The boys had to hustle a bit towards the end to get in an official game," added the *Herald*, but the Braves hitters were not quite ready to call it a day. Tobin, one of baseball best-hitting pitchers, who had slugged three home runs in a game in 1942, led off the Braves fifth with a double. Lefty Barney Mussill, in his only big-league season, relieved Barrett and was greeted by Holmes' double driving in Tobin. Second baseman Connie Ryan followed with a single to score Holmes. The Braves' offensive outburst concluded when first baseman Buck Etchison beat out an infield single, the team's ninth hit, plating Ryan for a 7-0 lead. Home plate umpire Ziggy Sears called the game after one hour and two minutes when catcher Phil Masi was retired for the final of the inning.

"There won't be the glamour attached to this one," wrote Malaney of Tobin's five-inning no-hitter.[10] Accounts of the doubleheader in Boston newspapers the following day led off with Tobin's feat, but Al Javery's 15-inning complete game received as much print or more. "There was almost a ho-hum attitude about the whole thing," wrote Ed Rumill of Tobin's second no-hitter and fourth shutout of the season.[11] His comments were not disparaging, but rather pointed to his belief that Tobin was as likely as any big-league pitcher to throw a no-hitter. "As long as he can get the knuckler in the strike zone," continued Rumill, "he is unhittable or close to it."[12] Tobin, however, never came close to another no-hitter, and tossed only one more shutout in his career, a four-hitter against the Dodgers in the first game of a doubleheader on September 17 as part of an impressive streak of eight consecutive complete games to conclude the 1944 season.

Melville Webb of the *Boston Globe* reported that the Braves departed by train several hours after the game to play an exhibition game against Fort Shanks, an Army base in Orangetown, New York, about 30 miles north of New York City, the next day.[13] A day later the Braves were at the Polo Grounds to play the Giants in the first of an exhausting 17-game road swing that included five more doubleheaders.

SOURCES

In addition to the Sources listed in the notes, the author consulted BaseballReference.com, Retrosheet.org, and SABR.org.

NOTES

1   Jack Malaney, "Hub Fandom Again Thumps Tub For Tobin," *The Sporting News*, June 29, 1944, 4.

2   Philadelphia had games suspended on May 16 and May 21; they subsequently won those games.

3   Jack Malaney, "Another No-Hitter For Tobin," *Boston Post*, June 23, 1944.

4   Malaney, "Another No-Hitter For Tobin."

5   Arthur Sampson, "Tribe Splits with Phils," *Boston Herald*, June 23, 1944, 22.

6   Ibid.

7   In Tobin's last appearance against the Phillies, a relief outing on June 15 at Shibe Park, Philadelphia nicked him for two hits and a run, saddling him with the loss.

8   Ed Rumill, "Tobin Apt To Make No-Hit Ranks Again," *Christian Science Monitor*, June 23, 1944, 15.

9   Malaney, "Another No-Hitter For Tobin."

10   Ibid.

11   Rumill.

12   Ibid.

13   Melville Webb, "Tobin Hurls Hitless Five Inning, 7-0, Win," *Boston Globe*, June 23, 1944, 17.

TOMMY HOLMES' GREATEST DAY AND GREATEST SEASON

JULY 6, 1945: BOSTON BRAVES 13, PITTSBURGH PIRATES 5 (FIRST GAME); BOSTON BRAVES14, PITTSBURGH PIRATES 8 (SECOND GAME) AT BRAVES FIELD

BY W.G. NICHOLSON

On June 6, 1945, Tommy Holmes of the Boston Braves began a hitting streak that ended as a modern National League record of 37 games; the record lasted until 1978 when Cincinnati's Pete Rose established the current (as of 2014) mark of 44 games. The Braves connection remained: Atlanta's Gene Garber stopped Rose in Atlanta on August 1.[1]

Thomas Francis Holmes, a chunky Brooklyn native, was a fine natural hitter. He had spent six years as a Yankee farmhand before joining Casey Stengel's

Tommy Holmes with "superfan" Lolly Hopkins.

Boston Braves in the spring of 1942. A Braves outfielder for the next 10 years, with right field his home from 1945 to 1950, he endeared himself to the fans with his easygoing manner, steady hitting, and his knack of turning routine fly balls into shoestring catches.

Holmes had his biggest year in 1945. He led the major leagues in slugging percentage (.577), hits (224), doubles (47), home runs (28), extra-base hits (81), and total bases (367).[2] Moreover, he struck out a mere nine times, and had one of the best home runs-to-strikeouts ratios in major-league history. It's not surprising that he was the darling of fans in the Jury Box, Braves Field's right-field bleachers. Braves fans had not had much to cheer about in the previous 28 years, finishing in the bottom half of the standings for all but three of those years.

For most of the season Holmes had been using a 35 ounce, 13-year-old bat that Johnny Frederick had used to hit six pinch homers for the 1932 Brooklyn Dodgers. Del Bissonette, a Braves coach and an apple farmer, had collected a number of bats when he played with the Dodgers. The well-seasoned bats had been lying in an attic in Winthrop, Maine, for years until Bissonette brought them to Boston in the spring of 1945. He succeeded Bob Coleman as Braves manager on July 30, 1945.

Holmes's streak began in Philadelphia on June 6 in a noteworthy series consisting of a twilight game, a night game, and a doubleheader. The Braves won all four as Tommy went 10-for-21, raising his average to .390. Another series at the end of the month against the Cardinals provided Holmes with an opportunity to extend his streak to 28 games and to raise his average to a heady .397. In those three games he went 7-for-10, hitting four homers and driving in nine runs.

The Braves met the Chicago Cubs on July 3 in Boston where Holmes broke the city's major-league record of 28 games with a hit set by George Metkovich of the Red Sox in 1944. And by singling three times against the Cubs' ace Claude Passeau he raised his average to .403. Holmes's second single, on a Passeau forkball, broke the 1932 bat he had been using; however, he singled again in the ninth inning with his own bat as the Braves bowed 24-2.

Holmes was one game short of tying Rogers Hornsby's modern National League hit-streak mark of 33 games (set in 1922) when the Braves opened a doubleheader at home with the Pirates on July 6, a gray day with intermittent showers. Both teams were mired in the second division: the Pirates (36-32) in fifth place and the Braves (32-35) in sixth. It was, however, a day that produced two of the most memorable games in Braves' history.

Braves manager Bob Coleman started Nate Andrews, a hard-living pitcher with a 4-6 record, while Pittsburgh's Frankie Frisch went with Al Gerheauser, one of his veteran starters. Holmes, as usual, played right field (as he did in every one of his team's 154 games that year) and batted third in the order. If Holmes had been nervous, he showed no sign of it as he hit Gerheauser's first pitch for a double, tying Hornsby's 23-year-old mark. He singled in the seventh and then hit his 13th home run in the eighth inning as the Braves won, 13-5. Andrews was the winning pitcher although he gave up eight hits and five runs in seven innings. Mort Cooper, the former St. Louis ace who had been traded to the Braves less than a month earlier, earned what would be defined today as a save for Andrews.

Don Hendrickson, an eight-year minor leaguer who had been called up from the minors and made his first major-league appearance on July 4, started the second game for the Braves. Frisch went with the ace of the Pittsburgh staff, Preacher Roe. It was not, however,

One thin dime got you a program at the Wigwam in 1945.

to be one of Roe's better outings. Holmes wasted no time breaking Hornsby's record when he hit a double on Roe's first pitch to him. The Braves star went on to hit two more doubles in the game as he led his team to 14-8 victory in a wild scoring game. Hendrickson pitched a complete-game victory, giving up 13 hits and eight runs. The umpires had collected both of the first-inning balls that Holmes hit for doubles and presented them to him as a rain-soaked crowd of 8,025 cheered. They had witnessed two of the most memorable games in Braves history. Holmes was now batting .407.[3]

The new record intact, Holmes' streak went to 35 games the next day thanks to the first break he had had since June 6. A bad-bounce single off Pirate first baseman Frank Colman's glove in the fourth inning saved Holmes, who went on to deliver hits in two more games against the Pirates. There was no All-Star Game

Tommy "Kelly" Holmes, idol of the "Jury Box" denizens.

The Boston sportswriters made up for any lack of attention to Holmes's achievement by awarding him the Peter F. Kelley memorial plaque as the city's outstanding player for the year. The Braves and their fans rewarded their hero with one of the most highly prized objects imaginable in the last of the war years, a new Ford sedan.[6]

As of the 2014 season, Holmes still held the Braves franchise record for most hits in a season since 1900 (224) and the longest hitting streak (37 games).[7]

SOURCES

Several personal interviews with Tommy Holmes at Boston Braves Historical Association events in the 1990s.

Wisnia, Saul. "Tommy Holmes," SABR BioProject, at sabr.org/bioproj/person/2c6097b4.

Baseball-reference.com.

Reichler, Joseph L., ed. *The Baseball Encyclopedia*, 6th edition (New York: Macmillan, 1985).

NOTES

in 1945, because of wartime travel restrictions, but at the break he had a .401 average and a 37-game hitting streak.[4]

The Braves faced the Cubs in a doubleheader on July 12 in Chicago. With Hank Wyse feeding the Braves sinkers and sliders before 30,000 fans, Holmes drove Peanuts Lowrey to the left-field wall to haul in a line shot in the first inning. He grounded out to second base in the fourth and sixth innings, and the hit streak was finally broken in the ninth when Tommy grounded weakly back to the box and Wyse completed a 6-1, three-hit victory.[5]

Although Holmes set four Braves hitting records in 1945, he lost the batting title on the last day of the season, .352 to .355 to Phil Cavarretta, the Cubs first baseman. He lost the league MVP title to Cavarretta as well, but *The Sporting News* named him the National League's Most Valuable Player, which the publication's *1946 Baseball Guide* said made him "one of the few second-division players ever selected for this distinction."

1   Holmes was present at Shea Stadium for the occasion.

2   Holmes also had an impressive 125 runs scored and drove in 117 runs.

3   *The Christian Science Monitor* said Holmes told reporters after the game that he used Joe Medwick's 36-ounce bat to break the record. He had asked Medwick if he could borrow it and Medwick said it was OK with him. "Joe Medwick Gets Assist as Holmes Sets New Mark," *Christian Science Monitor*, April 17, 1945.

4   The 1945 All-Star Game was canceled because of wartime travel curbs, but there were a series of regional games. The Red Sox beat the Braves before 22,809 at Fenway Park on July 10 and although not an "official" game, Holmes was the center of attention. He went 1-for-4 with a single.

5   As it happens, over the break, there was one game—the July 9 Boston United War Game, featuring the Braves against the Red Sox at Fenway Park. Holmes got a hit in that one, his 38th game in a row, but that was not a regular-season game.

6   Harold Kaese noted, "New automobiles being rather scarce in those troubled times, Holmes received his present several months after it was given to him." Harold Kaese, *The Boston Braves* (New York: Putnam Press, 1948), 260.

7   See *2014 Atlanta Braves Media Guide*.

"ROYALTY" GRACES THE WIGWAM

AUGUST 13, 1945: KANSAS CITY MONARCHS (NEGRO LEAGUE) 11, CHARLESTOWN NAVY YARD (BOSTON PARK LEAGUE) 1 AT BRAVES FIELD

BY RICHARD "DIXIE" TOURANGEAU

On occasion, the buildup exceeds the event. Such was the case in mid-August 1945 when Braves Field hosted a renowned Negro Leagues team, the Kansas City Monarchs. Though the Monarchs outclassed the local Charlestown Navy Yard Athletic Association, 11-1, the circumstances bookending the entire episode make it a classic in the ballpark's annals.

It was a simple enough idea. The Monarchs were journeying through the East Coast playing black, white, and mixed teams in various cities. The Navy Yard was enjoying a fine season in Boston's semipro, seven-team Park League and Braves Field was available for a night game since the Monarchs traveled with their own floodlight "arcs." On a much more important stage, World War II seemed to be finally coming to a conclusion. The game, agreed upon in late July, was slated for August 13. In the two weeks before the game, thousands more American fighting men would die in the final air and sea attacks Japan launched in its own last-ditch defense effort, ending with the United States dropping two atomic bombs.

Boston's weekly (Saturdays) black press, the *Guardian* and the *Chronicle*, started promoting the game in their first August issues. The invitational hook was that LeRoy "Satchel" Paige, the magnificent Monarch moundsman, would hurl at least four innings. In addition, Kansas City's newest phenom, "Jake" (as the promo ad put it) Robinson, UCLA's multi-sports hero, would play shortstop. It was only four months after Robinson was given "a Fenway Park tryout," but Robinson's signing with Tom Yawkey was not to be.[1]

The August contest at the Braves' Tepee was to be a grand encounter for Curt Fullerton's Navy Yard nine.

Fullerton was a decade beyond his minor-league pitching days in the Pacific Coast League and other leagues and nearly two decades from his less-than-stellar (10-37) short stay with the Red Sox in the 1920s. By the wartime 1940s he was a welder and shipbuilding helper at the Navy Yard.

In 1942 and 1943 the Charlestown squad was good enough to play for the Park League championship against the Dick Casey Club of Dorchester. The Casey Club had captured six straight crowns as the 1945 season began. Again they finished first, edging the Yardmen, 25 wins to 24, beating them 11-0 in a final regular-season matchup. But Fullerton rallied his second-place finishers and as August began so did the three semifinal playoffs, one pitting the defending champs against their Navy Yard stalkers. It was a best-of-seven grudge match, usually drawing large crowds at the neighborhood fields in Dorchester and East Boston.

The *Guardian* and to a larger extent the *Chronicle*, which was more sports-minded, trumpeted Satchel Paige's anticipated arrival.[2] *Chronicle* sports editor William "Sheep" Jackson wrote weekly treatises about why Negroes should be playing major-league baseball. Jackson, a Malden High (just north of Boston) sports star from the 1920s, was a community organizer who lived in Cambridge. The Monarchs visit gave him even more impetus to scroll his hopes for an integrated major league. Not playing favorites, Sheep was not shy in praising the two black players on the Navy Yard's color-blind club, Buster Reddick (sometime catcher for the local Colored Giants) and outfielder Billie Burke. There were notices and photos of Paige

Kansas City Monarchs, 1945. Back row; L to R: Hilton Smith, Enloe Wylie, Fred Davis, Satchel Paige, Frank Duncan, Jim LaMarque, Jack Matchett, Sammy Haynes and Booker McDaniel Front row; L to R: Lee Moody, Eddie Locke, Emory Long, Jesse Williams, John Scott, Dave Harper, Walt Thomas, Herb Souell, Chico Renfroe, and Jackie Robinson.

and other Monarch players in the black papers, but the white mainstream outlets (*Globe, Herald, Post*, and *American*) printed tiny, one-paragraph blurbs the day before and day of the game — all buried at the bottom of the sports pages. *Post* columnist Arthur Duffey did promote the game in his space that morning, calling Paige, "one of baseball's outstanding showmen."

As Monday, August 13, unfolded, the host Braves beat the Pittsburgh Pirates 6-4 despite Lowell, Massachusetts, native Johnny Barrett's greatest career day (four hits, two home runs, two RBIs). Attendance was about 2,100. Later that same afternoon the Navy Yard edged Casey Club, 5-4, to even their series at two wins each. An hour later, near 7:30, Fullerton's spent team was at Braves Field welcoming the flashy Monarchs to their Gaffney Street home, just off Commonwealth Avenue. Good seats were $1.20 (60 cents for the bleachers). War bonds were going to be raffled off to what became a crowd of nearly 5,000. Trumping all of this sports activity, however, was the slowly leaking news of the long-prayed-for official government confirmation that Japan was finished. People went crazy celebrating. Boston joined in (the *Post* said 750,000 celebrants hit the streets) and so the

ballgames immediately took a back seat. Yard players' emotions must have been swirling. By simple job definition they were more attached to the war effort than most Hub dwellers and had just played a cliffhanger with the Casey Club. Now they faced the star-studded Monarchs. There was plenty of hoopla but one thing was missing — Satchel Paige.

He didn't show up, and "Sheep" Jackson later reported that the announcement (blaming car trouble — more specifically a tire blowout) was not made to the expectant crowd until the eighth inning.[3] But the attending fans were not completely cheated because Monarch stalwart Hilton Smith stepped in and threw a five-hit, 11-1 win. During KC's Negro League championship years, Smith had done more pitching than vagabond Paige and was only a bit shy of Satchel's numbers in 1945, both then being age 38. Paige (5-4) was the drawing card, Smith (2-4) the lovable veteran, but the much younger Booker McDaniels was the team's real workhorse (7-4, 118 innings, more than Smith and Paige combined).

Much to the chagrin of researchers, there is no box score in any newspaper. Very short stories by the dailies gave the score, mentioned Smith and Robinson's play, critiqued the lights (fair), and all made note of Paige's absence. On Tuesday morning the *Globe* ran a line score showing that the Monarchs scored eight runs in the last two innings. (Its front page blared "SURRENDER DUE" and the North Shore's *Newburyport Daily News* had "JAPS GIVE UP" greet its readers, while the *Boston Post* proclaimed "WAR IS OVER"). Only Jackson saved future fans a bit of baseball history by giving some details the following week, and he included a second agenda. He was livid that Paige had not shown up despite the prideful black community's promotion. The outspoken writer came down heavily on anyone he thought to be insulting black people, be they white (usually) or in this case, black.

The front page of the competing *Guardian* of August 18, headlined, "Monarchs Win Easy Victory" but did not supply any details of play.

Jackson had glorified Paige's iconic baseball life in the August 11 *Chronicle*, and held back from any comment on August 18, but in the August 25 issue his "Sports Shots" column excoriated the missing Monarch. "... His actions towards the man who had planned, worked and spent all sorts of money for advertisement for the coming of the great colored baseball Messiah was little less than scandalous. He should stay in the midwest to clown and kid his way through the Negro baseball league. It is just another black mark against the Negro American League. ... Satch, in the eyes of Bostonians, is just a Great Social Error and Bust."[4]

Sheep was even more embarrassed because he had written a glowing column on Paige in the June 30 edition, a month before the Monarchs decided to make their Hub stop. After dealing with Paige on August 25, Jackson switched mood and gave the only game notes now available, applauding the efforts of those who exhibited their skills for the Braves Field crowd. "Though outclassed, the Navy Yard did itself proud," he noted, "with (John J. "Red") Chappie, (Charles "Gubby") McArdle, and black catcher Reddick playing as brilliantly as the pros themselves." He lauded Robinson's completeness as shortstop Jackie

had two hits (one a drag bunt), stole four bases (including home), and fielded with style. Of Hilton Smith (Hall of Fame 2001), the irked Jackson beamed, "... hurled better than Satch. (Bill) Williams at second base was better than all right." Jackson ended with, "The crowd was good, with many a white fan really enjoying the game and applauding Robinson and Smith on many occasions. It was the first time a night game was played in any Big League Boston (park). It might be the beginning."

As for the Navy Yard's quest for glory, they lost to the Caseys the next day, but then beat them twice, including a 1-0 classic, to secure a place in the finals against the Linehan Club. Jumping to a three-games-to-none advantage (plus a 0-0 tie), Fullerton's boys hung on to take the series, four wins to two, for their only Park League championship. Joe T. Callahan of East Boston (High School), who pitched for Northeastern University, the Bees (1-2 in a career of 32 innings), and six minor-league clubs, won the final game, 5-1. Sadly, Callahan would die of heart disease complications in May 1949 at age 32.

SOURCES

Baseball Reference.com (Monarch player stats from 1945).

Boston Park League website (history of league championships).

Minor League Baseball Encyclopedia, third edition, online (Navy Yard players).

Retrosheet.org.

Boston American, Boston Globe, Boston Herald, and *Boston Post.* August 1 through 14, 1945.

Boston Chronicle, June, July, and August, 1945.

Boston Guardian, July and August, 1945.

Boston Navy Yard News, May 5, June 16, June 30, July 28, August 11, August 25, and September 8, 1945. Courtesy of the Boston National Historical Park Archives (museum curator David J. Vecchioli).

NOTES

1   Under a front-page headline of "Big Time Game At Braves Field" on August 11, 1945, the *Boston Guardian* ran this brief account of Robinson's Fenway Park tryout within the promotional story: "After a recent workout with the Boston Red Sox, manager Joe Cronin said he (Robinson) was the best prospect he had seen for some time."

2 Ibid. The front page had a picture of Paige and a caption that said in part, "… he will be hailed by thousands of baseball fans and others who appreciate his amazing performances as contributing to better interracial understanding."

3 The *Guardian* gave a few details, score, crowd, who donated, and who won the war bonds but had an entire paragraph on Paige's absence. "It was announced that his car broke down on the way to the Hub. Newspaper reports from Washington said that Paige had been beaten by a DC policeman Thursday of last week. It is alleged that the officer punched him twice in the eye and that the injury might keep the star pitcher out of the game for a week. The cop is said to have accused Paige of failure to obey traffic directions." Though often found in various claimed eyewitness accounts, the DC story is never documented as to a paper source. It is not in the *Washington Post* or *Baltimore Sun* or *The Sporting News*, to name three. It is claimed that DC officer Robert Lewis, not knowing it was Paige, socked Satchel for nearly running him over at a tight intersection. Satchel's reputation with traffic laws was not good and he drove a big, fancy car, usually very fast.

The Monarchs schedule was exhausting. They played in Pittsburgh on August 8 and in Washington the next day. Icon/showboat Paige drove his own vehicle and came too late to pitch for his Monarchs in DC so he tossed three scoreless innings for the Birmingham Black Barons in the second game of the doubleheader, which they lost, 13-7. It was after that game on August 9 that he got into the fracas with the policeman. The blowout was mentioned in the *Boston Globe*, August 14, 1945.

4 William "Sheep" Jackson, "Sports Shots," *Boston Chronicle*, August 25, 1945, 7.

THE WEARING OF THE GREEN – OPENING DAY 1946

APRIL 16, 1946: BOSTON BRAVES 5, BROOKLYN DODGERS 3 AT BRAVES FIELD

BY BOB BRADY

Boston's baseball fans eagerly awaited the start of the 1946 baseball season. Red Sox owner Tom Yawkey had assembled a formidable post-World War II ballclub that many viewed as having a legitimate shot at the American League crown for the first time since 1918. Further down the road from Yawkey's Kenmore Square playground, Boston's Braves had been very active during the Hot Stove season. The ownership triumvirate, dubbed by Hub sportswriters as the Three Little Steam Shovels, had sought to improve Boston's longstanding National League representative by bolstering its roster and enhancing its home diamond. Through their actions, owners Lou Perini, Guido Rugo, and Joe Maney looked to transform the Braves from a perennial senior circuit second-division dweller into a pennant contender.

The Tribe's owners dug deep into a replenished treasury to lure manager Billy Southworth away from the Cardinals. "Billy the Kid" had skippered St. Louis to three consecutive NL pennants from 1942 through 1944 and claimed world championships in 1942 and 1944. It took a then unheard-of rich multiyear contract offer to induce the former 1921-23 Braves outfielder back to Boston. St. Louis owner Sam Breadon was unable to match the Braves' overture and reluctantly parted company with his skipper. The Cardinals proprietor's pockets weren't deep enough to meet Boston's contract offer of a reported base salary of $35,000 a season with incentive bonuses for placing fourth ($5,000), third ($10,000), second ($15,000), and first ($20,000). The princely sum of Southworth's guaranteed annual stipend was akin to $406,000 in 2014.

The Braves' ownership wasn't through raiding the Redbirds. In 1945 they had picked up three-time 20-game winner Mort Cooper for a token player and $60,000 and were now flashing a blank check in front of Breadon for Marty Marion, Whitey Kurowski, and Stan Musial. While the latter offers were wisely turned down, the Cardinals did ship outfielder-first baseman Johnny Hopp and first baseman Ray Sanders to the Hub in preseason deals. In return, the Braves sent $40,000 and $25,000 respectively to St. Louis. At Southworth's behest, other players with Cardinals connections would populate the roster over time to the extent that some Boston sportswriters began to refer to the Braves as the Cape Cod Cardinals.

In addition to roster upgrades, Tribe ownership invested $500,000 in undertaking significant offseason renovations to Braves Field. Just as the club had been the first Boston team to offer Sunday baseball, the Braves would initiate night baseball in the Hub in 1946. Eight light towers were positioned around the Wigwam's perimeter and new night-only uniforms, using a reflective satin material, were designed. The club introduced the now classic tomahawk-style jersey to both their evening- and day-game togs. A new outfield fence was constructed and shrubbery gardens were planted in the rear of the right-field pavilion and along the streetcar tracks inside the ballpark's confines.

All this activity was devised to lure fans into Braves Field's seats. The previous season witnessed a sizable increase in attendance, with the addition of more than 165,000 individuals passing through the park's turnstiles over 1944 figures. Still, the sixth-place Tribe drew only a bit more than 374,000 fans in 1945. In contrast, the neighboring Red Sox, a seventh-place finisher in the Junior Circuit, attracted over 603,000 to Fenway Park.

Upon their return north from Grapefruit League play, the Braves and Red Sox concluded the preseason exhibition schedule with their annual City Championship Series. In 1946 the competition for Boston baseball supremacy was held at Fenway Park on April 12-14. Boston's American League representatives handily took two of the three contests. The final game provided Boston's baseball fandom with an early example of the potency of the Sox' '46 lineup. The Crimson Hose humiliated the Tribe, 19-5, before the largest crowd in the history of this event, a paid attendance of 33,279.

In anticipation of commencing the 1946 championship campaign against Leo Durocher's Brooklyn Dodgers on Tuesday, April 16, workers performed a variety of pre-Opening Day housekeeping tasks at the Wigwam. Among their chores was putting a fresh coat of green paint on the field's 31-year-old wooden reserved-grandstand seats. The Home of the Braves, built by previous owner James E. Gaffney, stood at the ready to welcome the Tribe's followers to the dawning of a hoped-for new era of National League baseball in Boston.

Despite all of the offseason hoopla and perhaps as the result of the Braves' drubbing in the City Series, a disappointing crowd of 19,482 passed through Braves Field's portals on Opening Day. Those in attendance saw Johnny Sain outduel Brooklyn's Hal Gregg and deliver a 5-3 complete-game triumph. Billy Herman led the visitors' attack with four hits in his five at-bats and accounted for two of his team's tallies. (Herman later would join the Tribe in a June 15 swap.) The Braves and Dodgers were tied at 3-3 through the fifth inning. The lead was captured in the bottom of the sixth when Braves second baseman Connie Ryan scored an unearned run when right fielder Gene Hermanski's muffed a Tommy Holmes fly ball. An insurance run was plated the next inning on another unearned run occasioned by a Pee Wee Reese error.

The ballplayers' on-field performance was overshadowed by an unfortunate happening in the stands that is remembered to this day. As was the custom at season starts of yore, those in attendance often dressed up

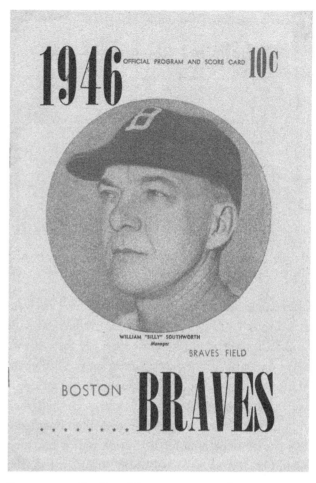

New manager Southworth's appearance on the cover symbolized a hoped-for franchise rebirth.

for the occasion and came attired in business suits and other noncasual wear. Early-spring weather in Boston is always unpredictable and, in 1946, had proved less than conducive for the prompt drying of the emerald paint that recently had been applied to ballpark's grandstand seating. Initially, upon discovering the stains, many irate Braves Field Opening Day patrons marched to the team's administration building at the park's main entrance to complain. Overwhelmed staff quickly ran out of cleaning fluid, forcing those affected to leave the ballpark with an unintended green paint souvenir spotting their suits, fur coats, and stockings.

The Braves front office reacted quickly to the first-game fiasco. An advertisement was placed in local newspapers the next day with the heading, "An Apology to Braves Fans." In print, the club promised full reimbursement of cleaning costs to all of those in

AN APOLOGY TO BRAVES FANS

The Braves management regrets the inconvenience to its patrons who sustained damage to their clothing at Tuesday's opening game due to recently applied paint in certain sections of the grandstand.

The management will reimburse any of its patrons for any expense to which they may be put for necessary cleaning of clothing as a result of paint damage.

For today's game the management assures its patrons that no section of the grandstand will be open for public sale where there is the slightest possibility of any similar damage occurring.

BOSTON BRAVES
JOHN QUINN, *General Manager*

Making amends in newsprint.

attendance suffering from stained clothing. Fans were reassured that those sections of the grandstand with undried paint would be closed off for the season's second game. Wednesday's contest drew a little over 11,000 to the Wigwam and while no further incidents were reported, those hearty souls witnessed the Tribe's first loss of the campaign. The team then boarded a train to Philadelphia for its initial road trip, which would keep it away from Boston until April 28. The Braves secured the loan of Fenway Park from Tom Yawkey for a brief return to the Hub for a Sunday doubleheader against the Philadelphia Phillies. Emerging victorious in both games of the twin bill, they left town until May 11, allowing ample time to cure the sticky chairs in the Wigwam's reserved grandstand. The Braves wisely waited until the club went on the road after the season's second homestand to complete their internal painting project. All other reserved seats received a maroon coating, while box seats were adorned in gold.

True to their promise, the Braves opened up a "paint account" at a local bank to house funds to reimburse those with damaged clothing. Two attorneys were retained to review claims for compensation. As a result of the incident's drawing national media attention, some dubious demands began to flow into Braves headquarters as evidenced by claims emanating from such faraway places as Florida, California, and Nebraska. All told, about 13,000 requests (representing approximately 67 percent of the day's official attendance) were received. The letters were processed over the summer months and the ballclub intentionally applied a fairly liberal standard in determining the legitimacy of the petitions. More than 5,000 claims were accepted with payouts averaging $1.50 and ranging as high as $50. Even though the blunder ended up costing the Braves around $6,000, the astute manner by which they addressed it brought about favorable free publicity and generated goodwill that aided an upsurge of attendance at the Wigwam. Despite the inauspicious start to the 1946 season, attendance at Braves Field increased to a club record of 969,673.

SOURCES

The author reviewed contemporary newspaper accounts as well as *The Sporting News;* Retrosheet; Harold Kaese, *The Boston Braves: 1871-1953;* and materials in the archives of the Boston Braves Historical Association.

LET THERE BE LIGHTS

first nite gone

MAY 11, 1946: NEW YORK GIANTS 5, BOSTON BRAVES 1 AT BRAVES FIELD

BY SAUL WISNIA

In their ongoing struggle to outdraw the Red Sox, their team's longtime rivals for the affections of New England baseball fans, owners of the Boston Braves usually finished on the losing end. Cavernous Braves Field, situated just off an unexciting stretch of automobile dealerships on Boston's Commonwealth Avenue, was no match for cozy Fenway Park and the more inviting hotels and restaurants of Kenmore Square. Whether longtime residents or businessmen in town for a quick junket, fans usually chose the Red Sox and Fenway—especially if Ted Williams was expected in the Red Sox lineup.

After World War II, however, new Braves majority owner Louis Perini seemed poised to finally make some major inroads in this uphill climb to city supremacy. A self-made success as a contractor, Perini began putting together a team that he hoped would be as impressive as any of his company's bridges or buildings. He used a breathtaking three-year, $100,000-plus salary to lure to town baseball's best manager—Billy Southworth of the St. Louis Cardinals—and as Southworth assembled an All-Star lineup, Perini turned his sights to sprucing up Braves Field. He put in new concessions stands and a new outfield fence before the 1946 season, but his biggest change could be seen by fans as they passed by the ballpark starting that February—eight new light towers rising into the sky.[1]

The Braves were 12th of the 16 major-league teams to begin playing night home games, but the first in Boston.[2] Fenway was still a day-game-only venue, and Perini planned on big crowds for each nocturnal contest. The $152,000 lighting system included four towers in the grandstand, three beyond the outfield fence, and one by the separate-admission bleacher section known as the Jury Box. Early accounts of its illumination potential described it as the equivalent of up to four times the average American living room, with the outfield lighting only slightly less.[3]

Of the 77 home games on the 1946 Braves schedule, nearly one third (24) were scheduled as night contests. The first was slated for Saturday, May 11, against the New York Giants, and there was tremendous buildup to the event. A special ticket booth was set up at Braves Field and opened for extended hours starting in early May specifically for the sale of night and Sunday doubleheader tickets, and new satin uniforms—then referred to as "sateen"—were designed for Braves players to wear in night games. The uniforms, the *Boston Globe* reported, would have "dazzling luster" to

Nanny Fernandez, Mike McCormick, and Danny Litwhiler model the new sateen uniforms designed for night game use.

Braves Field at night from the Jury Box.

make "a lot of hairy-chested athletes look like so many sparkling diamonds." The goal was to give fans in the stands a clearer view of the home club, and neon foul poles and gold-painted box seats were added for the same purpose.[4]

The opening night's agenda for May 11 was published in the *Globe* like a theatrical playbill. Prior to the Giants-Braves game at 8:30 P.M., there would be a concert from 7:00 to 7:30 by a 75-piece band; a shorter concert from 7:30 to 7:45 by the "Braves Field Troubadours," a trio of musicians who routinely played in the stands at home games; an appearance by baseball comedian Al Schacht from 7:45 to 8:00; fireworks from 8:00 to 8:25; and, finally, a spotlight introduction of the players. Schacht was told to stay in New York when a rainstorm earlier in the day dampened the field and made his act potentially treacherous to the diamond, but the rain had stopped by evening and the rest of the festivities went off well.

Among the 37,407 in attendance were 30 busloads of fans brought in from outside Boston to be on hand at the Saturday night soiree, and most were in their seats when Baseball Commissioner Happy Chandler's wife, Mildred, flicked the switch that brightened the 768-bulb, 112,220-volt system,[5] and National League President Ford Frick threw out the first ball.[6] Right-hander Johnny Sain took the mound for the Braves, third baseman Bill Rigney settled into the batter's box, and night baseball in Boston was officially under way.

Things were eventful but sloppy early on. Rigney walked and stole second, but Sain got through the first inning unscathed while recording the ballpark's initial night strikeout victim in Jess Pike. The Braves got two aboard in the bottom of the first off New York left-hander Monty Kennedy, who like Sain seemed to struggle initially with the darker setting by hitting Johnny Hopp and walking Tommy Holmes. But the promising frame ended when Ray Sanders struck out and Hopp was thrown out stealing to complete a double play, with the throw to second coming from Giants catcher Ernie Lombardi—a former batting champ with the '42 Braves and one of two future Hall of Famers (along with New York first baseman Johnny Mize) to play in the contest.

Despite more baserunners in the second inning—a walk for New York off Sain, two walks and a single for Boston off Kennedy—neither team scored (another double play, this time a 6-4-3 grounder by Stew Hofferth with Nanny Fernandez on first, hurt Boston). Both clubs, however, broke through in the third. The Giants went up 1-0 on a single by Lombardi to drive in Rigney, and the Braves tied it on an unearned tally when Ryan walked, went to second on a sacrifice bunt by Hopp, and scored when he stole third and Lombardi's throw to nab him got past third baseman Rigney.

Still in the third, the Braves blew a chance to move ahead when they suffered their third double play in as many innings on a 4-6-3 grounder off the bat of Sanders with Holmes at first. So many early squanders are usually a bad omen, and things only got more frustrating for the home fans when the Braves left two men on in the fourth inning without scoring after Sain had retired the Giants in order in the top of the frame (including the fifth of his seven strikeouts over seven innings).

New York's biggest inning against Sain came in the fifth, when they scored twice on four singles, including run-scoring hits to center by Mize and rookie center fielder Jack Graham. Sain settled down after this, but the Braves had exhausted their best chances against Kennedy early and were quiet the rest of the night.

Night game aerial view, circa 1948.

Boston still trailed in the eighth, 3–1, when young right-hander Steve Roser came on for the Braves in relief, and in the ninth the Giants padded their lead to 5–1 on a Johnny Rucker double, an RBI triple by Pike (who had struck out three times against Sain), and a run-scoring single by Mize. Kennedy (2–0 in the young season) went the distance, allowing eight walks but just one unearned run, while Sain fell to 3–3.

Despite the final score, which dropped Southworth's revamped club under .500 at 9–10, reviews of Boston's first major-league night game were positive. It was reported that outfielders had no problems with fly balls, and even with the rain earlier in the day the stands were nearly full. This would be the case for the rest of the summer, as the novelty of night ball and a competitive team that finished a solid fourth in the National League helped the Braves set a franchise attendance record of 969,673 (more than double their prior seasonal mark). But the Red Sox picked the same year to go 104–50 and romp to the American League pennant. Even without night ball, Ted Williams and Co. drew 1,416,944 to Fenway Park.

Perini was not deterred. Convinced that night games were the future of the sport, he proposed at the December 1946 winter meeting in Los Angeles that teams be given the right to schedule as many such contests as they wanted—a suggestion that was met with an uproar from many other owners. The three New York teams, for instance, had an agreement between them to have no more than 14 night games

apiece per season.[7] Perini was thinking more along the lines of 30 or 40, and by 1948 he had his wish.

Braves attendance peaked that year at 1,455,439, when the team captured its last NL pennant in Boston. The Red Sox, who added lights in 1947, were just a shade better at 1,558,798, but the Braves would never quite catch them. The crowds at Braves Field plummeted along with the team's fortunes over the next several seasons, and by 1952 Perini wondered if too many televised night games—TV was then the new rage, threatening the movie industry—were hurting the turnout as much as a seventh-place team.

"Should television programs become so attractive every evening of the week that they are keeping people at home," Perini told reporters at the December 1952 winter meetings in Phoenix, "baseball will have to go back to playing all its games in the daytime." He said he planned just 28 night games for the '53 season.[8]

Perini never would see how the change might impact his Boston crowds, however. By 1953, the Braves were playing all their home games—day and night—in Milwaukee.

SOURCES

"Lo, the Rich Indian's Wigwam is Ablaze With Light and Color," *Boston Sunday Globe*, May 11, 1946.

"37,407 See Braves Arclight Debut; Bonham Ends Red Sox Streak, 2–0," *Boston Sunday Globe*, May 12, 1946.

"TV May Force All Day Baseball Games—Perini," *Boston Globe*, December 2, 1952.

"37,000 Attend Night Game," *Boston Sunday Herald*, May 12, 1948.

"Giants Win, 5–1, before 37,407," *Boston Sunday Post*, May 12, 1948.

The Illumination of Braves Field in Boston, postcard produced by Boston Braves Historical Association, quoting from 1946 Vol. 1, issue 1 of *Braves Bulletin*, 2014.

"Braves Ask Unlimited Night Baseball as Majors Convene," *New York Times*, December 6, 1946.

Caruso, Gary. *The Braves Encyclopedia* (Philadelphia: Temple University Press, 1995).

Kaese, Harold. *The Boston Braves* (New York: Putnam Press, 1948).

Klapisch, Bob, and Pete Van Wieren, *The World Champion Braves: 125 Years of America's Team* (Turner Publishing, Atlanta, 1995).

NOTES

1 At the time Braves Field was being lighted, the Braves were
   run by the Three Little Steam Shovels ownership triumvirate,
   Perini, Rugo and Maney. (Perini didn't buy out his fellow majority owners until 1951-52.) However, Perini clearly was the "face"
   of ownership, assuming the top executive position, and was the
   principal decision-maker.

2 Given wartime restrictions, the Braves had to apply to the War
   Production Board to obtain approval for this construction.
   World War II had ended in Europe and was winding down in
   the Pacific. Approval was granted on July 14, 1945. Construction
   commenced on December 5, 1945, and by March 26, 1946, all
   towers were in place. A preliminary test of the lighting system
   occurred on April 24 and the final test was deemed a success on
   May 1. See William Sullivan, ed., *Braves Bulletin: A Newspaper
   dedicated to Sports Fans who follow the Braves*, May 11, 1946 issue
   (Volume 1, Number 1), and the Summer 2014 issue of the *Boston
   Braves Historical Association Newsletter*, 5.

3 Sullivan.

4 "Al Schacht, Bane, Fireworks—All at B's Night Game," *Boston
   Globe*, May 9, 1946.

5 Jerry Nason, "Lo, the Rich Indian's Wigwam Is Ablaze With
   Light and Color," *Boston Globe*, May 11, 1946. The *Hartford
   Courant* and Retrosheet both give attendance at 35,945.
   Regardless, the *Courant* reported that this was Braves' highest
   game attendance in 13 seasons, since 1933, when the Braves con-
   tended for the pennant late in the season. *Hartford Courant*, May
   12, 1946; *New York Times*, May 12, 1946.

6 "Giants Trip Braves With Kennedy, 5-1," *New York Times*,
   May 12, 1946.

7 John Drebinger, "Braves Ask Unlimited Night Baseball as
   Majors Convene," *New York Times*, December 6, 1946.

8 Hy Hurwitz, "TV May Force All Day Baseball Games—Perini,"
   Boston Globe, December 2, 1952.

A WAR HERO'S RETURN: WARREN SPAHN'S RETURN TO THE BRAVES AFTER WORLD WAR II

JULY 27, 1946: BOSTON BRAVES 5, ST. LOUIS CARDINALS 2 AT BRAVES FIELD

BY JIM KAPLAN

When Warren Spahn returned to the Braves midway through the 1946 season, he was 25, balding and weathered, a decorated World War II veteran of the Battle of the Bulge and the fight over the bridge at Remagen. "He was born old," a teammate said.

But he felt like a young man on the mound. "Before the war I didn't have anything that resembled self-confidence," he told the AP. "Then"—he had had a four-game cup of coffee with the 1942 Braves—"I was tight as a drum and worrying about every pitch. But nowadays I just throw them up without the slightest mental pressure."[1] As Spahn explained to another reporter, "Nobody's going to shoot me."[2]

Despite his three full seasons away from the majors, he was pitching like a world-beater. By the time he got his first Braves Field win, on July 27, Spahn had knocked off the Pirates, 4-1, on July 14, and the Cubs, 6-1, on July 19. In relief, he had given home fans an inkling of how he could go long when he pitched four innings of one-unearned-run ball at the St. Louis Cardinals on June 17—Bunker Hill Day in New England. "He was all grace," his biographer Al Silverman wrote, "kicking his right leg high in the air, his left elbow passing his right knee, just as his dad had taught him, then uncoiling and the ball snapping to the plate out of slapping sleeves and trousers, the ball streaking in and on the batter almost before he could measure it, blazing in like a freight train coming out of the darkness."[3]

Before Spahn's July 27 start, all grandstand seats were sold by 5 P.M. and the Braves Field "express" set a record with 36 buses carrying 1,500 customers from outlying communities. What Howell Stevens of the *Boston Post* described as a near-record "banner throng" of 33,732 "cash customers," plus 962 "service guests," attended the night game against the championship-bound Cardinals.[4]

"Spahn is pitching for the Braves," said Hall of Fame pitcher Dizzy Dean, then broadcasting Cardinal games. "Who in the world is Spahn?"[5]

Spahn showed him, not to mention the Cardinals. It was not just his impeccable control that his father, Edward, had taught him. Nor was it merely his high-kicking, arm-back, over-the-top delivery full of leverage that was hard for a batter to pick up. Because of an old football injury, Spahn had a strange and disruptive way of moving his right arm through a batter's sight line. All in all, he was a bewildering vision on the mound.

Spahnie returns to the Wigwam mound.

It was Spahn's fourth outing of the season against the Cardinals, but they still had little idea how to hit him. "The loose lefty with a war record as long as his south paw," as Will Cloney of the *Boston Sunday Herald* put it, no-hit the Cardinals through the first six innings, allowing only one baserunner when he walked Stan Musial in the fourth.[6] The Braves picked up a run in the second, when Phil Masi singled, took third after Carden Gillenwater's grounder went through first baseman Musial's legs, and scored on Nanny Fernandez' single. The same Braves made it 2-0 in the fourth when Masi singled, went to third on Gillenwater's hit and scored on a Fernandez fly ball.

The Cardinals tied the score in the seventh, but almost as much through fielding mistakes as their own hitting. Buster Adams doubled and Musial singled him home before the Braves made two errors on Whitey Kurowki's double-play grounder to Spahn. After Spahn threw wide to shortstop Dick Culler at second, Culler threw wide to first, leaving Musial on one corner and Kurowki on the other. Both Culler and Spahn were charged with errors. Musial scored on Enos Slaughter's fly.

The Cardinals took their own turn at give-away in the Braves' seventh. Fernandez singled and Connie Ryan reached when his bunt rolled untouched between pitcher Harry "The Cat" Brecheen and Musial. Brecheen hit Spahn, who was trying to sacrifice, on the left shoulder. With the bases loaded, Culler grounded to shortstop Marty Marion, whose throw home was low for an error, allowing Fernandez to score and the Braves to take a 3-2 lead. Mike McCormick rolled to Brecheen, who threw home to nip Fernandez, but Musial bobbled the return throw to first for another misplay, leaving the bases loaded. Then Johnny Hopp, the majors' leading hitter with a .379 average at game time, doubled to score Spahn and Culler: 5-2 Braves.

Miscues aside, a great fielding play helped save the day for Spahn. In the Cardinals eighth, Del Rice singled and after Terry Moore flied out, Red Schoendienst hit such a convincing drive to right-center that pinch-runner Joffre Cross had rounded second by the time Gillenwater made a diving catch. Gillenwater easily doubled Cross off first. Instead of having runners on second and third with one out, the Cardinals were out of the inning. Stevens wrote that Gillenwater "contributed one of the greatest catches of the year."[7] Cloney called it "the game's and perhaps the year's stickout defensive contribution."

But most plaudits went to Spahn, and rightfully so. He beat the Cardinals, 5-2, on three hits, striking out six and walking one. It was his third start, third complete game, and third win over 10 days, in which he allowed opponents four runs on 17 hits while striking out 12 and walking five in 27 innings. "He was almost kicking himself in the chin with his knee on his very loose movement, and his curve ball had the Cardinals breaking their backs," Cloney wrote. The *Globe*'s Hy Hurwitz added, "A 'skinny' 18-year-old schoolboy [actually 19] when he first reported to the Braves in 1941 [spring training], Warren now shapes up as the prize young southpaw of the senior circuit."[8]

Spahn took time off to get married on August 10, and went 3-4 after his honeymoon. But overall he went 8-5, with a 2.94 ERA, and impressed opponents plenty. In a conversation captured by a Philadelphia sportswriter, Phillies manager Ben Chapman and slugger Del Ennis traded impressions with New York Giants star Johnny Mize.[9]

Chapman: "Spahn has one of the greatest overhand curves I've ever seen."

Ennis: "Never mind the curve. What I have to watch for is the change of pace he throws. I swing at it before it is halfway to the plate."

Mize: "The curve and change of pace are all right, but it's that fastball. It does tricks as it reaches the plate."

The fans at Braves Field on July 27 couldn't have agreed more.

SOURCES

In addition to the other Sources cited in the notes, the author consulted Jim Kaplan, *The Greatest Game Ever Pitched: Juan Marichal, Warren Spahn, and the Pitching Duel of the Century* (Chicago: Triumph Books, 2011).

NOTES

1   Jim Kaplan, *The Greatest Game Ever Pitched: Juan Marichal, Warren Spahn, and the Pitching Duel of the Century* (Chicago: Triumph Books, 2011), 65.

2   Ibid.

3   Kaplan, 64.

4   *Boston Post*, July 28, 1946.

5   Kaplan, 65.

6   *Boston Sunday Herald*, July 28, 1946.

7   *Boston Post*, July 28, 1946.

8   *Boston Globe*, July 28, 1946. Spahn was born on April 23, 1921, which would have made him 19, almost 20 in 1941's spring training.

9   The three quotations come from Kaplan, 66.

BRAVES MEMORIAL DAY SWEEP SPOILS JACKIE ROBINSON'S BOSTON DEBUT

MAY 30, 1947: BOSTON BRAVES 6, BROOKLYN DODGERS 3 (FIRST GAME) AND BOSTON BRAVES 3, BROOKLYN DODGERS 0 (SECOND GAME), AT BRAVES FIELD

BY TOM MASON

Jackie Robinson's debut at Braves Field was originally scheduled for April 22, 1947. But the Dodgers' three-game series in Boston was a total washout because of rain. Robinson's first game was in the opener of a Memorial Day doubleheader on May 30.

Before both scheduled series, Robinson wasn't the biggest story in the local news. In April the yearlong suspension of firebrand Brooklyn manager Leo Durocher overshadowed Robinson's debut. Durocher was considered to be a master strategist and motivator. There were many questions about whether Robinson's addition offset Leo the Lip's loss. Durocher's temporary replacement, Burt Shotton, was a relatively undistinguished baseball lifer. Durocher brought excitement to the long baseball season. Without him, *Boston Globe* baseball beat writer Harold Kaese complained, "the Dodgers are as quiet as a nightclub at 10 o'clock in the morning."[1]

In May Braves diehards were beginning to believe that a subway World Series with the Red Sox could happen. At Ebbets Field in the year's opening series, the Dodgers swept the two-game set from the Braves. On May 12 the Dodgers again defeated the Braves, 8-3. The only team the Braves had not yet defeated was the Dodgers. Brooklyn was now in first place, just one game ahead of Boston. Braves manager Billy Southworth juggled his rotation to start his best pitcher, Warren Spahn, in the twin bill's first game. Spahn was looking to win his eighth straight game without a loss. The Braves were powered by rookie

first baseman Earl Torgeson and third baseman Bob Elliott, who went on to win the Most Valuable Player award that year. Batting seventh in the lineup, Torgeson was leading the National League in runs batted in at the time.[2] Southworth was thinking about changing the Braves' starting lineup to move Torgeson up to third and provide more pop against their Brooklyn rivals.

While the media frenzy about Robinson had diminished, record-breaking crowds turned out for his games. He was the first African-American to play major-league baseball in Boston. For the first scheduled series at Braves Field, local African Americans, such as MIT grad Anselmo Krigger, bought blocks

Robinson integrates Boston baseball at the Wigwam.

of tickets to see Robinson play.[3] Members of churches and civic organizations celebrated the day.[4]

But the ultimate goal was to have each Robinson appearance treated as just another game. The challenge for African-Americans was, according to William G. Nunn of the *Pittsburgh Courier*, to take his "accomplishment in stride" and "let him prove he's major league caliber."[5] The lack of hype for Robinson's appearance in Boston can perhaps be explained by the common practice of sportswriters of the era to stay away from social commentary. It may also be attributed to the initial success of the groundbreaking experiment. Robinson's play had already earned the respect of teammates and opponents alike.

The attendance on May 30 was 30,535 — a good crowd but not a sellout. Robinson started at first base and batted second in both games. In the opener Spahn faced Dodgers fireballer Rex Barney. With on out, Robinson walked in his first at-bat but was quickly picked off by Spahn, who was averaging about one pickoff a game.[6] The next three batters, Pete Reiser, Carl Furillo, and Dixie Walker, reached base. The Braves escaped damage when third baseman Cookie Lavagetto grounded into a bases-loaded forceout.

The Dodgers scored two runs in the second. Torgeson made his ninth error of the season when he flubbed a grounder by the eighth-place batter, shortstop Pee Wee Reese. A long double by pitcher Barney scored Reese. Barney moved to third on a missed cutoff throw by center fielder Johnny Hopp. And a sacrifice fly by second baseman Eddie Stanky drove in Barney.

The Braves, behind 2-0, responded in the sixth. Leadoff hitter Torgeson made up for his defensive lapse and doubled. He eventually scored on a single by left fielder Bama Rowell. Then the Braves played some small ball. Catcher Phil Masi singled to center, sending Rowell to third. Rowell and Masi executed a double steal to tie the game.

The Braves sewed up the game in the seventh inning. With men on second and third and one out, Torgeson was intentionally walked. The move backfired. With

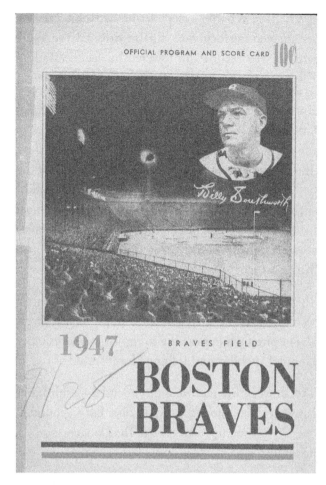

The first Boston major-league program to feature an African American in the scorecard.

the bases loaded, Elliott, the team's best hitter, singled to center, driving in two runs. Catcher Phil Masi's double to right gave the Braves two insurance runs. The Braves led, 6-2.

The Dodgers threatened in the ninth but Spahn hung tough and completed the game. Bobby Bragan walked and was replaced by pinch-runner Marv Rackley. Pinch-hitter Eddie Miksis struck out. Leadoff hitter Eddie Stanky singled. The Dodgers loaded the bases after Robinson dragged a bunt single down the third-base line. With one out, Reiser grounded into a force play at second. Rackley scored and Stanky moved to third. The last out of the game was a Furillo fly out. The Braves won, 6-3.

Spahn threw 150 pitches and walked six batters. The home team had two errors. Each team left 10 runners on base. The difference in the teams was clutch hitting.

Every Boston batter except Spahn had a hit. Despite his uneven performance, Spahn finished the game with an 8-0 record and lowered his league-leading ERA to 1.34.

Braves right-hander Red Barrett (1-3) and Dodgers left-hander Vic Lombardi (1-4) were the starters in the nightcap. In four at-bats, Robinson was hitless. The Braves scored their first run in the bottom of the first. Earl Torgeson drew a walk with two out. Elliott singled to right, moving Torgeson to third. It must have shocked the Dodgers when two of the Braves' slowest runners executed a double steal and Torgeson scored.

The Braves tallied their second run in the third inning. With the bases loaded and one out, Lombardi threw a wild pitch while pitching to the Braves' left fielder Danny Litwhiler, and Johnny Hopp scored.

The Braves now had men on second and third, but Litwhiler and shortstop Sibby Sisti both grounded out. No further runs were scored. The Dodgers escaped, down just 2-0.

The Braves' final run was scored in the sixth. Litwhiler led off with a walk, advanced to second on a sacrifice by Sisti, and scored on a base hit by second baseman Connie Ryan.

Scattering just five hits, Barrett struck out six without any walks for a complete-game 3-0 victory, played in 1 hour and 46 minutes.

Earl Torgeson's play gave Braves fans a lot to talk about. Southworth's move of his rookie first baseman to third in the batting order worked. In the two games Torgeson had two hits, drew five walks, scored three runs, and stole home. But he made a couple of bad baserunning mistakes. Torgeson was caught stealing and almost thrown out at second on a double. After pulling the ball down the first-base line, Torgeson didn't run and instead "stood transfixed at the plate until coaxed to run."[7] Torgeson's fielding was ugly. In each game, he made an error. After the Memorial Day doubleheader, the Braves first basemen already had made 10 errors in just 36 games. The strange but true

Rookie first baseman Earl Torgeson.

part of the day was that Torgeson, due to his fielding, gained a permanent place in baseball's record book. In the first game of the doubleheader, he became one of the few major leaguers to play a nine-inning game at first base without recording a putout.

There was a reason for fans to be satisfied with the day's outcome. Braves fans were happy that their team swept the Dodgers. The sweep allowed them to jump from fourth to second, still one game behind the New York Giants. And Robinson had a successful debut. Mabray "Doc" Kountze of the African-American weekly *Boston Guardian* wrote: "Jackie Robinson made a fine, quiet, well-received debut in Boston. He did not 'steal the show,' he was just another player in the lineup who did his part. That is good."[8]

SOURCES

The author consulted with a variety of Sources for this story. Retrosheet, with box scores and play-by-play accounts of the games, is a primary source. The *Boston Globe*, the *Boston Herald*, and the *Boston Post* had previews and firsthand accounts of the Memorial Day doubleheader. Boston's African-American newspaper, the *Boston Chronicle*, was also consulted. The author did a diligent search for African Americans' firsthand reaction to Robinson's visit to Boston. There was unfortunately very little information besides what was written in the *Chronicle*.

One of the most surprising things about researching this story is the lack of fanfare in newspapers regarding Jackie Robinson's first game in Boston. Writers focused their attention on action between the lines. This is consistent with how Jackie Robinson's games were covered by newspapers throughout the country.

The best available resource, in the author's opinion, to measure Robinson's major-league journey is *The Sporting News*. For many years, *The Sporting News* was considered to be the paper of record for baseball. The seemingly infinite statistics and tidbits provided ample information on Robinson. *The Sporting News* is still a great resource for understanding the tapestry of baseball information.

A native of West Medford, Massachusetts, Mabray "Doc" Kountze was a sportswriter for the *Boston Chronicle*, the *Boston Guardian*, and other black publications like the *Pittsburgh Courier*. In 1934 he was the first African American to receive a press pass to Fenway Park, to Braves games, and to the Boston Bruins. He opened doors by publicizing the accomplishments of great black athletes. He helped found an association of sports editors from African American newspapers who publicized black athletes by selecting All-America and All-Star teams. Doc believed that the spirit of abolitionism was an important part of Boston's heritage. For this reason, he believed that Boston would be the perfect place to desegregate baseball. With other African American sportswriters, he lobbied major-league baseball teams to give Negro League players tryouts. Doc met with officials of the Red Sox and Braves to argue that they should take a stand against discrimination. On the morning of April 16, 1945, the Red Sox gave a perfunctory tryout to Negro League stars Jackie Robinson, Sam Jethroe, and Marvin Williams.

NOTES

1 Harold Kaese, "Not the Same Bums!: Robinson Will Help Dodgers But They Need Durocher More," *Boston Globe*, April 21, 1947, 14.

2 A local sports newspaper, the *Boston Sport-Light*, held a contest and nicknamed Torgeson the "Earl of Snohomish." Outfielder Earl Averill, a former six-time All-Star who finished his career with the Braves, was the first to be given this nickname. Both players were given the same moniker to recognize their Washington state hometown. See also *The Sporting News*, June 4, 1947, 16.

3 "Negroes to Give Jackie Robinson Welcome Sunday," *Boston Globe*, April 17, 1947, 26.

4 Very little detail, if any, of the reactions of African Americans to Jackie Robinson's first visit to Boston is available in the local newspapers. In newspaper accounts of Robinson's first game in Brooklyn, coverage was similar.

5 "Good Contact by Negro Fans Urged," *The Sporting News*, May 21, 1947, 4.

6 "BRAVES BUZZINGS," *Boston Globe*, May 31, 1947, 4.

7 Ibid.

8 Mabray Kountze, "Boston Baked," *Boston Guardian*, June 7, 1947, 4.

THE OLD BRAWL GAME

APRIL 16, 1948: BOSTON RED SOX 19, BOSTON BRAVES 6
AT BRAVES FIELD (CITY SERIES)

BY SAUL WISNIA

For decades the Braves traditionally started each big-league season in Boston with a handful of "City Series" games against their crosstown rivals, the Red Sox.[1] Although these were exhibition contests, both teams played to win—and anybody doubting the intensity they brought to the diamond no longer felt this way after what unfolded in one of these grudge matches at Braves Field on April 16, 1948.

The home team entered the contest with the confidence that comes from positive reinforcement. After finishing the previous year with a fine 86-68 record, the Braves had improved their roster with the pickup of elite outfielder Jeff Heath, scrappy second baseman Eddie Stanky, and hot-shot rookie shortstop Alvin Dark. Adding this trio to a lineup that already included National League MVP Bob Elliot at third base, .300-hitting Tommy Holmes in right field, and up-and-coming Earl Torgeson at first, along with a pitching staff anchored by 20-game winners Johnny Sain and Warren Spahn, made the Braves the darlings of the preseason prognosticators. A poll of 238 members of the Baseball Writers Association of America by *The Sporting News* predicted a Braves-New York Yankees World Series, which would be the first for the Tribe since 1914.[2]

If the Braves fulfilled their end of this prediction and the Yankees faltered, many experts believed, the American League entry in the fall classic would be none other than their neighbors from Fenway Park. Although injuries to their three top pitchers had caused the Red Sox to drop to third place in 1947 from their tremendous 104-50, pennant-winning campaign of '46, they too had spent the offseason bolstering their

already formidable offense with the addition of slugging shortstop Vern Stephens to join Dom DiMaggio, Johnny Pesky, and Ted Williams atop their lineup. Sportswriters picking Boston's AL club as just a shade behind the Yanks were betting pitchers Boo Ferriss, Tex Hughson, and Mickey Harris would return to health, and that newcomers Jack Kramer and Ellis Kinder would round out the rotation.[3]

Another factor that bolstered the prospects of an all-Boston "Trolley Series" in October was the men leading the two teams. Braves manager Billy Southworth, with three pennants already to his credit

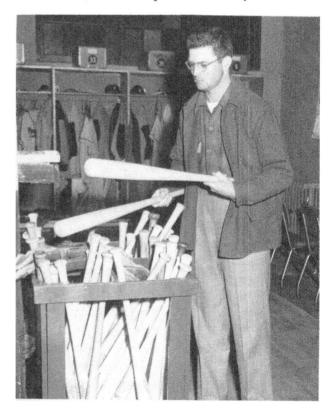

Torgeson conducts a pre-game bat inspection.

Ellis Kinder and Billy Hitchcock posing for the camera at Braves Field.

while at the helm of the St. Louis Cardinals, was generally considered the National League's top skipper. The Red Sox, with longtime pilot Joe Cronin moving up to general manager for 1948, were now under the leadership of the most successful manager of them all: Joe McCarthy. "Marse Joe" had guided the Yankees to eight AL pennants and seven World Series titles after capturing an NL pennant with the Chicago Cubs. The general consensus was that his Midas touch would be a big advantage for the Red Sox as well.

Long considered poor cousins to the Red Sox, the pumped-up Braves were determined to defend their home turf as 12,630 fans settled gathered at the Wigwam on April 16, 1948, for the third City Series game. Sain, coming off a 21-12 season, took the mound for the home team, but was driven from it in the second inning as McCarthy's potent lineup rocked him for five hits and two walks while taking a 5-1 lead. Lefty Clyde Shoun took over for Sain, and two batters later gave up a mammoth 450-foot home run over the center-field wall to Williams. The three-run blast helped end any speculation that the Splendid Splinter would be slow to show his usual power stroke after a preseason bout of appendicitis.

In the top of the fourth inning, with the Red Sox up 11-1, the day's main event occurred. Billy Hitchcock, a utility infielder who had come to the Red Sox from the St. Louis Browns in a separate trade a day after

Stephens the previous November, pinch-hit for pitcher Joe Dobson and grounded to Braves hurler Ed Wright. Wright's throw to Dark caught Sam Mele in a rundown between second and third, but after tagging Mele, Dark's relay to first baseman Torgeson to try to double off Hitchcock—who had rounded the bag widely—was low and wild. Hitchcock slid in under Torgeson to get back to first, and as Torgy attempted to untangle from the runner and chase after the ball, Hitchcock grabbed his legs.[4]

"Action became rapid," Burt Whitman of the *Boston Herald* wrote of what came next. "It looked like a free-swinging of fists, both from the supine Hitchcock and from the now thoroughly aroused Torgy. Players of both teams rushed to the center of the battle. Manager Joe McCarthy was there as soon as some of the players. So was Ted [Williams]. So was umpire [Charlie] Berry. They pinned the two men, now on their feet, and both were sent to the showers."[5]

After these fireworks, the rest of the contest was anticlimactic as the Red Sox continued to pour on the offense en route to a 19-6 win. By game's end the American Leaguers had 24 hits, with Dom DiMaggio, Sam Mele, and rookie infielder Billy Goodman collecting four apiece. The Braves had 11 hits, including two each from Eddie Stanky and catcher Phil Masi, but also made five official errors and several other fielding mistakes. Not surprisingly in such a one-sided battle, all anybody wanted to talk about in postgame interviews was the fight.

Both combatants were World War II veterans known to play tough. Hitchcock, a rock-solid 6-foot-1, 185-pounder, was a football star at Auburn University, and the 6-foot-3 Torgeson had gotten used to defending himself as one of the few major leaguers who wore glasses. Their scuffle, in which Torgeson landed two good shots to Hitchcock's face before Williams's intervention, was in Torgy's telling a rematch of sorts. He claimed that two weeks earlier, during an April 4 spring-training game between the clubs in Sarasota, Florida, Hitchcock had grabbed him on another play around the first-base bag—prompting a warning that any future such nonsense would result in a fight. "The

A new program for a new season.

first time could have been an accident,"Torgeson told Gerry Hern of the *Boston Post*. "But when it happens twice, that fellow's looking for it. You can't let anyone get away with stuff like that."[6]

John Drohan of the *Post* passed on that Hitchcock answered the query "Why didn't you pick on a guy your own size?" with the quick comeback "I couldn't find one."Torgeson, meanwhile, needed to get a new pair of glasses after his "cheaters had been broken in the scuffle."[7] Torgy was boastful to Henry McKenna of the *Boston Herald;* when McKenna asked if his glasses were broken on a punch by Hitchcock, the first baseman smiled and said, "Are you kidding? He hasn't hit me yet. The glasses were broken when someone jumped on them."[8]

Changing the subject away from the fight, and trying to account for the shellacking, Braves skipper

Southworth blamed it on the fact that "the wind favored their blows, pulling them away from our out-fielders, and dropping ours into their hands. That won't happen again in a blue moon—or an east wind." Southworth also joked that after seeing Ted Williams hit, he was hoping three or four Braves players would also come down with appendicitis.[9]

That would not happen, but by season's end it would be Southworth, Torgy, and the Braves who were still playing when the World Series rolled around. Although the Red Sox finished the year tied atop the American League with the Cleveland Indians, Ted and his team-mates missed their chance at an all-Boston fall classic by losing a one-game AL playoff to the Cleveland Indians at Fenway Park.

SOURCES

Baseball reference.com.

"Torgy, Hitchcock Scrap," *Boston Globe,* April 17, 1948.

"Wigwam Fight A Wow," *Boston Post,* April 17, 1948.

"Braves and Yankees Picked by Experts," *The Sporting News,* April 21, 1948.

Kaese, Harold. *The Boston Braves* (New York: Putnam Press, New York, 1948).

Wisnia, Saul. *The Jimmy Fund of Dana-Farber Cancer Institute* (Charleston, South Carolina: Arcadia Publishing, 2002).

NOTES

1   A complete history of the City Series may be found in Frank J. Williams, *The Battle forBaseball Supremacy In Boston: A Chronicle Of The Annual City "Championship Series" Between The Boston Red Sox And Boston Braves, 1905-1953* (Marlborough, Massachusetts: Boston Braves Historical Association Press, 1998). Williams tabulated wins and losses and reported, "Of the 104 games played, the Red Sox claimed 62 victories, the Braves 38 and four resulted in ties."

2   Carl Felker, "Braves and Yankees Picked by Experts," *The Sporting News,* April 21, 1948.The Braves were picked first in the eight-team NL by 102 of the 238 scribes polled, with the Cardinals second at 77; in the AL, the Yanks edged the Red Sox in first-place votes, 119-106. Making his own predictions, *The Sporting News's* editor, J.G. Taylor Spink, forecast a rematch of the 1946 World Series—with the Cardinals squaring off against the Red Sox. Spink picked the Braves and Yankees for second place.

3   Ibid. Stephens, Kramer, and Kinder all came to the Red Sox from the St. Louis Browns in a pair of blockbuster trades on November 17-18, 1947. The Browns, longtime doormats in the American League, had briefly moved up to respectability in the mid-1940s but were back to last place and struggling financially by '47—leading the front office to unload the trio for $310,000 of Sox owner Tom Yawkey's cash (with several lesser players also switching sides).

4   Bob Holbrook, "Torgy, Hitchcock Scrap," *Boston Globe,* April 17, 1948. Holbrook's account mentions Dark's throw hitting Hitchcock as he slid and bouncing 15 feet away from the first-base bag. Other writers did not mention the ball hitting Hitchcock, or said Hitchcock only grabbed one of Torgeson's legs. Several mentioned in good humor that Torgeson as a former Army private was an enlisted man who punched out an officer in Hitchcock—a former major.

5   Burt Whitman, "Red Sox Overpower Braves, 19-6," *Boston Herald,* April 17, 1948.

6   Gerry Hern, "Ted Strikes Out as Peacemaker," *Boston Post,* April 17, 1948.

7   John Drohan, "Wigwam Fight A Wow," *Boston Traveler,* April 17, 1948.

8   Henry McKenna, "Get in First Punch—Torgy," *Boston Herald,* April 17, 1948.

9   Drohan.

TWO WINS FOR JIMMY

MAY 23, 1948: BOSTON BRAVES 8, CHICAGO CUBS 7 AT BRAVES FIELD (FIRST GAME)
BOSTON BRAVES 12, CHICAGO CUBS 4 AT BRAVES FIELD (SECOND GAME)

BY SAUL WISNIA

Two early-season games at Braves Field on May 23, 1948, were quickly forgotten amid far more exciting contests from that championship season, but the events that unfolded around the Sunday doubleheader were significant for reasons that go far beyond baseball.[1]

The story starts a few miles from the ballpark. In the basement of what is now Boston Children's Hospital, Sidney Farber, M.D., was working in a one-room laboratory probing the mysteries of leukemia—a cancer that was then 100 percent fatal for children and adults. In November 1947 he found a drug that achieved temporary remissions in 10 of 16 pediatric patients, and his findings were reported in the *New England Journal of Medicine* in the spring of 1948.[2]

Members of the Variety Club of New England, a social and charitable organization connected with the theater and entertainment industry, were looking for worthy causes to support financially. When they heard about Dr. Farber's findings they decided to back his cause, and their fundraising efforts resulted in $45,536 and formation of the Children's Cancer Research Foundation, or CCRF (now known as Dana-Farber Cancer Institute). Next, hoping to bankroll a state-of-the-art research and treatment facility for Dr. Farber, Variety Club executive director William S. "Bill" Koster and fellow Boston-based member George Schwartz came up with a unique and winning idea.[3]

Using Schwartz's Hollywood connections, they arranged for a live nationwide broadcast of the popular Saturday night radio game show *Truth or Consequences* to be aired in part from the hospital bedside of one of Dr. Farber's patients. As the show's host, Ralph Edwards, asked questions in front of his California audience, they were heard and answered in Boston Children's Hospital by Einar Gustafson, a 12-year-old boy whom Dr. Farber had dubbed "Jimmy" to protect his privacy. Gustafson, a tall, blond farmer's son from tiny New Sweden, Maine, was being treated for Burkitt's non-Hodgkin's lymphoma, a form of cancer then fatal in about 85 percent of pediatric patients.

This is where the baseball comes in. Hearing that Gustafson's favorite team was the Boston Braves, Schwartz and Koster worked with Braves publicity director Billy Sullivan to arrange for members of the club to surprise Gustafson with a visit to his room during the live broadcast. After a 6-4 loss to the Cardinals that afternoon at Braves Field, players changed into their street clothes and made the trip to the hospital. There they were met by Sullivan and representatives from the Variety Club, who led them to Gustafson's room, where microphones had been hooked up beforehand.

"Mr. Team," Bob Elliott meets The Jimmy Fund team.

front of Boston Children's Hospital and handing coins and dollar bills over at the front desk. In the days to come thousands of envelopes marked "Jimmy—Boston, Mass." arrived at the hospital stuffed with change, and Braves players attended picnics, car washes, and other fundraising events that brought in more cash. Gustafson soon got his TV, and by summer's end, $231,485.51 was raised for the "Jimmy Fund."[4]

It was all heady stuff for young Einar "Jimmy" Gustafson, but what he remembered most was the Sunday doubleheader he attended as the guest of his heroes. The Braves entered the twin bill with a mediocre 14-13 record, and the sixth-place Cubs were just the tonic they needed. Although Chicago took a 5-1 lead in the third inning of the opener, the Braves got close in their half of the third on a three-run double by Jeff Health, and then moved ahead 8-5 with four more in the fourth—including two on a Phil Masi double. Catching both games of the doubleheader, Masi would go 6-for-9 with six RBIs to break a 6-for-54 slump.

Boston's bats were quiet for the rest of the first game, but the 8-5 lead stood up thanks to brilliant relief pitching by Clyde Shoun. Bailing out struggling starter Bill Voiselle, Shoun threw six innings of no-hit ball and retired 18 of the 19 men he faced. Making the feat even more impressive was that it was his first appearance in three weeks. "I was pleased and tickled pink,"

Einar "Jimmy" Gustafson in his replica Boston Braves uniform.

The crowd in Hollywood and listeners around the country heard Gustafson — known only as "Jimmy"—grow increasingly excited as players arrived one-by-one at his bedside with autographed balls, bats, and jerseys. Manager Billy Southworth came last with an authentic woolen team uniform tailored to Gustafson's size, after which a piano was rolled in so the group could sing "Take Me Out to the Ballgame." Gustafson, gloriously off-key, was heard above all the others. Southworth invited Gustafson out to the next day's doubleheader at Braves Field against the Cubs, and after the radio feed from Boston went out, Edwards made an appeal to listeners: If $20,000 could be raised for the CCRF, "Jimmy" would receive a television set on which to watch Braves games.

Before the broadcast had even ended, listeners who heard it on their car radios were driving up to the

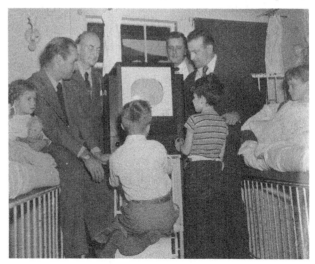

Jimmy receives his television with his Braves idols, Tommy Holmes, Johnny Beazley, and Phil Masi looking on.

"Jimmy" is presented with another television at a 1998 welcome-back ceremony at the Dana-Farber Cancer Institute.

manager Southworth said of the effort, noting that Shoun "has kept himself ready by warming up every day in the bullpen." Although he had often started in the majors previously, Shoun said he was fine with being used almost exclusively in relief due to Boston's strong rotation.[5]

A case in point came that same afternoon, when rookie Vern Bickford hurled a complete game in Boston's 12-4, sweep-completing victory. No comeback was needed in this one, as the Braves exploded for six hits, five walks, and eight runs in the third inning to move ahead, 9-1. Two-run singles by Masi and Frank McCormick were crucial in the early uprising, and both, as well as leadoff man Tommy Holmes, had three hits. All told, the Braves had 26 hits in the two games, but interestingly not a single home run. They didn't need any, thanks in large part to 20 walks (10 in each contest) given up by Chicago pitching.

The sweep moved Boston into a third-place tie with the Pittsburgh Pirates, and delighted the crowd of 31,693 on hand at Braves Field. Among those watching from a box seat, alongside his doctor and nurse, was Gustafson. Although he was not introduced to the crowd and Boston players didn't visit with him in order to continue preserving his privacy, "Jimmy's" new buddies smiled at him throughout the day. Gustafson left after the big third inning of the second contest because, as Arthur Siegel of the *Boston Traveler* noted, "he was beginning to droop a bit, and the doctor thought this had been quite a large day for the boy.

There was fear it would become too much for him. So Jimmy went back to the hospital and for him, because he does not know how seriously ill he really is, there loomed nothing but bright days ahead."[6]

Siegel was not being overly dramatic. Due to the grim statistics then associated with all children's cancers, Gustafson was not expected to survive. But as the Braves did in recovering from their early-season mediocrity to move into first place in mid-June and eventually win the pennant, the boy rallied. Gustafson was home on his family farm by that fall, and the tremendous fundraising surrounding his radio appearance was the springboard for the construction of a four-story cancer research and treatment center for Dr. Sidney Farber and the CCRF. Located less than a block from Boston Children's Hospital, it was named—appropriately—the Jimmy Fund Building.[7]

Here Dr. Sidney Farber and his colleagues would continue their noble work. When the Jimmy Fund Building opened in January 1952, Braves representatives at a celebration luncheon included owner Lou Perini, PR man Billy Sullivan, and player-manager Holmes. And even after the Braves moved to Milwaukee the next year, the connection between Boston baseball and Dr. Farber continued—as Red Sox owner Tom Yawkey accepted Perini's appeal to make the Jimmy Fund *his* team's official charity.[8]

Dr. Sidney Farber and "Jimmy" memorialized in bronze and granite in 2013.

What became of Einar "Jimmy" Gustafson? Continuing to live out of the spotlight, and presumed dead by almost all but his hometown and Dr. Farber (with whom he corresponded), Gustafson grew up to be a father of three, a grandfather of six, and a long-distance truck driver. In 1998 he emerged from a half-century of silence to help the Jimmy Fund celebrate its 50th anniversary, and in an emotional reunion put together by the Boston Braves Historical Association, he was able to thank Holmes, Sullivan, and several of the others who brought him joy and a pennant during the toughest summer of his life.[9]

His was not the only happy ending. The most common childhood leukemia is 90 percent curable, and survival rates for many other pediatric and adult forms of the disease continue making extraordinary gains — thanks in large part to the night a group of weary ballplayers stopped in to make a sick little boy happy.

SOURCES

Baseball Reference.com.

"Braves Whip Cubs, 8-5, 12-4," *Boston Post*, May 24, 1948.

"Baseball Therapy for Jimmy," *Boston Traveler*, May 24, 1948.

"Shoun's Wing, Masi's Bat Helped Braves Take Bill," *Boston Traveler*, May 26, 1948.

Dana-farber.org (history section).

Jimmyfund.org (Red Sox section).

Kaese, Harold. *The Boston Braves* (New York: Putnam Press, New York, 1948).

Wisnia, Saul. *The Jimmy Fund of Dana-Farber Cancer Institute* (Charleston, South Carolina: Arcadia Publishing, 2002).

NOTES

1   It is also notable that this day was the one on which Norman Rockwell visited Braves Field to take photographs in preparation for his work "The Dugout." See the separate essay at the end of this book.

2   Saul Wisnia, *The Jimmy Fund of Dana-Farber Cancer Institute* (Charleston, South Carolina: Arcadia Publishing, 2002). Dr.

Farber's findings were initially met with skepticism in the scientific community, since no drug had ever been proved effective against nonsolid tumors (those that are spread throughout the body and cannot be surgically removed). Those doctors intrigued enough to contact Dr. Farber received personal responses and an invitation to come to Boston with their patients.

3   Ibid. Over time, as more children had positive responses to his treatments, Dr. Farber found himself in urgent need of more space. He temporarily moved the CCRF into five rooms of an apartment building near Boston Children's Hospital, but it was clear a full-size facility was necessary. The Variety Club, whose members had become wealthy and well-connected during the movie craze before and during World War II, made funding such a structure their top priority.

4   Ibid.

5   Tom Monahan, "Shoun's Wing, Masi's Bat Helped Braves Take Bill," *Boston Traveler*, May 24, 1948.

6   Arthur Siegel, "Baseball Therapy for Jimmy," *Boston Traveler*, May 24, 1948.

7   As a subtle tribute to the team that helped make the structure possible, two medallions emblazoned with the Braves logo — a regal Native American chief in full headdress — were placed by the entrance of the Jimmy Fund Building. They are still there. In November 2013 a longtime Jimmy Fund supporter, Jim Vinick, donated two statues to the Dana-Farber Cancer Institute. They are placed on Binney Street in Boston and depict Dr. Sidney Farber looking up toward his then 12-year-old patient Einar Gustafson, "Jimmy," who is shown wearing his Boston Braves uniform.

8   The Jimmy Fund continues to be a vital part of Red Sox fundraising efforts, and a gleaming new Yawkey Center for Cancer Care (named for Red Sox owners Tom and Jean Yawkey) now sits a few feet away from the original Jimmy Fund Building. A Jimmy Fund billboard was for many years the only advertising allowed by Tom Yawkey inside Fenway Park, and stood for decades atop the right-field grandstand and the Red Sox retired numbers. When modifications to the ballpark forced the billboard's dismantling, a Jimmy Fund logo was placed on the Green Monster left-field wall — where it remains.

9   *The Jimmy Fund of Dana-Farber Cancer Institute*. Fifty years to the day after his radio appearance, Gustafson was re-introduced to Boston baseball fans on the field at Fenway Park on May 22, 1998. *Truth or Consequences* host Ralph Edwards was on hand for the ceremony, which included a recording of the original 1948 broadcast played over the loudspeakers. Gustafson spent the last years of his life making public appearances and helping with other fundraising efforts on behalf of Dana-Farber before dying on January 21, 2001, after suffering a stroke.

TELEVISED BASEBALL DEBUTS IN THE HUB

wow

JUNE 15, 1948: BOSTON BRAVES 6, CHICAGO CUBS 3 AT BRAVES FIELD

BY DONNA L. HALPER

It was Tuesday night, June 15, 1948, and 24,124 Boston Braves fans packed the Wigwam hoping to see their team take over first place. They were not disappointed: Johnny Sain pitched a six-hitter and the Braves beat the Chicago Cubs, 6-3. Once again the Braves showed that they were very successful when playing under the lights: This was their10th win out of 14 night games. But before the game was played, there was another story dominating the news: Tonight would be the first time a local baseball game was televised. Television had just come to Boston when WBZ-TV, Channel 4, debuted on June 9, and there were already an estimated 3,500 TV sets in the greater Boston area.[1] Plans to televise baseball had been in the works since early May; after several delays and considerable expense—the TV cameras cost between $20,000 and $25,000 each[2] -- everything was tested and ready to go. Tonight, fans would be able to see as well as hear the game from the comfort of their home or at their favorite tavern.

Television was such a novelty that several sportswriters were assigned to watch the game on a TV and report on what they saw, rather than go to the ballpark.[3] Even the Braves management recognized that this first televised game was a momentous occasion, so they held a pregame ceremony. As the Braves players stood along the third-base line and Cubs players stood along first, play-by-play announcer Jim Britt introduced the guest speakers, who included WBZ-TV program director Gordon Swan, representatives from the Narragansett Brewing Company and the Atlantic Refining Company, who sponsored the game, and the president of the Braves, Lou Perini.[4] But Perini's remarks did not go as planned—perhaps nervous because he was on television, he had an unfortunate slip of the tongue, praising "this hysterical occasion." To his credit, he recovered quickly, and praised "this historical occasion," explaining that he had been "hysterical" when the Braves came home from their latest road trip.[5]

As for the game itself, the Braves got off to a good start when they scored two runs in the first inning. From that moment on, they were never behind: in addition to their two in the first, the Braves scored a run in the third, another in the fourth, and two more in the seventh. They got 10 hits off three Cubs pitchers;

Announcer Britt and sponsor Narragansett easily made the transition from radio to TV.

"Big John" was always exhibited a commanding presence on the Wigwam mound.

they also had a stolen base, by first baseman Earl Torgesen (his 11th of the year). But as impressive as the Braves' victory was, they missed a number of opportunities to score even more runs: The team left 14 men on base. In fact, three times during the first four innings, Braves hitters left the bases loaded when they made the final out. Meanwhile, Cubs starting pitcher Russ Meyer struggled. His main problem was an inability to find home plate: He walked nine batters during the 3⅔ innings he was in the game; that included a bases-loaded walk to Braves outfielder Jim Russell in the fourth, at which point Cubs manager Charlie Grimm had seen enough and changed pitchers. (Meyer had also issued a bases-loaded walk in the first inning.) The Braves player who had the best day at the plate was Eddie Stanky, who had three hits, including a double. But after he injured his right shin while making a slide in the seventh inning, he had to leave the game. Fortunately for the Braves, the injury was minor, and reporters said Stanky would probably be back in the lineup the next day.

On the mound, Braves starter Johnny Sain earned his seventh win of the season, and demonstrated excellent control. He gave up only one walk, as opposed to the three Cubs pitchers, who gave up a total of 11. Sain pitched his way out of a couple of difficult spots, getting the big outs when he needed to; and although the Cubs scored three runs, only one was earned.

Sportswriters noted that with his 7-4 record, Sain looked as though he was well on his way to another 20-win season.[6] The one bright spot for the Cubs, who lost to the Braves for the seventh straight time this year, was Eddie Waitkus. The former star first baseman at Cambridge Latin School hit a triple, and also made an outstanding fielding play, knocking down a Jeff Heath line drive and preventing the Braves from scoring even more runs in the first inning.

As *Boston Traveler* reporter John Drohan noted the next day, it had been a night of "firsts"—the Braves took sole possession of first place, Johnny Sain won his first game at Braves Field (his other six wins had been on the road), and, of course, it was the first time in New England that baseball had been seen on television. And speaking of television, some of the fans who watched it complained that the picture was sometimes fuzzy, or that the cameras missed an important play. Others were frustrated because at least one tavern, the Bamboo Bar, made patrons stand while watching the game.[7] But the majority of the TV watchers expressed their satisfaction with what they saw. Also happy were the proprietors of taverns and restaurants who had decided to install a TV set in their establishment; they drew large crowds as a result.[8]

As for the Braves players, they were undoubtedly glad to be on top of the National League standings, the result of their win against the Cubs and the New York Giants' 2-0 loss to the Pittsburgh Pirates. But while

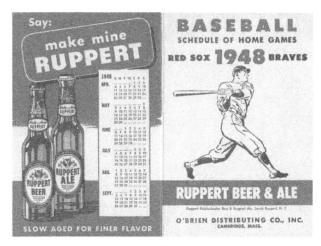

TV broadcast dates would start to appear on pocket schedules in Boston after 1948.

it was good to take over sole possession of first place, the players were well aware that it was only June 15. More than 100 games remained to be played, and there was plenty of work to do. In fact, the players were more concerned with improving their record at home: They had won 10 and lost just four during their recently completed road trip, giving them an impressive 19-9 record during away games. At home, however, the team hadn't been nearly as dominant. Even with this night's victory, the Braves still had a losing record of 9-12 at Braves Field. But the win against the Cubs was an encouraging way to begin the homestand, and the Braves now had 16 more games to play in front of their loyal fans before going back out on the road.

SOURCES

"Braves Game First Seen Here by Television," *Boston Globe*, June 16, 1948, 1, 7.

"Braves Take Undisputed Place at Top of League," *Springfield* (Massachusetts) *Union*, June 16, 1948, 18.

Drohan, John, "First Place Braves Just Loaded With 'Firsts,'" *Boston Traveler*, June 16, 1948, 21.

Kaese, Harold, "Braves Field Game Last Week in May Opens Television Here," *Boston Globe*, May 12, 1948, 23.

Keane, Clif, "Braves, Cubs Game To Be Televised Tonight," *Boston Globe*, June 15, 1948, 8.

Keane, Clif, "Braves Lead League by Full Game," *Boston Globe*, June 16, 1948, 22.

Lundquist, Carl, "Sain Red Hot—Braves Top N.L.," *Lowell* (Massachusetts) *Sun*, June 16, 1948, 17.

"Play of the Day: Braves," *Boston Traveler*, June 16, 1948, 21.

"Perini Gives TV 'Hysterical' Sendoff," *Boston Globe*, June 16, 1948, 22.

Siegel, Arthur, "Video Hurts Feet," *Boston Traveler*, June 16, 1948, 21.

Sampson, Arthur, "Braves Trade Aims End As Last Ditch Efforts Fail," *Boston Herald*, June 16, 1948, 35.

Sampson, Arthur, "Braves Whip Cubs, 6-3, Lead N.L.," *Boston Herald*, June 16, 1948, 35.

NOTES

1   Clif Keane. "Braves, Cubs Game To Be Televised Tonight," *Boston Globe*, June 15, 1948, 8.

2   Harold Kaese. "Braves Field Game Last Week in May Opens Television Here," *Boston Globe*, May 12, 1948, 23.

3   "Braves Game First Seen Here by Television," *Boston Globe*, June 16, 1948, 1, 7.

4   Arthur Sampson, "Braves Trade Aims End As Last Ditch Efforts Fail," *Boston Herald*, June 16, 1948, 35.

5   "Perini Gives TV 'Hysterical' Sendoff," *Boston Globe*, June 16, 1948, 22.

6   Carl Lundquist, "Sain Red Hot—Braves Top N.L.," *Lowell* (Massachusetts) *Sun*, June 16, 1948, 17.

7   Siegel, Arthur, "Video Hurts Feet," *Boston Traveler*, June 16, 1948, 21.

8   "Braves Game First Seen Here by Television," *Boston Globe*, June 16, 1948, 1, 7.

BRAVES BREAK OUT AS SPAHN PITCHES AND PICKS OFF

SEPTEMBER 6, 1948 (FIRST GAME): BOSTON BRAVES 2, BROOKLYN DODGERS 1 AT BRAVES FIELD

BY ROBERT GOODOF

As dawn turned to noon on this Labor Day, Boston fans reveled in the success of both major-league entries. The Red Sox led the Yankees by half a game, with the Cleveland Indians lurking 3½ games back. The Braves clung to a 2½-game lead over St. Louis and Brooklyn, but only a single game in the loss column over the Cards, Bums, and Pirates. Even the New York Giants were within hailing distance — four back in the loss column, with 19 out of their remaining 25 games at home to finish the season. Although they led, the Braves' September schedule was daunting — 17 of the remaining 24 games were against these four teams, including 14 home games.

The Braves sent Warren Spahn to the mound for the first game, and announced Johnny Sain for the nightcap — the third time the aces were to pitch on the same day this season. The Dodgers countered with 22-year-old Ralph Branca — a 21-game winner the previous year — in the first game, in front of the holiday crowd of 39,670 (second highest of the regular season).

Boston scored early, as Tommy Holmes led off the Braves end of the first with a single, moved to third on Mike McCormick's double, and scored on a liner to right by cleanup hitter Bob Elliott. The Dodgers evened the score in their next at-bat, as Carl Furillo doubled to deep center and scored on a Roy Campanella single to left.

The early scoring then gave way to an extended pitching duel, with both pitchers trading goose eggs over the next seven innings. Branca worked in and out of several jams over his nine-plus innings of work as Braves reached third base on a trio of occasions — Al Dark (three hits in each game, extending his hit streak to 14 games) twice — in the third and fifth, and Holmes near the end of Branca's stint on a wild pitch in the 10th inning. Branca also benefited from two Dodgers double plays during his effort.

Spahn cruised through the middle innings, retiring the side in order in the third, fourth, sixth, eighth, and ninth innings, although Bruce Edwards and Carl Furillo taxed him in the fourth with 10- and eight-pitch at-bats, respectively. The lefty scattered five hits and four walks and never allowed more than a single baserunner at a time after the second inning. He rose to the occasion in the ninth, falling behind by 3-and-1 counts to Pee Wee Reese and Edwards (both righties), and recovering to fan both.

A number of key plays, worthy of 20-20 hindsight, dotted the middle innings. Al Dark's fifth inning one-out triple went for naught as Mike McCormick's grounder to shortstop was not enough to score him from third. In the seventh Furillo doubled with one out, but was then caught in a rundown as Spahn nabbed Hodges' grounder and threw to second sacker Sibby Sisti, who made an excellent stretch grab and then ran down Furillo for the second out.

The deadlock rolled into extra innings, where much of the game's excitement took place The Braves loaded the bases in the 10th with one out on two singles (Holmes and Dark) and a walk, (Mike McCormick), chasing Branca for Rex Barney, who retired Elliott, and then Joe Hatten, who bested Clint Conatser (pinch-hitting for Jeff Heath) on popups. Jackie Robinson singled with two out in the 11th, but Spahn promptly picked him off first to end the inning.

The home team threatened again in the 12th as Spahn reached first when left fielder Bruce Edwards muffed a fly ball after an extended chase, and moved to second on Tommy Holmes's bunt. The Dodgers walked Dark on purpose. Mike McCormick followed with a line single to left, but Edwards atoned by throwing Spahn out at home by a good seven feet. Should Southworth have pinch-run for Spahn, who had thrown 150-some pitches? Or, absent a pinch-runner, should he have sent Spahn at all with a strong-armed catcher—albeit struggling outfielder—fielding and throwing from left? Southworth explained to the *Boston Globe's* Jack Barry that he liked Spahn's chances against Edwards' relatively weak arm and that he'd "do it again.' Dark and McCormick advanced to third and second on the throw home, but Conatser flied out (after another intentional walk) to end the threat.

The Braves loaded the bases again in the 13th on Earl Torgeson's single, Phil Masi's fielder's choice (safe at first on a sacrifice bunt), and Sibby Sisti's single. That brought Warren Spahn to the plate. Spahn had delivered over 160 pitches at the time but manager Southworth chose to ask him to execute a safety squeeze bunt, instead of pinch-hitting for him. But Hatten was able to field the bunt cleanly, force Torgeson at home plate, and nail Spahn at first, covered by second baseman Jackie Robinson. *Boston Herald* beat reporter Will Cloney wrote of " 'drugstore managers' who thought Torgeson should have been off with the pitch, i.e., a suicide squeeze." With a possibly overworked pitcher at bat?

The Dodgers continued to work to manufacture a run in the top of the 14th, as Billy Cox walked, and Robinson replaced him at first on a force out. However, Spahn caught him leaning the wrong way, and picked him off AGAIN, and then Reese popped up, ending the inning.

In their half of the 14th, the Braves finally broke through, as Conatser coaxed a two-out walk and scored on Torgeson's double to center, making Spahn a tired (177 pitches, two pickoffs) winner, and Branca a hard-luck loser.

Arguably, the day was a major turning point in the NL pennant race. The Braves won the nightcap, with Sain's five-hit, 4-0 shutout winning the second game. They stood with a four-game lead by Monday night, although the Pirates remained only a single game back in the loss column. (The Dodgers and Cards were both three back.) Spahn and Sain duplicated their Labor Day success in another doubleheader (after two offdays and then two rainouts) later in the week, and the Braves won 15 of the final 20 over the rest of the season, turning a one-game (loss column) lead into a seven-game advantage by the end of the regular schedule. Arthur Daley of the *New York Times*, ruminating on the prospects of an all-Boston World Series, proclaimed the Red Sox the most formidable team in the junior circuit. He wrote, "The Red Sox have been winning so consistently that they seem to defy the law of averages," and that "the fat cats of the National League would seem to be the Boston Braves," acknowledging a schedule with several offdays over the rest of the regular season.[1]

The offdays and postponements that followed led Southworth, on September 13, to outline his pitching plans for the next couple of weeks, largely riding on the left and right arms of his two best pitchers. His comments led *Boston Post* reporter Gerald Hern to pen the famous line "Spahn & Sain and followed we hope by two days of rain" in the September 14 edition. Thanks to several scheduled offdays, each of the aces continued their intense workload during the month—Spahn started seven games (winning four) and Sain eight (winning seven). Moreover, each started the October 2 doubleheader—one day before the end of regular season—even though the Braves had clinched the flag and had a 5½-game game lead. Workhorses, indeed!

SOURCES

Sources consulted for this article were Baseball-Reference.com and the September 7, 1948, editions of the *Boston Globe*, *Boston Herald*, and *Boston Post*.

NOTES

1 *New York Times*, September 8, 1948.

BRAVES WIN 1948 PENNANT

SEPTEMBER 26, 1948: BOSTON BRAVES 3, NEW YORK GIANTS 2 AT BRAVES FIELD

BY DAVID C. SOUTHWICK

For the first time in 34 years, the National League pennant returned to Boston thanks to Bob Elliott's 22nd home run, a three-run shot in the first inning. The Braves hung on to defeat the New York Giants, 3-2, before 31,172 jubilant spectators at Braves Field.

Boston manager Billy Southworth celebrated his fourth NL pennant. In his previous managerial stint, Southworth guided the St. Louis Cardinals to three pennants from 1942-44, winning the World Series twice, in '42 and '44. After the game, Southworth received a phone call from National League President Ford C. Frick to congratulate the champions.

It was an extra-special occasion for Southworth. As a Braves outfielder from 1921-23, he suffered through two seasons of 100-plus losses, playing in very poorly attended games.[1]

The Braves clincher took only 1 hour 46 minutes to play, a fast, quick pace to put an end to any thought of the second-place (and former defending champion) Brooklyn Dodgers or third-place St. Louis Cardinals staging a pennant-stealing drive.

The Braves would thus open the World Series, their first since the Miracle Braves of 1914, against the winner of the heated American League race between the crosstown Red Sox and the Cleveland Indians. After the 26th, the Indians held a one-game lead with five games to play.[2]

Elliott, the 1947 National League Most Valuable Player, delivered one of the most valuable hits in Boston's 72-year NL history with a high blast to right-center on a 2-1 pitch by Giants starter Larry Jansen (18-12).

Scoring on the play were Tommy Holmes and Al Dark, who had both singled. Elliott followed Earl Torgeson at the bat, after Torgeson failed to move the runners, flying out to left.

After Elliott's blast, the game settled into a pitchers' duel, Jansen settling down to keep the Giants in it by holding the Braves scoreless on two hits from the second on, while Braves starter Vern Bickford (10-5) shut down New York until the eighth, when the Giants attempted a comeback.

"I had the best stuff I had all year," said the jubilant winning pitcher. "I didn't tire, I never lost my stuff, they just got a couple of lucky hits."[3]

Bickford carried a two-hitter into the eighth when the Giants started swinging. Giants rookie left fielder Don Mueller singled to left and a fellow rookie, catcher Sal Yvars, singled over second to put two men on and raise Southworth's nerves a bit. As Nels Potter and Warren Spahn started to warm up in the Boston bullpen, former Brave Jack McCarthy was sent up by

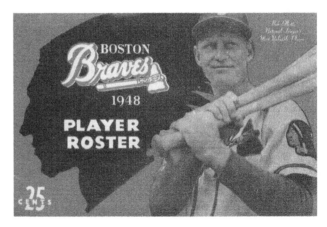

1947 NL MVP Elliott was a key contributor to the '48 pennant drive.

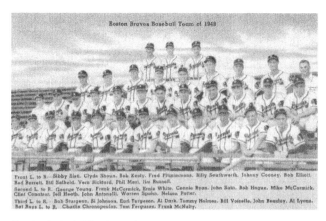

Boston's last NL champions.

Giants manager Leo Durocher to pinch-hit for Buddy Kerr. McCarthy responded with a lazy single to center. Mueller scored and Yvars went to third. The shutout was broken. Hal Bamberger ran for McCarthy. Another pinch-hitter, Lonnie Frey, batted for pitcher Jansen.

Southworth had seen enough. With a runner on third and the tying run at the plate, he brought in Potter. Frey grounded a 0-1 pitch to shortstop Dark, who got the ball to second in time to force Bamberger. But Yvars crossed the plate and brought the Giants to within a run. The score was 3-2 in Boston's favor.

Potter got Jack Lohrke to ground to Elliott, who forced Frey at second. Lohrke reached first, then ran all the way to third base when Potter threw wild to first in an attempt to pick him off.

Potter next faced Whitey Lockman and walked him on four pitches, putting runners on first and third with two out. Lockman then stole second to make matters closer. But the threat ended when Sid Gordon grounded a 2-and-1 pitch to Elliott, who threw him out at first, to the great relief of Braves fans.

After the Braves went down in order in the bottom of the eighth, it was up to Potter to seal the deal and secure the pennant. The Giants had Johnny Mize, Willard Marshall, and Mueller coming up, each hoping to extend the game, or postpone the celebration another day.

Potter wasted no time. It only took four pitches to bring the pennant home. Mize grounded to second, Sibby Sisti making a fine throw to first. Marshall popped a one-ball pitch to second, Sisti again in the middle of it all by making the catch on the edge of the outfield. With two down, the crowd now anticipated what had never been imagined back on Opening Day, a pennant of their own. It was up to Mueller, who had singled to begin New York's rally in the eighth. This time it was not to be: Mueller tapped the first pitch back to Potter, whose light toss to first clinched Boston's 87th win and set off a wild celebration by the crowd, players, and management alike. The 1948 National League pennant race was over with the Boston Braves finishing on top.

For several minutes after the final out, the many fans who stayed saluted each player as the Braves left the field to continue their own celebration in the clubhouse. The celebration included champagne flowing and players carrying Southworth around the locker room on their shoulders. The party lasted all night and probably would continue for days to come as the

The Braves Win The Pennant!

Wishing for an all Boston World Series that wasn't to be.

Braves hit the road to Brooklyn and New York for their final six games while leaving the front office the joyous task of assembling the order of World Series tickets. They waited to see who they would face in the American League, perhaps even their neighbors, the Red Sox.

After 34 years of anguish, disappointments, and losing seasons, the Braves were on top of the National League mountain, a mountain whose climb began in 1915 and ended in the grandest fashion.

Not long after the game, Braves president Lou Perini announced that all surviving members of the 1914 "Miracle" world championship team, a team that went from last place on July 4 to proud pennant winners followed by a just-as-miraculous World Series sweep of the powerful American League titlist Philadelphia Athletics, would be invited to attend the World Series as guests of the club. The first to hear of this was Hank Gowdy, the catcher for the Miracle Braves, who as fate would have it was coaching for the Giants at Braves Field that day when his former team won the championship.

SOURCES

"Hub Hails Gallant Braves' Pennant Drive," *Boston Globe*, September 27, 1948.

"Braves Win First Flag in 34 Years As Elliott's Homer Defeats Giants, 3-2," *Boston Herald*, September 27, 1948.

"Braves Conquer Giants and Capture Pennant for First Time in 34 Years," *New York Times*, September 27, 1948.

Retrosheet.org

NOTES

1   In Southworth's three-year playing stint with Boston, attendance never topped 381,627 in a season. In 1948 the Braves had a team record attendance of 1,455,439.

2   The Red Sox and Indians finished the regular season with identical 96-58 records. In the first one-game playoff in American League history, Cleveland defeated Boston, 8-3, to advance to the World Series against the Braves.

3   *New York Times*, September 27, 1948.

CLEVELAND INDIANS AT BOSTON BRAVES, OCTOBER 6, 1948

GAME ONE / 1948 WORLD SERIES

BY JOSEPH WANCHO

It had been a long time for both teams. A very long time since either the Boston Braves or the Cleveland Indians had won a pennant and earned a trip to the World Series. The Miracle Braves were a true rags-to-riches story, winning the 1914 World Series over the Philadelphia Athletics, after they had lost more than 100 games and finished in dead last in 1912. The Indians were not much better, having raised their first and only pennant in 1920. (They then bested the Brooklyn Robins to win the world championship.)

Those fans who perused *The Sporting News* on a regular basis were probably not surprised to read that in the April 21, 1948, issue the Boston Red Sox and the St. Louis Cardinals were picked to finish in the money. Still, the Braves were given strong consideration in the senior circuit: "Could be looking down at seven other clubs when the curtain drops on this current season," wrote John Drohan of the *Boston Traveler*. Ed McCauley of the *Cleveland News* was not as optimistic about the Indians, writing, "Enough improvement over last year to suggest third place finish." [1]

The Braves trailed the Brooklyn Dodgers on September 1 by a half-game. But Drohan's words proved prophetic as the Tribesmen posted a 21-7 record the rest of the season while the Dodgers broke even at 16-16. Boston finished a comfortable 6½ games over the second-place Cardinals.

The Indians had more drama to their pennant chase, as they tied the Red Sox at the end of the regular season. A one-game playoff was held on October 4, the day after the season ended, at Boston's Fenway Park. Behind two Lou Boudreau home runs and the

20th win for rookie Gene Bearden, the Indians punched their postseason ticket with an 8-3 triumph. One person who was in attendance at Fenway for the playoff game was Braves pitcher Johnny Sain. "I went over to Fenway Park to familiarize myself with the players on both teams," he said. "I stayed about six innings. It would have been nice to have an all-Boston Series, but I felt I'd have better success against Cleveland because I'd pitched against them more in spring training. I also liked Municipal Stadium more than Fenway Park. So I wasn't upset that Cleveland won." [2]

Game One was played at Braves Field as the fans were treated to an autumn-like day of 62 degrees. Although it was rather windy and gray, there was no threat of precipitation. Bob Feller (19-15, 3.56) started for Cleveland while Sain toed the rubber for the hometown heroes. The Braves' right-hander led the

Game One stub autographed by Sain and Feller.

Masi and Elliott in a pre-game pose before the backstop's date with Fall Classic fame.

NL in wins in 1948 (24-15, 2.60). The ballgame shaped up to be quite a pitchers' battle, and these two giants of the mound did nothing to sway that belief.

Both pitchers kept the crowd of 40,135 rather listless through the early innings of the game. As Paul Giguere of the *Boston Herald* wrote, "Yesterday's opening World Series game in Boston went into the books as one of the most subdued on record — not because there was any lack of spirit, but because of the close pitcher's duel. Most of the time the mammoth crowd was hushed. Peanuts cracking and the sound of the busy ambulance were all that could be heard."[3]

Marv Rickert's single to lead off the bottom of the fifth inning was the Braves' first safety of the game against Feller. Although the home crowd finally had something to cheer, Feller retired the side without incident.

And on it went, zeroes populated the scoreboard. Sain and Feller refused to give an inch to the opposition's batters. But this game would be decided by which hurler exhibited the best control. And on this fall afternoon, that was Johnny Sain.

Feller surrendered a walk to Braves catcher Bill Salkeld to lead off the bottom of the eighth inning. Salkeld, a reserve catcher, was a left-handed batter, and thus drew the starting assignment against the righty Feller. Phil Masi, the regular backstop for the Braves, was

sent into the game to pinch-run for Salkeld. Mike McCormick laid down a sacrifice bunt to advance Masi to second base. Eddie Stanky followed and Cleveland skipper Lou Boudreau elected to give The Brat a free pass. Although he was criticized later for the strategy, Boudreau explained that he was setting up a potential double play, as Sain stepped into the batter's box. However, Sain lined out to right field for the second out.

Feller and shortstop Boudreau then worked on some chicanery, as they attempted a pickoff play to try to nail Masi at second base. Seemingly, the ball arrived as Masi dove back to the bag on his belly. Second-base umpire Bill Stewart ruled Masi safe, although Feller and Boudreau argued vehemently that the runner had been tagged before he touched the base. "Boudreau tagged him up on the elbow," said Stewart. " It was just another decision."[4]

Leadoff hitter Tommy Holmes, who hit from the left side, represented the Braves' best opportunity to score a run. He didn't disappoint when he socked an outside offering from Feller down the third-base line and into left field to score Masi. The fans cheered with much delight as the Braves catcher crossed home plate, clutching his cap in his right hand. Holmes' single was only the second hit Feller gave up in the game.

The Braves needed three outs to secure the win and take a 1-0 lead in the Series. And with Warren Spahn scheduled to pitch in Game Two, the Braves had a 2-0 lead dancing in their heads, but first things first.

Holmes and Sain bask in after-game glory.

Sain retired the first two Cleveland hitters in the top of the ninth. Indians third baseman Ken Keltner then sent a grounder to third, but third sacker Bob Elliott airmailed the baseball over Earl Torgeson's head at first base. Keltner was awarded second base and some groans filled the stands. But Sain made quick work of Wally Judnich, striking him out with a curveball that reportedly broke about two feet. It was Sain's sixth K of the game, and he hadn't walked a man. He scattered four hits, and was behind in the count to only two Indians hitters.

Said Holmes of his game-winning hit: "(Feller) caught me on that (outside) pitch the last time up and I figured he was going to throw it again." "They gave me the hole at short, but I didn't want it. I was shooting for that line and I caught it. Hey, it's a wonderful feeling. I just knew Johnny would win this one."[5]

"We may not have many players who have been through a World Series," said Boston manager Billy Southworth,"but you never saw a cooler bunch in your life. They have courage. They played and waited for the break and when it came, they jumped."[6]

The Indians doffed their caps in admiration of the job Sain did. "I never saw so many rattlesnakes in my life," said Joe Gordon. "He's got quite an assortment. A curve overhand, then three-quarters overhand, then side-arm. I don't know how the fellow keeps throwing them—and over the plate all the time."[7]

The Braves received an unexpected lift before Game One. Jim Russell, their regular center fielder, was hospitalized with an ailing heart in Pittsburgh. Leo Egan of Boston radio station WHDH interviewed Russell a week before the Series began, with the thought that he might like to address the team before the game. The recording was played back to the ballclub before the start of the game. "There wasn't a sound during the playing," said Southworth, "and when it finished, all the players stood up, took another hitch in their belts and were really ready to charge out there. I held them for another minute, as I always do, and then out they went. It was great tonic to know that Jim was with them."[8]

NOTES

1   *The Sporting News*, April 21, 1948, 3.
2   Danny Peary, *We Played the Game* (New York: Hyperion, 1994), 84.
3   *Boston Herald*, October 7, 1948, 32.
4   *Boston Herald*, October 7, 1948, 33.
5   Ibid.
6   Ibid.
7   *Boston Globe*, October 7, 1948, 28.
8   *Boston Herald*, October, 7, 1948, 31.

"I GUESS THEY CAN'T WIN 'EM ALL"

OCTOBER 7, 1948: CLEVELAND INDIANS 4, BOSTON BRAVES 1 AT BRAVES FIELD
(GAME TWO OF THE 1948 WORLD SERIES)

BY ALAN COHEN

The favored Cleveland Indians had succumbed to the homestanding Boston Braves in the World Series opener on October 6, 1948, and the stage was set for Game Two. If the Braves won, they would take a 2-0 Series lead to Cleveland.

The pitchers were Warren Spahn for the Braves and Bob Lemon for the Indians, and as if two 20-game winners (Lemon was 20-14 and Spahn, who was 15-12 in 1948, had won 21 in 1947) were not enough to put a chill into some bats, the game-time temperature in the mid-50s made things even worse for the hitters, and winds that gusted to more than 20 miles per hour made it feel even colder for the 39,633 spectators. Not among the spectators was LoRene Spahn, Warren's wife, who had given birth to their son Greg on October 1 and watched the game on television in her hospital room.[1]

Neither pitcher was overpowering, but it was Lemon, pitching in and out of trouble all day (allowing the leadoff man to reach first four times), who emerged with the win. Spahn, on the other hand, was rewarded for his efforts with an early shower.

The Braves scored first on an uncustomary fielding lapse by the Indians' Joe Gordon in the first inning. He briefly bobbled a grounder off the bat of Alvin Dark that allowed the Braves shortstop to reach first base safely, or so said umpire Bill Stewart. It was the second close call in two games for Stewart. In the first game, when he was umpiring at second base, he called Braves runner Phil Masi safe when the Indians tried to pick him off at second with two outs. The decision was hotly contested by the Indians, but to no avail. The call allowed the inning to continue and Masi

scored from second for the game's only run on a single by Tommy Holmes. In the sixth inning of Game Two, as luck would have it, Masi was inserted into the game as a pinch-runner at second base. Remembering the incident from Game One, he told Indians shortstop-manager Lou Boudreau, who took the pickoff throw in Game One, "No tricks, now."[2]

Dark advanced to third on a single by Earl Torgeson. A single by Bob Elliot scored Dark, but the ball was hit so hard that Torgeson couldn't advance beyond second base.

Then came what was perhaps the turning point of the game. With Marv Rickert at the plate and the count at 2-and-2, Boudreau put on the pickoff play again. After giving a well-disguised signal to Lemon, Boudreau snuck in behind Torgesen and Lemon's perfectly timed pickoff throw arrived in time to catch the Braves first baseman.

Boudreau was known to Boston fans as creative. The prior season, he had initiated the shift against Ted Williams in which he moved his infielders to the right of second base to thwart the Boston left-hander. The shift became commonplace over the balance of Williams's career.

The evolution of the pickoff was capsulized by Hy Hurwitz in the *Boston Daily Globe:* Lemon bent way over, faking that he was having trouble seeing catcher Jim Hegan's signals. Meanwhile Boudreau crept stealthily to the rear of Torgeson. At the count of three, set in motion by a signal from Lemon to Boudreau, Lemon wheeled around and fired the ball to Boudreau. Torgeson was caught flat-footed. He didn't even have a chance to slide back.[3] Lemon struck out Rickert to end the inning. From that point on, the hosts were unable to put any runs on the board off Lemon.

Lemon's assist on this play was one of six assists he had during the game. He also tied a World Series record for pitchers with three putouts at first base on throws from first baseman Eddie Robinson.

The Indians, after being shut out in the opener and for three innings of the second game, broke through for two runs in the fourth inning against Spahn, who deserved a better fate. Boudreau opened the inning with a double off a Spahn changeup, and scored on a single by Joe Gordon. Boston left fielder Marv Rickert attempted to gun down Boudreau at the plate, but Boudreau scored easily. The throw home allowed Gordon to advance to second base. Columnist Red Smith categorized the hit as "the sort that would score a fast man from second, but Boudreau is so unsound he'd be ruled off any self-respecting horse track." Smith noted that Rickert's ill-advised throw "came fluttering in like a wounded dove. It dropped to earth not far beyond third base, too spent to permit a decent cut-off play."[4] Larry Doby's single to right field brought home Gordon.

The following inning, the Indians knocked Spahn out of the game. Dale Mitchell opened the inning with a single and went to second on a bunt by Allie Clark. Boudreau's single scored Mitchell and motivated Braves manager Billy Southworth to remove Spahn. Red Barrett put out the fire, but the Indians had what proved to be an insurmountable 3-1 lead. After the game Spahn said, "I'll be back. My change of pace was hanging too high. I couldn't get it down low, and that licked me."[5]

Both teams pulled off defensive gems. In the top of the sixth inning, Cleveland threatened. With one out, Eddie Robinson singled to center field off Barrett, but was quickly erased. Catcher Jim Hegan sent a fly ball to deep right field, seemingly beyond the reach of Tommy Holmes. Hegan was off at the crack of the bat, but Holmes caught up with the ball, reached out

'48 Series press pin given to members of the "Fourth Estate" by the Braves.

and grabbed it, and easily doubled Hegan off first base. It was the first double play of the World Series.[6]

The keystone combo of Gordon and Boudreau pulled off double plays in the sixth and eighth innings to thwart Braves opportunities. In the sixth, Eddie Stanky, a step slower than he had been in his prime, hit a grounder to Boudreau. Two throws later, the ball was safely in the glove of first baseman Eddie Robinson and Stanky was a dead pigeon at first base. In the eighth inning, Lemon induced Bob Elliot to hit into a double play with a steady diet of curveballs. With the count at 1-and-2, Elliot hit a groundball to Gordon, who sent the ball to shortstop Boudreau who fired on to first for the double play.[7]

The Indians added a run in the ninth as Hegan reached on an error by Dark, went to second and third on two groundball outs, and scored from third on a single by Bob Kennedy.

The difference in the game was timely pitching and defense. In both the second and fourth innings, Lemon got out number three with runners on second and third.

The Braves had not played well in losing. In two games at Boston, their hitting was quite feeble as they scored but one earned run in 18 innings. The press was not particularly kind to the Braves as they left for Cleveland. Harold Kaese wrote, "Except for hitting, pitching, fielding, and thinking, the Braves had everything in the clutch yesterday."[8]

The loss was the first ever in World Series play by the Braves in the 20th century. But then again, they had not played that often in the fall classic. They had swept to victory in 1914 and after an absence of 32 years they had won the opener in 1948. They never again won a World Series game in Boston.

SOURCES

Barry, Jack, "Stranding Men Not Way to Win … Southworth," *Boston Daily Globe*, October 8, 1948, 30.

Campbell, Gordon, "Indians Win 4-1," *Boston Traveler*, October 7, 1948, 1, 35.

Cole, Jean, "Mrs. Spahn Sure Braves Will Win," *Boston Daily Record*, October 8, 1948, 3.

Hern, Gerry, "Braves Baffled by Pickoff Play," *Boston Post*, October 8, 1948,

Hurwitz, Hy, "On to Cleveland," *Boston Daily Globe*, October 8, 1948, 1, 29.

Kaese, Harold, "Lapses by Torgy, Southworth, Rickert Contribute to Loss," *Boston Daily Globe*, October 8, 1948, 31.

Lee, Bill, "Lemon Hurls Cleveland to 4-1 Victory," *Hartford Courant*, October 8, 1948.

Malaney, Jack, "Bickford Is Hope of Braves Today," *Boston Post*, October 8, 1948, 1, 28.

Maloney, Alta, "Mrs. Warren Spahn Sees Lefty Pitch on Television," *Boston Traveler*, October 7, 1948, 37.

Smith, Red, "Patched Up Braves Starting To Fall Apart at Seams," *Boston Daily Globe*, October 8, 1948, 33.

Wolf, Al, "Indians Even Series, 4-1," *Los Angeles Times*, October 8, 1948, 1.

NOTES

1   Alta Maloney, *Boston Traveler*, October 7, 1948, 37.

2   Fred Foye, *Boston Traveler*, October 7, 1948, 1. The *Traveler*'s play-by-play of the game also shows Masi inserted as a pinch-runner in the bottom of the sixth.

3   Hy Hurwitz, *Boston Daily Globe*, October 8, 1948, 29.

4   Red Smith, *Boston Daily Globe*, October 8, 1948, 33.

5   Jack Barry, *Boston Daily Globe*, October 8, 1948, 30.

6   Gordon Campbell, *Boston Traveler*, October 7, 1948, 35.

7   Jack Malaney, *Boston Post*, October 8, 1948, 28.

8   Harold Kaese, *Daily Boston Globe*, October 8, 1948, 31.

BEARDEN DOES IN BOSTON – AGAIN

OCTOBER 11, 1948: CLEVELAND INDIANS 4, BOSTON BRAVES 3 AT BRAVES FIELD (WORLD SERIES, GAME SIX)

BY SAUL WISNIA

It is hard to find a more important date in Braves Field history than October 11, 1948. Not only was it Game Six of the World Series, a do-or-die contest for the hometown team, but it was also a chance for that club to take its biggest step yet toward reconquering the city it had lost nearly a half-century before.

The Braves trailed the heavily favored Cleveland Indians three games to two, but if they could capture this contest they had their ace Johnny Sain—whose four-hit shutout in the Series opener five days before was his 25th victory of the year—ready for Game Seven the next day.[1] And if the big right-hander came through in *that* contest, the Braves would not only be champions of the baseball world, but they would finally hold bragging rights over their crosstown rival Red Sox. The Red Sox had ruled Boston almost exclusively since the American League arrived in town for the 1901 season, and had won 104 games and an American League pennant just two years before. They lost to the St. Louis Cardinals in the World Series, however, so by capturing this fall classic the Braves would one-up their rivals.[2]

Braves fans had to feel pretty good about their chances. Although their club dropped three straight after Sain's Game One masterpiece, it had rebounded to crush strikeout champ Bob Feller and four Indians relievers for 12 hits and three homers during an 11-5 win in Game Five—played before the largest crowd in baseball history (86,288) at Cleveland Stadium. Now the Braves were hosting the last two games at home, with 6-foot-4 right-hander Bill Voiselle starting this one before a more modest sellout gathering of 40,103 and

Sain waiting in the wings. If Boston's bats could keep booming, the team's first world championship since 1914 was still a strong possibility.[3]

Game Two winner Bob Lemon, looking for his second road victory of the Series, started for the Indians. The righty kept Boston at bay for the first two innings, and in the third Cleveland broke through against Voiselle when Dale Mitchell led off with a double and scored on a blooped two-bagger down the right-field line by shortstop-manager Lou Boudreau that bounced out of the glove of a sprinting Tommy Holmes. The field general for the Indians was again proving a major thorn in the side of Bostonians after hitting two homers against the Red Sox in Cleveland's pennant-clinching 8-3 triumph at Fenway Park in the previous week's one-game AL playoff.

The Braves tied things 1-1 in the fourth, but lost a key opportunity to move ahead. Bob Elliott hit an infield single leading off, Bill Salkeld walked, and Mike McCormick drove in Elliott and sent Salkeld to second with a two-out single to center. Eddie Stanky walked to load the bases, but Voiselle grounded out, ending the inning. Braves manager Billy Southworth may have considered pinch-hitting for Voiselle (an .097 batter during the regular season) in such a crucial spot, but Big Bill had allowed just one hit in 3⅔ innings in Game Three and Southworth gambled that he could keep this contest close.

In the sixth inning the manager's hunch appeared to go sour. Joe Gordon led off for the Indians and crushed a homer over the left-field wall, and Voiselle also gave up a single and walk in the frame, with a second run scoring when Jim Hegan drove in Thurman Tucker from third on a groundout on which a high throw from Stanky prevented a double play. Cleveland's lead remained 3-1 into the eighth, when, with lefty Warren Spahn in for Voiselle, the visitors connected for three straight one-out singles. The last, by Eddie Robinson, made it 4-1. Time in the game and the season was running out for Boston, and the arc lights were ordered turned on by the umpires as the skies darkened.

Lemon had scattered just six singles to this point, but when Tommy Holmes led off the Boston eighth with number seven and went to third on a one-out double by Earl Torgeson, the home fans came alive. Elliott walked to load the bases, and Boudreau had seen enough. Heading to the mound from his shortstop position, the manager took the ball from Lemon and called for knuckleballer Gene Bearden. Rookie Bearden had been the talk of baseball with a 20-7 regular season capped by the pennant-clincher over the Red Sox, and had stopped the Braves cold in Game Two of the Series with a 2-0 shutout. Now he was being called upon to put out the season's most crucial brushfire, and Braves fans hoped the kid would finally blow a big one.[4]

He almost did. All season long Boston manager Southworth had proved a genius at platooning, and here he went to work again—calling back scheduled batter Marv Rickert (a right-hander) and sending up Clint Conatser (a lefty) to face the southpaw Bearden. Although a rookie, Conatser was older than many veterans on the Braves with five professional seasons under his belt and a .274 average against lefties during the regular season. This gamble proved a good one, as Conatser hit a screaming line drive to deep center that easily scored Holmes from third to make it 4-2. Torgeson, a fast runner on second, also managed to tag up and advance a base on the sacrifice fly as Boudreau wisely held the relay throw to keep Elliott (the tying run) on first.[5]

There were now two outs with men on first and third, and catcher Salkeld due up. Again Southworth made a move; although Salkeld was a left-handed batter, the manager knew that his other receiver, right-handed Phil Masi, might fare better, having faced Bearden three times in Game Three. Once more the hunch was dead-on, as Masi smashed a ball off the left-field wall for a double that scored Torgeson and sent Elliott to third. A few feet higher, and the Braves would have been ahead 5-4. If Boudreau had thrown to third a play earlier, thus letting Elliott reach second, it would be 4-4. Instead it was 4-3, and there it stayed as Bearden got McCormick on a sharp grounder to the mound.

Spahn quickly dispatched the shell-shocked Indians in the ninth, striking out the side swinging, and the Braves came up for their final whacks with the crowd and momentum on their side. Stanky led off with a walk against Bearden, and Southworth made yet another switch—sending up veteran utilityman Sebastian "Sibby" Sisti to hit for Spahn. This decision seemed particularly chancy; Spahn was going well, and was a good-hitting pitcher who batted left-handed. But Southworth considered Sisti the best bunter in

Ticket to the last World Series game played in Boston by its NL representative.

the National League, and Boston needed to get the tying run to second base.

Sisti did indeed bunt, but the ball went straight up instead of down. Catcher Jim Hegan grabbed the blooper, then gunned the ball to Joe Gordon covering first base to double off Connie Ryan (who, running for Stanky, was well on his way to second) for Cleveland's fourth twin-killing of the contest. Up stepped Holmes, who already had two hits in the game. The fan favorite had been a Game One hero by driving in that contest's only run, but Bearden got him here on an easy fly to left to end the game and the Series. For the second time in a week, the rookie pitcher was carried off a Boston baseball field after doing in the home team.[6]

Nearly in tears in the Boston clubhouse, Sisti blamed himself for the loss. Teammates tried to console him—it was you, they said, who helped save the season by starting at second base for several months after Stanky broke his ankle—but Sisti was real broken up.[7] It wasn't until early the next year, when he came to the Boston Baseball Writer's Dinner to pick up an award and a long ovation as the "Unsung Hero" of the 1948 season, that he was able to get over the pain.[8]

As a team, however, the Boston Braves never really got over Game Six. Dissension rocked the club in spring training of '49, and it finished fourth the next three seasons under Southworth and Holmes—who took Billy's post after the frustrated manager resigned in mid-1951.[9] A year later the Braves were a seventh-place outfit playing to mostly empty seats, and by the time they *did* win their second World Series, in 1957, they called Milwaukee's County Stadium home.

Could two more wins in '48 have kept the Braves in New England? That will never be known, but the confidence and good feeling that comes from winning it all might have been just what was needed to offset the problems that came the next spring—and may have also helped Boston fans to be more supportive (and visible in the stands) while waiting for the next great Braves team to develop.

SOURCES

Author interviews with Clint Conatser and Sibby Sisti, 1991-2008.

Baseball reference.com.

"Hustling Braves Rate Only Cheers," *Boston Herald*, October 12, 1948.

"Hub Warriors Losers in Hard Series Fight," *Boston Post*, October 12, 1948.

"Pop Bunt Hard for Sisti to Take," *Boston Post*, October 12, 1948.

"Indians Win Series By Beating Braves in Sixth Game, 4-3," *New York Times*, October 12, 1948.

Daley, Arthur. "Champions at Long Last," *New York Times*, October 12, 1948, 35.

Kaese, Harold. *The Boston Braves* (New York: Putnam Press, 1948).

NOTES

1   Sain had lost Game Four in Cleveland, 2-1, but allowed just five hits—giving him an impressive series line of 17 innings pitched, 9 hits, no walks, and an ERA of 1.06. The Indians did not want to face him in a Game Seven on the road, and some sportswriters even questioned Southworth's decision to start Voiselle ahead of Sain in Game Six even though Sain had thrown eight innings two days before.

2   Then officially called the Boston Nationals, the Braves had won eight pennants during the National League's first 25 seasons, including five in the 1890s alone. Their fans, known as the "Royal Rooters," were the most loyal in baseball—until the upstart American League came to town in 1901. The Boston Americans (later the Red Sox) used higher player salaries and lower ticket prices (25 cents versus 50 cents) to steal their neighbor's top talent and fans. During the decades to come, the AL club almost always had more success on the field and at the gate—and the gap widened once Ted Williams joined the Red Sox in 1939. The Braves had nobody to compete with Williams for hits or headlines, and Red Sox owner Tom Yawkey could not be outspent when it came to assembling a star-studded roster. Only now, with the Red Sox having lost a one-game playoff to Cleveland to deny Boston a chance at a "Trolley World Series," did the Braves finally have a chance to be top dogs in town.

3   It wasn't just Sain the Indians had trouble hitting against; Cleveland's cumulative batting average for the World Series was .199, one of the lowest ever for a Series winner. Larry Doby, at .318, was the only Indian to bat over .300. Earl Torgeson (.389) and Bob Elliott (.333, with five hits in the last two games) were Boston's top batsmen, but like Cleveland the Braves scored just 17 runs in six contests—and 11 of them came in Game Five.

4   Boudreau's decision to go to Bearden in the eighth was a gamble not just because it was a precarious place to bring a rookie into, even a battle-tested one, but because it precluded the manager from starting his hottest pitcher in Game Seven the next day. Steve Gromek, who had won Game Four with a 2-1 complete

game, would likely have gotten the ball against Boston's Johnny Sain in Bearden's place.

5   Author interviews with Clint Conatser. Nearly 45 years later, Conatser sat watching a video compilation of the '48 World Series on his living room TV and joked about how close he had come to being a hero. He remained friends with many of his old teammates for the rest of their lives, and with Alvin Dark's death in 2014 the 93-year-old Conatser was the last member of the Boston Braves still alive to have played in the '48 World Series.

6   Interestingly, many Braves players had been on hand and cheering at Bearden's first championship-clinching win exactly one week earlier. When the rookie beat the Red Sox, 8-3, to clinch the AL pennant for Cleveland at Fenway Park on October 4, the Braves knew that although they would not get a chance to beat their crosstown rivals in the World Series, their Series bonus shares—which were based on game attendance—stood to be much higher playing road contests in Cleveland Stadium (capac-ity 85,000-plus) than at Fenway Park (capacity 33,000). They were right; the $4,570 each Braves player earned was the highest losers' share to that point in World Series history.

7   Joe McKenney, *Boston Post*, October 12, 1948.

8   Author interviews with Sibby Sisti. Sisti's role in Boston's 1948 pennant was indeed significant. He played outstanding second-base defense while Stanky was out, and hit nearly .280 for the last four months of the season. In the 66 games he started, Boston's winning percentage was .600—higher than its overall mark of .595.

9   Stressful conditions in the 1949 Braves clubhouse led to Billy the Kid's mid-August leave of absence for "health" reasons, with coach Johnny Cooney temporarily taking over the steward-ship of the team for the rest of the season. See Jon Daly, "Billy Southworth," in Bill Nowlin, ed., *Spahn, Sain and Teddy Ballgame* (Burlington, Massachusetts: Rounder Books, 2008), 187.

CANNONBALL JACKMAN AT BRAVES FIELD

MAY 25, 1949: NEW ENGLAND HOBOS 3, BOSTON COLORED GIANTS 1 AT BRAVES FIELD

BY RICHARD "DICK" THOMPSON AND RICHARD "DIXIE" TOURANGEAU

St. Patrick's Church on Magazine Street in Roxbury was in need of funds to continue its charity work in what was slowly becoming the predominantly black section of Boston. It was May 1949, and the church decided to sponsor a baseball game at Braves Field, a three-mile line drive away and home of the NL-pennant-defending Braves. The plan was to herald one of its favorite adopted sons, pitcher Will "Cannonball" Jackman. Then 54, Jackman had been quietly pitching fewer and fewer games as the years went by. His real job for several years was as a Dedham doctor's chauffeur, but he happily agreed to hurl the game to enhance the church's donation box. Cannonball loved to pitch, anytime, anywhere, and against anybody.

Jackman (1895-1972)[1] was a fixture in the Roxbury neighborhood since the mid-1920s when he arrived from his semi-native Houston, Texas, area. He was born in rural Kyle, in Hays County, about 150 miles west of Houston, and as a teenager found his niche as an all-around player for the Houston Buffalos and a few other black ballclubs in east Texas. A right-hander, he was a workhorse, possessing a throwing arm that seemed tireless. In addition, he was a dandy hitter. In his lengthy baseball career, Jackman toiled for many teams—as chronicled by Dick Thompson in his 2007 *National Pastime* biography of the Negro legend. Jackman was part of black, white, and mixed clubs, like the 1929 East Douglas team in the famed Blackstone Valley League in south-central Massachusetts (with teammate Hank Greenberg) and the 1939 Portsmouth (New Hampshire) squad. But most of his outings were for black teams in the Boston

area such as the Boston Royal Giants, the Colored Giants, the Philadelphia (Boston) Giants, and even the Boston Night Hawks in the 1940s.

For one reason or another Jackman never made a point to join the Negro American or National League, apparently enjoying his role as a popular hurler for several semipro Boston-area black teams. Will always compared very well to his contemporary, icon Satchel Paige, with many baseballists not afraid to claim Will was better when in his prime. He was paid well for pitching and maybe the financial comfort and contentment of his Boston surroundings kept him from

Will "Cannonball" Jackman.

Jackman honored during his later years.

outside ventures. He said he was treated well from the day he arrived in the Northeast.

The May 25 contest was to pit drawing card Cannonball and his Boston Colored Giants pals against the New England Hobos, a team of mostly ex-minor leaguers who barnstormed much of the summer. Intrepid SABR researcher Thompson's relentless tracking of Jackman's exploits indicates that by the mid-1940s his appearances declined in frequency but certainly did not stop. Thompson was able to find a few dozen games per year, but that left dozens of others, most likely never printed by any outlet, to remain mysteries. By the late 1940s, the over-50 Jackman would take the ball only occasionally. So this sudden Wigwam charity game was a special treat for fans.

What transformed the idea into an "event" was a column by the *Boston Globe*'s Jerry Nason on May 24 announcing that it was possibly Jackman's 1,200th appearance. Nason's entire piece was a short biography and a sparkling promo for the following night. Other Boston dailies also had short pieces touting Jackman and his forever catcher/friend, Burlin White (1895-1971), as the "oldest battery" that was still competitive.[2] Nason claimed that Cannonball hurled 20 games in 1948, winning 17 (not documented or found by Thompson). The Jackman-White combo had emeritus-like status with the Giants but they were no longer the mainstays. White caught Jackman's tosses for at

least three Boston black teams, including the Colored Giants and the Royal Giants, which White managed on and off. Being the well-worn backstop, White had retired before his free-throwing pitching pal, but gladly came out of that state for this one game. Being May, it was Will's first game of the year.

Timing and baseball irony collide here. On Sunday, May 22, at Cincinnati's Crosley Field, the first black battery in modern major-league history carved out a 3-0 win for the Brooklyn Dodgers as rookie Don Newcombe got his first start (and win) while throwing to Roy Campanella (who scored one of the runs). Newk knocked home two Dodgers and Jackie Robinson the other, for a historic victory. The Jackman-White tandem could have been the first just as easily but were born too early.

As for the game itself, the *Globe*'s Herb Ralby provided the best coverage. His game account the next morning was headlined, "Just Getting in the Groove, Says Jackman After 8 Innings." The Hobos were fortunate to win, 3-1, on six hits before 4,266 chilled fans who eagerly contributed to the St. Patrick coffers. Three Giants errors gave the Hobos two runs in the second inning and the Giants left their two ninth-inning leadoff runners stranded, so it was a close, exciting match down to the last out. Scribe Ralby focused on Jackman's effort, "The cool weather and his previous inactivity caused Jackman to get away to a slow start. He had worked all day on his chauffeuring job and arrived at the park (Braves Field) in time to heat up his aging muscles with a self-administered rubdown and a ten-minute warmup."

"I couldn't get loose in those first few innings but after that I was fine. Sure I could go another full game now. I was just getting in the groove," claimed Jackman.[3] Using his trademark underhand knuckleball, sinker, and curveball, he threw 106 pitches in eight frames as the Hobos were granted home status at the Gaffney Street tepee. The opposing hurler and winner was 28-year-old Ray Louis Bessom (1920-2013), star of the 1937 Lynn Classical High School State Champions with schoolboy batterymate Jim Hegan (Indians) and winner of the "Little World Series" title game for East

Lynn Legion Post 291 the same year. Young Bessom served in World War II as a staff sergeant in France and Germany. Ray gave up eight hits and a walk while fanning eight; two of those whiffs came in the ninth while a groundout ended the cordial contest. Ray was 48-46 in the minors, ending his pro career in 1947. Other Hobos were Billy Cliggott, Joe Lehan, Tony Novello (two hits, run), Lucien Belanger, Charlie Maloney (two walks, run), and Joe Lynch. All had minor-league stints from the late 1930s to mid-1940s. Untraceable shortstop MacDonald (two hits) and catcher Shea (run) completed the roster that night. Ageless Jackman's fielders were Bob Thomas (ss, three hits, run), Spence (hit), Fran Matthews (hit), Charlie Thomas, Collins (hit), Adamson (hit), Griffin, sub John Neves, sub Sylvester Mills, White (hit), and Jackman. Art "Fats" Johnson was the manager of the then 3-and-2 Giants.

Local icon Jackman gave a grand showing as an effortless over-50 hurler, without any real "warmup" for the season, never mind this game. He faced and kept in check a team of recent minor leaguers a bit more than half his age. While fans across the nation were excited about the Newcombe-Campanella possibilities, Boston had its own less publicized version of breathing black baseball history that had already performed extremely well.

It is interesting to note that columnist Nason, who gave folks an extra reason to come out to Braves Field that May night in 1949 and gave modern researchers some background into Jackman's life to that point, still had his *Globe* writing slot in 1972 when Cannonball died. He typed not a single word of remembrance.

SOURCES

Boston Chronicle, May 21, 1949, and "Giants Lose in Charity Tilt," May 28, 1949.

Boston Globe, May 22, 24, 25, and 26, 1949.

Liston, Bill, "Hobos Beat Giants at Wigwam," *Boston Post*, May 26, 1949.

Lynn Daily Item, May 8, 2013.

Retrosheet.org.

SABR Minor Leagues Database, accessed online at Baseball-Reference.com.

Thompson, Dick. "Cannonball Bill Jackman, Baseball's Great Unknown, "*The National Pastime, A Review of Baseball History* (Cleveland: SABR, 2007), #27.

NOTES

1 Jackman's year of birth is up for some debate but not much. His tombstone and a Baseball Hall of Fame questionnaire that he filled out say 1897, but the 1900 and 1920 US Censuses do not confirm that year. They indicate late 1895 or early 1896. Texas birth records for blacks in rural communities are difficult/impossible to find.

2 "Ageless Jackman Faces Hobos," *Boston Globe*, May 25, 1949.

3 Herb Ralby, "Just Getting in the Groove," *Boston Globe*, May 26, 1949, 31.

A BARRIER PARTIALLY FALLS:
SAM JETHROE'S FIRST GAME IN BOSTON

APRIL 21, 1950: PHILADELPHIA PHILLIES 2, BOSTON BRAVES 2 (TIE)

BY BILL NOWLIN

More than nine years before Pumpsie Green first played for the Boston Red Sox—the last team in baseball to desegregate—Sam Jethroe played for Boston's first major-league team, the Boston Braves. Jethroe's first two games were on the road, against the Giants at the Polo Grounds, on April 18 and 19, 1950. He was 2-for-4 with a home run and two RBIs in his big-league debut.

His first appearance in Boston was in a City Series exhibition game at Braves Field on April 15. He went 2-for-4, scored one run, and drove in one run. He also played in the next day's game at Fenway Park, in a game—albeit an exhibition game—at the same park and on the fifth anniversary of the April 16, 1945 date when he and Jackie Robinson and Marvin Williams had tried out for the Red Sox in 1945.[1]

Jethroe's first regular-season game in Boston came on April 21. Considering that Jethroe playing at Braves Field represented the first integration of either of Boston's two teams, there was very little mention of race in the Boston newspapers leading up to the game.[2] The *Boston Post* devoted a preview to the team's home opener on April 21, but it contained just two sentences referring to Jethroe, neither of them noting his race. The *Boston Herald*'s preview just noted, "Sid Gordon … Sam Jethroe, and Willard Marshall in the outfield." The *Boston Globe* had a 20-paragraph story by Clif Keane on how the rookie Jethroe's home run in New York had dispelled some of his butterflies; there was not a word hinting at race. Nor did Harold Kaese's preview. The *Globe*'s Jack Barry mentioned Jethroe in passing as "the Negro star." And the *Boston Traveler*

suggested that "Sam Jethroe's Boston debut in a championship game vies for attention at the Braves opener with the return of Eddie Waitkus to major league action."[3] In the eighth paragraph, the *Traveler* noted that Jethroe was "the first Negro Boston regular."

Braves Field fans were excited to get a look at "Jet-Propelled Jethroe"—in 1949, he had set an International League record with 89 stolen bases for Montreal.

Manager Billy Southworth selected Vern Bickford as his starting pitcher for the April 21 game. The Braves had won the pennant in 1948, but plunged to a 75-79 fourth-place finish in 1949, 22 games behind the Brooklyn Dodgers. Southworth was, of course, hoping for a better showing in 1950 and the Braves had won both games against the Giants. The visiting Philadelphia Phillies were on the rise. Eddie Sawyer had taken over as skipper for the last third of the 1948 season, which

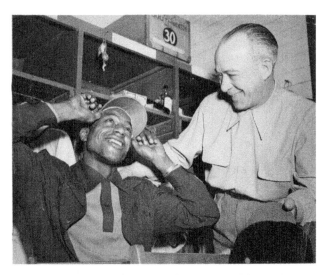

Billy Southworth welcomes the "Jet" to the Braves.

The Braves scored one run in the bottom of the second, thanks to a walk worked by Sid Gordon and then a two-out balk that moved him to second. Del Crandall struck a "clean single to center,"[5] and it was Phillies 2, Braves 1.

In the bottom of the fifth the Braves got one more, tying the game. With one out, Crandall singled over the second-base bag and into center field, and shortstop Buddy Kerr doubled him home with a drive off the fence in left field, even taking third on Hamner's errant throw to the plate—but there he languished.

The Phils failed to score in the top of the eighth. In the bottom of the inning, with the Braves' Connie Ryan at the plate pinch-hitting for Bickford, and with a 3-and-2 count on him, play was halted by plate umpire Lon Warneke. It had been raining for an inning and a half. After a 44-minute delay, removing the infield tarpaulin deposited "hundreds of gallons of water in short right field"[6] and the grounds were deemed too soggy for the game to continue. The score reverted to where it had stood at the end of seven and the game went into the books a 2-2 tie. Thus, the batter Bickford had walked in the top of the eighth was no longer part of the official record.

After the game, fellow pitcher Warren Spahn lamented, referring to the back-to-back complete-game wins that he and Johnny Sain had in the season's first two games, "Bick pitched a much better game than Sain or I and gets no credit for it. Except from the fans, teammates, writers, and Southworth."[7] Jethroe had been 1-for-3, a single with two outs in the third inning, thrown out trying to stretch it to a double. The hit was noted by the several Boston dailies, but no particular crowd reaction was reported. Heintzelman had given up only five hits—Jethroe's, the two by Crandall, Kerr's double, and a single by Bickford to open the third (he was shortly erased on a double-play ball hit by Ryan). In the seventh Bickford slashed a line drive down the left-field line, but it was about 12 inches foul—and he wound up popping up to second baseman Mike Goliat.

Boston's first African American major leaguer.

had seen them 66-88, in sixth place. In 1949 they'd climbed over the Braves into third place, six games ahead of them in National League standings. The Phillies were 1-1 coming into Boston. Sawyer started lefty Ken Heintzelman.

Phils leadoff batter Richie Ashburn singled to center and then Granny Hamner singled on a roller to third base. After Eddie Waitkus fouled out to the catcher, Del Ennis "plunked a single into short right"[4] and both baserunners advanced two bases, Ashburn scoring. Willie Jones flied out to second, but Dick Sisler drove in Hamner with a single to right, getting cut down himself for the third out while trying to take second base. Still, the Phillies had a quick 2-0 lead. In the bottom of the inning the Braves couldn't get the ball out of the infield, going down 1-2-3.

After the first inning, Bickford settled down and allowed only three more hits in the game. He didn't walk a batter until the eighth—a walk that doesn't show up in any box scores.

Boston baseball integration pioneers Robinson and Jethroe meet at Braves Field in 1950.

There had been a bit of thunder and lightning and even a very brief snow flurry at one point. The threatening weather had kept the paid crowd to 7,308, though the *Post* estimated that over 10,000 in all came to Braves Field, what with all the various dignitaries. Governor Paul A. Dever had thrown out the first pitch. Mayor John B. Hynes was there, as well as the governors of Rhode Island and New Hampshire. A contingent of Marines saw to the raising of the flag, and the music was provided not by The Three Troubadours, who had previously regaled Braves fans, but by John Kiley playing an electric organ that had been installed "in the photographers' cage under the third-base roof."[8]

The game itself was replayed at a later time and did not go into the books as a tie, but all individual stats remain a part of baseball's historical record.

Not one of the game stories in Boston's three newspapers mentioned Jethroe's race.

In 1950 Jethroe led the league with 35 stolen bases, more than double those of second-place finisher Pee Wee Reese. He scored an even 100 runs and won the National League Rookie of the Year award.

NOTES

1   The trio reported never having heard a word from the Red Sox after what has widely been termed a "sham tryout." See several articles on the subject in Bill Nowlin, ed., *Pumpsie and Progress: The Red Sox, Race, and Redemption* (Burlington, Massachusetts: Rounder Books, 2010).

2   Readers knew of Jethroe's race, dating at least from the time of his acquisition from the Dodgers and from coverage of spring training, but even then mentions in the Boston papers were notably sparse.

3   *Boston Traveler,* April 21, 1950. Waitkus came from Cambridge, Massachusetts, and had been shot by a crazed female fan, a story later fictionalized into part of the book and movie *The Natural.*

4   *Boston Herald*, April 22, 1950.

5   *Boston Globe*, April 22, 1950.

6   *Boston Herald*, April 22, 1950.

7   *Boston Globe*, April 22, 1950.

8   *Boston Post*, April 22, 1950.

PUGILISM AT THE BALLPARK/THE WIGWAM WELCOMES TWO FUTURE CHAMPS IN ONE EVENING

JULY 10, 1950

BY BOB BRADY

On occasion over the years, some of Boston's Green Cathedrals have served as venues for outdoor boxing programs. Fenway Park staged its first fight on October 9, 1920, and would continue to host fisticuffs within its confines through 1956. Braves Field got a later but more auspicious start. Just three days later, on October 12, more than 15,000 fans gathered at the Wigwam to witness a battle for the welterweight championship of New England. The *Boston Globe* of the following day declared that the attendees comprised "the largest crowd that ever saw a fight in New England." But for rain in the forenoon and threatening weather later in the day, at least an additional 10,000 individuals would have come to the contest, according to the newspaper.

In all, Braves Field played host to around 70 boxing programs, most featuring multiple matches, through July of 1951. The majority of these events occurred during the Depression years as Braves ownership leased the ballpark to generate revenues to stay afloat financially. According to Bob Fuchs in *Judge Fuchs and the Boston Braves*, Boston Garden boxing promoters attempted to stage evening boxing cards at the Wigwam directly after afternoon Braves games in hopes of retaining the baseball crowd. The promoters paid $25,000 for such rights but soon found that the Tribe's fans were not interested in sticking around and quickly negotiated a buyback.

International Boxing Hall of Famers such as welterweight champion Jack Britton (The Boxing Marvel), heavyweight champion Jack Sharkey (The Boston Gob), light-heavyweight champion Paul Berlenbach (The Astoria Assassin), heavyweight champion James J. Braddock (The Cinderella Man), featherweight champion Willie Pep (Will o' the Wisp), bantamweight champion Manuel Ortiz, and middleweight champion Theodore "Tiger" Flowers (The Georgia Deacon) all made appearances at Braves Field.

Well before African American ballplayers took to the field at the Wigwam and Fenway Park, minority pugilists performed before crowds in temporarily assembled rings on the respective diamonds. Tiger Flowers, the first African American to become world middleweight champion, fought at Braves Field in 1925, well before Jackie Robinson's barrier-breaking season of 1947 and Sam Jethroe's integration of Boston home-team baseball in 1950. Similarly, Fenway Park opened its doors to black boxers such as Cuba's Kid

Rocky moves a step closer to the world heavyweight title.

Chocolate in 1932, many years in advance of its primary tenant's 1959 welcoming of Pumpsie Green to the home turf.

A landmark boxing event at Braves Field took place on July 10, 1950. The Braves abandoned the Wigwam on July 9 after a 13-inning victory over the Giants to embark upon a road trip and the All-Star break that wouldn't have them return to action at their Gaffney Street residence until July 25. Given ownership's past receptivity toward leasing out the premises to nonbaseball events when the field was otherwise vacant, an evening of boxing featuring local pugs with championship potential was set up. The site also proved to be an attractive venue as the ballpark possessed its own internal streetcar stop, allowing fight patrons quick and easy inexpensive public transportation to and from Braves Field.

With the Boston region's large Italian-American community, it seemed only natural to put together a boxing card involving two up-and-coming slugging *paisanos*: welterweight Leonardo Liotta and heavyweight Rocco Marchegiano. Upon embarking upon professional careers in the ring, both underwent name changes — Liotta fought as Tony DeMarco while Marchegiano battled as Rocky Marciano. Liotta assumed the DeMarco moniker upon borrowing the latter's birth certificate to fight professionally while still under age.

The Wigwam's alternative use as a boxing battleground did not seem out of place for Marciano. As a youth, Rocky was torn between baseball and the fight game. Through the auspices of a *Boston Herald* sportswriter, he had been invited to the Chicago Cubs' annual tryout camp in 1947, conducted at their Fayetteville, North Carolina, Tri-State League facility. While Rocky showed promise as a hitter, he was unable to throw accurately from his backstop position to second base because of an arm injury incurred during his time in the Army. According to Ed Fitzgerald in the January 1953 issue of *Sport* magazine, Rocky reported, "My arm was dead. I couldn't throw." Given the local publicity that had surrounded his baseball trip south, Rocky was reluctant to return home upon failing the tryout.

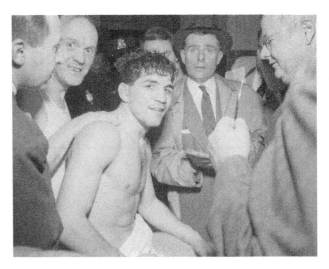

Tony DeMarco, pride of Boston's North End.

An acquaintance referred him to the Goldsboro (North Carolina) Goldbugs of the Class-D Coastal Plain League. The unaffiliated club was short of catchers and he sought a job with them. As Rocky related to Fitzgerald, "I played for a couple of weeks, maybe three altogether, and I got my hits, but I couldn't throw. The manager finally told me I'd better go home." Rocky would ultimately make it to Boston's National League ballgrounds wearing boxing gloves instead of the "tools of ignorance." Two of his younger brothers, Louis (Sonny) and Peter Marchegiano, would follow in Rocky's baseball footsteps, playing a few seasons of low-level minor-league baseball. Peter, in fact, signed in 1962 with the Braves, albeit the Milwaukee version, at Rocky's former catching position.

Tony DeMarco (11-2-0) appeared on the Braves Field undercard of July 10. His contest, against journeyman Roger Ringuette (11-9-0) of Fall River, Massachusetts, was scheduled for four rounds. The pride of Boston's North End pummeled his opponent, sending him to the canvas three times in the first round. Mercifully, the referee stopped the bout and handed DeMarco a technical-knockout victory. He would go on to claim the world welterweight crown in 1955. Perhaps not wanting to show favoritism toward either of Boston's baseball parks, DeMarco would later fight to a unanimous victory at Fenway Park on June 16, 1956, representing, as of 2014, that site's last boxing card.

Rocky's 28th bout on his way to the heavyweight crown was the main event of the July 10, 1950, boxing program at Braves Field. Marciano's opponent was former Italian amateur heavyweight champ Gino Buonvino (22-11-7) of Bari, Italy. Joe Zapustas, a former South Boston athlete of some renown, drew the refereeing assignment. Zapustas, had had a "cup of coffee" as an outfielder with the 1933 Philadelphia Athletics and had played offensive and defensive end for the '33 NFL New York Giants, who lost that season's league championship game to the Chicago Bears, 23-21.

The rainy July evening resulted in a disappointing gate as only 4,900 filed through the turnstiles. Another noted negative to the bout was the antique ring used for the contest. It was in a dilapidated condition and several feet smaller than regulations required. Fight patrons also suffered from poor lighting of the ring, causing a chant of "LIGHTS" to often arise from grandstand spectators during the bout.

The future champ started strongly, knocking Buonvino to the canvas with a left hook to the jaw for an eight-count in the first round, but was unable to quickly put his opponent away. Buonvino fought back valiantly but began to tire noticeably by the seventh round. Knocked down in the ninth, Buonvino was saved by the bell. The exhausted Italian faced a relentless barrage of Rocky's blows in the next round until the referee stepped in and stopped the fight for a TKO. Rocky commented about his Braves Field experience, "[W]hat a ring. It was really small and tilted. I felt like I was fighting uphill all night." Writer Arthur Siegel of the *Boston Traveler* panned Rocky's performance, opining that the heavyweight ranks must be weak in talent if a "good club fighter" like the Brockton Blockbuster was considered a leading contender. Marciano and Buonvino would meet one more time with even worse results for the former Italian champ. On April 21, 1952, in Providence, Rhode Island, Rocky kayoed Buonvino in the second round. Buonvino hung up his gloves after this defeat. Rocky took the heavyweight title on September 23, 1952, knocking out Jersey Joe Walcott in the 13th round of their championship bout. He retired undefeated (49-0-0) after his final bout in 1955.

Braves Field was but a brief stop along the road to boxing glory for Tony DeMarco and Rocky Marciano. Today, their achievements in the ring have been commemorated in statutes of each in fighting poses. DeMarco's sculpture resides at the entrance of Boston's North End. Marciano is memorialized by a two-ton, 20-foot statue in Champion Park on the grounds of Brockton High School.

SOURCES

In addition to the Sources identified in the text of this article, the author utilized BoxRec.com.

THE LAST NO-HITTER PITCHED BY A BOSTON BRAVE

AUGUST 11, 1950: BOSTON BRAVES 7, BROOKLYN DODGERS 0 AT BRAVES FIELD

BY RICK SCHABOWSKI

Vern Bickford came close to a no-hitter on September 5, 1947, pitching eight hitless innings in the American Association as a Milwaukee Brewer against the Minneapolis Millers, losing the no-hitter on a lead-off single in the ninth by pinch-hitter Andy Gilbert. But he would not be denied on August 11, 1950, seven days before his 30th birthday, pitching a no-hitter against the Brooklyn Dodgers at Braves Field. The no-hitter was the only one during the 1950 season.

There was some question about Bickford's availability for the starting assignment that night. Four days before, he had been hit on the elbow by a ball hit by Pete Reiser during batting practice. But he was given the okay to start.

The 1948 pennant chant of "Spahn and Sain followed by rain" wasn't needed in 1950. After Bickford's no-hitter, the Braves trio had won 44 of the Braves' 59 victories, and Bickford accounted for 14 of them. The 1950 Braves were in a pennant race, entering the game in second place, six games behind the Philadelphia Phillies and leading the Dodgers by a half-game.

A raucous crowd of 29,008 fans packed Braves Field to watch Bickford square off against Carl Erskine, making his first start since being recalled by the Dodgers from Montreal.

Bickford breezed through the first inning, striking out Pee Wee Reese and getting groundouts off the bats of Gene Hermanski and Duke Snider. The Braves had a two-out uprising in the bottom of the inning. With Sam Jethroe on first base after a walk, back-to-back doubles by Bob Elliott and Walker Cooper, then

a single by Sid Gordon on which Duke Snider made an error, gave the Braves a 3-0 lead.

Bickford set down the Dodgers in the second, getting Jackie Robinson and Carl Furillo on groundouts and striking out Gil Hodges. Furillo's groundball was sharply hit and after the game third baseman Bob Elliott recalled, "It took one big hop and was stung pretty good. I guess maybe it was the best shot they had all night."[1] In the bottom of the inning the Braves added another run, on a two-out single by Roy Hartsfield, an error on a pickoff attempt by Erskine, and a single by Sam Jethroe. Dodgers manager Burt

Vern Bickford warming up.

222

Spahn congratulates Bickford.

Shotton had seen enough and brought in Joe Hatten, who struck out Earl Torgeson.

The no-hitter was almost lost in the third inning when Joe blooped a pitch into right-center field. Jethroe, Hartsfield, and Willard Marshall all converged on the ball. Jethroe and Hartsfield fell down and Marshall made a diving catch. After the game Hartsfield said, "Any one of the three of us could have had it, but when we got close to it, the only one who hollered was Marshall. He said, 'I got it,' so I fell to the ground to keep away from the ball. When I hit the ground somebody toppled over me and I guess it was Jethroe."[2] Marshall said, "There was a collision between the two fellows just as I reached for the ball. I caught it about hip high and then I bumped into Jethroe when he was falling over Roy, but I didn't juggle the ball at all. I just sort of brushed against Sam's side when I caught it."[3]

In the fourth inning Bickford lost his perfect game, issuing a one-out walk to Gene Hermanski.

The Braves added another run in the fifth inning. Earl Torgeson stroked a one-out single and advanced to second base on yet another error on a pickoff attempt by a pitcher, this time by Hatten, and scored on a single by Bob Elliott, giving the Braves a 5-0 lead.

Two more Braves runs came across the plate in the seventh inning. Torgeson drew a walk from Dan Bankhead, Elliott singled and went to second as rifle-armed Carl Furillo tried in vain to get Torgeson at third. Both scored on a single by Sid Gordon for a 7-0 Braves advantage. The eighth inning was very easy for Bickford, who retired Gil Hodges, Roy Campanella, and Billy Cox on six pitches. The Braves got two hits in the bottom of the inning but didn't score.

Bickford entered the ninth inning having thrown only 77 pitches. He had to throw 19 more to nail down his no-hitter. He walked pinch-hitter Jim Russell, got Pee Wee Reese on a fly ball to center, then walked Gene Hermanski. "All I wanted was the game," Bickford said later. "That was all. No, I didn't think anything about it for eight innings but truthfully, I did in the ninth. Especially when I walked those two hitters. Nobody had said a word all through the game to me. I didn't hear anything. I guess the Dodgers were yelling something at me, but I didn't pay any attention to them."[4]

An elated Vern Bickford.

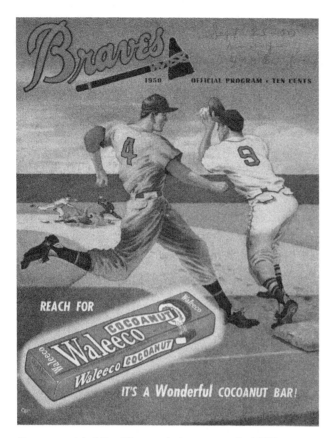

Program sold at the Wigwam to keep score in 1950.

With Russell and Hermanski on base, the next hitter was the dangerous Duke Snider. The first pitch was a ball, high and wide. Bickford evened the count with a slow curve. The count went to 2-and-1 with a pitch in the dirt. After two foul balls, one of them a long drive down the left-field line that went foul aided by the wind, Bickford threw another curveball. Snider hit it to shortstop Buddy Kerr, who turned it into a game-ending double play. "Boy, what a feeling that was when Snider hit the ball to me," Kerr said. "I was right close to second base as I put my left foot on it and threw to Torgy. I just coaxed the throw right to him and I felt like jumping a mile high when I saw the out sign by the umpire."[5]

Of that last pitch, Bickford said, "I guess you could call it the happiest pitch I ever threw in my life."[6] Bickford's no-hitter was the first in the major leagues since the Dodgers' Rex Barney no-hit the Giants on September 9, 1948, and the first by a Brave since knuckleballer Jim Tobin accomplished the feat against the Dodgers on April 27, 1944. The Braves stormed out of the dugout and carried Bickford off the field to the accompaniment of cheers of "Bickie!"

Manager Billy Southworth said, "It was a great pitching performance. He had wonderful stuff."[7] Catcher Walker Cooper thought that "Bickford had everything. I'd say he had the best curve ball he had all year, but he threw everything good. It was a hell of a game he pitched. I don't think they hit any balls real good."[8]

Bickford gave credit to his teammates. Pointing to Cooper, he said, "That's the guy who pulled me through, and don't forget those great plays by Bob Elliott and Willard Marshall."[9]

It was a long but happy postgame for Bickford as well-wishers, telegrams, and phone calls congratulated him on his effort.

Nine months later, on May 6, 1951, the Braves were no-hit themselves in the second game of a doubleheader at Braves Field by the Pirates' Cliff Chambers.

Bickford's no-hitter was the first night game no-hitter in Boston, a feat that would not be repeated until June 26, 1962, when the Red Sox' Earl Wilson no-hit the California Angels.

NOTES

1 Clif Keane, "Started Thinking About It in 9th—Bickford," *Boston Globe*, August 12, 1950.

2 Ibid.

3 Ibid.

4 Ibid.

5 Ibid.

6 "Bickford Hurls No-Hit Shutout," *Boston Post,* August 12, 1950.

7 "Started Thinking About It."

8 Ibid.

9 "Vern Bickford Credits New Slider For No-Hit Job Against Brooklyn," *Hartford Courant*, August 12, 1950. Bickford's no-hitter was the first for Dodgers announcer Vince Scully and the only one where he did not make the call of the final out. Since Scully joined the Dodgers in 1950, there have been 15 no-hitters pitched by the Dodgers and seven pitched against them, the most notable being Don Larsen's perfect game.

THE RETURN OF THE "MIRACLE MEN"

JUNE 2, 1951: CHICAGO CUBS, BOSTON BRAVES 5 AT BRAVES FIELD

BY BOB BRADY

Special events were scheduled throughout the senior circuit season of 1951 to celebrate the league's Diamond Jubilee 75th anniversary. National League ballclubs commemorated this historic event with a variety of ceremonies. The Boston Braves chose to bring back surviving members of the 1914 Miracle Braves World Series championship team as the Tribe's jubilee contribution. A three-day affair was put together by Braves owner Lou Perini, culminating in pregame festivities at Braves Field before the Saturday, June 2, match-up with the visiting Chicago Cubs. Fittingly, Boston and Chicago were the only National League clubs to have operated continuously since the circuit's formation in 1876.

Time had taken its toll in the 37 years that had elapsed since the Braves' last (and final) world championship. Eleven of the 34 ballplayers on the Tribe's 1914 roster were now deceased. First to depart the scene was pitcher Otto Hess in 1926, followed in 1929 by manager George Stallings. The last survivor was utility infielder Jack Martin, 93, whose death closed this chapter of Miracle Braves history on July 4, 1980.

On Friday evening, the celebrants of Saturday's jubilee events met in the Hotel Somerset lobby to reminisce with reporters. Asked what it was that led them on their triumphant march to the pennant, they cited team spirit. George Stallings' deft leadership was duly noted. Pitcher Bill James stated, "We belonged in eighth place when we were there and without Stallings we belonged there at the end of the season." Catcher Hank Gowdy seconded James' opinion: "George made us a great team." Even in 1951, old-timers grumbled about baseball's changing salary structure. Staff ace and 1914 26-game winner James remarked that his

largest contract was for $2,600 or about what he figured to be a week's paycheck for Red Sox star Ted Williams.

First sacker Butch Schmidt entertained all with an anecdote of his own. He proclaimed that the Braves could have acquired Babe Ruth in 1914 from the International League Baltimore Orioles. Schmidt had played in Baltimore from 1908 to 1912 and was an acquaintance of club majority owner Jack Dunn. "I scouted Ruth myself when he was pitching for St. Mary's Industrial School [and] recommended him to Gaffney when the Baltimore Orioles were breaking up," Schmidt revealed. Dunn was under significant

Drumming up interest for the NL anniversary celebration.

Surviving Miracle Braves members gather at a hotel before the game.

financial stress brought about by competition from the upstart Federal League Baltimore Terrapins who forced him to relocate his club to Richmond, Virginia, in 1915. (The Orioles returned to Baltimore in 1916, after the Federal League folded.) Schmidt claimed that for $10,000, Gaffney could have picked up not only the Babe but also pitcher Ernie Shore and catcher Ben Egan. However, Gaffney said "$10,000 was too much to pay for ballplayers." Instead, the Red Sox jumped at the deal. Schmidt's tale indicates that the "Curse of the Bambino" might have been cast upon not one but both of Boston's baseball franchises!

Festivities kicked off on June 2 with a parade along Commonwealth Avenue to Braves Field. The old-timers assembled at the host hotel at noon for the trek to the Wigwam. Lou Perini and Ford Frick headed up the delegation, which was driven to the field in antique automobiles provided by Brookline's Larz Anderson Museum. The procession commenced at 12:45 P.M. under the escort of the police and a detachment of US Marines. When the parade reached the Commonwealth Armory, it was joined by the almost 100-piece Harvard University band. As Harvard was in the midst of final exams, the bandsmen had to wear their uniforms to their tests. They then were given box lunches and hustled onto a bus that was driven to the Allston destination with the way cleared by members

of the Cambridge police. Inside the armory nearly 3,000 Little Leaguers from Massachusetts, Maine, New Hampshire, and Rhode Island had assembled in uniform waiting to join the procession. Units from the Army and Navy added to the throng that entered the ballpark for the 1:15 kickoff of festivities. The Mutual Broadcasting Company was on hand to air the day's special events and the ballgame to over 352 of its affiliates and to the armed forces overseas.

The Diamond Jubilee celebration preceded the day's Braves-Cubs contest at the Wigwam. Fans cheered as the parade of old-time automobiles circled the playing field, passing before the visiting and home dugouts. In each of the ancient jitneys was a member of the Marine Corps holding a sign that identified the honored guests in the buggy. Paraded before the crowd in addition to Gowdy, Mitchell, James, Smith, Schmidt, and Tyler were outfielder Herb Moran, catcher Bert Whaling, outfielder Les Mann, third baseman Charlie Deal, pitchers Dick Crutcher and Paul Strand, batboy Willie Connors, and George Stallings, Jr., substituting for his father. Instead of donning replicas of their '14 togs, the guests appeared in current Tribe tomahawk-style uniforms.

Each of the old-timers was called out onto the field by National League President Ford Frick to assume his former position. Mitchell and Stallings Jr. reported to the first- and third-base coaching boxes, respectively. Gowdy and Whaling, catcher's mitts in hand, stood behind home plate. James, Tyler, and Crutcher took to the mound while Schmidt and Smith ambled to first and third base. Deal subbed for the late Johnny Evers at second base while Messrs. Mann, Strand, and Moran walked to their outfield positions. The placement of pitcher Strand in the outfield was not entirely out of place as an accommodation to the dearth of reunion representatives at that position. In 1915 he appeared in five games in the outfield for the Braves in addition to performing his normal mound duties, and finished his career as a fly chaser. As would be expected, batboy Willie Connors was situated on the sidelines.

Pre-game festivities.

Fan favorite Rabbit Maranville drew the day's greatest ovation as he was introduced and jogged to his position at shortstop. The diminutive infielder had missed the parade as he had had to make a quick trip to New York to fulfill a commitment to a sandlot baseball group. Flying back to Boston on Lou Perini's private aircraft, he rushed from the airport in time to dress and just make it to the Wigwam for the introductions. Maranville "warmed up" by taking a few groundballs, flipping one behind his back to Deal at second. When announcer Les Smith informed the crowd that the irrepressible Rabbit would perform his legendary "vest pocket" catch, a roar came from the stands. Hank Gowdy threw a ball high in the air toward the peppery shortstop and Maranville gingerly backed up toward left field, cupped his hands and caught the ball at belt level to the delight of all. Rabbit then twisted his cap sideways on his head as he had done throughout his playing days.

Watching the day's events and the game from the stands was 91-year-old C.A. Brown who claimed to have been present at Boston's first National League game on May 30, 1876. Unfortunately, he and the other 15,127 in attendance witnessed the Braves go down to defeat, 7-5, despite some ninth-inning attempted heroics. Tribe starter Warren Spahn had one of his infrequent poor outings, lasting less than two innings, yielding four runs on six hits and two walks. Earl Torgeson provided some excitement, blasting an

eighth-inning two-run homer, five rows into the Jury Box. Cubs "senior citizen" reliever Dutch Leonard squelched a rally in the bottom of the ninth, retiring the side after coming in with no outs and two Braves on base.

Seated behind home plate during the game, the "Miracle Men" couldn't help but contrast "Stallings' baseball" against the current version. At one point when the Braves filled the bases and the next batter swung at the first pitch and hit into a double play, Bill James reflected, "Under Stallings, the batter wouldn't swing at the first pitch. Maybe the pitcher would have walked the next man up and forced in a run." James remarked that Stallings always said, "Let the pitcher lick himself, if possible." Les Mann and Red Smith both observed, "We won the pennant in 1914 by bunting. It's a different game today." The old timers got caught up in the excitement of the last-inning rally and later expressed their appreciation to the present-day Braves for trying pull out a win for them.

Despite all of the hoopla surrounding the celebration, the turnstile figures were disheartening, especially when one considers that the grand total was a bit "padded." Passes were handed out to the 2,985 Little Leaguers, 157 servicemen, and 2,001 Knothole Gang members, leaving just 9,984 paying guests. The lukewarm reception drew an editorial rebuke in the June 13 issue of *The Sporting News*. Baseball's "Bible" expressed disappointment toward the fans' "So what?"

Commemorative anniversary ticket stub.

reaction to the jubilee commemoration and honoring of the game's pioneers. As the *TSN* editorialist opined, "The game owes a great deal to these old-time heroes, whose achievements helped the majors over a period of struggle and made possible the sport's present solid place in American life."

SOURCES

The original extended version of this piece appeared in *The Miracle Braves of 1914: Boston's Original Worst-to-First World Series Champions* (Phoenix, Arizona: Society for American Baseball Research, 2014).

JURY BOX HERO TAKES THE HELM

JUNE 30, 1951: BOSTON BRAVES 19, NEW YORK GIANTS 7 AT BRAVES FIELD

BY JOE SCHUSTER

During his full-time playing days with the Boston Braves (1942-1950), outfielder Tommy Holmes was a particular fan favorite, especially among those who populated the right field grandstand known as the Jury Box, where fans often carried on a conversation with Holmes as he stood in his position.[1] Twice an All-Star (1945, when he was elected to the NL roster although there was no All-Star Game that year, and 1948), Holmes hit .304 over those nine seasons, finished among the top 10 in batting five times, and barely missed the NL batting title and MVP award in 1945, when the Chicago Cubs' Phil Cavarretta edged him out in both races, although Holmes had superior numbers in nearly every other offensive category. In 1948 he was one of the pivotal players on the Braves' first NL championship team since 1914.

After the 1950 season, the Braves asked Holmes to manage their Class-A team at Hartford in the Eastern League for 1951. Then 33, Holmes thought he still had some years in him as a major-league player but recognized that if he turned down the managing job, he would likely be the number four outfielder for the Braves in 1951; the minor-league job would give him a shot at staying in baseball and one day managing in the major leagues.[2] Holmes even suggested at the time that the Braves had hinted they had pledged the big-league managerial job to him whenever it next opened up. "They made me a pretty nice promise," he told reporters.[3]

As it turned out, Holmes did not have long to wait. In mid-June, Braves manager Billy Southworth resigned abruptly, citing the team's continuing mediocre play and his disappointment that the organization was unable to acquire any players who might help the team out of its doldrums.[4] To replace him, Boston turned to Holmes, who at the time had his Hartford team in first place. Braves general manager John Quinn told reporters that Holmes was the only person on the team's short list of candidates: "[We] considered Tommy and nobody else. In a few months at Hartford, he proved to us that he can handle men, that he can produce winning baseball for us."[5]

Tommy Holmes in his playing days.

Holmes ascends the Braves administration building staircase as for the first time as Tribe manager.

With the Braves at 28-31 and 10½ games out of first place, Holmes debuted as manager on June 20 against the Cubs in Wrigley Field and guided Boston to a 9-0 victory, which the *Boston Globe* took as an omen for the balance of the team's season. Declaring "a new era opens," the newspaper ran the game story under the headline, "Holmes Brings Tribe Back to Life," and reported that the team seemed to have renewed enthusiasm under the new skipper.[6]

Although the team went but 1-3 over its next four games to close out Holmes's road debut at 2-3, he returned to Braves Field to significant acclaim. "I haven't had too much time to sleep [since assuming the manager's job]," he told reporters. "It's been a whirl ever since I took over. ... Press conferences and calls and letters ... from everywhere. ...There are some [that] tell me they haven't been to a Braves game all season but they'll be coming down now."[7]

Holmes made his home debut on Saturday, June 30, 1951, facing the second-place New York Giants, sending Boston's Vern Bickford (8-7) against the Giants' Sal Maglie (12-3), who was on his way to arguably his best season as a starting pitcher.

The game drew 10,812 spectators despite the threat of rain, and before the first pitch fans in the Jury Box celebrated Holmes's return by presenting him with

some good-luck charms, including rabbits' feet and four-leaf clovers and what the reporter from the *Boston Herald* described as "a miscellaneous assortment of magic potions."[8]

The charms seemed to do their work early on. Bickford retired the Giants without allowing a run in the top of the first inning, though he hit Willie Mays, who had just completed his first month in the major leagues. There was a 12-minute delay before the Braves' first hitter could step to the plate when the skies opened up and the grounds crew covered the mound and the plate, but the downpour ended before they could deploy the tarp.[9] Then the Braves gave Holmes what the *Boston Globe* described as a "jubilant opening."[10] They scored four runs off Maglie in the first inning, the big blow a two-run, 425-foot homer to center field by left fielder Sid Gordon.[11]

The lead held up only until the top of the third, when Bickford began to struggle with his control, walking two consecutive hitters after striking out the leadoff man. He nearly got out of the inning when the Giants' Al Dark hit what should have been a double-play ball to Braves shortstop Sibby Sisti. But Sisti booted it, loading the bases. Willie Mays grounded to second for the second out, but then Bickford allowed three consecutive hits, tallying five unearned runs. The Giants added two more in the fifth to take a 7-4 lead, helped by another Braves error, this one when first

Holmes points to his image on the team photo of the 1948 NL pennant winners.

Tommy Holmes dresses for the first time as the Braves playing manager.

baseman Earl Torgeson dropped a throw from second baseman Roy Hartsfield.

But then the game shifted.

To lead off the bottom of the seventh, Holmes sent pinch-hitter Bob Addis to the plate for Bickford, and Addis singled to left. Then the Braves started what was their biggest one-inning offensive explosion of the season. (They matched it in a game on August 26.) Maglie did not retire a batter in the inning, allowing Hartsfield to single and then hitting Sam Jethroe to load the bases. On a 1-and-1 pitch, Torgeson made up for his error in the top of the inning by launching his first career grand slam into the Braves bullpen. After Maglie walked third baseman Bob Elliott, Giants skipper Leo Durocher lifted him for right-hander Sheldon Jones, but the Giants seemed undone: Jones allowed four singles, threw a wild pitch and Giants right fielder Don Mueller added a throwing error before Durocher went to his bullpen again and bought in Dave Koslo, who finally retired the side — but not before the Braves had tallied eight runs in the inning.

The Braves were not finished. In the bottom of the eighth, after reliever Max Surkont set the Giants down in order, Boston went back on the attack, aided by more porous New York defense. Two hits and a walk loaded the bases and catcher Walker Cooper singled, scoring two runs when center fielder Willie Mays

booted the ball, although he recovered in time to nab Cooper trying to go to second on the miscue. After a single by Sisti, Surkont fouled out to first, but then Giants second baseman Eddie Stanky made errors on two consecutive plays, allowing one run to score and putting two on base for Torgeson, who had been struggling nearly all season to that point, his average down to .236 at game time. Torgeson launched his second home run of the game, to collect his seventh RBI, his career best for one game. His blow ended the scoring for the game, which gave Holmes a 19-7 victory as a homecoming present. Holmes inserted himself into the lineup in the top of the ninth, playing right field, and received a standing ovation from the fans in the Jury Box.[12]

Sadly, Holmes did not last long as Braves manager and he did not, as the *Globe* declared, bring the team back to life: They went 48-47 under his guidance for the rest of the 1951 season, finishing fourth, 20½ games behind pennant winner New York. After the team got off to a 13-22 start for the 1952 season, the Braves replaced Holmes at their helm with Charlie Grimm, this time GM Quinn saying that Holmes "needed more experience" before he was ready to return to the major leagues.[13] Holmes managed in five more seasons in the minors but never returned to the big leagues as a manager.

SOURCES:

Boston Globe

Boston Herald

Lowell (Massachusetts) *Sun*

The Sporting News

Society for American Baseball Research Tommy Holmes Biography

Baseball-Reference.com

Retrosheet.org

NOTES

1 Saul Wisnia, "Tommy Holmes," SABR Biography Project sabr. org/bioproj/person/2c6097b4, accessed November 23, 2014.

2 Bob Ajemian, "Holmes Gives Up Braves Berth to Make Pilot Bow at Hartford," *The Sporting News*, March 28, 1951, 10.

3   Steve O'Leary, "New Skipper Was Popular With Players," *The Sporting News*, June 27, 1951, 7.

4   Steve O'Leary, "'Braves Good Enough to Win'—Holmes," *The Sporting News*, June 27, 1951, 7.

5   O'Leary, "New Skipper."

6   Clif Keane, "Holmes Brings Tribe Back to Life, *Boston Globe*, June 21, 1951, 15.

7   Bob Holbrook, "Lil Holmes Still Floating on a Cloud," *Boston Globe*, July 1, 1951, C31.

8   Will Cloney, "Braves Crush Giants 19-7," *Boston Herald*, July 1, 1951, 37.

9   Frank Sargent, "Braves Explode at Plate to Hammer Giants, 19-7," *Lowell Sunday Sun*, July 1, 1951, 17.

10 Hy Hurwitz, "Braves Trounce Giants, 19-7," *Boston Globe*, July 1, 1951, C30.

11 Sargent.

12 Ibid.

13 Jack Barry, "Braves Name Grimm Manager," *Boston Globe*, June 1, 1952, C1.

"THE GREATEST RHUBARB IN THE HISTORY OF BRAVES FIELD"

SEPTEMBER 27, 1951: BOSTON BRAVES 4, BROOKLYN DODGERS 3 AT BRAVES FIELD

BY BOB BRADY

So said *Boston Traveler* sportswriter John Drohan in the September 28, 1951, edition of his newspaper, remarking upon the happenings at the previous day's Braves-Dodgers tilt at the Wigwam.

Brooklyn's Dodgers were struggling to retain the top spot in the senior circuit's standings. Their advantage over the second-place New York Giants had evaporated from 13 games to 2½ games by the time they visited Boston for four contests, commencing with a September 25 twi-night doubleheader. The Braves were returning home after six straight road losses and in the throes of wrapping up another disappointing season. The Billy Southworth era had ended on a sad note on June 19 when the overwhelmed Braves skipper finally threw in the towel, and Jury Box hero Tommy Holmes was summoned to take the parent club's reins from his novice managerial assignment with the Eastern League Hartford Chiefs.

The Braves swept the doubleheader. The first game featured Warren Spahn capturing his 22nd victory while wearing a teammate's borrowed number-22 jersey for good luck. Now only a game ahead of the Giants, Brooklyn regrouped the following day and humbled the Braves, 15-5, behind big Don Newcombe.

With every game a "must win" for the Dodgers, tensions were high on September 27 when the Bums sent ace Preacher Roe to the mound to face rookie lefty Chet Nichols. Roe was seeking his 23rd win of the season while Nichols had a shot at capturing the National League ERA crown. Braves players were incensed over Jackie Robinson's perceived "bush" steal

of home the previous day after the Dodgers had already locked up a lopsided victory. Despite the drama associated with this contest, the ballpark was sparsely populated for the Thursday afternoon Ladies Day game, even with the addition of 321 female fans. The *Boston Globe's* Gene Mack, Jr. later commented that it was a "crime that only 2,086 Bostonians turned out to witness probably the most exciting game played in the Hub this season."

Umpire Frank Dascoli.

The hard-fought contest was tied 3-3 heading into the bottom of the eighth. Braves left-fielder Bob Addis led off with a single to center, followed by a Sam Jethroe single that sent Addis to third. Earl Torgeson bounced to Jackie Robinson at second and Robinson threw to Roy Campanella at the plate. Robinson's throw was a bit outside, causing Campy to pivot to the right. This provided an opening for Addis to reach the plate with the eventual winning run in a spikes-first slide as the Dodgers catcher made a half-spin tag. Home-plate umpire Frank Dascoli signaled that Addis was safe.

Campanella vehemently protested the call. In doing so, he slammed down his mitt, resulting in an immediate heave-ho by Dascoli. The angry visitors then swarmed the arbiter. Coach Cookie Lavagetto was booted as well. Emotions failed to cool and the Dodgers continued to ride Dascoli from the first-base dugout. Out of patience, Dascoli ordered the entire Brooklyn bench to their internal dressing room, excepting manager Chuck Dressen and coach Jake Pitler. The layout of Braves Field required the players to cross past Dascoli toward the third-base dugout to enter the tunnel accessing the clubhouse. Future Boston Celtic and Basketball Hall of Famer Bill Sharman, a late-season call-up, was among the Dodgers exiled but not ejected. He would never officially appear in a major-league contest. John Gillooly of the *Boston Record American* described the eviction trek as a "pitiable procession; no doubt stingingly profane."

Campanella's ouster had a significant bearing on the game and, ultimately, Brooklyn's drive for the pennant. Campy, who later in the year would be voted the NL Most Valuable Player, was replaced in the lineup by Rube Walker. In the top of the ninth, Pee Wee Reese doubled and advanced to third on a Robinson groundout. Deprived of Campanella's clutch bat at this critical juncture, Dressen chose to pinch-hit for the weaker-hitting substitute backstop. To make the move, Dressen had to send his batboy, Stan Strull, to the distant clubhouse to retrieve sequestered utility infielder Wayne Terwilliger, delaying the game. Terwilliger grounded out to third and Nichols struck out Andy

1951 Rookie and NL ERA leader Chet Nichols is flanked by fellow rookie moundsmen George Estock (L) and Dave Cole (R).

Pafko to secure the win. Only a half-game now separated the Dodgers and Giants. The Braves clinched fourth place, securing a few hundred dollars for each player, and freshman portsider Nichols captured the National League ERA title with a 2.88 average.

The Dodgers' anger continued unabated after the game. The umpires' room was closely situated between the players' quarters beneath Braves Field's stands, allowing the disgruntled Bums a further opportunity to complain. What followed would later be headlined in the *Boston Herald* as a "riot under [the] stands."

Dascoli and his crew had retired to their dressing room and locked its door. An attendant claimed that Jackie Robinson kicked the door repeatedly, splintering its upper and lower panels, while "screaming unprintable words of indignation and resentment." Campanella, now in civvies, was said to have been among others taking part on this incident. Braves Field grounds superintendent Al Oliver and six Boston patrolmen assigned to the Wigwam were summoned to the scene but arrived after order had been restored.

Reporters at the scene indicated that the battle had turned verbal behind the locked doors of the Dodgers' and arbiters' rooms. "Player—'You are a ___ ___ ___.'" "Umpire—'The same goes for you.'" "Player—'You can go to ___.'" "Umpire—'And that's for you.'" Said a Braves player, "I've seen fist fights, but I've never

The Braves' '51 program cover commemorated the NL's 75 anniversary.

seen anything like those guys pounding on that door. If they don't get suspended, nobody will ever get suspended."

When questioned, Robinson angrily denied the allegations. "Anybody who says I did it is a damned liar. … Whenever I'm in a crowd and something happens, right away it's me." Robinson couldn't resist adding, "He [Dascoli] was run out of the International League he was so bad, and then they let him work up here. … He chokes up worse than the players."

Preacher Roe admitted to knowing the guilty party but refused to identify the culprit. "But it wasn't Jackie, I'll take an oath on that." Another Dodgers player said, "Quite a few of our boys either kicked or pounded it on their way to our dressing room."

Dodgers coach Clyde Sukeforth issued damning statements not only against Dascoli but also Commissioner Ford Frick, then also the acting National League president. "Dascoli is a bad umpire, that's all. No other umpire would have acted so hastily. … I don't blame Dascoli, though. He is more to be pitied. He's not big enough for so important an assignment. I lay the blame on Frick. He must know, as everybody else does, that Dascoli is incompetent. He never should have assigned him to a series as important as this." Chuck Dressen added, "He's just not competent, that's all." "We've had trouble with him all year — as far back as spring training."

After Dascoli emerged from the dressing room, he offered his take on the matter. "Campanella didn't touch Addis until his feet crossed the plate." Robinson's hurried throw was sufficiently off the mark to provide the opening to Addis. As to Campanella's ouster, Dascoli waved him out of the game not because of language or physical contact. "He threw his glove. When they throw their glove, it's automatic. It's got to be. If you didn't, the next time they'd throw the center field bleacher at you."

The Braves supported Dascoli's account. Addis, a former Brooklyn farmhand, unflinchingly claimed that he was safe. Manager Tommy Holmes stated, "He got in under him. I saw the whole play." Many of the Braves felt that Brooklyn's furious protestations were totally unjustified and that Campanella's reaction was only a gesture to cover up his failed tag.

Boston Globe columnist Harold Kaese opined that most observers agreed with Dascoli's decision. However, Kaese added that the umpire had the reputation of having "more notches in his right thumb than Wyatt Earp ever had on the butt of his six-shooter." In the scribe's opinion, the arbiter from Danielson, Connecticut, had always been too quick to eject players. "He is allergic to protests. Players say he has the biggest rabbit ears in the business."

The day's events were reported to Ford Frick. For such bad behavior, the national pastime's top official decided to fine Robinson and Campanella $100 each and Roe $50. Frick said that "these fines are not for actions on the field, but for those in the runway on the way to the clubhouse." Other loose-lipped participants in the melee escaped punishment.

The Braves weren't through influencing the 1951 senior-circuit pennant race. They finished the season at home against the Giants. Despite their best efforts, the Tribe could not stop the New York juggernaut and lost both contests, setting the stage for the "Shot Heard 'Round the World."

SOURCES

The author used various contemporary Boston newspaper accounts as noted above and *The Sporting News* of October 10, 1951.

BRAVES QUIT HUB

SEPTEMBER 21, 1952: BROOKLYN DODGERS 8, BOSTON BRAVES 2 AT BRAVES FIELD

BY SAUL WISNIA

The last home game of the 1952 season at Braves Field was played before 8,882 fans and nearly 32,000 empty seats on a Sunday afternoon in late September. Under the circumstances, this wasn't much of a surprise.

There are plenty of numbers one can use to describe the '52 Braves, most of them bad. Boston's National League club finished in seventh place at 64-89, had no starting pitcher with a winning record, and batted .233 as a team. Although rookie third baseman Eddie Mathews hit an impressive 25 home runs, including three in one game, he had so few teammates getting on base ahead of him that he managed only 58 RBIs.[1] Given such a substandard product to watch, just 281,278 fans ventured to Braves Field—the worst attendance in the major leagues and a cataclysmic decline of more than 80 percent from the 1,455,439 who had seen the 1948 pennant winners do battle four years before.[2]

Just how dismal were things at the Wigwam? The Braves drew 4,694 fans on Opening Day, and soon settled into a pattern in which the home crowds rarely went above that total. For the May 14 game against the Pittsburgh Pirates, the announced figure was 1,105, and *Boston Globe* photographer Paul J. Maguire took a photo that showed a vast expanse of the third-base pavilion in which one fan was seated all by himself in the last row. Sportswriters were so convinced that the 1,105 number was inflated that they decided to hand-count the fans themselves from the press box. They came up with less than 900, and the *Globe* claimed the official figure was later changed to 825—the lowest in the 37-year history of Braves Field.[3]

By the time the Braves faced off against the Brooklyn Dodgers in their home finale, which came in the midst

of a 10-game losing streak, Boston had fallen 30 games behind the visitors, who were on the verge of clinching the National League pennant. Brooklyn's All-Star lineup featuring future Hall of Famers Jackie Robinson, Pee Wee Reese, Duke Snider, and Roy Campanella, and Cooperstown-worthy Gil Hodges. Boston manager Charlie Grimm countered with youngsters and old-timers whose best days were ahead of or behind them, including a pitcher in Jim Wilson who ended the season leading the league in earned runs allowed.[4] Dodgers starter Joe Black, in contrast, was a favorite for both the National League Rookie of the Year and MVP awards with a 14-3 record, 15 saves, and a 2.03 ERA.[5]

It was a mismatch on paper, but most of the game played out as a very close affair. After the Dodgers took a 1-0 lead in the second inning on Campanella's 22nd homer, the Braves went ahead on a wild play in the fourth. Johnny Logan opened the frame with a

Opening Day's sparse crowd commenced a season-long pattern of low attendance at the Wigwam.

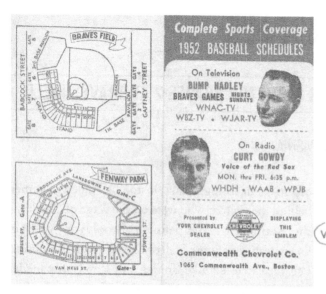

The Red Sox and Braves no longer shared broadcasting teams.

single, and then Mathews hit a shot that bounced over Hodges' head at first base. Normally dead-on-accurate right fielder Carl Furillo charged the ball with his eyes set on getting Mathews at second, but his hurried throw went past the bag and deep into left field—allowing both Logan and Mathews to score.

The two unearned runs gave Boston a 2-1 edge, but Furillo atoned somewhat in the sixth when he doubled and came around to tie the game on two infield outs. According to Larry Claflin of the *Boston Evening American*, the crowd got ugly as the day wore on. Fans were particularly harsh on center fielder Sam Jethroe, the former NL Rookie of the Year now struggling with a batting average of .235 and a variety of fielding lapses, and Earl Torgeson, the once powerful and productive first baseman, who looked washed up at age 28 as a .227 singles hitter.[6]

Boos grew louder in the eighth, when the Dodgers got to Wilson and rookie reliever Virgil Jester for six runs—all of them scoring with two outs. There were four hits and three walks in all, including a two-run single from Black in support of his own cause and more atoning from Furillo in the form of a two-run double. Interestingly, Jester was lifted in the bottom of the frame in favor of pinch-hitter Warren Spahn, but Spahn would never go in to pitch. Manager

Grimm, wanting to spare his ace left-hander the indignity of losing his 20th game of the year, was keeping Spahn and his 14-19 record away from the mound. Sheldon Jones came on instead to hurl an uneventful ninth for Boston, after which Black retired the Braves 1-2-3 to complete his three-hitter.

All told, Black had gotten the last 10 men in order and wound up not allowing an earned run. "Joe's responsible for at least eight other wins for us that don't show in his record," Jackie Robinson (three hits in the contest) said after Black lowered his ERA to 1.90. "[NL umpire] Dusty Boggess says he's the difference between us finishing first and third. He was great today and he's been great all year. In my book he's the most valuable player in the league." Robinson wasn't the only one excited, as he reported that he saw Black after the game "jumping up and down and saying, 'I went nine! I went nine!'" He had gone eight innings on August 5, among his 54 relief assignments, but going the distance was a new experience for the rookie.[7]

While the program cover portrait of the Tribe manager lasted the entire season, Holmes, as the Braves skipper, didn't.

Although the game did nothing for the Braves but bring them one day closer to the end of a horrid season, it was an important victory for Brooklyn. Coupled with a 6-2 loss by the New York Giants, it gave the Dodgers a six-game lead over New York with just six games to play. The worst Brooklyn could now do was tie for the pennant, and it would wind up clinching the flag in its next game with a September 23 win over the Philadelphia Phillies before the home folks at Ebbets Field.

It's a good bet that the gamblers huddled in their usual spots in the Braves Field grandstands during the September 21 game did not wager much on the home team, but they would have given pretty big odds on one thing: Boston would still have two big-league clubs come the next spring. After all, the same 16 teams in the American and National leagues had played in the same 11 cities for half a century, and even though Braves majority owner Lou Perini had done some grumbling in the newspapers about how much money he was losing with the franchise, he had plenty of it in reserve, right?

"We are picking up the greatest check in baseball history this season," Perini was quoted in the *Boston Globe* as saying after the home finale, estimating that his losses were currently reaching $30,000 per week. He said he intended to keep the team in his hometown for the time being, but added that "I'm not going to be stubborn about this thing. I don't intend to spend 10 years here when people don't want to see the Braves."[8] Eventual estimates were that the team lost Perini and his associates $580,000 for the year and more than $1.2 million from 1950 to 1952.[9]

According to Larry Claflin, Perini's timeframe for patience was actually much smaller. "Lou Perini admitted today the Braves are in danger of losing their Boston franchise unless attendance improves in the next year or two," Claflin wrote on September 22. Claflin said that a month earlier, during an exhibition game between the Braves and the Milwaukee Brewers, their top minor-league affiliate, in Milwaukee, Perini had suggested that the city was ready for a big-league team with construction of a 30,000-seat stadium (expandable to 80,000) already well under way. Perini did not go so far as to say that team could be the Braves, but he did, according to Claflin, predict that "a major league team would be playing in the new [Milwaukee] stadium soon."[10]

This might be the case, astute Braves fans surmised, but they knew that *their* team had several strong young players to build on—and would likely be a much improved club the next spring. Besides, said the armchair speculators, Perini was a Boston native with a big family that he surely didn't want to uproot. The Hub had fielded an NL franchise since 1876, and it would do so again in 1953. As they quietly walked onto the "Braves Field" trolley cars that rolled down off Commonwealth Avenue and right into the ballpark, the disappointed crowd leaving the finale could at least be sure of that.

What they did not know, and what they may not have believed even if they could read between the lines of Larry Claflin and other columnists, was that outside forces would soon intervene to threaten the loyalty, patience, and tradition Perini was trying hard to uphold.[11]

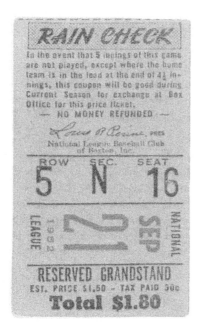

Little did attendees at the time know that their stub would represent the final major-league game of Boston's Braves at Braves Field.

SOURCES

Baseball reference.com

"Lou Perini Admits He Might Sell or Shift Braves," *Boston Evening American,* September 22, 1952.

"281,000 Fans See Braves This Year," *Boston Evening American,* September 22, 1952.

"Black Holds Braves to Three Hits, 8-2." *Boston Globe,* September 22, 1952.

"Perini Sticks With Boston Despite 'Greatest Loss in Baseball History,'" *Boston Globe,* September 22, 1952.

"Private Audience at Braves Field," *Boston Globe,* March 17, 1953.

"Black Goes Route, Beats Braves for Leaders, 8-2," *Boston Herald,* September 22, 1952.

"Braves Lose in Home Finale, 8-2," *Boston Post,* September 22, 1952.

Kaese, Harold. *The Boston Braves* (New York: Putnam Press, 1948).

NOTES

1   Future Hall of Famer Mathews garnered a meager one point in the Rookie of the Year balloting. Joe Black ran away with the award with 19 points. Black was a 28-year-old Negro League veteran and MLB "rookie," who had performed for the Baltimore Elite Giants from 1943 to 1950, with time out for World War II military service.

2   The largest "crowd" the Braves drew at home all season was the 13,405 who saw Boston face these same Dodgers in a night game on July 5. Even that number was tainted, as the game marked the return of fan darling Tommy Holmes—who had been fired by the Braves as manager

a month earlier and signed on as a spare outfielder for his hometown Brooklyn club. The sub-9,000 crowd at the finale was actually the second highest attendance mark of the year at the Wigwam—and the largest for a day game.

3   "Private Audience at Braves Field," *Boston Globe,* March 17, 1953.

4   Wilson and Murry Dickson each allowed 110 runs in 1952.

5   Howell Stevens, "Braves Lose in Home Finale," *Boston Post,* September 22, 1952. Black's gaudy record to that point had been compiled exclusively in relief, but Dodgers manager Charley Dressen surprised Black when he arrived at the ballpark by telling him he was getting his first major-league start against the Braves. Although Dressen would not confirm it, it was assumed the move was a test to see if Black could handle a starting assignment in the World Series. It worked; his strong performance against Boston earned Black the opening-game start in the fall classic against the Yankees, and he would go the distance in a 4-2 win—although he lost two later starts in the series, including Game Seven.

6   Larry Claflin, "281,000 Fans See Braves This Year," *Boston Evening American,* September 22, 1952.

7   Henry McKenna, "Black Goes Route, Beats Braves for Leaders, 8-2," *Boston Herald,* September 22, 1952. Robinson's MVP sentiments, however accurate, were not shared by the sportswriters. They voted the award to Hank Sauer of the Cubs in what is considered by baseball historian Bill James as one of the worst MVP selections in history.

8   Bob Holbrook, "Perini Sticks With Boston Despite 'Greatest Loss in Baseball History,'" *Boston Globe,* September 22, 1952.

9   Harold Kaese, *The Boston Braves* (New York: Putnam Press, 1948), 283.

10 Larry Claflin, "Lou Perini Admits He Might Sell or Shift Braves," *Boston Evening American,* September 22, 1952.

11 Perini did go ahead and solicit season-ticket packages for the 1953 season in Boston and printed the tickets for the entire 1953 campaign. The team also issued a Boston Braves 1953 Press, Radio and Television Guide for use during spring training. Dual Red Sox-Braves pocket schedules (the usual format over the years) for 1953 had been printed for distribution and had to be hastily stamped on the Tribe side "Left Town." Only 420 season tickets had been sold when the shift to Milwaukee was announced. On April Fool's Day 1953, some 1,274,216 now useless tickets to games at the Wigwam were torched in a bonfire in the former major-league ballpark's outfield.

While the rumors of a move abounded, Warren Spahn and his investors felt confident enough to spend the offseason preparing for the grand opening on Opening Day 1953 of Warren Spahn's Restaurant, an ill-fated diner situated at 966 Commonwealth Ave., across from the Wigwam.

Boston Braves fans did get a chance to say goodbye to their beloved team when the Milwaukee Braves returned to Boston to play the Red Sox at Fenway Park as part of the pre-move commitment to the annual exhibition City Series, now awkwardly dubbed the "Cross Country Series." The two games in Milwaukee were rained out. On April 11 the Red Sox triumphed, 4-1, and in a bone-chilling drizzle the following day, 7,873 saw the Braves emerge victorious by a similar score.

A LOOK BACK AT BRAVES FIELD

BY MORT BLOOMBERG

Ugly, old, barn-like, sooty, rat-infested, and the "House That Ruth Quit" are a sample of the disparaging phrases attributed to the ballyard that used to exist on Gaffney Street in Allston near the banks of the Charles River. To me, though, it was a home away from home where my childhood heroes like Bama Rowell, Earl Torgeson, Sam Jethroe, Willard Marshall, Bob Chipman, Chet Nichols, Bobby Hogue, and Johnny Logan jogged onto the field each game in the belief that they could defeat their National League rivals.

My first Wigwam trips were by car with Dad to weekend and night games (first pitch at 8:30 P.M.). Gazing to the right when we crossed the Cottage Farm Bridge (later dubbed the BU Bridge) offered a picture-perfect bird's-eye view of the only Boston "green cathedral" I ever cared about. In the evening with arc lights beaming from its tall stanchions, Braves Field looked even more inviting. No problem parking, since the back lot of a nearby tire company on Commonwealth Avenue with which Dad did business was always open to us.

From there we walked to Hayes Bickford's cafeteria, up the block maybe 15 minutes away at the corner of Babcock Street and a short distance from Warren Spahn's yet-to-be-built, ill-fated diner (its grand opening was scheduled for April 1953, one month after the National League approved the Braves' shift to Milwaukee). I always ordered their chicken pot pie, to this day the best I ever ate in a restaurant. Only my grandmother did it better ... and that was minus a recipe.

Dad worked in downtown Boston, where the Braves recently had installed a ticket outlet (in Gilchrist's department store, as I recall). Yet on most occasions he purchased our seats on the day of the game at the Gaffney Street box office. We sat frequently in the "unreserved" section (the back 10 to 12 rows) of the first-base grandstand. Priced at $1.20, these seats were easily accessible from the signature ramp that older fans may recall was built only on the right-field side of the ballpark. In the final years before the Braves left town, I would take the bus from Winthrop to Orient Heights (part of East Boston), board the MTA, and 45 minutes later arrive with friends or by myself at the special entrance to the ballpark built for trolley cars.

Having attended games from 1947 to 1952, I had the chance to view the game from several other locations. The sight lines from the reserved grandstand were poor because it was sloped so gradually that spectators in front often blocked your view, particularly if they wore hats (still popular in the post-WWII era). Fans in the 2,000-seat Jury Box next to the right-field foul

Ramp leading to the Braves Field grandstand.

The Wigwam's massive electric scoreboard.

pole adopted Tommy Holmes and a love affair soon was born. Throughout each game, win or lose, Tommy could be heard chirping in his high-pitched Brooklyn accent with his many devoted admirers. When Willard Marshall, known for his rocket arm, joined the Braves as part of the deal that sent Eddie Stanky and Al Dark to the New York Giants, Billy Southworth placed him in right field. Not for long, though. Holmes's fans became so indignant that soon thereafter Tommy received a hero's welcome home as he went back to right and Marshall became the new left fielder.

Kids attending a Saturday morning baseball quiz program hosted by Jerry O'Leary on WHDH radio were eligible for free Braves tickets in the third-base pavilion. There were wood bench seats there, and an oversized (for 1948) electric scoreboard which from that angle was difficult to see and on a sunny day impossible to decipher. On the other hand, those fans were up-close and might get to interact with coach Bob Keely and members of the Braves bullpen, which was situated down the left-field foul line out in the open directly in front of the pavilion.

The best gift I ever received from my parents was tickets to 12 games of my choice for the 1951 season. The seats they gave me were called field boxes, but in truth were below ground level just beyond the visiting team's dugout, on the first-base side. Comparable seats

were available on the opposite side of the field. But given that first baseman Earl Torgeson was one of my favorites and that in the course of a typical game more action occurs on the right side of the diamond, my preferred location was an easy pick. More good news: first row! Feeling a bit like a surfer who encounters the perfect wave, I decided to cram as many double-headers as possible into my game selection. One memorable twin bill in early May was against the Pirates. In the opener Warren Spahn blanked the Bucs, 6-0, for his second straight shutout. But what made the day historic was journeyman Cliff Chambers' no-hitter in the nightcap. As Roy Hartsfield, Sid Gordon, Walker Cooper, Luis Olmo, and others came to the plate in the late innings, my prayers for a base hit grew. At the same time, an odd situation was evolving in the stands. Many of the 15,492 fans in attendance rooted for Chambers to make history. To me, that was nearly as blasphemous as cheering for Boston's other team. Four footnotes on the game: It was the final no-hitter hurled at Braves Field; Chambers surrendered eight bases on balls; Braves starter George Estock took the loss in his big-league debut and that would turn out to be his only pitching decision in the majors; and—finally—three Braves went to the Pirates clubhouse after the game to offer their congratulations: Vern Bickford (a no-hit author himself in 1950), ex-Pirate star Bob Elliott, and future Pirate for two games Sam Jethroe.

In its finest hour, Braves Field's public address system was adequate at best. It would not surprise me, nevertheless, if big John Kiley's organ renditions of the national anthem were audible in Kenmore Square, especially after the Braves introduced a new state-of-the-art organ in 1950. Braves rallies were his cue to play the "Mexican Hat Dance," which began with a soft, slow beat, increasing gradually in volume and tempo. But for good humor or earaches or both, nothing matched the serenades of the Three Troubadours. Banned as persona non grata at Yawkey's Yard because their musical comedy routines did not fit the Fenway philosophy, they were a smash hit at every Braves Field performance. Even its mediocre PA system could not repress this slightly madcap trio.

My favorite was their chorus of Hawaiian belly dance music when Marv "Twitch" Rickert came to the plate on account of his wiggle as the pitcher got ready to deliver the next pitch.

Since our pregame cafeteria stop guaranteed that trips to Braves Field's concession stands were infrequent, there's nothing firsthand I can say about the ballpark food or merchandise. Thanks, though, to a 1952 scorecard, here is a price list of items that were then available: hot dog, 25¢; hamburger, 25¢; egg salad sandwich, 25¢; hot pastrami sandwich, 50¢; orange drink, 10¢; beer, 35¢; peanuts, 10¢; ice cream, 15¢; pencil, 10¢; minibat, 40¢; pennant, 50¢; hat, $1.00; uniform, $6.00; and warmup jacket, $7.00.

In a related vein, Tommie Ferguson, one of the team's batboys in the postwar era, gave me this tidbit about clubhouse manager Shorty Young. Between games of a doubleheader he would go to the stand and purchase for 30 cents apiece ham and cheese sandwiches for the Braves players. Catered postgame spreads in the clubhouse were a long way off in the future. And finally, many fans are aware that the Braves were the first team to sell fried clams. Did you know they were also the first team to remove this tasty treat from the menu when complaints were made by those in nearby seats that the frying process diverted their attention from the game? So in 1949 the suddenly unpopular clams were replaced by baked beans. This item also was a temporary addition to food sold at the Wigwam since it did not appear on the aforementioned 1952 menu (probably because it, too, carried unwelcome side effects!).

Last among the Wigwam's deficiencies was an eyesore as well as a potential health hazard: smoke bellowing from Boston & Albany steam engines behind the

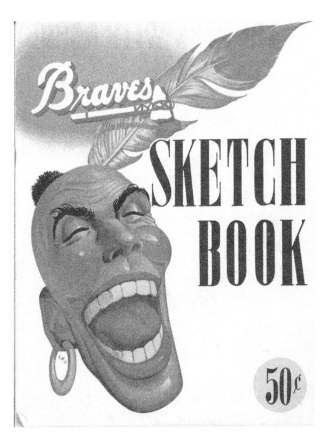

1950 yearbook sold at the park.

left- and center-field fence. Nonetheless, I really loved the place the Braves called home until the transfer of the franchise to Milwaukee, and in my heart it will always remain a shrine. As it approaches its centennial, Braves Field is the last major-league baseball facility built in Boston. Guaranteed it will not receive the accolades or attract the pomp and circumstance that marked the 100th anniversary of the ballpark their former American League neighbors own. Yet the Home of the Braves for 38 colorful seasons occupies a unique role in the history of our sport that hopefully will be recognized and celebrated for generations to come.

THE PARK WITH NOBODY IN IT: BRAVES FIELD 1957

BY JOHN DELMORE

with apologies to Bob Cooke and Joyce Kilmer

Whenever I go to Allston,
on the subway called the "T,"
I pass by a poor old ball park,
where the turnstiles rust by degree.
I know I've passed it a hundred times,
but I always stop for a minute,
and look at the park, the tragic park,
the park with nobody in it.

This park on the way to Allston,
needs forty thousand pairs of eyes.
And somebody ought to cheer it up,
by coming out there under the skies.
It needs new life and laughter
and the seats should be occupied.
'Cause what it needs the most of all
are some people sitting inside.

Now if I had a lot of money
and all of my debts were paid.
I'd put a gang of men to work
with brush and saw and spade.
And I'd buy that park and fill it up
the way it used to be.
With fellows like Sain and Tommy Holmes
and a great guy named Torgy.

They say the park's not haunted,
but I hear there are such things
that hold the talk of the Braves of old
and their mirth and sorrowings.
I know this park isn't haunted,
but I wish it were, I do.
For it wouldn't be so lonely,
if it had a ghost or two.

A park that has done what a park should do.
A park that has sheltered life.
Has put its loving concrete arms around
a Braves fan and his wife.
A park that has echoed a baseball song
and held up a rookie's feet,
is the saddest sight when it's left alone
that ever your eyes could meet.

So whenever I go to Allston
with the help of the MBT.
I never walk by the empty park
without pausing in hopes I won't see,
a park there empty and barren,
with seats that are falling apart.
And I can't help thinking the poor old park
is a park with a broken heart.

*Reprinted from the 1994 Special Membership
Edition of the Boston Braves Historical Association
Newsletter.*

244

THE FIRST HOMERS OVER THE FENCE AT BRAVES FIELD

BY BILL NOWLIN

When Fenway Park opened in 1912, people looked at its now-legendary left-field wall and said no one would ever hit a home run over the fence. After all, it was—at best—300 or more feet from home plate and stood—at the time—31 feet tall.

How long did it take? Five games. In just the fifth regular-season game ever played at Fenway Park, Hugh Bradley hit one out. It was April 26, 1912. The *Boston Post*'s game notes declared, "Few of the fans who have been out to Fenway Park believed it possible to knock a ball over the left field fence, but Hugh Bradley hit one that not only cleared the barrier but also the building on the opposite side of the street." His homer, wrote Paul Shannon, was "a feat that may never be duplicated."[1]

It wasn't something that happened often, during the Deadball Era. In 1913, not one homer was hit over the fence. Nonetheless, it had been done.

Some 40 months later, Braves Field opened, in August 1915. It was a more capacious park, and could hold many more people.

When Ty Cobb first visited brand-new Braves Field, he saw that both the left-field and right-field fences were 375 from home plate, and straightaway center was a full 440 feet distance. To the deepest corner in right-center field, it was 542 feet. Baseball writer F.C. Lane noted, "Even at that remote distance a lofty wall girdles in the grounds."[2] The fence was apparently 10 feet tall.[3]

Cobb said, "No home run will ever go over that fence." And then he added, in approval, "This is the only field in the country on which you can play an absolutely fair game of ball without the interference of fences."[4]

How long did it take? Considerably longer. Ever heard of Walton Cruise? He was an outfielder from Alabama

who played in 736 major-league games from 1914 to 1924, the first five of those seasons for the St. Louis Cardinals and the final six for the Boston Braves.

Given how unlikely it was considered that someone would ever hit one out, it was perhaps superfluous to have erected a wire screen that rose 15 or 20 feet above the wall of the bleachers, thus creating a barrier that rose in all to about 25 to 30 feet.[5]

On May 26, 1917, somewhat early in Braves Field's third season of play, Cruise was with the Cardinals and in the eighth inning the left-handed hitter whacked a Pat Ragan pitch, a "gosh-awful home run … into the previously inviolate right-field bleachers." The *Herald*'s Burt Whitman continued, writing, "The

WALTON CRUISE
OUTFIELD, BOSTON NATIONALS

1922 E120 American Caramel baseball card.

245

Cruise crash was the hardest, the longest, the most spectacular fair hit the Wigwam has seen in its young and brilliant career, two world series included." [6] It was hit into what later became known as the "Jury Box." The *Boston Globe* said the ball landed about halfway up in the seats.

The Cardinals won the game, 6-1. It was only the second homer of any sort hit that season at Braves Field. Cruise had hit the earlier one, too, two days earlier, an inside-the-park one to right-center.

On May 17, 1919, the Braves purchased Cruise's contract from the Cardinals.

When was it that a member of home team hit one out? Fans had to wait four more years and almost three months on top of that. On August 16, 1921, the Chicago Cubs were in town. In the bottom of the first inning, there were two Braves on base, facing the Cubs' Grover Cleveland Alexander. The next batter stepped into the box and hit a home run to almost the very same spot, though this one was more of a line drive than a high, arcing blow. What was the batter's name? Walton Cruise.

The *Boston Globe* reminded readers, "This was the second time this stunt has been performed since the park was built, and Cruise was the one who turned the trick the first time." [7]

NOTES

1   *Boston Post*, April 27, 1912.

2   F.C. Lane, "The World's Greatest Baseball Park," *Baseball Magazine*, October 1915, Vol. XV, No. 6, 31.

3   The height of the fence and the distance to right-center are both cited in Philip J. Lowry, *Green Cathedrals* (New York: Walker & Co., 2006), 32. Lowry reports that it was 402.5 feet to both right and left, not the 375 cited by Lane's contemporaneous account.

4   F.C. Lane, op. cit.

5   The wire screen is noted in Burt Whitman's game account in the May 27, 1917, *Boston Herald*.

6   Ibid.

7   *Boston Globe*, August 17, 1921.

THE BAMBINO'S WIGWAM WALLOPS

BY BOB BRADY

Some might be surprised to learn that Babe Ruth hit memorable regular-season home runs at the "Home of the Braves" while wearing the uniform of the New York Yankees as well as in his Boston Braves togs. Popularly referred to as the "Wigwam" during most of its existence, Braves Field was not unfamiliar territory to the legendary Bambino. In his first World Series start, Ruth had hurled a masterful complete-game 14-inning, 2-1 victory for the Red Sox over the Brooklyn Robins in Game Two of the 1916 fall classic at the Hub's National League diamond. During Babe's Yankees years, the Red Sox would borrow Braves Field to play Sunday home games when its principal tenant was on the road. Restrictive so-called Blue Laws prevented the Red Sox from using Fenway Park on the Sabbath due to its close proximity to a house of worship.

Even on a Sunday afternoon with the "home team" Red Sox destined for a last-place finish, a visit by the Yankees was guaranteed to draw a crowd. Some 25,000 fans filed into Braves Field on June 30, 1929, as Miller Huggins' reigning World Series champions took to the unfamiliar senior-circuit turf. Boston valiantly battled the powerful New Yorkers but could not overcome the heroics of George Herman Ruth, who drove in four of the Yankees' six runs in the visitors' 6-4 triumph. In the top of the fifth inning, facing Deacon Danny MacFayden, the Babe blasted a baseball approximately 470 feet into the top row of the center-field bleachers. It was his 16th circuit clout of the campaign. These bleacher seats had not been part of the ballpark's original design but had been hastily installed in 1928 to reduce Braves Field's huge outfield dimensions that reflected its pre-Ruthian Deadball Era design. This seating lasted only a few seasons before being permanently dismantled. The innovation had failed to produce benefits to the home occupant that outweighed advantages gained by their opponents.

A near replay of that June day's events took place as the 1929 season drew to a close. The Yankees came to town for a one-day visit on Sunday, September 1. The Wigwam's turnstiles rapidly spun some 28,000 ticket holders into the friendly confines. Again the Red Sox went down to defeat by a 6-4 score. In the first inning, the Sultan of Swat stepped up to the plate and drove southpaw Billy Bayne's second pitch like a rocket to center field, where it eventually banged into a billboard that sat atop the bleacher stands. Ruth's 40th circuit clout carried as far as his June shot before it was stopped by the interfering barrier.

The Bambino awaits his at-bat.

Alleyway between the Jury Box and pavilion where Ruth's last Boston home run landed.

The Bambino's mightiest Braves Field blast took place the succeeding season. On May 18, 1930, New York routed the Red Sox, 11-0, as 25,000 folks looked on. In a first inning at-bat, Ruth sent a pitch by Big Ed Morris into the ballpark's famed "Jury Box," where it finally landed about two rows in front of the elevated back scoreboard. A contemporary newspaper account called the clout "one of Babe's heartiest hits in his whole career."[1] The reporter further commented that the homer was "the longest drive ever hit to right field in Braves Field since they first fenced in the land on the banks of the Charles, fifteen years ago." Some speculated that Ruth had exerted such force on the spheroid that it would have reached the Commonwealth Armory (the current site of the Agganis Arena) across Gaffney Street (now Agganis Way), 490 feet from home, had it not been impeded by clipping the top scoreboard portion of the Wigwam's tiny right-field section and rebounding into the stands.

The Wigwam was the site of a rare nonbatting Ruthian event on the ending day of the 1930 season. New York sat in third place in the junior circuit while Boston owned its basement. On Sunday, September 28, the Babe was handed the ball and took to the Braves Field mound for the first time there since his 1916 World Series triumph. He hadn't pitched in a major-league contest since 1921. Showing a little rust, Ruth allowed 11 hits and three runs in hurling a complete-game 9-3

victory. Teammate Lou Gehrig also took the opportunity to play out of his traditional position at first base for the only time that year and patrolled the Wigwam's left field. Ruth "cursed" his former team with its 102nd defeat of the campaign.

Ruth's final majestic blow at Braves Field occurred during his National League debut, on April 16, 1935. The 40-year-old slugger had been unceremoniously waived by the Yankees and was lured back to Boston by financially strapped Braves owner, Judge Emil Fuchs. Opening Day was designated "Judge Fuchs Day," in part for this apparent early attempt to "reverse the curse." Despite the frigid weather, 20,000 fans came to watch the historic event and were not disappointed. With all eyes upon him, the Bambino responded in the fifth inning the way he had done 723 times before in regular and postseason play. Facing future Hall of Famer Carl Hubbell, Ruth bludgeoned an offering 430 feet into the narrow runway between the right-field pavilion and the Jury Box, driving in what proved to be the game-winning run. Part of that runway and a portion of the pavilion exist today within the confines of Boston University's Nickerson Field. You still can actually stand near the landing area of Ruth's last home run in Boston!

Ruth also provided the contest's fielding gem. Although he was originally penciled in to play first base, a pregame strategic change found him in left field. There, in the fifth, Ruth had to madly dash in, plunging headlong to spear a shot off of Hubbell's bat and prevent a Giants comeback. During the sixth inning, snowflakes began to drift down on the field, causing an attending band to strike up "In the Good Old Summer Time" followed by "Jingle Bells." Unfortunately for the Babe, the inaugural game was not an accurate predictor of what was to come. An aged and aching Ruth would soon unhappily retire, believing that he had been deceived regarding the club's alleged promise of front office/managerial duties. The "Ruth-less" Braves would win only 37 more times during the 1935 season (losing 115) and a deluge of "red ink" would force Judge Fuchs to abandon his ownership position.

Two other Boston Braves and Braves Field tidbits relating to the mighty Babe are also worthy of mention. Ruth made his last appearance as an active player at Fenway Park during the April 14, 1935, City Series preseason exhibition game between the Red Sox and Braves. Performing for the "visiting" Tribe, first baseman Ruth failed to get a hit in three at-bats during the Braves' 3-2 triumph over their in-town rivals in a contest that also marked the Boston debut of new Red Sox player-manager Joe Cronin.

Babe Ruth's final regular-season visits came as a member of Brooklyn Dodgers manager Burleigh Grimes' "brain trust." During the 1938 season, Ruth served as a coach for Brooklyn, but as in his Braves

days, was employed more for his appeal as a gate attraction. In Boston the Bambino assumed his post in the first-base coaching box opposite the visitors dugout at a ballpark that was now nicknamed the Beehive. When Boston's senior circuit entry renamed itself the Bees in 1936, Braves Field was rebaptized as National League Baseball Field. The Bambino's official appearances for four different big-league teams (Red Sox, Yankees, Braves, and Dodgers) is unique to this former National League ballpark, adding further luster to the site's importance as a part of baseball history.

NOTES

1   *New York Times*, May 19, 1930.

HOW THE WIGWAM BECAME A BEEHIVE

BY BOB BRADY

Judge Emil Fuchs' 12 seasons of stewardship over the Boston Braves concluded in 1935 after a valiant but futile last-gasp attempt to achieve solvency by luring an aged and ailing Babe Ruth back to Boston. At the direction of the National League, the team undertook a corporate reorganization at the end of the year. The Boston National League Baseball Company terminated its existence in favor of the newly organized Boston National Sports, Incorporated. Judge Fuchs' principal financial backer, Charles F. Adams, was precluded from converting his substantial financial advances to the ballclub into a front-office position or even become an active shareholder in the new entity because Commissioner Kenesaw Mountain Landis objected to Adams's ownership of the Suffolk Downs horse racing track.

At Adams's behest, 66-year-old J.A. (James Aloysius) Robert "Bob" Quinn returned to the Hub from an executive post with the Brooklyn Dodgers to direct the destiny of the city's National League entry. No stranger to Boston, Quinn had been the leader of a syndicate that bought the Red Sox from Harry Frazee in 1924 and operated the team until it sold out to Tom Yawkey in 1933. During his tenure, the cash-starved Quinn once considered selling Fenway Park and having the Red Sox become a tenant at Braves Field.

With a limited budget, Quinn's challenge of restoring the Braves to a competitive footing in Boston with the neighboring Red Sox was made extremely difficult given Tom Yawkey's willingness to deploy his vast wealth toward bettering the American League franchise seemingly regardless of cost.

Quinn decided to start from scratch and consigned the "Braves" nickname to the scrapheap, along with such associated epithets as Tribe, Wigwam, Tepee, Warriors, etc. He never cared for the name Braves,

possibly because of its linkage to former owner James Gaffney and his association with New York's Tammany Hall political machine. The team's recent poor performance under that title further warranted a rebranding in his opinion to symbolically signal a new beginning. Seeking to stimulate some positive publicity, Quinn opted to solicit potential nicknames from the fans.

The proposed transformation met with only tepid resistance from a fan base that had rooted for the National League franchise as the Braves since 1912, when then new club president James E. Gaffney opted for a team characterization that reflected his ties to Tammany Hall. That political machine had derived its name from a Native American chief, Tamanend, of a clan within the Delaware Valley Lenni-Lenape Nation.

Senior circuit followers had become accustomed to periodic name changes dating back to the club's charter membership in the National League in 1876. Starting out with nicknames linked to their apparel during the years 1876-82 (Red Stockings, Reds, or Red Caps), the

National League Baseball Field.

team assumed a more local "flavor" when it was referred to as the Beaneaters from 1883-1906. Changes in ownership brought about the shorter-lived Doves (after the Dovey brothers, John and George; 1907-10) and Rustlers (after William H. Russell; 1911). Gaffney's ascendency established an identity that was also reflected for the first time in team history as a logo on the players' uniforms. An Indian in full headdress appeared on jersey sleeves and chests during his regime.

Quinn and company quickly launched a contest among club followers and the general public. A committee of regional sportswriters was charged with picking the winning replacement name. As an inducement, prizes would be awarded to lucky entrants who made the panel's final cut. Quinn hoped for an outcome that would deliver a title associated with Boston or Massachusetts.

The contest exceeded expectations. The club's office staff spent three weeks opening and sorting mail. Some 13,000 individuals throughout the United States expressed their preferences. Many sent in multiple choices, including one prolific entrant whose letter listed 73 potential candidates, none of which were ultimately chosen. Some 1,327 distinct monikers emerged from the mountain of correspondence. The pool of choices covered titles starting with every letter of the alphabet except "X." Entries with a negative association to the disastrous past were quickly rejected (*e.g.*, the Bankrupts, the Basements, *etc.*). As had been expected, hundreds offered Pilgrims, Beacons, Puritans, Minute Men, Sacred Cods, Bunker Hills, and other titles related to the history of the area. Also among the mix were such strange submissions as Aspirins, Comics, Pill Boxes, Hamburgers, Lemons, Zulus, and Zippers. Whittling down the list to a more manageable seven candidates, the jury of 25 sportswriters and one cartoonist deliberated for two hours in a room at the Copley Plaza Hotel. The group's spokesman, senior journalist James "Uncle Jim" O'Leary of the *Boston Globe*, was charged with announcing the results. Receiving over half the ballots, the Bees led the pack with 14 votes. Following as also-rans were the Blue Birds (4 votes), Beacons (3 votes), and Colonials (2

votes). In the back of the pack, with only a solo vote each were the Bulldogs, Blues, and Bulls.

Allegations immediately arose that the newspapermen were motivated towards the winning submission because its brevity provided an ideal fit for headlines and that the title easily lent itself to wordplay and cartooning. In fact, it didn't take long for the latter to commence. In announcing the name change, *The Sporting News* couldn't resist the headline, "Boston Club Given Honey of a Name." The publication extended its wishes that the newly christened team would experience a flow of honey at the turnstiles.[1]

In addition to his official designation of ballclub president, Bob Quinn soon became referred to as the King Bee and his manager, Bill McKechnie, as the Bee Keeper. Sports pages later would describe times when the Bees "swarmed" the field, "stung" their opponents and were "swatted" by adversaries. Famed

J.A. Robert "Bob" Quinn.

scribe and club historian Harold Kaese summarized his feelings about the superficiality of this affair involving a perennial second-division ballclub by restating a well-known Shakespearean quote. "What's in a name? That which we call a skunk cabbage by another name would smell as foul."[2]

Thirteen fans had submitted the Bees nickname in the contest. A random drawing was conducted to award prizes. O'Leary drew the grand-prize winner's name out of a hat. Arthur J. Rockwood, a sheet-metal worker from East Weymouth, Massachusetts, and the father of nine, received two season tickets for all Bees home games during the 1936 season. Eleven others were given pairs of tickets to the club's home opener. To compensate the 13th fan, an out-of-towner from Chicago, a pair of passes to the first Bees-Cubs tilt of the season at Wrigley Field was sent his way.

When reporters expressed an intent to describe the former Wigwam as the Beehive, Quinn railed that they could call it whatever they wished but the ballpark would be formally titled National League Park.[3]

Reflecting Quinn's preference, the entomological nickname was absent on tickets, programs and roster booklets. In its place appeared a bland "Boston National League" reference. However, Quinn's edict seemed to soften as the years passed as the Boston Bees title found its way onto the cover of the 1938 spring-training roster booklet and a golden beehive and "Home of the Bees" slogan was placed on official stationery of the late 1930s.

Quinn was true to his word, with one minor alteration. The title of the ballpark, prominently displayed on the administration building above the field's front entrances, received a new paint job. Gone was "Braves Field" and in its place appeared "National League Baseball Field," and not "Park" as Quinn had earlier remarked. While the ballpark was referred to colloquially by some as "The Hive," many stubbornly stuck to "Braves Field" when describing the Gaffney Street

diamond. Following Quinn's edict, the center entrance trolleys (a/k/a "cattle cars") that delivered and picked up patrons at the ballpark replaced the Braves Field designation on the streetcars' destination sign scrolls to now read "National League Park."

Subtle changes occurred within the park's confines. The Horace Partridge Company replaced the past use of "Braves" on its outfield wall advertisement to now read "Athletic Outfitters To The Bees." Lifebuoy Soap followed suit and proclaimed that the Bees used their product to "stop 'B.O.,'" which often drew the sarcastic retort that the team still stunk. Fans peering out into center field were urged to "Follow The Bees" on WAAB, a Boston radio station heading up a regional radio network from its studio at the nearby Hotel Buckminster in Kenmore Square.

The Boston Bees lasted until their "extermination" on April 29, 1941. On that date, the team's ownership, influenced by the addition to its ranks of the "Three Little Steam Shovels"—Lou Perini, Guido Rugo, and Joseph Maney, voted to bring back the Braves designation and return the ballpark's title to Braves Field, restoring the "Wigwam" nickname.

SOURCES

A version of this story first appeared in Brady, Bob, *The Bees of Boston: Baseball At The Hive 1936-1940* (Boston: Boston Braves Historical Association Press, 2012). That account was based upon contemporary local newspaper articles as well as from *The Sporting News*, Kaese, Harold, *The Boston Braves* (New York: G.P. Putnam's Sons, 1948), the Harry M. Stevens photographic archives, and the files of the Boston Braves Historical Association.

NOTES

1   *The Sporting News*, February 6, 1936, 1.

2   Harold Kaese, *The Boston Braves 1871-1953* (Boston: Northeastern University Press, 2004, first published 1948 by G.P. Putnam's Sons), 235.

3   Bob Brady, *The Bees of Boston: Baseball At The Hive 1936-1940* (Braintree: Boston Braves Historical Association Press, 2012), 2.

"SPAHN AND SAIN AND PRAY FOR RAIN"

BY GREG ERION

One of baseball's most enduring quotes had its genesis in a short poem written by Gerald V. Hern, sports editor of the *Boston Post*. His verse forever linked Warren Spahn and Johnny Sain as a two-man pitching rotation to their efforts leading the Boston Braves to the 1948 National League pennant. The piece, capturing a moment in time, appeared on September 14, 1948, in the *Post* as the Braves were making their final drive toward the championship. Hern's offering:

"First we'll use Spahn then we'll use Sain
Then an off day, followed by rain
Back will come Spahn, followed by Sain
And followed, we hope, by two days of rain"

As originally published, his wording did not contain the more popular "Spahn and Sain and pray for rain" or its variant, "Spahn and Sain and two days of rain" with which baseball fans are familiar. How Hern's prose came to its present form is of interest, but of greater significance is to ask: How close was his rhyme to events on the field?

This question is not unique to Hern's piece. It has frequently been asked about baseball's most famous poem, Franklin Pierce Adams's "Baseball's Sad Lexicon," which contained the immortal, "Tinker to Evers to Chance" phrase, generating the vision of an efficient double-play combination. Like Hern, Adams's poem reflected an image, his of Chicago Cubs infielders Joe Tinker, Johnny Evers, and Frank Chance's defensive abilities.

Over the years, Adams's work has been critiqued as to accuracy, primarily because his stanza is often credited with their being elected to the Hall of Fame in 1946.[1] While analysis will doubtless continue, there is no argument that they were significant cogs on a team that won four pennants and two World Series within five years.

Thus, how important were Spahn and Sain in the Braves winning the pennant in 1948? Virtually any reference to the 1948 Braves mentions their contributions.

Sain (24-15) and Spahn's (15-12) combined 39-27 contributed largely to the Braves' 91 wins that year, but their joint effort was hardly unique that season. Cleveland's Gene Bearden and Bob Lemon teamed to go 40-21, while Yankees pitchers Vic Raschi and Ed Lopat posted a 36-19 mark. The fifth-place Giants' Larry Jansen and Sheldon Jones's 36-20 record compared favorably to the Bostonians. Given their record in 1948, while solid, it was not unique. What caused Spahn and Sain's effort to gain lasting resonance?

First, of course, is that the Braves won the pennant—the Yankees and Giants didn't. Second is the alliterative nature of Spahn and Sain's names. Bearden and Lemon, or Raschi and Lopat, would challenge the best of poetic talent. Jansen and Jones suggest rhythmic potential, but the Giants' fifth-place finish made any lyrical endeavor inconsequential. Third, Hern's piece captured a crucial time in the pennant race during which his description was decidedly on the mark. A

The subjects of Hearn's poem.

Sain and Spahn reminisce about the glory days.

combination of unique events came together to make it so.

Early in September, Boston was in a tight pennant race with Brooklyn. On the morning of September 6, Boston held a slight two-game lead. While Sain, Spahn, and rookie Vern Bickford were pitching well, the fourth man in the rotation, Bill Voiselle, wasn't. After developing a 10-6 record through early July, he fell off, losing seven of his next 10 decisions. Voiselle's loss to the Phils on September 4 was his third in a row.

With that defeat, manager Billy Southworth took Voiselle out of the rotation essentially augmenting Spahn and Sain's starts by giving them Voiselle's.[2] In August Sain, Spahn, and Voiselle had each started seven of the 31 games Boston played that month. In September, of the 24 games played, Sain started eight, Spahn seven, and Voiselle just that one game in early September before being pulled from the rotation.

On September 6 Spahn and Sain threw complete-game victories against the Dodgers in a doubleheader. Two off days and two rainouts brought them into a doubleheader against the Phils on the 11th. Bickford had been scheduled to pitch in the rained-out game of the 9th, but Southworth elected to go with Sain and Spahn, who again supplied complete-game wins. The next day Red Barrett and Bickford pitched, splitting a second consecutive doubleheader with Philadelphia. The 13th was an offday; Southworth

came back with Sain on the 14th and Spahn on the 15th against Chicago. Two more complete-game victories. An offday on the 16th, then Sain and Spahn against Pittsburgh. Again, two complete-game wins. During a 13-day stretch, Boston had gone 9-1. Sain and Spahn won four games apiece, each a complete-game effort. At that point Boston's lead over Brooklyn had grown to six games with two weeks left to play. From then on, Bickford was back in the rotation. On September 26, Boston clinched the pennant.

Sain's 24 wins topped the majors, but Spahn's 15-12 record was just above average, certainly below his 21-10 performance in 1947. Over the years efforts have been made to analyze their combined deeds before, during, and after the 1948 season. One article offered, "The implication (Hern's poem) is that for a period of several years after World War II, Hall of Famer Warren Spahn and 4-time 20-game winner Johnny Sain were the only good pitchers on the Boston Braves."[3] Valid points, but Hern was not writing about past seasons, other contributors or the 1948 season. He had a specific point of view. As did Adams on Tinker, Evers, and Chance. Adams's stanza contained the phrase, "Ruthlessly pricking our gonfalon bubble."

His mention of a gonfalon, or banner, alluded to the National League pennant. Adams's poem first appeared in July 1910 when the Cubs and Giants were fighting for first place. The Giants, a close second behind Chicago, should not have given cause for the overall gloominess Adams's poem projected. His outlook was not driven by a particular game but by the fact that Chicago's dynastic run had consistently thwarted the Giants' hopes. It was out of that setting, not a capacity for double plays, that Adams created his work.

The reverse was true of Hern. While what Spahn and Sain did during previous years, as well as the efforts of others, had pertinence, his focus was on two individuals carrying the day for Boston.[4] Their exploits are still recalled because of Hern's self-described "ode," which Sain years later said was inspired by Southworth. Soon after Sain and Spahn threw their second set of wins, Southworth described his revised pitching rotation to reporters as "Spahn on one day, Sain the next." [5]That comment gave impetus to Hern's poem, published the next day.

Both pitchers appreciated that it kept them forever in the minds of fans." It's not so much my pitching people know, but that little poem about me and Johnny Sain with the forty-eight Braves. We got it [the jingle] because it rhymed," Spahn mused years later. While he appreciated being remembered, he did not like the phrase because it failed to account for the efforts of others—"… guys like Vern Bickford… and Nelson Potter… had good years and they're not remembered.[6] Sain pointed out that theirs was an intense burst of effort. He recalled tiring late in games, indicating this sustained level of performance could not be continued. Sain felt a degree of reluctance as to its popularity– "Unfortunately, that diminishes the contributions of our other starters that year"— recalling Voiselle's and Bickford's roles.[7] Voiselle, when asked years later if he resented being overlooked, agreed: "I reckon I was, in a way. We had some pretty good pitchers on that team— Spahn, Sain, Vern Bickford. Nelson Potter did real good that year and so did Red Barrett."[8]

Spahn, Sain, and others who later commented were right; the poem did take away from the efforts of Bickford, Voiselle, and the rest of the pitching staff. But Hern, almost certainly unaware of how this stanza would carry over time, was not concerned with anything but the situation facing the Braves in September 1948.

Hern's original prose is at variance with today's familiar phrasing. His original lines:

> "Back will come Spahn, followed by Sain,
> And followed, we hope, by two days of rain"

have of course, given way to:

> "Spahn and Sain and pray for rain,"

Or

> "Spahn and Sain and two days of rain."

Various references vaguely explain the transformation in wording. The poem "was eventually shortened conversationally" as described in a biography of Billy Southworth.[9]Jim Kaplan's book *The Greatest Game Ever Pitched* notes that "the poem was shortened popularly" to its present form.[10] On the Internet, Spahn's entry at Wikipedia relates that "popular media eventually condensed" to today's phrasing.[11]

"Eventually" seemed quick; three weeks after Hern's poem appeared, Whitney Martin, writing for the *Washington Post* about the ensuing World Series between Boston and Cleveland, observed, "The slogan up here in the cod country during the Boston Braves' regular season was "Spahn and Sain and two days of rain."[12] As early as this recognizable verse is, it has to stand behind Hern himself. His verse came in an article titled "Braves Boast Two-Man Staff." The subheading in part was "Pitch Spahn and Sain, Then Pray for Rain." Thus Hern not only came up with a poem about Spahn and Sain but with the phrase that immortalized them.

NOTES

1   See for instance, Rob Neyer and Eddie Epstein, *Baseball Dynasties: Greatest Teams of All Times* (New York: W.W. Norton & Company, 2000), 35-40.

2   sabr.org/bioproj/person/230d3efb, SABR BioProject, *Bill Voiselle*, by Saul Wisnia.

3   baseballevolution.com/keith/sainrain.html.

4   Roger Birtwell, "Red-Hot Sain Heats the Beans for Boston," *The Sporting News*, September 29, 1948, 6.

5   Gerry Hern, "Braves Boast Two-Man Staff, *Boston Post*, September 14, 1948.

6   baseball-almanac.com/poetry/po_rain.shtml; Jim Kaplan, *The Greatest Game Ever Pitched, Juan Marichal, Warren Spahn and the Pitching Duel of the Century* (Chicago: Triumph Books, 2011), 68.

7   Danny Peary, ed., *We Played the Game: 65 Players Remember Baseball's Greatest Era, 1947-1964* (New York: Hyperion, 1994) 59.

8   John C. Skipper, *Billy Southworth: A Biography of the Hall of Fame Manager and Ballplayer,* (Jefferson, North Carolina: McFarland & Company, Inc., 2013), 160.

9   Skipper, 159.

10   Kaplan, 68.

11   wikipedia.org/wiki/Warren_Spahn#.22Pray_for_rain.

12   Whitney Martin, "'Sain, Rain, Back With Sain' Lone Series Hope for Braves," *Washington Post*, October 8, 1948, B4.

BOSTON BRAVE STARTING PITCHERS — 1948

Month	Red Barrett	Johnny Beasley	Vern Bickford	Glenn Elliot	Bobby Hogue	Nelson Potter	Jim Prendergast	Johnny Sain	Clyde Shoun	Warren Spahn	Bill Voiselle	Total Team Starts	Spahn/ Sain % of Starts
April	2	2	-	-	-	-	1	3	-	2	2	12	41.6%
May	3	-	3	-	-	-	-	5	-	5	6	22	45.4%
June	2	-	5	-	-	-	1	7	1	7	7	30	46.7%
July	1	-	5	-	1	2	-	7	1	7	7	31	45.1%
August	2	-	4	-	-	4	-	8	-	6	7	31	45.2%
September	3	-	4	1	-	-	-	8	-	7	1	24	62.5%
October	-	-	1	-	-	1	-	1	-	1	-	4	50.0%
TOTAL	13	2	22	1	1	7	2	39	2	35	30	154	48.1%

"SPAHN AND SAIN AND PRAY FOR RAIN"

Date	Pitcher	W/L Record	Opponent
September 6	Spahn	1-0	Dodgers
September 6	Sain	1-0	Dodgers
September 7	off day		
September 8	off day		
September 9	rain out		
September 10	rain out		
September 11	Sain	2-0	Phillies
September 11	Spahn	2-0	Phillies
September 12	Barrett	0-1	Phillies
September 12	Potter	1-0	Phillies
September 13	off day		
September 14	Sain	3-0	Cubs
September 15	Spahn	3-0	Cubs
September 16	off day		
September 17	Sain	4-0	Pirates
September 18	Spahn	4-0	Pirates

BRAVES FIELD INSPIRES A MASTERPIECE: NORMAN ROCKWELL VISITS THE WIGWAM

MAY 23, 1948

BY BOB BRADY

Pennant fever had yet to grip the Hub when the fourth-place Boston Braves and sixth-place Chicago Cubs played a doubleheader at the Wigwam on Sunday afternoon, May 23, 1948. While the Tribe convincingly swept both games (8-5 and 12-4), advancing one rung in the standings and adding two more victories to aid in their pursuit of their first National League pennant since the Miracle Braves season of 1914, our tale focuses not on the particulars of those contests but, instead, on the actions of one of the 31,693 in attendance that day.

Famed American painter and illustrator Norman Rockwell journeyed from his home in Vermont to Braves Field to collect ideas for a baseball-related portrait scheduled to appear on the cover of *The Saturday Evening Post*, a nationally distributed weekly magazine that traced its roots back to Benjamin Franklin. Rockwell had performed many cover assignments for the periodical over the previous 30 years. His overall *Post* portfolio eventually would include several iconic baseball images. As was his custom, Rockwell would scope out future artwork by staging scenes at particular sites and have an assistant take photographs for later reference. Upon returning to his studio, he would use such pictures as inspirations for his illustration.

The artist did not focus his attention on any of the notable ballplayers populating the rosters of either team. Instead, he called upon Braves 17-year-old batboy Frank McNulty to serve as his primary model. McNulty had joined the Tribe in 1945, working as a clubhouse boy under team custodian George "Shorty" Young. He next became the home team-supplied visitors' batboy. Upon gaining further seniority, he moved to the home dugout and acted as the Braves batboy until the club departed for Milwaukee.

Before the start of the opening contest, Rockwell approached McNulty and offered the lad the sum of $5 to dress up in a Chicago road uniform. He posed him in front of a white sheet held up by fellow Braves batboys Tom Ferguson and Charlie Chronopoulos. McNulty was instructed to stare forlornly toward the diamond, pretending to be suffering from the prospect of another Cubs loss. Rockwell struggled to obtain the desired expression of sadness from McNulty. Over the course of a couple of hours, he would change the tilt of the batboy's cap and request a variety of facial expressions from his model. Finally Rockwell suggested to his subject that he pretend that his dog had just died. McNulty recalled that the photographer accompanying Rockwell snapped about 25 photos for later use.

Rockwell enlisted a number of folks to occupy the grandstand seats in back of the dugout and mimic his instructions to pretend to jeer at the Braves' opponents. The grouping of volunteers included Helen Fitzsimmons, the daughter of a Braves coach, and Terese Prendergast, the wife of a Braves pitcher. As he sometimes did in his finished works, Rockwell later would insert himself among the boisterous Braves Field crowd.

The famed illustrator took the results of his Braves Field trek back to his studio and proceeded to paint one of baseball's most memorable images, "The Dugout," which appeared on the front of the September

4, 1948, issue of *The Saturday Evening Post*. In addition to using McNulty's pose, Rockwell included the disheartened images of pitcher Bob Rush, manager Charlie Grimm, catcher Al "Rube" Walker, and hurler Johnny Schmitz in the Cubs dugout.

So great was the artist's reputation that the Cubs had not voiced an objection to being portrayed in defeat on the *Post* cover. Selecting the Windy City's National League representative for this treatment was not fortuitous. By the magazine's cover date, Chicago found itself mired in eighth place. The Cubs would finish the season in the senior circuit's basement, 27½ games in back of the league-leading Braves. Some believe that the reputation of the Cubs as "lovable losers" can be traced back to the *Post* portrait.

At an after-publication pregame ceremony at Braves Field, Rockwell presented McNulty with a signed copy of the *Post* cover. In the fall the Braves' batboy was rewarded with a World Series ring. Charlie Grimm, who later would serve as the last Boston Braves manager, was gifted with a charcoal draft of "The Dugout," inscribed by Rockwell, "To Charles Grimm, a long suffering but wonderful manager." The original watercolor used by the magazine now resides in the Brooklyn Museum.[1] An earlier Rockwell preliminary study of the scene was once sold at auction for well over $600,000.

Then and now: McNulty (center) reunites with fellow batboys Ferguson (right) and Chronopoulos (left).

McNulty eventually went on to serve as the president of *Parade Magazine*, a position he held until his retirement. In 2002 he was inducted into the Boston Braves Hall of Fame.

SOURCES

The author relied on notes taken at Boston Braves Historical Association reunions, the archives of the Norman Rockwell Museum and Neil D. Isaacs, *Innocence & Wonder: Baseball through the Eyes of Batboys* (Indianapolis: Masters Press, 1994).

NOTES

1   The Brooklyn Museum's website contains illustrations of a Rockwell reference photo and the *Post* cover: brooklynmuseum. org/exhibitions/norman_rockwell/dugout.php.

BRAVES FIELD TO NICKERSON FIELD: BASEBALL, FOOTBALL, SOCCER, AND EVERYTHING IN-BETWEEN

BY DOUGLAS CHAPMAN

When Braves Field opened on August 18, 1915, it had the largest capacity of any stadium in professional baseball at 45,000. A century later, with only the right-field pavilion remaining and with just a quarter (10,412) of that overall capacity, Boston University's Nickerson Field is one of the largest soccer-specific college stadiums in the country.

A total of 2,871 major-league baseball games were played at Braves Field from 1915 to September 21, 1952, including 2,811 by the Braves and 60 by the Boston Red Sox, plus the 1936 All-Star Game, as well as games in the 1915, 1916, and 1948 World Series.

While Braves Field was built to be a cathedral of baseball for Boston's National League club, it became over its long history a multi-use venue for football, soccer, and nearly every field sport imaginable. Before the ballpark was built, the site hosted a different sport as part of the Allston Golf Club.

The field was home for Boston's original National Football League franchise, the Boston Braves, who finished with a 4-4-2 record in 1932. The football Braves were evicted after a rent dispute with their baseball brethren. Owner George Preston Marshall moved the team less than two miles down Commonwealth Avenue to Fenway Park, where he renamed the team the Redskins. Four seasons later they relocated to Washington, D.C., where they captured their first NFL championship in 1937.

Even before Boston University took ownership on July 29, 1953, Braves Field hosted local college football games. BU played its first football game there with a 1921 season-opening 52-0 victory over Worcester Tech.

In addition to the Terriers, Boston College also used Braves Field for football games that required a greater capacity than the Eagles' original Alumni Field. A Braves Field record crowd of 54,000 watched BC edge Holy Cross, 17-13, on December 2, 1922.

Braves Field hosted 70 boxing cards through July 1951, with most occurring during the Depression years as the Braves owners attempted to keep the franchise financially afloat. Boston Garden boxing promoters paid to host evening cards following afternoon Braves games, hoping to retain the baseball crowds, but without much success.

Several Boxing Hall of Famers fought at Braves Field, including Rocky Marciano (The Brockton Bomber), Willie Pep (Willo the Wisp), Jack Britton (The Boxing Marvel), Jack Sharkey (The Boston Gob), Paul Berlenback (The Astoria Assassin), James J. Braddock (The Cinderella Man), Manuel Ortiz, and Tiger Flowers (The Georgia Deacon).

Marciano won his 28th bout en route to the world heavyweight championship at Braves Field, stopping Italy's Gino Buonvino in the eighth round on July 10, 1950. Only 4,900 paid to see the fight, which took place in a small, dilapidated and tilted ring under poor lighting. Marciano commented that he felt as if he were "fighting uphill all night."[1]

In addition to its many sporting uses, Braves Field also was the site of rodeos, circuses, jazz concerts, dancing, movies, political rallies, and religious gatherings while still a baseball venue. Judge Emil Fuchs, the Braves owner, even attempted to bring in dog racing during the Depression, without success.

In the summer of 1953, BU was notified by the Commonwealth of Massachusetts that its home field in Weston (also called Nickerson Field) would be taken by eminent domain for the construction of the

Massachusetts Turnpike. Boston's National League franchise had abandoned Braves Field earlier that year and moved to Milwaukee. BU needed a new field and Braves owner Lou Perini had a stadium he no longer had any use for, so a deal was struck. Perini sold Braves Field to BU for $585,000, believed to be only a fraction of what the property was actually worth.

Led by head football coach Aldo "Buff" Donelli, BU coaches and players removed the outfield fences, mowed the grass, and cleaned and refurbished the seats, getting the former ballpark ready for the 1953 football season.

The stadium has undergone numerous changes and refurbishing's since BU took ownership.

The grandstand, left-field pavilion, and the "Jury Box" were demolished in 1955. The right-field pavilion was squared off on the west side and filled in on the east side where the right-field foul pole and bull-pens had been.

The current stadium design, with a press box mounted on top of the old right-field pavilion, came about in 1960, when the university partnered with the Boston Patriots of the fledgling American Football League. New lighting, new sod, and additional seating, costing more than $300,000, became part of the reconstruction project.

The Patriots playing at Boston University Field was homecoming for team owner Billy Sullivan, who was for many years the public-relations director for the Boston Braves.

The first regular-season game in the history of the AFL was played at Boston University Field on September 9, 1960. The Denver Broncos beat the Patriots, 13-10, in front of a Friday night crowd of 21,597. There was no television, tickets cost $5, and the gate receipts were carried to the bank in a shoebox, according to retired Broncos PR director Jim Saccomano.[2] The game was played on a Friday night to avoid competing against Harvard and BC home games on that Saturday or the New York Giants television broadcast into New England on Sunday.

Still there: the Wigwam's administration building/main entrance is now Boston University's police station at Nickerson Field.

Patriots defensive end Bob Dee, a former Holy Cross star, scored the new league's first points when he recovered a Broncos fumble in the end zone for a safety. The quarterbacks were Butch Songin (ex-BC) for the Patriots and Frank Tripucka (Notre Dame) for the Broncos.

The vagabond Patriots spent three seasons playing at Nickerson Field before moving on to BC's Alumni Stadium, Fenway Park, and Harvard Stadium, ultimately settling in Foxboro.

In 1963 University Field was renamed Nickerson Field, in honor of William E. Nickerson, a longtime booster of Terrier athletics and donor of BU's original field in Weston in 1928.

Nickerson Field was also the home of the Boston Breakers of the United States Football League in 1983.

The Breakers added temporary stands to three sides of the ground, to bring the capacity back over 20,000. The Breakers, coached by Dick Coury and led by veteran quarterback Johnnie Walton, finished with an 11-7 record but were one of only two teams with average attendance of less than 14,000. The franchise moved to New Orleans after one season in Boston.

Nickerson Field got another facelift in 1968, when the four Braves Field light towers were dismantled and it became the second college field in the United States to install an Astroturf carpet playing surface. The Patriots returned to use it as a practice field whenever they would go on the road to play an Astroturf opponent.

It was refurbished again in 1973, with the additions of a 400-meter turf track, three tennis courts, and the Harold C. Case Physical Education & Athletic Center, including Walter Brown Arena, along with the three high-rise student dormitories — Sleeper, Claflin, and Rich — that overlook the field and give an indication of where the original Braves Field grandstand once stood.

While Boston University's football team was the primary tenant up to 1997, playing to mixed results in the Yankee Conference, the stadium had become a favored venue for professional soccer.

The Boston Astros of the American Soccer League called Nickerson Field home from 1969 to 1975, with the exception of a few games in '73 while the new turf was being installed.

"It was a good place for us to play," recalled Astros owner/coach John Bertos after his 2014 induction into the New England Soccer Hall of Fame. "We had no problem with BU. They were good to us. But at the time, we still had to educate fans about soccer and it was difficult getting them to games at Nickerson Field."[3]

Nickerson Field's capacity was ideal for professional soccer at the time. Bertos remembers only a few times the 10,412 capacity was exceeded.

"When we were doing well, we'd have about 4,500 fans," he said. "We got some big crowds when we

Inside the Wigwam, 1948 and today.

Bertos. "We raised ticket prices from $5 to $10. We were hoping to make enough money from that one game to keep us going for the whole season."

The fog rolled in from the Charles River that evening, making it almost impossible to see across the narrow 75-yard field.

"I wanted to postpone the match for a day, but we had to play that day. We ended up taking a bath."[4]

The ASL Astros shared Nickerson Field with the Boston Minutemen of the North American Soccer League in 1975. It didn't work out for either franchise.

"We gave free clinics all over the area, hoping to draw fans to our games," said Bertos. "The Minutemen, who had moved over from Boston College, gave their tickets away for free. We couldn't compete with that."

Bertos, whose team finished in first place in 1975, relocated to Lowell. The Minutemen, featuring Portuguese superstar Eusébio, also finished in first place in '75 and then moved south and became nomads, playing in Foxboro, Quincy, and New Bedford before dissolving the following year.

"We both had good clubs, and one of us could have made it," said Bertos, "but the pie was not large enough to share."[5]

The Minutemen had one memorable match during their lone season at Nickerson Field that remains part of New England soccer lore, on July 9, 1975. While world superstars Eusébio and Pelé had several high-profile clashes when the "Black Panther" played for Benfica of Portugal and Pelé starred for Santos of Brazil, they also had a few head-to-head battles in the NASL, with Pelé's New York Cosmos facing Eusébio's Minutemen.

The official attendance was recorded as 18,598, more than 4,500 over the listed capacity. The real attendance was said to have easily exceeded 20,000, in violation of the stadium's safety codes.

As reported in *People* magazine: "After a scoreless first half, Eusébio booted a free kick into the Cosmos' goal to give Boston a 1-0 lead. Then, moments later, Pelé threaded through the Boston defense like a sapper, darted in front of the goalie with a defender right on his back and lofted a push shot for what appeared to be a score. With a fearful roar the mob poured onto the field and swarmed over the Brazilian wonder. Fortunately his instincts told him to fall limp on the ground, but by the time Cosmos general manager Clive Toye, Boston police and other soccer officials were able to get to him with a stretcher, Pelé had suffered a pulled knee muscle and a sprained ankle, had his shoes and uniform ripped—and learned that his goal had been disallowed on a technicality. He was hustled into the Cosmos' dressing room, and a semblance of order was restored. Boston went on to win 2-1 in overtime, but that didn't matter. What did was that Pelé's very precious life had been risked."[6]

Boston University takes over the abandoned Wigwam.

Nickerson Field also played host to the New England Tea Men (1979) of the NASL, as well as the Boston Beacons and Boston Bolts (1988-90). It was the site of the ASL championship match in 1989, when the Bolts fell to the Fort Lauderdale Strikers, 2-1, in another match played in rain and fog.

BU's men's soccer team has been a successful tenant at Nickerson Field. The Terriers' 1994 squad finished 19-1-1 and was ranked No. 1 in the nation.

A large gray platform was added to the field in 1989 to accommodate commencement speakers President George H.W. Bush and French President Francois Mitterand, and remained until 2008.

The Astroturf was replaced in 2001 with a newer, safer FieldTurf surface as part of a deal that brought the Boston Breakers of the Women's United Soccer Association to Nickerson Field. Individual seats were also added to the lower area of the old right field pavilion, replacing the aluminum bleachers.

Nickerson Field was the first in the country to have its FieldTurf surface certified for international play by FIFA, world soccer's governing body.

With BU no longer playing football (it dropped the sport after the 1997 season), Nickerson Field became a soccer-specific venue and football lines were not repainted. That also ended it as a host site for Massachusetts High School Football Super Bowl Games.

The Breakers lasted for three years until the WUSA shut down for a couple of years before restarting.

The stadium was also home to BU field hockey for many years, including hosting an international match involving the US National Team in 1980. It also played host to the 2006 NCAA Women's Lacrosse Tournament.

It was also home of the Boston Cannons of Major League Lacrosse from 2004 to 2006.

The field was expanded and given a new turf in 2008.

In addition, Nickerson Field annually plays host to BU's extensive intramural program, including sports like softball, flag football, ultimate Frisbee, and anything else that can be played outdoors on a turf field.

Braves Field's old parking lot area on Babcock Street became home to the $27 million New Balance Field in 2013, a university sports complex that houses women's field hockey and other university club and intramural sports. The space under the elevated field is still used for parking, as a garage instead of an open lot.

Boston University has taken great care to ensure the historical connection between Nickerson Field and its Braves Field origins. A plaque commemorating its Braves Field origins (courtesy of SABR and the New England Sports Museum) sits outside the entrances to the former right-field pavilion at Nickerson Field. The alleyway between Harry Agganis Way (formerly

Gaffney Street, named after former Braves owner and Braves Field builder James Gaffney) and Babcock Street is named Braves Field Way, with signage at both ends courtesy of the Boston Braves Historical Association. There are also three large panoramic photos of Braves Field construction in 1915 prominently located in the Walter Brown Arena lobby inside the Case Athletic Center.

BU students participating in recreational activities are often surprised to learn they are treading the same ground where Babe Ruth completed his baseball career after seeing the signage.

There is a statue of Agganis, nicknamed the Golden Greek, outside the arena that bears his name on Commonwealth Avenue and the entrance to Agganis Way, leading to the former Braves Field offices, which now house BU campus police. There are twin ironies at work here, as Agganis, a football and baseball star at BU before signing with the Red Sox, never played a game at Braves Field. Nor did he play ice hockey or basketball, the sports the Terriers play at Agganis Arena.

Boston's NL baseball team spent 38 of their 81 seasons at Braves Field. It has now been the home of BU's Terrier teams for considerably longer (60-plus years).

SOURCES

Boston Braves Historical Association newsletter.

Boston University sports information archives.

New York Daily News (First AFL game).

Seamheads.com.

SoccerStats.us.

NOTES

1   Saul Wisnia, Boston Braves Historical Association Newsletter, Fall 2008.

2   Hank Gola, "Broncos and Patriots have come a long way since playing first AFL game 53 years ago," *New York Daily News*, January 18, 2014.

3   Interview with John Bertos, November 29, 2014.

4   Bertos interview.

5   Bertos interview.

6   Mark Goodman, "The Peerless Pele Comes to Gotham to Put US Soccer on the Map," *People*, August 4, 1974.

BU begins demolition work on the ballpark.

Crough

"STAYIN' ALIVE" – PELÉ'S DEBUT AT NICKERSON FIELD MARRED BY RIOT

JUNE 20, 1975: BOSTON MINUTEMEN 2, NEW YORK COSMOS 1 (RESULT NULLIFIED DUE TO POOR PLAYING CONDITIONS)

BY TOM MASON

Over the years, Braves Field, which Boston University administration named Nickerson Field, has hosted many professional soccer games. Elevens from the North American Soccer League, the American Professional Soccer League, the American Soccer League, and the Women's United Soccer League called the old ballpark home.

Two of the greatest male soccer players of all time played at Nickerson Field on June 20, 1975. Pelé and Eusébio squared off in a North American Soccer League contest.

The illustrious Pelé, who had recently signed a three-year $ 4.5 million contract with the New York Cosmos, led the visiting Cosmos against the Boston Minutemen.[1] The Brazilian star was signed for more than his playing ability. Bringing the world's most famous athlete to America, it was hoped, would jump-start interest in the world's most popular sport A US record TV audience of 10 million watched Pelé's debut with the Cosmos five days earlier.[2]

Minutemen owner John Sterge didn't stand idle. To counteract the Cosmos, he signed a player who he thought could match up with Pelé. Portuguese World Cup star Eusébio, considered by many to be one of the 10 greatest players of all time, was the Boston striker. Eusébio, who played for international soccer power Benfica, was once the all-time leading scorer for the Portuguese national team. At the time of his signing, Eusébio had been playing for the Rhode Island Oceaneers of the American Soccer League, the NASL's rival circuit. Minutemen management thought that Eusébio would be a drawing card for the large Portuguese fanbase in New England.[3]

According to a United Press International preview of the game, "the messiah (Pelé) has arrived to convert pagan Bostonians to the religion of soccer."[4] It didn't seem to bother the fans that Eusébio (32 years old) and Pelé (34) were past their prime. Normally only several thousand fans attended Minutemen matches. For this one, more than 18,000 fanatics jammed the 12,000-seat stadium.

The NASL and the Minutemen were totally unprepared for hosting the two international greats. There were long lines to enter the stadium. The Minutemen didn't provide enough seats, parking, or security. Before the start, firefighters had to put out a fire beneath the stands.

If this wasn't enough to sour Boston, a healthy dose of soccer hooliganism made it worse. Eusébio scored the game's first goal. Pelé apparently responded with a point-blank strike on a rebound off a save by goalkeeper Shep Messing to tie the match at 1-1. But the referee called a foul on Pelé for an illegal pushoff of a defender in front of the net. His goal was disallowed. Hundreds of fans, unhappy with the call, stormed the field in protest. Pelé barely escaped being trampled and was carted from the field on a stretcher. He only had minor injuries. John Powers of the _Globe_ wrote: "You would expect this to happen in Rio de Janeiro or Lisbon. You did not expect this to happen in Boston."[5]

After order was restored, the Minutemen scored the winner in overtime. The Cosmos protested the results and the game's playing conditions. Their protest was upheld by NASL Commissioner Phil Woosnam and the match was replayed at Nickerson Field on August 3. Neither Pelé nor Eusébio played in the rematch, which the Minutemen won, 5-0.[6]

Many have doubted soccer's ability to attract American fans. The Minutemen's attendance at Nickerson Field was poor. By the end of the 1976 season, the Minutemen, like all previous professional soccer teams in Boston, had failed. The NASL and the Cosmos went out of business in 1984. But in 2014 an average audience of more than 18 million American fans watched the US team play Portugal in the World Cup on television.[7] Major League Soccer (MLS), North America's highest professional league in the sport, saw growing attendance and achieved lucrative television contracts. The New England Revolution, an original franchise in the MLS, owned by New England Patriots owner Robert Kraft, were the 2014 Eastern Conference champions, losing the MLS Cup to the Los Angeles Galaxy in a 2-1 overtime match. Plans were launched to eventually move the Revolution from Foxboro's Gillette Stadium to a soccer-specific stadium in Boston. Pelé's visit to Nickerson Field was an unforgettable chapter in United States soccer history.

SOURCES

The firsthand accounts of Pelé's game at Nickerson Field are mainly drawn from the *Boston Globe*. An excellent comprehensive history of the Boston Minutemen can be found at: funwhileitlasted.net/2013/08/25/1974-1976-boston-minutemen. There are abundant reSources available about Eusébio and Pelé. Eusébio died on January 5, 2014. Portugal held a national day of mourning for him.

NOTES

1 Pelé had previously played in a June 30, 1972, exhibition match at Nickerson Field featuring the Boston Astros of the ASL vs. the Brazilian Santos team. About 1,100 attended. Pelé had three goals and Santos won, 6-1. The crowd was held down because of erroneous reports that the game had been canceled due to excessive fog.

2 nasl.com/page/slug/a-review-of-the-golden-era#.VKGFOF4Ao.

3 A statue to honor Eusébio was unveiled next to Gillette Stadium on May 6, 2006. It is a replica of a statute in front of Benfica's home stadium.

4 "Pelé the Lure at BU Tonight," *Boston Globe*, June 20, 1975, 31.

5 John Powers, "Frenzied Fans Rough Up Pelé," *Boston Globe*, June 21 1975, 17.

6 Francis Rosa, "Minutemen Ramble Over Cosmos, 5-0," *Boston Globe*, August 4, 1975, 25.

7 forbes.com/sites/maurybrown/2014/06/23/u-s-a-vs-portugal-highest-rated-ever-world-cup-match-for-espn/.

THE LAST STEAL OF HOME AT BRAVES FIELD

BY BOB BRADY

The final theft of home plate at Braves Field did not take place during a regular-season game but instead on a cold late-March Boston day in 1953 in an empty park, shortly after the ballclub announced its shift to Milwaukee while encamped in sunny Florida.

Despite the dismal 1952 attendance figure (281,278) that prompted owner Lou Perini to move his team to the Midwest, the Braves always had a core of rabid supporters, especially among local youth. Back in days of the deep Depression, Tribe owner Judge Emil Fuchs launched the "Knot Hole Gang" to provide an inexpensive way to attract youngsters to the sparsely populated ballpark. The team supplied thin cardboard membership cards to area youth groups such as the YMCA and city recreation agencies for distribution. The card enabled its holder to enter Braves Field for the nominal price of 5 cents and sit in a designated section of the left-field pavilion near the bullpen area. In order to retain this privilege, such attendees were expected to conform with guidelines printed on the back of the card.[1]

With a few precious coins in their pockets to cover admission, a streetcar ride and, possibly, a ballpark snack, local lads would set out to the Wigwam to enjoy an afternoon Braves game. This marketing program was unique to the Braves; the neighboring Red Sox did not offer a comparable arrangement to youngsters. It remained a popular feature through the Boston Braves' final season of 1952.

The announced loss of the Braves and the Knot Hole Gang program was an unexpected and harsh blow to a group of teenage friends who resided in the vicinity of Braves Field. The boys billed themselves the "Mountfort Street Gang" at a time when "gang" had a more benign connotation. The reports of the Tribe's departure sounded a call to action to these Braves' kid loyalists. Something had to be done to reflect and preserve their ties to a team that was abandoning its "home."

A plan was hatched to sneak into Braves Field and remove an artifact that would forever symbolize their youthful days happily spent at the "Home of the Braves." In a commando-like operation, the gang traversed Gaffney Street down to the adjacent Boston and Albany rail yard area and found an entry spot from outside the park's left-field wall. A decision was made to capture and remove home plate. The compacted clay soil surrounding the treasure was additionally hardened by the past long New England winter. With only bare hands, the gang members scratched into the soil some 17 inches until the plate was liberated from the ground. The gang quickly secured their prize and departed from the diamond undetected.

Their purloined prize lay hidden for many years thereafter. It was shared among the members of the Mountfort Street Gang through adulthood, residing in cellars and attics, under beds, and in various other secretive locations until it emerged in 1988 on the occasion of a 40th-anniversary commemoration of Boston's last National League pennant. In an event

Braves Field home plate on display at the Sports Museum.

sponsored in part by the Sports Museum of New England and the Society for American Baseball Research, a former gang member turned over the beloved relic to the museum, where the historic dish now resides on display.

The Mountfort Street Gang's pilferage ranks as the greatest "steal" of home at Braves Field since it secured an important piece of Boston's baseball heritage that would otherwise have been lost.

SOURCES

The author relied on the notes that he took at the 1948 Boston Braves Reunion Celebration on August 5-7, 1988, where the above described return of the Braves Field home plate took place, as well as on the shared memories of other Boston Braves Historical Association members who also were in attendance.

NOTES

1 The "Knot Hole Gang Agreement of Membership" included promises not to skip school to attend a game and not travel to the Wigwam against a parent's wishes. Members were expected to "uphold the principles of clean speech, clean sports, and clean habits." Cardholders could not smoke cigarettes at the game or use profane language, and had to comply with all rules and regulations imposed by the ballclub.

Schedule printers also were caught by surprise.

THE MOUNTFORT STREET GANG

BY BILL NOWLIN

For those who have followed the Whitey Bulger saga and the Winter Hill Gang, thrilled to Martin Scorsese's *The Departed*, read Dennis Lehane's novels such as *Mystic River*, feared the Boston Strangler, were appalled by the murders at Sammy White's Brighton Bowl, or even remember the Great Brinks Robbery, the activities of the Mountfort Street Gang may seem a bit pale by comparison.

Advocates of the "broken windows" theory of policing, however, believe in zero tolerance and would spare no one. They believe that failure to prosecute "quality of life" crimes such as public drinking, littering, and the breaking of windows leads good citizens to retreat to their homes and abandons public spaces to the miscreants.

The men in the Mountfort Street Gang who committed a crime in Boston back in 1953 stayed out of the public eye until 1988—some 35 years later. Two or three may still be hiding out, in fear of the long arm of the law.

What was this crime in Boston and who committed it?

Mountfort Street runs from Commonwealth Avenue in Boston, across from the BU bridge, more or less parallel to and to the south of the Mass Pike, eventually connecting to Beacon Street, just a large parking lot away from Fenway Park. Before the Mass Pike sliced through Boston in the mid- to late 1950s, the street was lined on both sides with three-story stone tenement houses—triple-deckers—and was a fairly quiet residential street in the Back Bay. In a sense, it ran more or less between Boston's two major-league ballparks: Braves Field and Fenway Park. When the turnpike construction began, one entire side of the street was torn down. Gone forever.

When the Braves announced in early 1953 that the franchise had been moved, more or less in the dark

of night, to Milwaukee, Braves fandom was stunned. True, the Red Sox almost always outdrew the Braves, but the Tribe had its loyal followers. Many were bereft. Others were aggrieved. Some, even into the twenty-first century, decline to patronize the Red Sox.

A handful of young teenagers from Mountfort Street—three or four of them, 13-14 years old—took a measure of action on a March night in 1953. They couldn't stay out late, but it's still sufficiently dark in March that they could have the protection of darkness. One has since come forth to confess.

They went to Braves Field. There were no cops in sight. "It was in the evening, later on, probably about 7 or 8. The left-field wall, over on the side of the tracks, was only about eight feet [high]," recalled Arthur Haley, born in 1939 and the only member of the gang known to us today.[1] "Everybody gives 10 fingers and props people up and over. It was an adventure."

They were in. There was no one around. They stole home plate.

Why home plate? "Once you—so to speak—break into a joint, what else are you going up there for? Let's see what we can get."

1953 pocket schedules required a quick modification.

2015 view of Montfort Street, with Fenway Park in the background.

It wasn't easy work. "Yeah, but we were industrious. It's not as though we had shovels. It was mounted on 2-by-3's underneath. It wasn't just sitting there by itself." They dug it out of the clay with their bare hands. They lugged home plate back home to Mountfort Street, then hid it in the cellar of one of the boys' homes. Adrenaline was pumping; had they been caught, the punishment could have been severe. "If our fathers found out, they would have booted us in the can, and taken us down to the police station."

With the purloined plate in the basement, gang members were getting a little worried. "We actually passed it around for a week at a time. We didn't know if we were going to get arrested."[2]

But no one ratted. No one turned state's evidence. No one went into witness protection. Things settled down and the "hot goods" settled into Haley's care. Within a couple of years, his family moved to Framingham and the plate went with him. He graduated from high school, then spent three years with the Air Force in Germany. Little did the Air Force know it had unwittingly enabled a lawbreaker to leave the country.

Haley's father was a salesman for Sunshine Biscuit, but Haley had no doubt he himself would have been hauled down to the station had his father known. Arthur had grown up in Boston and played ball over at the Fens; he played CYO ball for St. Cecilia's. "We used to walk by Fenway Park from Mountfort Street. The lights from Fenway Park would light up our street."

Haley himself worked as a radar operator for the Air Force at the airport in Munich, then got a job for 30 years taking x-rays for Arnold Greene Testing Laboratories in Natick, eventually becoming general manager. They would x-ray paintings for authenticity but also aircraft engine parts and nuclear submarine component castings. At present, in 2015, he is manager at Thielsch Engineering of Cranston, Rhode Island. Quite coincidentally, his oldest son married Julie Bresciani, niece of the late Red Sox executive Dick Bresciani.

In 1988 Haley read in the *Boston Herald* that Dick Johnson of the Sports Museum of New England was looking for memorabilia to help mark the 35th anniversary of the closing of Braves Field. Haley knew he had home plate and called the Sports Museum. He brought it in and left it with them … but Museum staff was not certain they could accept stolen property. Counsel advised that the statute of limitations had long since passed.

It was safe to see it all as a bit of "light-hearted larceny."[3] Haley was invited to formally present the plate at a banquet held on August 5, 1988, at the Prudential Center in Boston. Some of the Boston Braves were there, as was Billy Sullivan, former publicity director for the Braves, and even a couple of members of the Perini family, who would have had a claim of ownership had the event not happened so long in the past. A Perini publication dubbed Haley the "kingpin" of the gang.[4]

Whether any of the gang members went on to a hardened life of crime is not known. Word has it that a Jimmy Jango might have been another member of the Mountfort Street Gang but we were unable to locate Mr. Jango. Haley may be protecting his partners in crime, or he may simply not remember their names, but the others who helped with the heist are names at present lost to history. Rather than simple vandalism or juvenile delinquency, gang members had preserved an artifact that might itself otherwise have become lost to history.

The unanticipated abandonment of Braves Field led to separate bonfires at the park of 1953 season Boston Braves baseball and Boston College football tickets. Pictured in this Leslie Jones photograph is a dump truck delivering the college pigskin passes to the Wigwam to meet the same fate as had befallen Tribe tickets previously.

A 1953 Boston Braves ticket that somehow escaped the flames.

NOTES

1   After reading Bob Brady's article, "The Last Steal," the idea of tracking down a gang member was too appealing to pass up. All quotations are from an interview with Arthur Haley on December 31, 2014. Haley did say the gang had never snuck into either ballpark to catch a game. A Doctor Manfredi lived on Mountfort Street (Haley noted that the doctor's son was not part of the gang that night in 1953) and he had four season tickets to both Braves Field and Fenway Park. Whenever he wasn't using them, they were available to his son and his friends.

2   The Mountfort Street Gang wasn't the only small group to visit Braves Field after the mid-March announcement that the Braves were decamping for Milwaukee. The March 19, 1953 *Boston Daily Record* reported that four teenage boys had scaled the wall the night before and smashed 10 windows in concession and telephone booths with long sticks they poked through the windows, "apparently in retaliation for the Braves' moving out of Boston." They were "working their way along the booths to the main office of owner Louis Perini" when the vandals were interrupted by caretaker Jerry Palazoo who gave chase until they escaped over a wall.

3   Daphne Hurford, "Yet Another Game for a Boston Hero," *Sports Illustrated*, December 10, 1990.

4   *Perini News*, September–October 1988.

CONTRIBUTORS

ERIC ARON has been a SABR member since 2002 and has contributed several bios for both the "team" book projects and BioProject website. In addition to his writing for SABR, he has contributed to other websites and magazines, including Throughthefencebaseball. com, NewEnglandFilm.com, and Imagine Magazine. He lives in Boston and holds a Master's degree in Public History & Museum Studies. He enjoys documentaries, playing hoops, and laughter Yoga.

FR. GERALD BEIRNE has been a priest in Rhode Island since 1962, but his history with baseball goes back to a game at Braves Field in the late 1940's; his next was a night game also at the Wigwam. However the Red Sox now have a never-ending hold on his baseball passion. He still regrets that "Willoughby and Clemens were taken out." His most exciting sport memory will always be—sitting to the right of home plate on October 1, 1967, when the "Impossible Dream" Red Sox vanquished the Twins to win the American League championship, and he has made that experience into a 20-minute sermon. He has been a member of SABR since 1983 when his first and only book *The New England Sports Trivia Quiz Book* was published.

MORT BLOOMBERG is a retired psychology professor with a lifelong magnetic attraction to the Boston Braves. He does not often write, but nowadays when he does…Mort's subject matter spotlights the post-WWII inhabitants of Braves Field.

BOB BRADY joined SABR in 1991 and is the current president of the Boston Braves Historical Association. As the editor of the Association's quarterly newsletter since 1992, he's had the privilege of memorializing the passings of the "Greatest Generation" members of the Braves Family. He owns a small piece of the Norwich, Connecticut-based Connecticut Tigers of the New York-Penn League, a Class-A short-season affiliate of the Detroit Tigers. Bob has contributed biographies and supporting pieces to a number of SABR publications as well as occasionally lending a hand in the editing process.

Doug Chapman spent 19 years as a sports writer at the *Providence Journal*, covering the Boston Bruins for 11 of them, and has been a high school (Somerset Berkley) and college tennis coach (UMass Dartmouth, Roger William, and Bridgewater State) for more than 35 years. While a journalism student at Boston University, he hit home runs into the old right-field pavilion at Braves Field in intramural softball games. He is a season ticket holder for BU men's hockey and had a season ticket to the USFL's Boston Breakers. He resides in Somerset, Massachusetts.

ALAN COHEN is a retired insurance underwriter who has been a member of SABR since 2011. He has written over 20 biographies for the SABR BioProject, and done several game summaries for the SABR games-project. A native of Long Island, he now resides in West Hartford, Connecticut with his wife Frances, two cats and two dogs. He graduated from Franklin and Marshall College with a degree in history in 1968. His article on the Hearst Sandlot Classic, which launched the careers of 88 major leaguers, appeared in the Fall 2013 edition of the *Baseball Research Journal*, and he is currently expanding his research on this topic. During the baseball season, he serves as data-caster (stringer) for the New Britain Rock Cats of the Eastern League.

WARREN CORBETT is the author of *The Wizard of Waxahachie: Paul Richards and the End of Baseball as We Knew It*. His baseball writing has appeared in the *Hardball Times*, *The National Pastime*, *Baseball Research Journal*, and more than a dozen books. He lives in Bethesda, Maryland.

HERB CREHAN is in his 20th season as a contributing writer for the Boston Red Sox. He has written well over 100 feature articles for the team's official program. He is the author of *Lightning In A Bottle: The Sox of '67* and *Red Sox Heroes of Yesteryear*, and he has contributed chapters to five other books on Boston baseball history. Crehan speaks extensively on Boston baseball history including appearances at the Baseball

Hall of Fame in Cooperstown, New York, WBZ radio, NPR's "All Things Considered," Forbes.com, and numerous Society of Baseball Research (SABR) meetings.

BRIAN DAVENPORT is assistant professor of Leadership and Organizational Studies at the University of Southern Maine's Lewiston-Auburn College. His research interests include leadership and coaching, technologies impact on leadership, and the experiences of undocumented students. He is an avid Red Sox fan.

JOHN DIFONZO is a first-time SABR author who grew up in Somerville, Massachusetts where he was the sports editor for his high school newspaper. He is a lifelong Red Sox fan and season-ticket holder since 2004 currently living on Beacon Hill with his wife, Gabriella. John is a graduate of Tufts University and holds a Master of Science in Finance from Bentley University and is a CFA chartholder.

GREG ERION is retired from the railroad industry and currently teaches history part-time at Skyline Community College in San Bruno, California. He has written several biographies for SABR's BioProject and is currently working on a book about the 1959 season. Greg is one of the leaders of SABR's Baseball Games Project. He and his wife Barbara live in South San Francisco, California.

SCOTT FERKOVICH is the leader of the SABR Ballpark Project. He is a contributing editor to the annual *Emerald Guide to Baseball*, and blogs about Detroit Tiger history for Detroit Athletic Co. He also writes for Seamheads.com, TheNationalPastimeMuseum. com, and *Spitball* magazine. Scott was the editor of *Detroit the Unconquerable: The 1935 World Champion Tigers*. A graduate of Columbia College in Chicago, he was a judge for the Casey Award in 2014.

TIM GOEHLERT is the author of *Baseball Franchise Rankings*. Tim has worked professionally as a marketing manager for 10 years at various companies in the Boston area. He received his Bachelor of Science in Marketing from Salem State University in 2004 and his Master of Business Administration in Marketing

from Suffolk University in 2012. Tim teaches marketing courses at Fisher College as an adjunct professor, has a wife and two sons, and lives in Danvers, Massachusetts.

BOB GOODOF has been a devotee of baseball history since reading the first edition of the original *Baseball Encyclopedia*, cover-to-cover, and back again, around the age of 9, in search of players with his birthday ("Stinky" Davis, who played in the 1880s), and then memorizing the winners and records of World Series contestants from the Beginning. As board member of a historical museum in Back Bay, Boston, Bob has founded and produced "Victorian Baseball Night" (with SABRs great help) since 2012.

CHIP GREENE, a SABR member since 2006, has contributed to numerous SABR book projects. Additionally, he contributed sports biographies to the four-volume encyclopedia, *American Sports: A History of Icons, Idols and Ideas*, published in 2013 by Greenwood. Chip edited *Mustaches and Mayhem: Charlie O's Three-Time Champions*, a SABR biography book project that chronicles the three-time champion Oakland Athletics. The grandson of former Brooklyn Dodgers pitcher, Nelson Greene, Chip lives with his wife, Elaine, and daughters, Anna and Haley, in Waynesboro, Pennsylvania.

DONNA L. HALPER is an Associate Professor of Communication at Lesley University, Cambridge, Massachusetts. A media historian who specializes in the history of broadcasting, Dr. Halper is the author of six books and many articles. She is also a former broadcaster and print journalist.

TOM HUFFORD is one of the 16 Founding Members of SABR (1971), and served as the group's Secretary in 1976 and on the Board of Directors 2004-13. His autograph collection includes the signature of every Braves player since 1925 and every member of the Red Sox since 1927.

JIM KAPLAN is the author of 19 books, including *The Greatest Game Ever Pitched: Juan Marichal, Warren Spahn and the Pitching Duel of the Century*.

BOB LEMOINE grew up in South Portland, Maine, long after the Braves had moved from Boston. His grandfather used to tell of the time "when me and a few fellas took the train to Boston to try out for the Braves. We hit a few balls and caught a few fly balls. Then they told us 'You fellas may as well go back home.'" It has only been since joining SABR in 2013 that Bob has learned that this tale probably actually happened and wasn't just another of Grampa's stories. Bob lives in Rochester, New Hampshire and works as a high school librarian. He has master's degrees in education and library information science.

LEN LEVIN could never understand the animus some Boston Braves fans felt for the Red Sox. When the Braves were in town, he liked both teams. A retired newspaper editor, he lives in Providence, Rhode Island, and has been a copyeditor for many of SABR's books.

MIKE LYNCH was born in the heart of Red Sox Nation in the year of Yastrzemski and has been a diehard Red Sox fan ever since. A member of SABR since 2004, he lives in West Roxbury, Massachusetts. His first book, *Harry Frazee, Ban Johnson and the Feud That Nearly Destroyed the American League*, was published by McFarland Publishing in 2008 and was named a finalist for the 2009 Larry Ritter Award in addition to being nominated for the Seymour Medal. His second book, *It Ain't So: A Might-Have-Been History of the White Sox in 1919 and Beyond*, was released by McFarland in December 2009. His work has also been featured in SABR books about the 1912 Boston Red Sox and 1914 Boston Braves.

TOM MASON is an attorney and an accomplished freelance writer with dozens of articles to his credit. His work has been published in the *New Bedford Standard-Times*, the *Brockton Enterprise*, and the *Quincy Patriot-Ledger*. He was the primary author of the *Maple Street Guide to New England Ballparks* and contributed to the Pawtucket Red Sox yearbook. A graduate of the Wharton School of Finance and Boston University Law School, Tom has lived in Lakeville and Lexington, Massachusetts. As a boy, Tom would go to Nickerson Field to watch Boston University play football. He's

also seen United States Football League and professional soccer games at the ballpark formerly known as "Braves Field."

DAN MCCLOSKEY is a native downstate New Yorker who's been a Boston area resident for the past 18 years. His interest in the Boston Braves evolved from a specific fascination with the St. Louis Browns to a general desire to celebrate the less-celebrated teams from historic baseball towns. A medical librarian by day, and baseball writer, craft beer enthusiast and amateur music critic by night, Dan's work has appeared in *USA Today Sports Weekly* as well as various web sites such as highheatstats.com and beergraphs.com.

RAY MILLER, a member of SABR since 1995, has written articles on old ballparks for SABR and *The Baseball Digest*, and is the author of *A Tour of Braves Field* (Boston Braves Historical Association, 2000). He lives in Maine, and has recently retired after teaching at Bowdoin College for 30 years. He is a writer, songwriter, and musician, and plays second base for the Giants of the Maine Woods 45 senior baseball league.

W.G. NICHOLSON is a retired independent school administrator and teacher who has published over 50 articles, edited two books, and written two others. He lives in Osterville, Massachusetts.

BILL NOWLIN has been vice president of SABR since 2004. Most of his nearly 50 books have been Red Sox-related, though he's also written about musical and political history. He was a co-founder of Rounder Records and lives across the Charles River but really not all that far from Fenway Park, where the Boston Braves played home games in the 1914 World Series. Sadly, he never saw a game at Braves Field.

MARK PESTANA has been a SABR member since 1990. He began following baseball in 1967 when his family moved to the Boston area in the summer of the Impossible Dream Red Sox. He currently lives in Dunstable, Massachusetts, has written for *Moonstone Magazine* and *The Pearl*, both of Lowell, Massachusetts, and he published and edited a local literary/news journal, *The Scrawl*, from 1981 to 1985. He has previously contributed work to the SABR 19th Century Committee's book *Inventing Baseball: The 100 Greatest Games of the 19th Century*, and to the Deadball Era Committee's forthcoming book on World Series of the Deadball Era.

MIKE RICHARD is a lifelong Red Sox fan who was not even born when the Braves played in Boston. He retired as a guidance counselor from Gardner (Massachusetts) High School and is a sports columnist for the *Worcester Telegram & Gazette*. A Massachusetts high school sports historian, he has authored two high school football books: *Glory to Gardner: 100 Years of Football in the Chair City*, and *Super Saturdays: The Complete History of the Massachusetts High School Super Bowl*. He has also documented the playoff history (sectional and state championships) of all high school sports in Massachusetts. He lives in Gardner and also owns a home in Sandwich on Cape Cod with his wife Peggy. They are the parents of a son Casey, a daughter Lindsey, and have a grandson Theo.

PAUL ROGERS is a law professor at Southern Methodist University, where he served as dean for nine years. When not writing about antitrust law or legal history, he has co-authored four baseball books, including two with his boyhood hero Robin Roberts, *The Whiz Kids and the 1950 Pennant* and *Throwing Hard Easy*. His most recent collaboration is *Lucky Me — My 65 Years in Baseball* with Eddie Robinson. He is also president of the Ernie Banks — Bobby Bragan DFW SABR Chapter, has authored a score of biographies for the SABR BioProject, and in 2014 served as a judge for the Casey Award.

BOB RUZZO is an attorney practicing real estate and affordable housing law at Holland and Knight, LLP in Boston. Before becoming a Red Sox fan, his father rooted for the Boston Braves, and so the spirit lives on. Bob's articles about Braves Field and the Federal League have appeared in SABR's *Baseball Research Journal*.

RICK SCHABOWSKI is a retired machinist from Harley-Davidson and is currently an instructor at Wisconsin Regional Training Partnership in the Manufacturing Program, and is a certified Manufacturing Skills Standards Council Instructor. He is President of the Ken Keltner Badger State Chapter of SABR, Treasurer of the Milwaukee Braves Historical Association, and a member of the Hoop Historians.

JOE SCHUSTER is the author of *The Might Have Been*, a novel that was a finalist for the 2012 CASEY Award as best baseball book of the year, and *One Season in the Sun*, about players whose major-league careers lasted only a few weeks. He is a member of the faculty of Webster University, is married, and the father of five rabid Cardinals fans.

HARVEY SOOLMAN joined SABR in 1972 and was among its first 100 members. He grew up in Brookline less than a mile from Braves Field, but alas, the Beehive and the Jury Box were slightly before his time. His dominant boyhood memory of the park is his shagging fly balls on Boston University's rock-hard Astro-Turf, where if you didn't catch it there was a lot of chasing to do. He lives in Medford, Massachusetts, now, manages and still occasionally plays in the Boston Park League and has written and produced a play, *Ballplayer*, about an old amateur athlete who just cannot give it up because playing baseball is what he has always done.

DAVID C. SOUTHWICK is the former publicity coordinator of SABR's Boston Chapter. Despite a lot of good times at Fenway Park, his most enjoyable moment at Braves Field/Nickerson Field was in 1992 when he witnessed his North Quincy High School win the state football championship.

LYLE SPATZ is the Chairman of SABR's Baseball Records Committee. He has authored and edited several books on baseball history, most recently. *Willie Keeler: From the Playgrounds of Brooklyn to the Hall of Fame*, and *The Colonel and Hug: The Partnership that Transformed the New York Yankees* (co-authored with Steve Steinberg).

MARK S. STERNMAN has written extensively on the Deadball Era with multiple book reviews for *The Inside Game* (the quarterly newsletter of the Deadball

Committee), and BioProject profiles of Scotty Ingerton and Fred Tenney, the latter of which also appeared in slightly different form in *Deadball Stars of the National League* (Brassey's, Inc., 2004). Sternman also contributed the World Series game accounts and a chapter on the Johnny Evers ejection record to the recent book *The Miracle Braves of 1914: Boston's Original Worst-to-First World Series Champions* (SABR, 2014).

CECILIA TAN is a professional writer and editor in the Boston area. She has served as SABR's Publications Director since 2011 and has written for *Baseball Prospectus*, *Baseball Ink*, *Yankees Magazine*, *Mudville*, and many other places.

RICHARD J. "DICK" THOMPSON was stellar SABR researcher and friend to all. Mostly he enjoyed digging up stories on unknown ballplayers and giving them their due notoriety. Among the many stories he authored for SABR was his book *The Ferrell Brothers of Baseball* in 2005. Dick was also a multi-champion of several SABR trivia contests. His final and maybe most lasting SABR article was the 10-page, 2007 *National Pastime* biography of Will Jackman, now definitive, and he continued looking for more Jackman-pitched games until his untimely death. He left us much too soon in early January 2008.

RICHARD "DIXIE" TOURANGEAU was recruited for SABR by Hall of Fame Librarian Cliff Kachline back in 1981. That was the same year Dixie started writing the "Play Ball!" baseball calendar for Tide-Mark Press, which he retired from with the 2005 issue. He has authored a half-dozen articles for *The National Pastime* but only one for the BioProject, a situation he hopes to improve upon in the coming years having enough material on file for about three dozen more. He has paid the Red Sox for four Field Box season tickets since 1988 and lives one mile from home plate. SABR member Marilyn Miller, several kitties, and 900 baseball books share his Mission Hill triple decker. Born the day Bill Veeck signed Larry Doby and raised in south-central Massachusetts, Dixie is a retired National Park Service ranger-public affairs person (1983-2012).

Joseph Wancho lives in Westlake, Ohio and is a life-long Cleveland Indians fan. He has been a SABR member since 2005 and serves as Chair of the Minor League Research Committee. He edited a Bio Project Book on the 1954 Cleveland Indians, *Pitching to the Pennant*, (Nebraska Press, 2014.

SAUL WISNIA is the author of seven baseball books, including *Miracle at Fenway, Fenway Park: The Centennial*, and *For the Love of the Boston Red Sox*. He has coauthored, edited, or contributed essays to numerous others, including the SABR volumes *Spahn, Sain, and Teddy Ballgame*, *The 1967 Impossible Dream Red Sox*, and *The Fenway Project*. Wisnia is a former contributing writer for the *Washington Post* and feature writer for the *Boston Herald*, and has also written for *Sports Illustrated*, the *Boston Globe*, and *Red Sox Magazine*. A SABR member (Boston chapter) since 1990, he keeps the city's National League roots alive as a board member of the Boston Braves Historical Association as Publications Editor at Dana-Farber Cancer Institute, whose Jimmy Fund charity the Braves helped launch during their final years in Boston. Wisnia lives 5.8 miles from Fenway Park and shares his "Fenway Reflections" at saulwisnia.blogspot.com.

A lifelong Pirates fan, **GREGORY H. WOLF** was born in Pittsburgh, but turned his back on the Smoky City and now resides in the Windy City area with his wife, Margaret, and daughter, Gabriela. A Professor of German and holder of the Dennis and Jean Bauman endowed chair of the Humanities at North Central College in Naperville, Illinois, he served as editor of the SABR book, *Thar's Joy in Braveland: The 1957 Milwaukee Braves* (April 2014). He is also editor of two additional SABR books, on the 1929 Chicago Cubs and the 1965 Minnesota Twins, to be published in 2015.

JACK ZERBY, a retired attorney and trusts/estates administrator, acquired his interest in the Boston Braves through research on Wally Berger for one of the earliest SABR Biography Project posts. He writes and edits regularly for the BioProject and the new SABR Games Project. Jack lives in Brevard, North Carolina, with his wife Diana, a professional violinist. He divides

his in-season baseball attention among the Atlanta
Braves, the Asheville Tourists, and the Cliff Melton
Fantasy Baseball League.

Join SABR today!

If you're interested in baseball — writing about it, reading about it, talking about it — there's a place for you in the Society for American Baseball Research.

SABR was formed in 1971 in Cooperstown, New York, with the mission of fostering the research and dissemination of the history and record of the game. Our members include everyone from academics to professional sportswriters to amateur historians and statisticians to students and casual fans who merely enjoy reading about baseball history and occasionally gathering with other members to talk baseball.

SABR members have a variety of interests, and this is reflected in the diversity of its research committees. There are more than two dozen groups devoted to the study of a specific area related to the game — from Baseball and the Arts to Statistical Analysis to the Deadball Era to Women in Baseball. In addition, many SABR members meet formally and informally in regional chapters throughout the year and hundreds come together for the annual national convention, the organization's premier event. These meetings often include panel discussions with former major league players and research presentations by members. Most of all, SABR members love talking baseball with like-minded friends. What unites them all is an interest in the game and joy in learning more about it.

Why join SABR? Here are some benefits of membership:

- Two issues (spring and fall) of the *Baseball Research Journal*, which includes articles on history, biography, statistics, personalities, book reviews, and other aspects of the game.
- One expanded e-book edition of *The National Pastime*, which focuses on baseball in the region where that year's SABR national convention is held (in 2015, it's Chicago)
- 8-10 new and classic e-books published each year by the SABR Digital Library, which are all free for members to download
- *This Week in SABR* newsletter in your e-mail every Friday, which highlights SABR members' research and latest news
- Regional chapter meetings, which can include guest speakers, presentations and trips to ballgames
- Online access to back issues of *The Sporting News* and other periodicals through Paper of Record
- Access to SABR's lending library and other research resources
- Online member directory to connect you with an international network of SABR baseball experts and fans
- Discounts on registration for our annual events, including SABR Analytics Conference & Jerry Malloy Negro League Conference
- Access to SABR-L, an e-mail discussion list of baseball questions & answers that many feel is worth the cost of membership itself
- The opportunity to be part of a passionate international community of baseball fans

SABR membership is on a "rolling" calendar system; that means your membership lasts 365 days no matter when you sign up! Enjoy all the benefits of SABR membership by signing up today at SABR.org/join or by clipping out the form below and mailing it to SABR, Cronkite School at ASU, 555 N. Central Ave. #416, Phoenix, AZ 85004.

✂ —

SABR MEMBERSHIP FORM

	Annual	3-year	Senior	3-yr Sr.	Under 30
U.S.:	❏ $65	❏ $175	❏ $45	❏ $129	❏ $45
Canada/Mexico:	❏ $75	❏ $205	❏ $55	❏ $159	❏ $55
Overseas:	❏ $84	❏ $232	❏ $64	❏ $186	❏ $55

Add a Family Member: $15 for each family member at same address (list on back)
Senior: 65 or older before 12/31/2015
All dues amounts in U.S. dollars or equivalent

Participate in Our Donor Program!

I'd like to desginate my gift to be used toward:

❏General Fund   ❏Endowment Fund   ❏Research Resources   ❏_____
❏ I want to maximize the impact of my gift; do not send any donor premiums
❏ I would like this gift to remain anonymous.

Note: Any donation not designated will be placed in the General Fund.
SABR is a 501 (c) (3) not-for-profit organization & donations are tax-deductible to the extent allowed by law.

Name _____

Address _____

City _____ ST_____ ZIP_____

Phone _____ Birthday _____

E-mail: _____
(Your e-mail address on file ensures you will receive the most recent SABR news.)

Dues $_____

Donation $_____

Amount Enclosed $_____

Do you work for a matching grant corporation? Call (602) 496-1460 for details.

If you wish to pay by credit card, please contact the SABR office at (602) 496-1460 or visit the SABR Store online at SABR.org/join. We accept Visa, Mastercard & Discover.

Do you wish to receive the *Baseball Research Journal* electronically?: ❏ Yes   ❏ No
Our e-books are available in PDF, Kindle, or EPUB (iBooks, iPad, Nook) formats.

Mail to: SABR, Cronkite School at ASU, 555 N. Central Ave. #416, Phoenix, AZ 85004

CPSIA information can be obtained
at www.ICGtesting.com
Printed in the USA
LVOW03s1323191115

463332LV00022B/357/P